Preparing
America's
Teachers

A HISTORY

James W. Fraser

TEACHERS COLLEGE PRESS

Teachers College
Columbia University
New York and London

Published by Teachers College Press, 1234 Amsterdam Avenue, New York, NY 10027

Library of Congress Cataloging-in-Publication Data

Fraser, James W., 1944–
    Preparing America's teachers : a history / James W. Fraser.
       p. cm. — (Reflective history series)
    Includes bibliographical references and index.
    ISBN-13: 978-0-8077-4734-6 (pbk. : alk. paper)
    ISBN-13: 978-0-8077-4735-3 (cloth : alk. paper)
    ISBN-10: 0-8077-4734-3 (pbk. : alk. paper)
    ISBN-10: 0-8077-4735-1 (cloth : alk. paper)
    1. Teachers—Training of—United States—History.   I. Title.
    LB1715.F697 2007
    370'.71'1—dc22

                                        2006025072

ISBN-13:   ISBN-10:
978-0-8077-4734-6 (paper)   0-8077-4734-3 (paper)
978-0-8077-4735-3 (cloth)   0-8077-4735-1 (cloth)

Printed on acid-free paper

Manufactured in the United States of America

14   13   12   11   10   09   08   07   8   7   6   5   4   3   2   1

REFLECTIVE HISTORY SERIES

Barbara Finkelstein and William J. Reese, Series Editors

4/08

To

ROBERT WOOD LYNN

Contents

Acknowledgments

More than others I have previously written, this book became possible because of the support of many others. James Stellar, David Hall, Pat Meservey, and my colleagues at the School of Education at Northeastern University in Boston supported me in the most basic possible way: they gave me time, arranging a yearlong sabbatical—the first ever in my career—that allowed me to ponder, engage in research, and write this book. Mary Brabeck, Jonathan Zimmerman, Rene Arcilla, Robby Cohen, and many other new colleagues at the Steinhardt School of Education at New York University welcomed me into their community for this year and offered a wonderful mix of space, time, and intellectual resources to write this book, while also offering all of the wonderful distractions of their friendship, Greenwich Village, and alternative preoccupations that kept this book from taking over my life. Finally, The Marion and Jasper Whiting Foundation and its program officer Robert G. Bannish provided funds to support my research. Without the Whiting grant to travel to archives across the country, the local case studies would not have been possible. I am very grateful to my friends and colleagues at Northeastern University, New York University, and the Whiting Foundation for all of their support.

Karen Hallman, then a student finishing her undergraduate program in History, English, and Education at Northeastern University and now a public school teacher in Massachusetts, became my research assistant for a year while this book was in its infancy. She, like Gina Sartori and Elizabeth Wallace before her, taught me—and I hope some of my colleagues—the significant value of undergraduate research assistance in the humanities as well as the sciences. Without Karen Hallman's careful research and keen insight, this book, and especially chapter 10, would be much weaker.

Archivists and librarians in many places helped me in my search for obscure documents, old sources, and the buried treasures that historians find in likely and unlikely places. Daphne Arnaiz-DeLeon, Director, Archives and Historical Services Division, State of New Mexico State Records Center and Archives, and her staff, especially Barry Drucker, worked patiently with me to find the sources that have allowed me to develop the New Mexico case studies. Archivists at the New Mexico Highlands University in Las Vegas were also very helpful in tracing that institution's history. Mark Burnette, Coordinator of Circulation and Archivist at the National-Louis University in Evanston, Illinois, could not have been more helpful or thorough in providing me materials for understanding the development of schools for kindergarten teachers such as the one that became the National College of Education. I am also grateful to archivists at the Library of the Haskell Indian Nations University in Lawrence, Kansas, who offered me valuable materials on the development of their school and the parallel developments in teacher education for American Indians and for African Americans; and also to archivists in the Government Documents Room of the Harold Washington Public Library in Chicago, which holds a treasure trove of documents on the governance of education in the city of Chicago and the state of Illinois; as well as to the staff of that most complete of research libraries, the Library of Congress in Washington, D.C., the documents from which, both original manuscripts and hard-to-find government publications, enriched this study. Finally, I must acknowledge the extraordinary staff and the wealth of historical resources that are contained in the Elmer Holmes Bobst Library at New York University. I was fortunate to be able to travel around the United States to do the research for this book, but a substantial amount of research was also done in that library a block from my New York apartment.

Several colleagues went above and beyond the call of duty in reading and commenting on drafts of this manuscript. I am very grateful to David Imig, Joan Malczewski, Christine A. Ogren, and Jonathan Zimmerman for detailed comments, questions, and suggestions. While I must, of course, absolve them of any responsibility for errors—or for opinions with which they still disagree—each of them saved me from embarrassing errors and made this a much stronger book.

As with everything in my life, my daughters and granddaughters, my beloved wife, Katherine, and our companion, Snowball, have made the time spent on this research so much richer than it could otherwise have been.

The dedication of this book to my first academic mentor, Robert W. Lynn, who guided me through years of graduate study and who first engaged me in serious study of professional education through the Lilly Endowment's history of theological education project, reflects one of my life's great and most pleasant debts.

Introduction

David F. Labaree has described a reality that anyone engaged in the field of teacher education knows all too well. In *The Trouble with Ed Schools* he writes:

> Institutionally, the ed school is the Rodney Dangerfield of higher education: it don't get no respect. The ed school is the butt of jokes in the university, where professors portray it as an intellectual wasteland; it is the object of scorn in schools, where teachers decry its programs as impractical and its research as irrelevant; and it is a convenient scapegoat in the world of education policy, where policymakers portray it as a root cause of bad teaching and inadequate learning.[1]

If Labaree's analysis is true, and there is certainly a great deal of evidence that however unfair it represents a view held by many, the question for the historian is, "How did this situation come to be?" And the question for anyone concerned with tomorrow's children and their teachers is, "What can we do to improve the situation?"

My study of the history of teacher education in the United States from the time of the American Revolution to the present will point to some of the reasons that such views are held but will also note that they are not new; indeed, that in virtually every generation from the early 1800s to the dawn of the 21st century, there have been many urgent voices calling for far-reaching reform in the preparation of the nation's teachers and many reforms designed specifically to respond to the critiques raised.

At the beginning of a new century many people are currently concerned about the state of teacher education in the United States. The federal government, private foundations, and state governments are spending millions of dollars and devising new laws and regulations to improve the preparation of a new generation of teachers. Reports filled with critiques and recommendations continue to be issued with predictable regularity. Colleges and universities are restructuring their teacher education programs, closing some, opening others, and radically restructuring most. And in the middle of all of this activity, many assumptions are being made about the past that are wide of the mark, sometimes quite wildly so. Teacher educators and their critics talk of decline without remembering that it is only in the last half-century that teachers were required to have a baccalaureate degree. They talk of the importance of testing teachers and changing the process of licensure without any sense of the history of teacher testing and licensing, which has gone on in some form in this country since at least the 1830s, not always with happy results. The list can go on. I wrote this book in part out of the conviction that the current public policy debates could be significantly elevated if they were informed by a better historical sense of what has gone before—among teacher educators and among their many critics in the university, government, the press, and the foundations.

At the same time, my interest in doing this study is not only to inform policy. As I have studied this topic I have become convinced that the history of teacher education is one of the most overlooked topics in the history of American education today. As Ellen Lagemann noted in the Preface to *An Elusive Science*, she wrote in part to help understand how past debates about research help us understand some of "the most difficult educational problems that exist in the United States today," but also because the lack of a good overview of the history of educational research prior to her work constituted "a rather egregious vacuum in the historical literature."[2] Larry Cuban said much the same of the issue of classroom instruction prior to his writing *How Teachers Taught*. As he noted, the fundamental questions, "How did teachers teach? Why did they teach as they did?"[3] have been overlooked by historians more concerned with the political and social context in which teaching took place. The same is true of teacher education today. While case studies and carefully detailed monographs that explore one region or one institutional structure in great depth are terribly important, there is also an essential role for the big picture study of a major theme be it research, classroom instruction, or teacher education. *Preparing America's Teachers: A History* seeks to be one step toward filling the gap in both the historical research and the education policy literature.

In the Introduction to one of the most useful studies of teacher preparation in the United States, John I. Goodlad noted that "Successive cycles of educational reform are as certain as the succession of the seasons. The diagnoses and proposals of one are resurfaced in the next, usually devoid of critical comparative analysis."[4] This is certainly true across a very wide spectrum in the field of education and it is painfully true in teacher preparation. As a historian of education myself who has spent most of the last two decades engaged in implementing a series of reform efforts in teacher education, I confess some embarrassment that it has also been true of my own professional life. Only lately have I come to understand that some of my efforts—implementing the Holmes and Carnegie recommendations in the state of Massachusetts in the 1980s and building a new set of connections between the faculty of arts and sciences and the faculty of education at Northeastern University in the 1990s—represented efforts that could trace their history to parallel efforts decades, even a century, earlier. Thus it seemed appropriate to me personally, as I happily laid down the responsibilities of being the dean of one school of education, to take up my historian's pen and study my own field—the preparation of the nation's teachers—in this context.

In beginning my research I quickly found that while there was a dearth of materials written about this topic, there were extraordinarily rich documentary resources for pursuing the research. Goodlad himself cites David Tyack's wise and still all too true observation "that educational historians have largely neglected teachers and teaching," and then goes on to note that, "They have largely neglected teacher education too." Ellen Lagemann also had noted that the "history of teacher education is still so understudied that one can only venture" an occasional hypothesis about the context for any specific report or innovation. My goal, in this volume, is to make a small contribution toward correcting that gap in the historical literature.[5]

While I have found that dissatisfaction and calls for reform can be found in every generation, it is also true that teacher education, like everything else, has changed dramatically in the United States over the past centuries. There is no golden age, no moment in the past when people felt—or should have felt—that they had gotten it right. There certainly have been improvements as well as other changes that may, in retrospect, seem more like mistakes. Although they have seldom been satisfactory to many, major reforms have taken place over the decades, and the preparation of teachers in the United States is probably better today than at any previous time.

For most of the history of the United States, from the American Revolution until well into the 1950s and 1960s, teacher preparation was a haphazard affair. The majority of teachers had no formal preparation, whether it was John Adams going from college to a teaching position in Worcester, Massachusetts, in the 1750s or a thirteen-year-old Lucia Downing taking the teaching exam as a lark in the 1880s, passing, and soon being hired to teach; it was often the case that teachers were simply hired by school boards seeking the best person willing to work for the low pay offered.

Nevertheless, during the first almost two centuries of the nation's history a number of programs did develop for the more specialized preparation of teachers. Be they the specialized academies like Emma Willard's at Troy, New York; or the normal schools that spread from Horace Mann's Massachusetts across the nation; or the short-term teachers' institutes that were developed to mirror the normal school curriculum in abbreviated form; or the urban high schools that offered some students, generally women, a postelementary curriculum in pedagogy, all of these differing routes to teaching, with all of their differing names and standards, had certain common characteristics. When Francis Parker described the yearlong post-high school program that he offered at Cook County Normal School in 1890 he made it clear that though the time was short, the goals were high. Parker said that "the mere study of methods, [as important as they were to Parker] per se, can not be substituted for the deficiency in knowledge of subjects taught." And, in the end, his goal was to bring aspiring teacher "face to face with the grave responsibilities and duties of the work which should be done in the school room."[6] In nearly all cases the schools, programs, and institutes offered for teachers combined Parker's three significant elements—subject matter knowledge, understanding of pedagogy and the learning process, and dedication to the work of teaching and the success of students. And for the most part, like Parker, the leaders and teachers in these differing programs simply refused to separate any of the essential elements.

Beginning in the 1890s, but more substantially only after World War II, teacher education began its most drastic shift. As universities created their own education chairs, departments, and schools in the 1890s, and then as the former city and state teachers colleges rushed to become all-purpose colleges in the 1950s, teacher preparation became one among many university responsibilities. The move to university status had many positive results for teacher preparation. For the first time students in the programs were expected to be high school graduates when they began their work, they were expected to study both subject matter and pedagogy at a college level, and they were expected to stay at it long enough to receive a baccalaureate degree. Indeed, by the 1960s both a baccalaureate degree and some amount of specialized study of education had become virtually a universal requirement for those entering teaching. But the move of education into the universities did not come without cost—substantial cost.

In 1920 a research team commissioned by the Carnegie Foundation for the Advancement of Teaching warned that teacher education schools needed to maintain a single-minded focus on that enterprise and "no consideration whatever should divert such schools from their task."[7] In spite of such clear recommendations, this was a road not taken. Single-purpose teachers colleges devoted exclusively or at least primarily to the preparation of teachers mostly disappeared in the United States, replaced by programs offered within multipurpose colleges and universities.

Unfortunately, universities have too seldom been welcoming places for aspiring teachers. In a hierarchy that places theory above practice and content knowledge above pedagogical knowledge, and, indeed, that adopts a condescending attitude toward students preparing for practical fields and the specialized faculty who attend to them, education departments—whether in research universities or in recently renamed normal schools—are almost universally considered the bottom of the university pecking order. Any concern on the part of the arts and sciences faculty to take seriously the ways to teach even their own discipline has tended to be greeted with derision as well beneath the theoretical leaders of the field who inhabit disciplinary departments.

On the other hand, as they have taken their place as members of one department or school in a larger and more diverse university world, education faculty members have tended to adopt all too many of the university's structures and pretenses. If being a member of a university faculty means being a specialist, education professors have tended to develop their own specialized research and their own impenetrable jargon. They, too, have distanced from practice, but they have also—perhaps more seriously—distanced themselves from concern with disciplinary content. They have, instead, tried to make education its own discipline, rather than a means of conveying the content of other disciplines, often, as David Labaree has noted, with disastrous results. And at the same time, being embedded in university structures, education departments and schools have sought control over more and more of the student's time, giving more courses in pedagogy while leaving less and less time for the academic disciplines that are, as Parker knew so well, essential to good teaching. Only the student who is majoring in education was expected to merge theory and practice, content and pedagogy. The faculty in the disciplines and in the education programs were above such mundane matters.

Finally, and perhaps most seriously, the third leg of the older preparatory tripod—the deep commitment to the work of teaching and the success of teachers—has virtually disappeared from professional preparation in education. The words of normal school students and professors from a century ago often seem quaint, but their sense of passion for a high calling, a calling that included doing whatever needed to be done to ensure student success, would be a welcome addition to the curriculum of many a 21st-century school of education.[8]

This view of history should not be seen as a romantic call for a return to the good old days of the normal schools. Those days were not that good after all; instruction was often pedantic and at far too low an academic level. Again, Labaree is correct when he writes, "Even if the normal school had survived as a separate institution with a purely professional mission, its science, math, social studies, and English professors would by no means be considered comparable to their counterparts in the disciplines, and the teachers who graduated from these institutions would correctly be considered even weaker in subject matter knowledge than the graduates of today's university-based education schools."[9] Nevertheless, I do conclude this historical study believing that there is something fundamentally wrong with the structure of teacher education today. The modern research university, even the modern teaching-focused college, is not the receptive home for the professional preparation of teachers that it should be. Teachers, and more important, the coming generations of young Americans who will be taught by them, deserve better. Until universities can honor practice on an equal plane with theory, until they can honor professions that focus on children as much as professions that focus on adults, and, perhaps most fundamentally, until they can honor professions where the majority of practitioners are women as much as they honor professions that have traditionally been dominated by men, we will not have the teacher preparation we need and that our children deserve. Much remains to be done if the next chapters of this history are to report the progress that our children deserve.

As we use this complicated historical story to seek better ways to move into the future, one conclusion of my study is that a diversity of institutional arrangements and paths to teaching probably serves future teachers better than maintaining "one best system." In this conclusion I am probably at odds with many of my contemporary teacher education colleagues. Nevertheless, as a result of writing this book, I have come to believe more strongly than ever that a diversity of routes into teaching serves teachers and their students better than a single route—a diversity governed by high standards for all options, but a diversity nonetheless. From the days of the nation's beginnings to the present the history of this field has more often than not been a story of wonderful diversity. There has never been "one best system" for preparing teachers and there is not likely to be one soon, and probably should not be one.

Certainly it is the case that all too often, diversity in the modes of preparation has allowed low standards for too many of those women and men who entered the classroom. Throughout the 19th century, as normal schools, teachers' institutes, and high schools began to offer specialized programs to prepare teachers, many elementary-level teachers—perhaps the majority—made little use of the new institutions and, in fact, did little in terms of initial preparation beyond completing elementary school themselves. Even with the widespread growth of high schools late in the 1800s, many high school teachers had not themselves studied far beyond the high school level, while others were college graduates. And in the first half of the 20th century, as 2-year normal schools became 4-year teachers colleges and these in turn became multipurpose colleges with their own graduate programs, and as universities established their own departments and schools of education, the most substantial report ever done on teacher education in the United States, the *National Survey of the Education of Teachers*, published in the early 1930s, voiced the hope that someday every teacher in the country might have at least 2 years of education beyond high school, a goal that was not within sight as that report went to press. It was only after World War II that a college education, usually including substantial study in a school or department of education, became the accepted route into teaching.

Yet in the midst of the diversity that characterized teacher preparation between the 1770s and the 1950s, teachers also fashioned careers for themselves, careers that involved continued learning even as they were teaching. Indeed, the very variety of institutional options allowed teachers to take charge of their own education rather than following a path proscribed by others. Young women, and some men, began teaching fresh out of school and then attended teachers' institutes year after year to hone their skills and exchange information with one another even as they built up their professional commitment. Others began teaching at a young age and then took time off to attend, and sometimes complete, a college education. Women and men whose own education had been severely limited, in the case of Southern African Americans by slavery, in the case of Northern European American women by gender constraints, founded institutions—missionary colleges, kindergarten training schools—that would allow the next generation of teachers to have a more advanced level of preparation than had been possible for the founders. There are certainly disappointments and setbacks in the story told in these pages, but this is also a story of high ideals and of a sense of agency among many individual teachers, as well as teacher educators, who used the diversity of institutions, and less formal agencies available to them, to create a system of professional preparation far higher than the minimum of the day and more diverse than a simple look at institutional histories would imply.

Nevertheless, the key to the future is not a return to the past. While this study of the history of teacher preparation in the United States leaves me dissatisfied and with a renewed sense of urgency for future changes, it also leaves me proud, proud for at least two reasons. Teacher education has always been a professional field where at least some of the practitioners in every generation are driven by a deep sense of moral purpose, a commitment to providing a better education for the next generation of young people in the nation and a commitment to what has recently come to be called the social justice agenda, to using that education to make the nation itself, in the words of John Dewey, a place that is "more lovely, worthy, and harmonious." While education is hardly alone in this commitment, it is a professional field that has attended seriously to ethical claims.

The last two decades have seen significant progress in meeting goals long espoused. For all of the ways in which educational research has sometimes been an obscurantist search for prestige by individual faculty members bent on distancing themselves from the practice of teaching—and it has been that—educational research has also brought us much closer than any previous generation to actually understanding how students learn and therefore how teachers might teach effectively. Education is far from being a science; indeed, it probably never will be, for there is too much richness in the strange human interaction in which one human being supports another in the process of learning and growth. But we do know more—a lot more—about how to teach effectively and how to do it with a more diverse group of young people than we have before. In the last two decades there has been a renewed commitment on the part of individuals and institutions to the preparation of teachers. Much as many of us might disagree with one another—and we certainly do disagree—there are many today who are seeking to do more, and to use evidence to determine what should be done. Something is afoot in teacher education in the United States in the early years of a new century, and it will make the next years most interesting to see where it leads and what the next chapter in this history has to tell.

A word about what this study does and does not do and about terms used is in order in this Introduction. I have tried, as best I can, to keep the focus on the preparation of teachers. Each chapter opens with a brief biographical sketch of an individual who used one or more institutional structures to craft their own education in ways that are illustrative of some of the larger patterns of their era. I have also tried to offer case studies where possible so that a larger theme is illustrated in a specific location. But the focus here is teachers, elementary teachers and high school teachers. The preparation of many other educators, administrators, guidance counselors, and policy leaders is also very important, but the history of their preparation is a different volume.

I have not pursued all of the organizations or policy debates that have been significant during the last two centuries. The American Association of Colleges for Teacher Education, which has been so important in my own professional life, gets very little attention, as do accrediting agencies, research bodies, and those committed to policy analysis. I have tried, with varying levels of success, to stay close to the story of what was actually happening in each generation in those institutions—formal and informal—that prepared teachers and to look at national movements and organizations as they impacted those institutions. I have tried to give equal attention to institutions that are the predecessors of contemporary places where teachers are taught and to those that were once important but are no longer. On the other hand, this is an institutional history. While I have used the stories of individual teachers to examine various institutional options, the rich stories of the lives of aspiring teachers and the continuing educational stories of these individuals as they have moved through their careers are simply beyond the scope of this book. I have also tried to organize the book more or less chronologically but even more by the differing institutional types so that the chapters tell the story of one significant institutional structure that was adopted for some period of time and in which a large number of teachers were educated.

Readers of this book who are familiar with contemporary teacher education are bound to be disappointed at times that I have left out important organizations and significant institutions. In seeking to cover over 200 years of educational history in a volume of reasonable length, I have had to cut material dear to me and others and leave out examples that might have enriched the story. Especially in studying the last two decades, the gaps are inevitable.

Finally, I note that this is a study of the history of teacher preparation in the United States. I can already hear my friend Harry Judge saying, "You cannot study that topic in isolation; you need international comparisons." I must simply confess that while I ultimately agree, such a study is also the topic for another book.

A word about terms is also in order. I have generally used the terms as they were used during the time period under consideration. Thus, in the earlier parts of the 19th century I have alternated between talking about elementary school teachers as a generic term and using the terms *primary school teachers* (which generally referred to grades 1 through 4 or the equivalent) and *grammar school teachers* (which generally referred to grades 5 through 8 or the equivalent). As these distinctions disappeared into a more comprehensive 1st- through 8th-grade elementary school, I have silently switched to the term of use, "elementary teachers." In the same way, through most of the history, teachers sought certification for approval to begin their work—from a district or later a state—though more recently the language has changed to *initial licensure*, with certification being something achieved at a much higher level of status. But that was not the way people talked in 1920 or 1870, and so it is not the language I have used in describing the events of the 1870s or 1920s.

No history is written without bias, and I have tried to be clear about my own biases and assumptions in writing about this history of teacher preparation. My biases have certainly colored the stories that I have chosen to tell and the way in which I have told them. At the same time, I have tried, within the constraint of writing a book that can be read in a reasonable amount of time, to offer enough information for a reader to arrive at quite different conclusions than my own. Most of all, I have sought to fulfill my primary goal, to add one piece to the historical literature and to give some useful background to those who care about the coming chapters in the history of this enterprise.

1

Schooling Teachers for a New Nation

1750–1830

Late in the summer of 1755, a young John Adams, one of that spring's 25 graduates from Harvard College, made the 60-mile horseback ride from his home in Braintree, Massachusetts, to Worcester to take up his duties as the master of a grammar school in that central Massachusetts town. For Adams, teaching was his first job in a career that would lead him in time to success as a lawyer in Massachusetts, a leading proponent of the Declaration of Independence, and, indeed, to the White House itself. But in 1755, taking a position as a teacher before moving on to other employment was not unusual for a recent graduate of one of the colonial colleges in what would be—some 25 years later and with significant help from Adams—a new nation.

During his senior year in college Adams found himself leaning toward a career in law, though he had not entirely ruled out the ministry or medicine, but all of these fields required further study, and "A Lawyer must have a Fee, for taking me into his Office." The next step was obvious. "I therefore gave out that I would take a School, and took my Degree at College undetermined whether I should study Divinity, Law or Physick." Also attending the Harvard commencement that year was a "Mr. Mccarty of Worcester who was empowered by the Select Men of that Town to procure them a Latin Master for their Grammar School [and who] engaged me to undertake it." Adams was on his way to his new career.[1] Adams stayed at his school in Worcester for 3 years and during the last two he also read law at night in the home of a Worcester attorney, James Putnam. At the end of those years, having completed his studies with Putnam, Adams was admitted to the Massachusetts bar, and that was the end of his teaching career.[2]

Adams had decidedly mixed reactions to teaching the dozen or so boys and girls who appeared in his school. He wrote in his diary that "I find by repeated experiment and observation, in my School, that human nature is more easily wrought upon and governed, by promises and encouragement and praise than by punishment, and threatening and blame." And he seemed to revel in the times when his encouragement and praise worked. At other times, he fell into the deepest of depression, writing, "I long to study sometimes, but have no opportunity. . . . I have no books, no time, no friends, I must therefore be contented to live and die an ignorant, obscure fellow." Nevertheless, in March 1756, Adams recorded,

> I sometimes, in my sprightly moments, consider my self, in my great chair at school, as some dictator at the head of a commonwealth. In this little state I can discover all the great geniuses, all the surprising actions and revolutions of the great world in miniature. . . . Is it not then the highest pleasure my friend to preside in this little world, to bestow the proper applause upon virtuous and generous actions, to blame and punish every vicious and contracted trick, to wear out of the tender mind every thing that is mean and little, and fire the new born soul with noble ardor and emulation. The world affords no greater pleasure.

But one thing was absolutely clear to Adams, whatever pleasure it afforded him: teaching was temporary work, to be done until he could get on with his real career.[3]

COLLEGES

Adams's lack of specialized preparation and his assumption that teaching was temporary work before he went on to more serious and extended professional ventures was typical of his time, as it would be of many later points in history. In the colonial era teaching was often something young women did at home and young men did between the end of college and the beginning of what they saw as their real careers, often as lawyers or ministers. For a young man, home from college on the 4-to-6-week winter vacation that coincided with the school term in many communities or recently graduated from college, teaching was a way to earn money to continue their education or to keep themselves gainfully employed while waiting for other—and better—opportunities. Indeed, in the 18th century some college officials saw providing teaching opportunities as a way to award scholarships to poor students and adjusted their schedules accordingly.[4] And as many as 40 percent of the graduates of Harvard College in the 140 years between its founding in 1636 and the American Revolution in 1776 taught at some point in their lives. For Yale, the number was closer to 20 percent. But for both, the vast majority of these taught for a year or two and then moved on.[5]

These colonial college students and recent graduates did not teach because Harvard or any of the other colonial colleges offered a course or program to prepare them to be teachers. None of the colonial teachers had such specialized courses. Of course, the colonial colleges did not offer vocational preparation for the ministry or the practice of law, either, though those fields were the eventual destinations of the majority of their graduates.

Colonial collegiate education, following the English model, was broadly liberal in a 17th- and 18th-century understanding of liberal. It focused on the Greek and Roman classics, supplemented with considerable study in the natural sciences and mathematics and on the development in the students of both "mental discipline" and oratorical skills that could be demonstrated. The curriculum did not include anything a modern observer would recognize as professional preparation for teaching, law, medicine, or the ministry. Well into the 19th century, college leaders debated whether a college education should include practical preparation for any profession. While the spirit of the revolution of 1776 led some to experiment with more practical courses, well into the 19th century the majority of colleges followed the lead of Yale's faculty, which in 1828 proclaimed, "Our object is not to teach that which is peculiar to any one of the professions; but to lay the foundation which is common to them all."[6]

Those who wanted to pursue careers in the ministry or law usually "read divinity" or "read law" as an apprentice living in the home and studying with and modeling their plans on the work of a respected master of the vocation. The first professional school in the United States, Andover Theological Seminary for the preparation of ministers, did not appear until 1808.[7] But throughout the colonial era and well into the 19th century the assumption was that teaching did not need an apprenticeship or other professional preparation. These college students and graduates believed they already knew how to teach; after all, they had been students themselves and had watched others do it. Almost any relatively well-educated citizen, certainly any college graduate, was thought ready to teach.[8] On the other hand, few teachers in the colonial era stayed in the teaching profession for more than 5 years. Teaching for a colonial college graduate was always a beginning rather than an end of professional life.

In the years after the American Revolution, colleges proliferated in the United States at an amazing rate. There were nine recognized, degree-granting colleges in the colonies at the time of Independence. Between 1799 and 1861, 160 new permanent colleges were founded—19 prior to 1802. The result of such rapid college founding was generally a decrease in academic standards as too many colleges fought for too little money and too few students. Every community and every religious group wanted its own college for, as Theodore Rawson Crane noted, "A college sounded more imposing than a preparatory school, though many so-called colleges were little better than academies." There were major battles about the appropriate curriculum, although in general a broad liberal foundation and a strong emphasis on character development and morality were preferred to any specific professional preparation.[9]

Colleges generally remained white male bastions, although starting in the 1830s a few—led by Antioch and Oberlin—began to admit a limited number of women. More opportunities for women are discussed in the next chapter, but it is important to note that separate women's colleges began to be available with the founding of Troy Female Seminary in 1821, Mount Holyoke Seminary in 1837, and the Wesleyan Female College of Macon, Georgia, the first to offer academic degrees, in 1836. The college population was also overwhelmingly European-American. In spite of efforts dating to the earliest foundations of the colonial colleges to offer programs for American Indians, very little ever came of such efforts. And while some colleges—again led by Antioch and Oberlin—did include African Americans in their student bodies, the vast majority of Americans of African descent remained in slavery and by Southern law required to stay far from the classrooms of any educational institution. Christopher Lucas estimates that not more than a total of twenty-eight college degrees had been awarded to African Americans prior to the Emancipation Proclamation, in spite of Antioch and Oberlin and the opening of other schools like Avery College in Allegheny City, Pennsylvania, in 1849, Wilberforce University in Ohio in 1856, and Lincoln University of Pennsylvania in 1858.[10]

The small minority of college graduates who devoted themselves to teaching as a lifelong career were noteworthy. Perhaps the most famous was Ezekiel Cheever. Born in England and educated at Emmanuel College, Cambridge, Cheever came to North America in 1637 and taught school first in New Haven, Connecticut, then for 11 years at Ipswich, Massachusetts, and finally for 37 years from 1671 until he died in 1708 at the age of 93 at Boston Latin School. Cheever was remembered by one of his students, Cotton Mather, as "A learned master of the languages" who "taught us first good sense to understand." There were others like Cheever in the colonial era—a few others. Lawrence Cremin has estimated that only 3 percent of Harvard's colonial graduates remained in teaching for their entire careers.[11]

The Latin grammar schools were especially well served by having college graduates as their teachers. Their only purpose, after all, was to prepare young men for college by teaching them the Latin and Greek that were required for admission. It is a mistake to view the colonial grammar schools that were a prominent part of the educational system of New England and present in other colonies as forerunners of the modern high school. The grammar schools were highly specialized schools preparing a small subset of the population for college admission. Far more diverse, and showing much greater variety, were the schools known as petty or sometimes dame schools that offered a basic education. Sometimes in separate schools for reading and others for writing and arithmetic, sometimes sponsored by towns, often representing very informal arrangements, the petty schools were the heart of colonial education. And while teaching in grammar schools obviously required a knowledge of the Latin and Greek languages that were at the heart of their curriculum—a knowledge best acquired by college attendance—the requirements to teach in the petty schools were much less stringent.[12]

The pattern of young men moving from colleges into teaching did not end with the American Revolution or the rise of specialized teacher preparation schools. As William J. Reese notes, "Throughout the nineteenth century, Harvard educated most of the male masters, submasters, and tutors of Boston's Latin School, English High School, and the girls' secondary school. Yale educated many teachers for Connecticut's larger high schools, including prestigious Hartford High." For the prestigious urban high schools that offered the best chances of attending elite colleges—like Boston Latin School and Hartford High—a degree from those same colleges seemed logically to be the best possible preparation for the teachers.[13] These were hardly the schools of the majority of the nation's young citizens, but they were those for many of the local and national elite, and it mattered to members of this elite where their children's teachers had gone to school.

While some college graduates found lifelong careers in the nation's emerging high schools, many more continued to view teaching as the last resort or more often as temporary work. Well into the 19th century, clergy waiting for a church post to open up, farmers and merchants seeking a supplemental income in the winter, and men who had failed at another profession or were in transition kept school for a period of time. The baccalaureate degree was seen by most school board members who did the hiring as far exceeding the job requirements. But for those grammar and emerging high schools that were specifically preparing their students for college, a college degree was an excellent preparation for the teacher even if not an essential one.

ACADEMIES

Douglas Sloan described the place of academies in American education prior to the American Revolution: "Much of the formal higher education available in the southern and western settlements of the eighteenth century took place in academies founded by Presbyterian ministers. . . . While a primary purpose of the academies was to provide for ministerial education, they also accepted young men preparing for all the learned professions, and focused on college preparatory and when possible college level instruction."[14] And among these professions was teaching. Like the college graduates, some academy graduates taught for a short period of time before moving on to other work, while others made teaching a career, sometimes in another academy. Nevertheless, as the author of one of the most careful studies of the history of the academy movement says, "The early academies made no special provisions or definite attempts to train teachers for schools of a lower grade. Such teachers were at first only a by-product. This instruction was incidental, unorganized, unrecognized by the State, and even unnoticed for a time by the academy officials themselves."[15] In this the colonial academies were very much like the colleges that many of them sought to become. All of that would change, however, in the 19th century.

In another perceptive essay, Douglas Sloan also reminds us that we need to be very careful using 20th- or 21st-century institutional definitions when we look at the 18th or early 19th century. At least until the Civil War, whether one used the term *college* or *academy* or a host of other terms such as *seminary, institute,* or, later, *normal school,* the specific term did not tell a great deal about either the purpose or the academic quality or level of the institution. Academies were the forerunners of both high schools and colleges, and in a few places normal schools, depending on institutional trajectory. What did characterize an academy was, first, that unlike a public school, it was private in that it was controlled by a self-perpetuating board of trustees rather than an elected body—though it often received public funds—and secondly that it often had a more diverse and practical curriculum than either the college preparatory Latin grammar school or the colonial college. Nevertheless, in their antebellum incarnation academies often fulfilled, among other things, the role of both college preparation and college itself. Certainly, among their many roles, pre–Civil War academies also prepared teachers.[16]

While the colonial academy, like the colonial college, was almost always launched by one Protestant denomination both to prepare ministers and to ensure the development of a broad-ranging civic leadership that was sympathetic to their values, national independence brought change more quickly to the academies than it did to the colleges. With a few important exceptions, colleges tended to be founded by religious groups, at least until the Civil War. After the Revolution, however, the academy-founding movement as a whole was far more secular than was the case of the antebellum college. Speaking of the founding of academies between the Revolution and the Civil War, Theodore Sizer wrote, "Local communities needed schools of the lower grades far more than they needed colleges. . . . Far fewer sectarian than non-sectarian academies were founded in Vermont; the same was true in Mississippi. Only about one-third of Indiana's academies were sectarian . . ." Local communities wanted something that would educate some youth above the level offered in the common schools. Community leaders were usually confident that their academy, like the common school and the college, would teach a broad and generally Protestant morality without engaging in denominational squabbles. An academy's curriculum could be broader than its predecessor the Latin grammar school, which taught a fairly narrow curriculum, designed exclusively to prepare boys for college. The academy could prepare boys and girls for participation in a variety of fields and for civic life in general. And it could explicitly prepare teachers.[17]

In one example, Sizer notes, "Of the five 'purposes' of Barre Academy in Vermont, two are quite specific—college preparation and teacher training; two are vaguely humanistic—'sound, practical education' for boys and 'a liberal education' for girls; and only the last has a somewhat moral tone—'to promote virtue, morality, and piety in the young.'"[18] Barre was hardly alone in its focus, among many others, on teacher preparation.

After the Revolution, New York State developed by far the tightest level of state control of its schools and colleges with the creation of what was called—then and now—the University of the State of New York in 1784 with a powerful Board of Regents. The university had no students of its own but was a vehicle for the state to exert its influence on all the other schools from Kings College, renamed Columbia, on down. And very soon after their launch, the Regents began to exert their influence on the academies of the state. Although schools above the elementary level had existed in some form in New York since the grammar schools of New Amsterdam were established in the mid-1600s, in the decades after the Revolution the New York Regents brought a level of order to higher education in their state not seen elsewhere.[19]

In 1821, the Regents specifically embraced the place of the academies in the preparation of New York's teachers, reminding the state legislature of the need to support poor students who wanted to attend academies, since "it is to those seminaries that we must look for a supply of teachers for the common schools." The legislature was convinced. During the 1820s Governor DeWitt Clinton and other New Yorkers argued in favor of separate county-level teacher training schools for teachers, but the Regents and the legislature continued to support the existing academies. In 1826 a State Senate committee responded to Clinton that his message "respecting the establishment of an institution expressly for the purpose of educating teachers, will not answer the exigencies of the case." The Regents insisted that "teachers for common schools must generally be derived from the academies." And the money, mostly in the form of scholarships for students, followed the route preferred by the Regents and the legislature.[20]

Various efforts were made to encourage academies to do more to meet the teacher shortage. In 1834 the Regents selected 8 academies, later expanded to 16, and funded the development of their teacher preparation programs, and in 1838 the legislature required every academy that received $700 or more in state funds to maintain a department "for the instruction of common school teachers." Finally, between 1849 and 1889 New York developed a tightly organized system in which one academy in each of the state's 44 counties received state funds on the condition that it establish a program for at least 20 students in the "science of common school teaching."[21]

Reports to the Regents show that for the most part, these programs were efficiently run. There were always debates about the quality of the programs. The leaders of the academies defended their programs. Noah T. Clarke, principal of the Canandaigua Academy, reflected on his 31-year association with the institution:

Upon entering Canandaigua Academy, in April 1837, I found the teachers department in full operation. The "teachers class" numbered about thirty young men, and was mainly under the instruction of the principal, the late Mr. Henry Howe. The time of the class was about half of it spent in the "teachers" course of study. That course consisted in studies and recitations of the common branches; a daily drill upon the best methods of teaching, lectures upon the theory of teaching, and also upon geology, natural and mental philosophy, physical geography and history, upon warming and ventilation, the laws of health, teachers associations, school houses and blackboards, also upon the teacher's social habits and duties as a member of the community in which he might be placed . . . although I had taught school before, yet I found the instruction of that course of incalculable value; and if I have ever been able to accomplish anything as an instructor of youth, I owe it, in no small degree, to the exercises of that teachers class.[22]

However defensive, the words seem to represent a real respect for the institution.

Not everyone agreed. In 1882 the chancellor of the University of New York criticized the program, since "during these forty years in which we have been applying the money of the State to teachers classes, the application has often been very improper, because the service performed was not good." For all the ongoing debates about the quality of the academy programs—similar in some ways to the debates about every other program that has ever been offered for teachers—it was the case that in the middle decades of the 19th century, about one-fourth of New York's teachers were graduates of the teacher preparation programs offered at the academies, while other academy graduates entered teaching without benefit of specialized training. Given the alternatives available, George Miller's conclusion that "on the whole, it seems that the academies sent out the best teachers available for the elementary schools" seems warranted.[23]

No other state had New York's level of centralized control of education in the 19th century and no other state kept its records so well. Nevertheless, in many places academies played a more or less central role in teacher preparation between the Revolution and the Civil War. One of the most famous of the academies, Phillips Academy in Andover, Massachusetts, opened a Teachers' Seminary in 1829. Since Andover was also the home of Andover Theological Seminary, the first separate graduate school for the preparation of ministers, the opening of a separate teachers' seminary may not be surprising. Unlike the theological school, which was designed primarily to offer advanced work for college graduates, the Teachers' Seminary offered a course parallel to the classical/college preparatory one, which was and is at the heart of Phillips Andover's mission.[24]

In fact, the Teachers' Seminary was part of a larger reform effort at Andover in the 1820s. Following the model of the newly emerging high school, especially Boston's English Classical High School, Andover's trustees decided that in addition to the classical curriculum preparing boys for college, they needed a separate program that would prepare others who were "without the means of acquiring a collegiate degree," for immediate employment including as "teachers in the lower grades." Thus in 1830 they opened a school, of which, they said, "The most prominent object is to educate Instructors of common and other schools. Another object is to educate practical men, for all the departments of common life." As chapter 5 will show, offering teacher preparation as one of the major courses at a new high school was the norm, not the exception, for much of the 19th century. What was unique at Andover was the fact that on the same campus there was to be a traditional Latin grammar school preparing one group of young men for college and parallel to it a high school preparing teachers and men of business.

The first principal of the new school was Samuel Read Hall, who already in 1823 had launched one of the first schools to prepare teachers in Concord, Vermont. Hall was famous not only for his school but also for his *Lectures on School-Keeping*, which became perhaps the most widely used textbook of a range of teacher education institutions throughout much of the 19th century. Students generally took a 3-year high school–level program whether they were preparing to teach or to go into business, though the records make it clear that as with many other schools, students dropped in and out on a fairly regular basis. Tuition was collected by the week. Records of the school show that in the winter term of 1839 some 75 to 100 students from the school—the majority of the student body—were actually away from their studies earning money teaching in Massachusetts district schools.

Offering the curriculum of a high school, including teacher preparation, alongside a classical Latin school curriculum was too much for one institution. Rivalries between the two never ended, with "those connected with the classical Academy . . . inclined to look with contempt on the Teachers' Seminary . . . ," and in 1842 the programs were officially merged, though in fact the high school was simply closed and the traditional program at the academy took on a slightly stronger English Department. Though short-lived, the Andover experiment offers a useful case study of three different models of secondary education that coexisted in antebellum America—the older traditional Latin grammar program of college preparation; the multipurpose academy with a broad curriculum that might, or might not, prepare one for college; and the more explicitly vocational teacher preparation program that could be conducted in a high school or a separate institution that would come to be called, in many places, a normal school.[25]

HOME SCHOOLING, DAME SCHOOLS,
AND A NEW COMMON SCHOOL TEACHER

Writing in her diary in 1828, a then 10-year-old Lavinia Bailey Kelly reviewed the schooling she had received over the previous 5 years of her life:

> The first school that I attended was kept by Miss Mary Frost, of Andover, Mass. . . . in the summer of 1822. In the summers of the following years I attended school kept by Miss Frost, 1823, Miss Matilda Prentice 1824, Miss Martha Mead 1825, Miss Prentice 1826, Miss Harriet Nealey 1827. In the winters I never attended school. In the spring this year I was at Warner, and attended a school kept by Miss Sally Lyman about a fortnight.

Moving into her 10th year, Kelly began a more formal education at "the young ladies school kept at Mr. Hills in this town [Northwood, Massachusetts], by Miss Mary Hiddes and Miss Caroline Boynton of Dunstable," in which there were 24 pupils studying geography and writing and learning to work lace.[26] Except for the last experience, Kelly's schooling seems to reflect that of many young people, male and female, for at least the previous century. They attended very informal schools kept on an irregular schedule taught by women, and occasionally men, who wanted to make a little money and perhaps even do a little good. Nancy Cott is certainly right when she says, "Many of these must have been ephemeral establishments, lasting only as long as a teacher's need for money, and ability to find students, complemented each other."[27] Known as petty or dame schools (the latter because of the gender of the teacher), they were also the places where generations of European Americans learned to read and often to write. Up to the time of the American Revolution, and for a generation afterward, they were the backbone of the educational system. And we know surprisingly little about those schools or the teachers who taught in them.

Dame schools, as such, tended to be strongest in New England, though similar informal arrangements existed elsewhere. Varying mixes of individual payments and support from the towns maintained the teachers. In 1682, Springfield, Massachusetts, agreed with "Goodwife Mirick to encourage her in the good work of training up children, and teaching children to read, and that she should have three pence a week for every child that she takes to perform this good work for." Other towns in Massachusetts, Connecticut, and New Hampshire have similar notations in their records from the late 1600s and early 1700s. We do not have any reliable information about how Goodwife Mirick or her counterparts prepared themselves for their responsibilities.[28]

The dame schools generally met in the homes of the women who ran them. The 18th-century hornbook that offered the alphabet and the creed, and similar resources for introducing students to reading, writing, spelling, and some arithmetic, seem to have been the core of the curriculum. David Tyack and Elisabeth Hansot describe the dame school:

> The typical private dame school consisted of a few girls and boys under six or seven years of age meeting in the home of a woman who was paid a small sum by parents for supervising their children. She was expected to teach them to stay out of mischief, to mind their manners, to learn a catechism or short psalter, and to do simple tasks about the house, such as shelling beans. She often had to manage her own household while doing this.

While simple—and all too easily disparaged by contemporary and later commentators—these were, in fact, the tools of basic literacy that seem to have been available on a fairly widespread basis to European-American girls as well as boys. And based as they were in homes, the schools seemed like a simple extension of women's maternal sphere. They also provided a foundation that in later generations would slowly become the first female-led summer sessions—while the men were busy elsewhere—and eventually common schools taught by women teachers.[29]

Memories of the schools yielded a diverse evaluation. When Miriam Wood of Dorchester died in 1706, her epitaph called her, "A woman well beloved of all her neighbors; For her care of small folks education, their number being great." On the other hand, a teacher in Industry, Maine, described as "An old maiden lady [who] was employed occasionally a short time to teach children their letters and to spell out words," and was someone who "was quite incompetent."[30]

In the middle and Southern colonies, similar sorts of informal instruction were offered. The *New York Gazette* for December 16, 1762, carried an advertisement:

> Wants Employment, A single woman who can be well recommended for her honesty and fidelity, is well qualified to instruct children of both sexes in all that is necessary for their years and would go in a gentleman's family, in Town or Country, on reasonable Terms.

During the same time period, German immigrants in Pennsylvania—both Lutheran and Moravians—created elementary-level schools at their churches while Quaker women offered perhaps the most formal instruction in places like Anne Parrish's school for poor girls in Philadelphia. With very few exceptions—Parrish's school continued for 129 years until 1923—these schools opened and closed as employment or contracts were needed or terminated.[31]

As time passed, these informal educational opportunities became more formal. Private dame schools became the summer term of a town's common school. Other towns followed Springfield and helped pay the costs of the schools. As David Tyack and Elisabeth Hansot note, "By almost imperceptible steps, and not by abrupt shifts in policy, the people of Massachusetts began to blur the sharp gender distinction between the formal public schooling that was open only to boys and the informal education that was available to both girls and boys. In the process, girls as students and women as teachers gained a foothold in public education." After the Revolution, as Massachusetts created a new system of education, it required that schoolmistresses as well as school masters be certified by the town officials as being of good moral character, a recognition that gave them "a new kind of prestige in their communities." The same was true to greater or lesser degrees, and on differing timelines, in all of the American colonies.[32]

The reality is that the women who offered this initially informal instruction, who taught basic reading and sometimes writing and mathematics to young girls and boys prior to their entry into more formal schooling, are largely an anonymous lot. We know that the schools existed. We know from autobiographical and other sources how important they were. But we know far too little about the teachers who taught in these informal but essential schools and certainly almost nothing about their preparation to teach.

If it is true that for the 18th and much of the 19th centuries the meaning of institutional terms—*college, university, academy, seminary*—is ambiguous, and it certainly is, then the meaning of what constituted a school, and therefore a schoolteacher, at the same point in history is even more confusing. Lawrence A. Cremin was certainly correct when he wrote:

> It is difficult to generalize with any degree of precision about the extent of schooling in provincial America, largely because of the phenomenal variation in types and modes of instruction and the consequent difficulty of determining exactly what to call a school. We do know, as has already been indicated, that there were individual teachers of reading, writing, ciphering, grammar, bookkeeping, surveying, navigation, fencing, dancing, music, modern languages, embroidery, and every conceivable combination of these and other subjects; that these teachers taught part time and full time, by day and by evening, in their homes, in other people's homes, in rented rooms, in churches and meetinghouses, in abandoned buildings, and in buildings erected especially for their use; that they were self-employed and employed by others (acting as individuals or through self-constituted, self-perpetuating, or elected boards); and that they were paid with funds obtained from employers, patrons, subscriptions, lotteries, endowments, tuition rates, and taxes.[33]

In such a context, to speak with any degree of precision about the preparation of the teachers for these heterogeneous schools is simply ludicrous. Nevertheless, some generalizations are possible.

Early in the European development of all of the English colonies that would become the United States, the longstanding English notion that schoolmasters should be licensed to ensure their religious orthodoxy quickly took root. Starting in 1654, Puritan Massachusetts made it the responsibility of the selectmen of each town and the faculty of Harvard College to ensure that no teacher remain in office "that have manifested themselves unsound in the faith, or scandalous in their lives . . ." When the English took control of New Amsterdam and renamed it New York in 1664, the governor and later the Archbishop of Canterbury was responsible for licensing all teachers. And in Virginia, beginning in 1683 the royal governors required every schoolmaster to present themselves in Jamestown "in order to present evidence of their intellectual competence, uprightness and sobriety, and general conformity to the doctrines of the Church of England." In reality, many of Virginia's teachers never bothered to make the trip, Dutch teachers continued to teach in New York for another half-century after the English gained control, and even in the more tightly controlled Massachusetts the law was hard to enforce. But the notion that there was a baseline for teaching—one far more focused on religious orthodoxy than scholarly or pedagogical skills—started early in the development of European-style schooling. And the assumption that the key requirement for any teacher is good moral character and a quasi-religious enthusiasm for the work has persisted long after the more formal tests for religious orthodoxy disappeared.[34]

The higher the level of institution, the more we know about the teachers. We have solid biographical information, including knowing their own academic preparation, on the early faculty of Harvard, Yale, and William and Mary as well as on many of the academies and quite a few of the grammar schools. We know less—much less—about the women who taught in the dame schools that were at the foundation of the colonial educational edifice. Whether these women had themselves learned at school or at home, we can assume that they were usually quite literate enough to offer effective instruction to their charges. Writing half a century ago, Samuel Eliot Morison estimated that in New England, and probably in at least some of the middle colonies, female literacy among women of European origin had risen from something in the range of 40 percent in the mid-1600s to 62 percent by 1700, while European male literacy remained stable at around 90 percent. Somewhat more recently, Kenneth A. Lockridge estimates that while female literacy rose from around one-third in the 1670s to about 45 percent of women for the rest of the colonial and early national periods. Morrison also notes that the differing studies that all point to these generalizations focus on the ability to write—or at least sign one's name—and that the colonial school laws focused only on reading, so there may have been many others, "not only in New England but in the Middle Colonies and Virginia, who were unable to write their names could read the King James Bible and other simple English texts."[35]

Given such rates of female literacy, one wonders at statements like Christopher J. Lucas's that "Many in the 1600s were housewives and widows, barely literate themselves, who organized what were colloquially called 'dame schools.'" While Lucas is certainly right that "Acquaintance with the common subjects imparted to children was considered sufficient qualification for practically anyone to teach," a quick look at literacy rates, and at the expectations that colonial citizens would be literate, leads to a fairly logical conclusion that such acquaintance involved a fairly high level of literacy.[36] David Tyack and Elisabeth Hansot may be closer to the truth when they write that "The negative stereotype of dame schools perpetuated by historians who have focused only on public institutions and the professionalization of teaching may reveal a male bias."[37]

Beyond the assumption that the keepers of dame schools and other petty school arrangements were more often than not drawn from the half of women who were literate, we simply do not have enough information to say much about the preparation of the teachers in these places or other women who were their contemporaries. Many probably learned at home and then taught at home. Some may have found a way to sit in on the lessons offered to their brothers. Certainly many, like Abigail Adams, learned to read on their own and then read voraciously, finding "great pleasure and entertainment from it,"[38] while others may well have been much more indifferent readers. But the preparation and the life work of these teachers remains largely unexplored territory.

MISSIONARIES AND INDIGENOUS TEACHERS

In 1759, four years after John Adams had set out for Worcester to teach his school, Samson Occom was ordained as a Congregational minister in Connecticut and moved to Long Island, New York, as both a missionary and a teacher. He stayed there for 12 years, reporting:

> My Method in the School was, as Soon as the Children got together, and took their proper Seats, I Prayed with them, then began to hear them. I generally began (after Some of them Could Spell and Read) with those that were yet in their Alphabets; So around, as they were properly Seated, till I go through; and I obliged them to Study their Books, and to help one another . . .

While Occom's teaching style was probably very similar to that used by Adams, his background could not have been more different. Occom was a young Mohegan Indian who had been converted to Christianity during one of the great colonial revivals and who had, at age 20, gone to Reverend Eleazar Wheelock asking to be taught to read. Wheelock had recently founded Moor's Indian Charity School and he welcomed Occom, teaching him not only reading in English but, as with all his students, Greek, Latin, and Hebrew so that they could read both the Bible and the Latin classics in the original and, as good Protestants, make their own interpretation of the former. Boys and girls at Moor's Indian Charity School rose at 5:00 A.M., prayed, studied a traditional colonial classical collegiate curriculum, and helped earn their own keep as well. Occom, who would go on to a successful career as both a minister and a teacher, and who helped substantially in the fundraising that eventually allowed Wheelock to move from Moor's School to found Dartmouth College, was certainly one of the more highly educated teachers of any race in the United States when independence was declared.

While he was far from typical, Occom was not alone. There were many classically trained missionaries, many of them college graduates, who became teachers among the Indians of North America whether they were English Protestants along the Atlantic coast, Catholic priests in the Spanish-controlled Southwest or coming south from French Canada, or the case Alaska Russian Orthodox missionaries who by 1867 had founded over 50 schools in that territory.[39]

Indeed, the range of teachers in the lands that would become the United States—and their preparation—is extraordinary. The first schools—in the European understanding of schooling—in the West and Southwest were founded and taught by Spanish missionaries, mostly Franciscan priests who had been educated in the Catholic seminaries of Spain and Mexico. In the early 1700s, the London-based Society for the Propagation of the Gospel in Foreign Parts began to send missionaries to the colonies who would both preach and teach. The teachers, like the preachers, had to be ordained, at least as deacons, and this meant that they had to be graduates of Oxford or Cambridge. And Puritans in New England, Lutherans and Moravians, Presbyterians and Quakers in the middle colonies all imported European college graduates as both clergy and as teachers and often saw little distinction between the two roles.[40]

At the other end of the educational spectrum—in terms of formal preparation—were not only the teachers in the dame schools, but also the teachers who never called themselves teachers at all or who dared not let others know that they were teaching. The issue of the education of former slaves will be explored in detail in chapter 6, but it is important to note that some slaves learned to read and write in spite of extraordinary difficulty. In the colonial era, many believed that an educated slave was of greater value than an illiterate one. James Albert, Olaudah Equiano, and Phillis Wheatly were all born free in Africa, brought to America as slaves, and in time became highly literate voices for freedom, as in Wheatly's prayer that "Others may never feel tyrannic sway."[41]

With the slave rebellions of the early 1800s—rebellions, like Nat Turner's, often led by literate slaves—nearly all Southern states made it illegal to teach a slave to read or write, following the logic of North Carolina's 1831 statute that began, "Whereas the teaching of slaves to read and write, has a tendency to excite dissatisfaction in their minds, and to produce insurrection and rebellion . . ."[42] Still slaves did learn to read and write.

Many scholars estimate that at the time of the Civil War 5 percent of slaves had learned to read in spite of legal prohibitions. Some were taught by whites who "have ventured to teach them but they dare not let it be known they have done so." James Graham remembered, "When the white children would come from school, my mother's people would get instruction from them." Slaves also taught other slaves to read and write. Will Capers had "conducted a secret night school for men during plantation days" on St. Helena Island. And these illegally literate slaves formed the backbone of the first teachers of the freedmen and women when the Union armies brought emancipation to the South in the midst of the Civil War.[43] No one at the time thought of a slave child's surreptitious learning from a white child or another slave as a form of teacher preparation, but it was, as assuredly as the experience of a young white woman who herself might attend a dame school and then teach in one or a white man who might attend college or academy and then teach for a few years. All were teachers and all had been prepared, however haphazardly, for their work.

CONCLUSION

For the first several decades of the national life of the United States, as in the colonial era, the reality was that if one sought to be a teacher, whether as a missionary to Indians, as an informal tutor in literacy to a fellow slave, as a private tutor collecting what fees could be found from willing families, or as a paid teacher in a common school or even a prestigious urban grammar school, the only real requirements for the job were a willingness to declare oneself fit to teach and, if one wanted to be paid, someone, be they individuals or a town hiring committee, who would pay. Throughout the early national period the whole structure of schooling, even the very meaning of the words *school* and *teacher*, were extraordinarily fluid and flexible, and this variety was fully reflected in the preparation and qualification of those who taught.

While the colonial colleges did prepare teachers—John Adams's experience was not atypical—colleges never prepared a substantial portion of the teachers in the colonial or early national period. With rare exceptions, the college graduates never stayed in teaching long enough to make a meaningful impact. While 40 percent of Harvard's colonial graduates may have taught, only 3 percent stayed in teaching as a lifetime career. The graduates of the academies and of the more informal routes to teaching followed similar patterns. Most men taught for a year or two before moving on. Most women taught for only a couple of years after they completed school themselves and before marriage, though some women continued to teach or returned to teaching as widows. But certainly prior to 1830 the average teacher was only in the profession for a couple of years and the majority had only modest preparation. As a generalization, Carl F. Kaestle is probably correct that "Local common-school graduates, or those with a bit of academy training, sufficed where college students never trod."[44]

In the early decades of the 19th century this almost total fluidity of preparation began to change and, very slowly, formal programs of preparation for teachers began to emerge. It would be a long time before such programs began to impact the majority of schools or teachers—indeed, throughout the 19th century the majority of those who taught had very informal preparation—but something new was emerging on the American scene, formal teacher preparation. In the beginning, formalized teacher preparation had two groups of advocates. First there were women, such as Emma Willard, Mary Lyon, and perhaps most of all the indomitable Catharine Beecher, who sought to create a new career opportunity for women outside the emerging domestic role assigned to middle-class white women and who believed that formal preparation for a career in teaching would serve women, and their students, well. Then there was a second group of reformers, mostly men like Horace Mann in Massachusetts and Henry Barnard in Connecticut, who wanted to replace the informal, almost chaotic arrangements for schooling in their states with a much more tightly organized school system and who saw formal teacher preparation, ensuring basic standards in every schoolroom, as an essential element in their campaign. It is to these efforts to create institutions and systems of teacher preparation in the first half of the 19th century that we now turn.

2

Educating Women, Women as Educators

1800–1860

In 1856 Mary Buffington Adair took a teaching position at the Caney Creek School in what was then the autonomous Cherokee Public School system in the Indian Territory that would, in 1908, become a part of the state of Oklahoma. Her classmates Caroline Elizabeth Bushyhead began teaching at the Muddy Springs School, and Lucinda M. Ross started at the Oak Grove School at about the same time. Several of their classmates also began teaching in other of the Cherokee Public Schools in the years just before the start of the Civil War. Adair, Bushyhead, Ross, and their classmates were all recent graduates of the Cherokee Female Seminary, which, between 1851 and 1909, prepared more than 90 young women, all themselves Cherokee, to teach in the common schools that were administered by the autonomous Cherokee Nation.[1]

The Cherokee Female Seminary, along with the Cherokee Male Seminary, had been created by the National Council of the Cherokee Nation in November 1846 without any federal or missionary aid. The council ordered that "two seminaries or high schools be established, one for males, the other for females: in which all those branches of learning be taught, which may be required to carry the mental culture of the youth of our country to the highest practicable point." For the females, one key way of carrying forward the mental culture of the Cherokee youth was to become teachers in the Cherokee school system. The *Cherokee Advocate* noted that "there are no inducements for female teachers to come to this country," so the council intended to prepare their own teachers who would want to teach Cherokee youth and who would, because of their background, be much better prepared to do so than outsiders might be.[2]

When it became time to plan the curriculum and staff the new female seminary, Cherokee leaders turned to Mount Holyoke Female Seminary in South Hadley, Massachusetts. Mount Holyoke would be the model for the Cherokee Female Seminary in terms of institutional structure and curriculum and the source of the majority of the school's teachers. European-American missionaries among the Cherokee had long had New England roots, at least three of them had sent their own daughters to Mount Holyoke, and a Mount

Holyoke alumna, Mary Avery, already taught among the Cherokees at one of the mission schools. Those Cherokee leaders, who had converted to Christianity, liked Mount Holyoke's religious emphasis as well as its strict course of study and focus on preparing teachers. They had amazingly little interest in any cultural sensitivity on the part of either the teachers for the new seminary or within the curriculum that would prepare Cherokee to teach Cherokee.

When two Cherokee leaders visited Mount Holyoke in 1850 the principal, Mary Chapin, recommended Ellen Rebecca Whitmore and Sarah Worcester as teachers for the school. They were offered the positions and accepted, and in late 1851 they opened the Cherokee Female Seminary, modeled in every way on the curriculum of their own school. While there was a fairly regular turnover of the seminary's teachers—Whitmore married a missionary in 1852 and moved to Hawaii and Worcester married another missionary in 1853— Mount Holyoke continued to send a steady stream of its graduates to the school near Tahlequah, Indian Territory.[3]

The relatively unknown story of the Cherokee Female Seminary offers a fascinating glimpse into the intersections of gender, race, and, even more difficult to track, class in the story of the development of teacher education in all parts of what is now the United States. It is fascinating the degree to which the Cherokee—so recently the victims of the terrible 1838–1839 Trail of Tears, when the federal government, having previously signed treaties giving the Cherokees perpetual rights to remain in their homelands in Georgia, forced the tribe against their strenuous resistance to move a thousand miles to the west to desolate lands in Indian Territory—now embraced European-American patterns of schooling. In fact, the Cherokees had already developed schools of varying levels in their old homes in Georgia. In Indian Territory they set out to replicate the system, developing common schools and then the two high schools or seminaries. While there was no outside aid or control of the schools, they were controlled by the elite of the nation, and the majority of the students were the children of the elite, who tended to be of mixed blood. Poorer youth, full-blooded Cherokee, and those who sought to stay closer to the ancient ways were always highly underrepresented in the seminary. Acculturation into the ways of the United States was always a goal of the Cherokee elite, and few vehicles of acculturalization are more effective than schooling.[4]

The story of the Cherokee Female Seminary is a useful case study of a new institution for the education of women and specifically one for the preparation of women teachers that spread across the United States in the early decades of the 19th century—the female seminary. Beginning with only a few models— notably Mount Holyoke Female Seminary in South Hadley, Massachusetts, and Troy Female Seminary in Troy, New York—a new kind of institution specifically offering something close to a college-level education for women and strategically preparing these women to use their education as professional teachers spread across the United States. The female seminaries, of which the Cherokee school was one of many, were arguably the first professional schools for teachers in the United States. And their leaders consciously sought to change both the preparation of teachers and the gender of the practitioners of the teaching profession.

SEMINARIES FOR WOMEN TEACHERS—TROY, IPSWICH, MOUNT HOLYOKE, AND MORE

Before the Cherokee Female Seminary, before Mount Holyoke, there was Troy. The Troy Female Seminary, founded by Emma Willard in 1821, was not the first higher-level institution for women. In the glowing aftermath of the American Revolution, several academies for women—Philadelphia Young Ladies Academy and the Moravian seminary among the first—were founded that offered women essentially the same curriculum as the male colleges and academies. Revolutionary leaders—Benjamin Rush comes to mind quickly—argued that women in the new democracy, even if not the equals of males, needed a basic education to fit them to be effective mates and mothers. And sending one's daughter to a female academy became a new mark of distinction among the colonial elite. But Troy was different. It was the first to offer a specific intellectual ideology that, among other things, embraced the role of preparing women not only to be democratic mothers, but also democratic citizens (however quiet the school was on the specific issue of the vote) and professionals in their own right as teachers.[5]

Willard, born Emma Hart in Berlin, Connecticut, in 1787, began her own teaching career as most teachers of her generation, male and female, did. She completed the district school in her town, which she found unremarkable, but then had the good fortune to attend a newly opened academy in the town for 2 years. Just after she had turned 17 she began teaching with the usual formalities of the day. She recalled, "Mrs. Peck proposed that a children's school in the village, should be put into my hands," and it was. Peck was a respected citizen of the town, and her recommendation was quite good enough to decide the qualifications of the schoolteacher. There were no educational requirements and no exams.

Willard remembered, "At nine o'clock, on that first morning, I seated myself among the children to begin a profession which I little thought was to last with slight interruption for forty years." Though she remembered that first morning as "the longest of my life," she was more successful than many teachers and 3 years later was appointed the director of a female academy in Middlebury, Vermont, a college town where she could view the education offered to men firsthand.[6] Two years later, in 1809, she married John Willard, a physician 28 years her senior, who supported her interest in women's education, as she said, with a "zeal for the sex whom, as he had come to believe, his own had unjustly neglected." Dr. Willard was also, happily for his new wife, a Jeffersonian Republican in a region still dominated by Federalists.

As for many in New England, the War of 1812–1815 brought hard times to the Willard family. In 1814 they opened a boarding school in their own home, which not only helped their income but also became the springboard from which Willard could develop her ideas about the proper education for women. Indeed, in her own writings, Willard saw no discontinuity between the school she opened in her Vermont home in 1814 and its more formal successor in Troy, New York, that began in 1821. While she operated her Vermont school her ideas became clearer and clearer, and with encouragement from many of the leading citizens of her day she made a formal proposal to the state of New York, where she thought she would have a more receptive audience for her plan than in Vermont.[7]

In 1818 Willard addressed a lengthy letter to New York's Governor De Witt Clinton urging him to support her "Address to the Public, particularly to the Legislature of New York, proposing a Plan for Improving Female Education." Her proposal gave many reasons why the current arrangements for educating women were insufficient and the many benefits women and the larger society would receive through her plan, which called for public money to be specifically allocated for the education of women something not done in the United States at that time. She justified her plea with an appeal to the need for educated mothers who would shape the character of an increasingly prosperous nation and also on the need of women for greater intellectual challenges and specific professional opportunities.[8] One of the many elements of her address was the key role of higher education for women in preparing women teachers, which she also outlined in detail.

> That nature designed for our sex the care of children, she has made manifest by mental as well as physical indications. She has given us, in greater degree than men, the gentle arts of insinuation, to soften their minds, and fit them to receive impressions; a greater quickness of invention to vary modes of teaching to different dispositions; and more patience to make repeated efforts.

Thus she began a line of arguments that would be popularized by herself and others, most of all Catharine Beecher, that women were uniquely fitted to teaching for it was an extension of motherhood.

Willard, also like her successors, had more practical, economic arguments for making women teachers:

> There are many females of ability, to whom the business of instructing children is highly acceptable; and who would devote all their faculties to their occupation. They would have no higher pecuniary object to engage their attention, and their reputation as instructors they would consider as important; whereas when able and enterprising men, engage in this business, they too often consider it, merely

as a temporary employment, to further some other object, to the attainment of which, their best thoughts and calculations are all directed.

But finally Willard proposed something quite new, an idea that teachers needed professional preparation. "If then women were properly fitted by instruction," she wrote, "they would be likely to teach children better than the other sex . . ."[9]

At a point when the vast majority of the nation's teachers, at least those who were teaching outside the home, were still men, and well before others had made similar arguments, Willard outlined the primary arguments for offering formal preparation to women and allowing them to assume careers in the teaching profession, arguments that would be used so successfully in the coming decades. Teaching, she said, was an extension of motherhood, and therefore in women's sphere. With a rapidly expanding economy, men would want to pursue other fields while women would remain committed to teaching —and could be hired more cheaply. But, she insisted, in order to fulfill this ordained role of teacher, women needed a top-flight professional education.

Willard's arguments received much encouragement, but no money, from the New York State legislature. However, citizens of the town of Troy, New York, wanted a school in their midst and they, along with other Willard supporters, launched the Troy Female Seminary as a private venture in spite of the legislature's failure to act.

From its opening day, the Troy Female Seminary was a unique venture in American secondary or higher education. Willard had selected the name *seminary* to avoid the controversy that would have attended launching a college for women when none existed. But she meant to launch a college. She might diplomatically tell the New York State legislature that the seminary "will be as different from those appropriated to the other sex, as the female character and duties are from the male," but in fact the energy that launched Troy came from her own experience operating her boarding school near Middlebury College, which made her "bitterly feel the disparity in educational facilities between the two sexes." She was determined to "effect an important change in education, by the introduction of a grade of school for women, higher than any heretofore known," i.e. a college.[10]

When she opened Troy Seminary in 1821 Willard modeled the school on colleges she knew well—Middlebury especially, but also Brown, Amherst, Williams, Dartmouth, and Union. Like the presidents of these schools, Willard taught the capstone course in Mental and Moral Philosophy. She used the same curriculum and the same textbooks as the colleges, including the standard texts in rhetoric, logic, and philosophy, especially moral philosophy, and also mathematics, including algebra and geometry, and the French and Spanish languages.[11] She did depart from the standard male college of her day by being more willing than they to experiment with more engaging student discussions, in contrast to the lectures and recitations that characterized the early-19th-century college. She

also insisted that the seminary students meet the same standards as college
students she knew. While still at Middlebury, Willard invited the president and
professors of the college to attend her examinations, though she was excluded
from theirs.[12]

There was one substantial difference between the male colleges of the day
and Troy, however. The male schools prepared teachers accidentally; Troy
prepared them intentionally: While at least one commentator has argued that
the "receiving of girls expressly for education as teachers was at first accidental," Willard's own petition to the New York legislature in 1818, like other things
she wrote, was quite explicit. The success of her school, Willard said, "would
probably place the business of teaching children, in hands now nearly useless
to society; and take it from those, whose services the state wants in many other
ways." Men, Willard hoped, could now turn more fully to other matters and
make room for the women whom she and others would prepare to take their
places in the classrooms of the nation.[13]

While preparing teachers was a central part of Troy's program from the
day it opened, the seminary did not offer any courses specifically in pedagogy.
Troy's curriculum was the college curriculum of the day. Teacher preparation
at Troy happened in several ways. When the seminary opened at Troy, Willard
had already been teaching for almost two decades. She knew what her methods were, and she had reflected on teaching as few teachers or professors of
any age do. She described a system she had developed beginning with the boarding school at Middlebury in 1814 in which she organized each course into three
distinct parts. First she would do most of the talking, trying to explain the subject so that the students would understand it. Even then, however, she knew
that while talking the teachers needed to attend to what was actually being
learned, "for it was ever my maxim, if attention fails the teacher fails." Having
taught, she then asked the students to recite what they had learned to be sure
that they could remember it. And, finally, she asked the students to communicate what they had learned, to be able to show their understanding by explaining the subject to another. This three-part system of understanding,
remembering, and communicating became the Willard system, and she talked
of it constantly. In the process, she thus modeled pedagogy and told her students what forms of pedagogy she was modeling even as she taught them not
pedagogy but literature, science, and mathematics.[14]

In addition, Troy was suffused by a commitment to teaching. Willard
asked more advanced students to communicate their mastery of a subject by
teaching others. Following the Willard method, subject matter at Troy was
always learned and taught at the same time, and in the process students, sometimes to their own surprise, came to recognize themselves as teachers. In addition, Willard created a financial aid program for future teachers. Willard
offered loans to any woman who was preparing to be a teacher at Troy as long
as they would agree to pay the funds back from their salaries as teachers. In

the process Troy came to be open to many who could not have afforded the tuition or the living expenses. And a cadre of dedicated teachers was created. Like the normal schools that would emerge a decade or two later, Troy came to be suffused with a sense of commitment to teaching as a calling that offered opportunities for self-fulfillment and for service that could not be had elsewhere. No wonder its impact on American education was so great.[15]

Anne Firor Scott has noted that as important as the structure of the curriculum was, the atmosphere that Willard created at Troy told young women that "they could learn any academic subject, including those hitherto reserved to men, that they should prepare themselves for self-support and not seek marriage as an end in itself." And at the same time Troy's culture told young women that there was a profession open to them; indeed, one they had a duty to pursue. No wonder that Troy was the educational home of some of the century's best-known feminists, including Elizabeth Cady Stanton, while it also sent hundreds of teachers out to teach schools and at least 146 alumnae founded or administered mini-Troys across the country.[16]

Willard was not only an effective teacher and administrator, but she also knew how to create disciples and build a network eventually formalized as the Willard Association for the Mutual Improvement of Teachers. Julia Pierpont had studied with Willard in Middlebury but returned to Troy in 1824, then moved to South Carolina and opened a South Carolina version of Troy in Barhamville. One historian has traced over 100 women in South Carolina who were connected with either Barhamville or Troy itself. Urania Sheldon graduated from Troy in 1824 and opened a school in Washington County, New York, and then led schools in Schenectady and Utica. Caroline Livy graduated in 1841 and opened the Female Academy of Rome, Georgia. And the list goes on and on, with between 150 and 200 schools modeled on Troy. Something new had appeared on the American stage—an institution offering a college-level education to women, and an institution calling many of these women to teach.

Emma Willard and the model of the Troy Female Seminary were far from the only forces expanding the educational opportunities for women in the early 19th century and leading many of the newly emerging cadres of educated women to spend at least a few years as public school teachers. But Troy was one significant part of a larger effort that dramatically changed the teaching profession as a whole, so that by the time of Willard's death in 1870 over half of the nation's 200,515 teachers were women, a change made possible, in large part, because of the ideological arguments that she first made.[17] Schools directly modeled on Troy, and often led by Troy graduates, were emerging in every part of the country. But social, cultural, and economic changes in the United States in the 1820s, 1830s, and 1840s meant that still other schools emerged with similar missions, though from different roots.

Zilpah Polly Grant was born in western Connecticut in 1794, attended the district school there, and at age 15 began teaching in the school. A decade later, she had the good fortune to be able to extend her education when she attended an academy for young ladies opened by Joseph Emerson in Byfield, Massachusetts. After a six-month term at the academy in Byfield, Grant was invited to join Emerson as his assistant in teaching. In November 1823 she was asked to lead the Adams Female Seminary in Derry, New Hampshire. Grant led the school for 4 years and then moved to the Ipswich Female Seminary in Massachusetts, which she led until 1839. Like Troy, the Ipswich seminary under Grant's leadership also had a revolving fund from which graduates who promised to enter the teaching field could borrow funds to complete their education to be paid back out of the proceeds of their meager teacher salaries. During the decade of the 1830s, the seminary in Ipswich sent 88 teachers west and south to schools in the Mississippi Valley in addition to those who took teaching jobs closer to home. Grant, like Willard, illustrated in her own career the informal movement of antebellum women in and out of teaching as some, like Willard and Grant taught, then studied further, then taught more, while both encouraged their students to emulate the same career pattern whether for only a few years before marriage or as a lifetime career.[18]

Joining Grant in Derry and Ipswich was another important figure in the development of female seminaries and teacher preparation, Mary Lyon. Lyon was born in Buckland in the remote Massachusetts Berkshire hills in 1797 and began teaching at that town's school at the age of 17. In 1834 after almost a decade with Grant, Lyon left Ipswich to start her own school. She envisioned "a residential seminary to be founded and sustained by the Christian Public." The school Lyon founded in 1837, Mount Holyoke Female Seminary, received the public funds—from Massachusetts—that Willard had been denied by the state of New York. It also received substantial private funding and was the first school for women to have its own endowment. From the beginning, Lyon also established a 4-year curriculum so that students at Mount Holyoke not only studied the same subjects as their male counterparts who attended colleges, but studied them for as long and at similar depth. And Mount Holyoke produced even more teachers than Troy.[19]

When Lyon first began planning her own school, she had called it the New England Female Seminary for Teachers. Her early plans reflected a school designed to increase the number of well-prepared teachers and to allow teachers like herself, Grant, and Willard, who had begun with virtually no preparation, an opportunity to return for a substantial education. When the school was finally opened as Mount Holyoke Female Seminary in 1837, its purposes were broader but its emphasis on teacher preparation was still significant.

Like Troy and Ipswich, Mount Holyoke in these years did not offer courses specifically in pedagogy. Indeed, Thomas Woody's often-cited study of the subject matter listed in the catalogues of 107 different female academies between 1830 and 1871 does not include pedagogy or a related course in any of them. The leading courses included natural philosophy, 90 percent of the schools; chemistry, 90 percent; rhetoric, 88 percent; astronomy, 85 percent; algebra, 83 percent; English grammar, 84 percent; botany, 82 percent; mental philosophy, 82 percent; moral philosophy, 80 percent; and a range of other subjects, including 59 percent of the schools that offered Latin, 50 percent that offered Evidences of Christianity, down to 5 percent that offered Plain Needlework. How to teach, however, was handled elsewhere in the life of these schools.[20]

From the beginning Lyon organized an alumnae association, called the Memorandum Society, which about half of Mount Holyoke's graduates joined. Of that number, well more than half became teachers. In 1847, before Lyon's death, the society had 593 members of which 279 were teachers, and at the college's semicentennial in 1887 more than 2,000 of the 3,033 members had taught after leaving Mount Holyoke. Much as she and her successors strongly encouraged their graduates to teach, Lyon was also tough in her negotiations with those who sought Mount Holyoke graduates for their schools. Although she admired Catharine Beecher, she would not send graduates to her because she feared Beecher offered only "an unknown field with an unknown salary." She insisted she have "a particular place by name . . . and a salary of say only $100," before making any recommendations of candidates for teaching jobs. Nevertheless, Mount Holyoke's emphasis on a rigorous education and on the importance of service, and a strongly religious emphasis on sacrifice, meant that its graduates were prepared to go to many places and were widely sought, whether by the Cherokee Female Seminary or by hundreds of other schools across the nation.[21]

Margaret Nash, having noted the ways in which Mary Lyon, like most of her counterparts among early-19th-century women educators, deferred to the reigning philosophy of the day and agreed that there were limits to the "public stations" that women could occupy. But Nash also noted, "Lyon apparently had a narrow definition of the 'public stations' from which women ought to retire, given that there were many public arenas in which she thought women belonged. She trained women to be both teachers and missionaries, both of which took women away from their firesides." And she trained a lot of women to enter these professions and offered a model for other women's schools to follow.[22]

PREPARING WOMEN TO TEACH—FROM INDIVIDUAL SCHOOLS TO A NATIONAL MOVEMENT

The person destined to have the greatest impact on the transformation of teaching from a male to a female profession, and from a temporary and accidental profession for men to one for which women received a specific education, was Catharine Beecher. Beecher's own teaching career began when she moved from her family home in Litchfield, Connecticut, to the state capital in Hartford to open her own Hartford Female Seminary in 1823, shortly after Willard had moved to Troy and at about the same time Grant and Lyon were beginning their efforts. But unlike Willard, Grant, and Lyon, Beecher showed little interest in teacher preparation for almost a decade.

The Hartford Female Seminary, which under Beecher's leadership quickly grew to be a large school with over 100 students and its own buildings and endowment, educated the social elite first of Connecticut and then many parts of the United States. Beecher emphasized both religious conversion and the development of a strong morality for her students as well as the social graces expected of elite young women in the early decades of the 19th century. But the Hartford Female Seminary of the 1820s resembled other academies for women that had begun in the late 18th century, preparing their students to be thoughtful wives and mothers who would have the social graces of society's leaders without the professional emphasis that Willard had pioneered. But beginning about 1830, that emphasis changed.[23]

During the late 1820s, Catharine Beecher had been teaching the course in moral philosophy usually taught by the head of a school, be they female seminary leader or male college president. But in the process, Beecher had also been writing her own textbook and rethinking the very nature of morality, especially for women. Beecher's *Elements of Mental and Moral Philosophy* was published in 1831, but more important for the future of teacher preparation, the emphasis of the Hartford curriculum was changing in her last years at the school. One prospective student, the future abolitionist Angelina Grimké, visited Hartford in the summer of 1831 and found that Beecher taught the students "to feel that they had no right to spend their time in idleness, fashion and folly, but they as individuals were bound to be useful in Society after they finished their education, and that as teachers, single women would be more useful in this than in any other way."

At this point, Hartford became a teacher education school. The emphasis on teaching was a natural expansion of Beecher's growing conviction that morality required women "not to *shine* but to *act*." It fit with her concern, shared with her famous father, Lyman Beecher, to save the nation from infidelity, but unlike her father, as Kathryn Kish Sklar has noted, "Catharine Beecher not only wanted to 'save' the nation, she wanted women to save it." And finally, as a single woman, Beecher wanted to carve out options for single women—perhaps a temporary option prior to marriage but also for some, like Beecher herself, a life's work. Again, Sklar is right in noting, "Teaching was important to Catharine also because it provided women with a respectable alternative to marriage. The single woman need no longer become merely a spinster aunt." As Beecher herself said, teaching "is a *profession*, offering influence, respectability and independence." No wonder she wanted to make it the focus of her efforts.[24]

With her growing conviction that teaching was both a moral duty and an extraordinary opportunity for educated women, Beecher quickly found Hartford too small a stage for her efforts. She resigned from the seminary she had founded in the fall of 1831. Rather than try to remake the school into one preparing teachers, Beecher wanted to work at a national level. In the spring of 1832, Beecher and her father traveled to Cincinnati, Ohio, where he took up duties as president of the new Lane Theological Seminary for the education of Presbyterian ministers, and she began what would be a two-decade-long effort to promote "the cause of popular education, and as intimately connected with it, the elevation of my sex by the opening of a profession for them as educators of the young."[25]

In Cincinnati Catharine Beecher launched the Western Female Institute in 1833. Like her seminary at Hartford, the Cincinnati school was designed as an academy for young women, but it was more. The Western Female Institute was to be the first model seminary for what was intended to become a national system of interlocking schools, privately funded, that would prepare women to become the nation's teachers. In fact, owing to the fact that Beecher was often distracted with other matters and to the divisions within Cincinnati society, her school floundered and closed in 1837. But Beecher's campaign to transform teaching was a smashing success.[26]

To raise funds for her Cincinnati school and also as the first announcement of something much bigger, Catharine Beecher published an *Essay on the Education of Female Teachers* in 1835. This essay was to Beecher's efforts what Willard's 1818 appeal to the New York legislature had been, a blueprint for all that followed even if its immediate fiscal aims failed.[27] In the essay Beecher laid out her goals in no uncertain terms. Teaching, Beecher argued, was women's work. "What is the most important and peculiar duties of the female sex?" she asked. And her answer was, "It is the care of the health, and the formation of the character, of the future citizen of this great nation. Woman, whatever are her relations in life, is necessarily the guardian of the nursery, the companion of childhood, and the constant model of imitation." Thus she began with her key argument—teaching was an extension of mothering and should be regarded, like motherhood, as part of woman's sphere.

Having established her ground, Beecher went on to make several key points for her proposals. First, she insisted that teaching, like motherhood, was an important duty that called women to meaningful service, so society should not foster "the fainting, weeping, vapid, pretty play-thing, once the model of female loveliness," but rather "those qualities of the head and heart that best qualify a woman for her duties." Women needed the opportunity to do serious work, she insisted. At the same time, society needed the influence of well-prepared and tough-minded, virtuous women. She insisted that "few are aware how much influence a teacher may exert," but, in fact, "children do, to a very great extent, form their character under influences bearing upon them at school."

The United States needed better-trained teachers, and it needed the services of a Catharine Beecher to match the teachers to the schools in which they were needed. A generous public could only solve the first problem. "Here, we have no despotic monarch to endow seminaries for teachers . . . It is the people who must voluntarily do it, or it will remain undone." At the same time, "it has been heart-sickening to witness the intense interest that exists in all parts of the nation to obtain good teachers, and at the same time to know the earnest longing of many energetic and benevolent females to secure such situations as were offered . . ." But there was a solution. Beecher proposed to create both a network of schools to prepare the teachers and a kind of national placement service to link the teachers with the schools that needed them. In fact, she did both.[28]

As Kathryn Kish Sklar has argued, "teaching was in 1830 not a woman's profession. Although Emma Willard had for a decade linked her curriculum at Troy with preparation for a teaching career, Catharine Beecher was the first to envision teaching as a profession dominated by—indeed exclusively belonging to—women." Between 1843 and 1846 Beecher criss-crossed the nation, speaking in city after city on the importance of preparing women to teach in the emerging communities of the West, mostly the states of the current Midwest, Ohio, Indiana, Illinois, Michigan, and Wisconsin, but also as far west as Oregon. She published her speeches as pamphlets that were circulated broadly; gained the endorsement of other leading educators including Horace Mann, Henry Barnard, Samuel Lewis; raised substantial sums of money; and created an organization that eventually became the National Popular Education Board. In 1846 she capped her efforts by convincing Vermont's governor, William Slade, who was just then finishing his term in office, to become the full-time agent for her society.[29]

The National Board recruited young women who were willing to make a 2-year commitment to teach in the school in which they were placed, and it worked with school districts and communities to ensure that the schools would be there. But the National Board also created its own teacher preparation program. Many of the young women who responded to the National Board's appeal had already taught school for some period of time, and they were generally well-educated, having attended schools and academies, though only a small minority had graduated. But Beecher and her co-workers believed that special preparation was essential for those going west both as a means of skill-building and as a way to raise the level of commitment to the cause.

Beginning in Albany, New York, in the spring of 1847 and then again back in Hartford, Connecticut, in the fall of that year, Beecher led a monthlong training institute for those who were about to go west. Based on her own experience, Beecher lectured the aspiring teachers on how to teach in schools that lacked decent facilities or books, how to build moral habits among children "when all domestic and social influences tend to weaken such habits," how to inculcate religious values—for the National Board was a distinctly Protestant, religious venture—without running afoul of any one Protestant denomination, and perhaps most of all how to be a moral influence and moral example in the communities to which they were sent. In addition to the instruction, Beecher focused on building up the moral and religious fervor of the teachers so that years later, looking back, many remembered most of all "those seasons of social communion and prayer at Hartford."[30]

Having led the first two institutes, Beecher returned to her national role as writer, speaker, organizer, and fundraiser. She hired Nancy Swift, an experienced teacher and academy leader, to take over the institutes—now expanded to 6 weeks and permanently established at Hartford. Swift stayed with the National Board for 6 years and organized a total of 10 institutes for some 25 young women at a time, who were then sent to new posts in the Midwest and far West. Other well-known educators, Lucy Tappan Grosvenor, Linda Guilsford, and later Zilpah Grant herself, now long retired from Ipswich, led National Board institutes.

Under their different leaders, and with the help of a range of guest lecturers, the National Board institutes sought to prepare young women, most of whom had taught school already, but had done it close to home in familiar surroundings, for the rigors of the West. They also introduced a set of teaching methods in which the National Board was invested. Schools were to awaken the morality as well as the literacy of their students, and the use of the Protestant Bible was strongly recommended wherever community opposition was not too great. Practical matters, like using blackboards to teach writing, were recommended. Hartford's Thomas Gallaudet, pioneer teacher of the deaf, lectured on Pestalozzi's educational philosophy. Institute students also had an opportunity to review and be tested in a range of school subjects, including English composition, spelling, music, and algebra. They engaged in daily calisthenics to stay healthy. And they attended church and heard inspirational lectures designed to foster their evangelical commitment to their mission.[31]

Arozina Perkins, who participated in one of the Hartford institutes from September to October 1850, recorded one fast-paced day in her journal that included morning worship, then "instruction is given in music . . . Three minutes recess; then spelling, after which the ladies practiced calisthenics." There were also various lectures, some by the institute's leaders on subjects such as "Mechanical Letter Writing" and "Monochromatic Painting," but also by visitors, including one by Samuel S. Greene on "Language," and several by Gallaudet, including one especially valuable one on "School Government," as well as one or two sermons every Sunday in Hartford's many churches. There was also a strong feeling of camaraderie and of commitment to a cause greater than they were, as well as all of the petty squabbles that could confront any group of 25 young people thrown together in tight quarters and not quite knowing what would come next in their lives.[32]

In the decade after it was launched in 1846, the National Board sent some 600 single women from New England and upstate New York to the Midwest and beyond to Iowa, Nebraska Territory, and Oregon and California. Women made a 2-year commitment before being sent, though a few returned earlier either because of illness or discouragement. However, of those whose life histories can be traced, some two-thirds made new lives for themselves in the new country either through long teaching careers or marriage. Beecher herself had a falling-out with Slade and left the National Board to concentrate on founding other female seminaries and on her writing and lecturing. Other groups mirrored the National Board's efforts, some in coordinated projects and others quite independently. But far beyond the efforts of the organization itself, the image of teaching as "woman's 'true' profession" that Catharine Beecher so insistently portrayed was one that changed teaching—and the preparation for teaching—dramatically in the years between the American Revolution and the Civil War.

When the Civil War came, and when religious organizations, private philanthropies, and the federal government looked for Northern teachers to send to the South to teach the newly freed slaves, there was virtually no question as to the gender of the teachers to be sought. Ronald Butchart has noted the impact of the feminization of teaching on the teachers invited South during and after the war:

> The freedmen's teachers were predominantly female, both because most men either were in uniform or were needed to fill the depleted civilian positions, and because the teaching profession in the North had been largely feminized by the 1860s. The associations played on the abundance of women teachers when they spoke of the peculiar nature of the work that required presumed womanly qualities: "Who can minister to the hundreds of thousands of aged, poor, ignorant, sick, but woman?" they asked.

And at the same time, Jacqueline Jones has noted, the majority of these women teachers who went South were themselves graduates of female academies and seminaries. During Reconstruction the impact of Willard, Lyon, Beecher and their colleagues was far greater than they had dreamed or imagined.[33]

PREPARING WOMEN TO TEACH—CHANGES IN IDEOLOGY, CHANGES IN PRACTICE

David Tyack and Elisabeth Hansot have summarized the extraordinary impact on teaching and teacher education that came from the work of Emma Willard, Zilpah Grant, Mary Lyon, and Catharine Beecher:

These four women were the centers of widespread networks of educated women and their male allies. Through these associates they placed their graduates in teaching positions and encouraged the creation of secondary schools for women and the spread of coeducational public schools. These women and their alumnae were pedagogical Jenny Appleseeds, planting schools across the nation.

Troy sent almost 600 women into teaching between 1839 and 1863, while four-fifths of Mount Holyoke graduates between 1837 and 1850 taught at some point in their lives, Ipswich sent a smaller but steady stream of teachers, and the National Board sent another 600. And many of these teachers founded or led their own schools, modeled on what they had experienced—including, of course the Cherokee Female Seminary and countless others—so that the model was replicated over and over again.[34] While later historians of education have concentrated their attention on the normal schools (described in the next chapter), the reality is that at least until 1850, the female seminaries founded by Willard, Grant, Lyon, Beecher, and their disciples prepared more teachers and had a greater impact on the nature of the teaching profession than the normal schools.[35]

What had once been a male enterprise—albeit temporary and unprofessional—was by 1850 a female one. By 1870 59 percent of all of the teachers in the United States were women, and in the populous North Atlantic area almost three-quarters of the teachers were women. The gender ratios were not even across the country. Regional differences were substantial, with large numbers of men remaining in teaching in the South and West. The trend, however, would only continue. By 1888 63 percent of the nation's teachers were women, and in the major urban areas women were 90 percent of the teachers. Catharine Beecher's goal of women replacing men in the profession had been accomplished beyond anything she might have dared dream in the 1830s.[36]

One need ask, of course, at what cost did this transformation in the professional preparation and professional lives of women come? Certainly not all women were affected equally by the changes. For the most part the 19th century's teachers were middle-class Protestant women of European origin. There were some African Americans among them, small numbers from the free black communities of the North, and there were some poor women who had received scholarships and other unusual opportunities to enter teaching. There were also Catholic teachers, but the vast majority of these were women who entered religious orders, whose route to teaching was quite different, though with some surprising parallels to those proposed by Willard and Beecher.

Kathryn Kish Sklar has described the compromise that Beecher and her colleagues made regarding women's place in society. At a time when industrialization was changing the nation, and the nation's work, beyond recognition, at a time when feminists like Sarah and Angelina Grimké were demanding full equality in all spheres of life, "Catharine generally participated in the bargain then being struck between women's social role and domesticity. If women would agree to limit their participation in the society as a whole so the pact has been described, then they could ascend to total hegemony over the domestic sphere." Catharine Beecher's only additional stipulation was that teaching be included in the domestic sphere![37]

Historians have long debated the costs and values of the compromise that Beecher and others struck. For example, Anne Firor Scott argues persuasively that seminaries like Troy opened important opportunities for women, while she notes that Keith Melder saw the same schools, with their emphasis on separate spheres, as perpetuating the oppression of women. Other historians, notably Geraldine Joncich Clifford and Jackie M. Blount, have looked carefully at the impact of the fact that from Beecher's time on teaching was seen as a gendered, female profession, even when men were engaged in it in substantial numbers. And reflecting on the educational work of Willard, Beecher, and Lyon, Margaret Nash has wisely said, "There may indeed have been a 'cult of true womanhood' emphasizing piety, purity, obedience, and domesticity, but simultaneously there were people who believed that a 'true' woman was strong, courageous, self-sufficient, rational, assertive, and, above all, intelligent."[38]

In a brilliant essay on the compromises that allowed women virtual dominance of the teaching profession, but at the cost of a permanent second-class status for the profession, Nancy Hoffman has written:

> By 1860, young women . . . had a profession of their own. The "sacred office" gave them public status, the claim to a decent income, freedom to marry only for "pure affection," and their own institutions of higher education. But like many victories for women, this one was contradictory and qualified. . . . By the end of the nineteenth century, the profession of teaching had moved to the position that it would hold for the next century and beyond; less than equal in status to male professions, *and* a source of satisfaction and power for women. Teaching was to remain "shadowed," but also "special."[39]

This shadowed but also special nature of teaching would also continue to impact every development in the professional preparation of teachers, from the normal schools and teachers' institutes that followed quickly on the heels of the female seminaries to the latest 21st-century battles about the best means of preparing teachers for the schools of the United States. In all of these institutional structures and debates, gender is always at the heart of the matter, as it has been since the days when the female seminary advocates of the 1820s and 1830s specifically sought to place it there.

3

The Birth of the Normal School

1830–1870

Charlotte L. Forten was one of the hundreds of women to go South during and after the American Civil War to teach newly freed slaves, in Forten's case on the Sea Islands of South Carolina. Her earlier career was far more prosaic but wonderfully illustrative of the lives of many aspiring teachers in the middle decades of the 19th century. In her diary for June 18, 1856, several years before she first thought about teaching on the Sea Islands, Forten wrote:

> Amazing, wonderful news I have heard to-day! It has completely astounded me. . . . I have received the offer of a situation as a teacher in one of the public schools of this city,—of this conservative, aristocratic old city of Salem!!! Wonderful indeed it is! I know that it is principally through the exertions of my kind teacher, although he will not acknowledge it.—I thank him with all my heart. I had a long talk with the Principal of the school, whom I like much. Again and again I ask myself—"Can it be true?" It seems impossible. I shall commence to-morrow.—[1]

Thus this 18-year-old woman, herself just a little over a year out of grammar school, received the joyful news that she had been hired as a teacher at the Epes Grammar School in Salem, Massachusetts.

Though the joyful emotions on hearing of her success at gaining her first teaching job could be shared by thousands of other 19th- and early-20th-century normal school graduates, and indeed by new teachers of every generation, Charlotte Forten's life was different from that of most antebellum teachers for one critical reason: She was African American. Forten had grown up in an abolitionist free black family in Philadelphia and received her early education at home because her father did not want her to attend the racially segregated schools of Philadelphia. In 1854 her family reluctantly agreed that she could travel north to Salem, Massachusetts, where the schools were racially integrated and she could live with a family friend, another well-known abolitionist, Charles Lenox Remond. In the spring of 1854, Forten enrolled in the

Higginson Grammar School in Salem. She moved quickly through the curriculum and graduated in February 1855.[2]

Forten wanted to be a teacher, and Salem boasted one of the few schools in the nation at that time designed specifically to prepare young women and men to be teachers, the Salem Normal School. Her diary for Tuesday, March 13, 1855, recorded her success: "Went through the examination and entered the Normal School." A year later she was taking her final examinations at the Normal School, receiving the happy news of her first teaching job, and participating with her classmates in the July 1856 graduation ceremonies while she had already begun her teaching career at the grammar school. A year of grammar school education, a year at the normal school, and she was back at another grammar school in the same town as a teacher. In this, as in few other things, Forten's career is an exemplar of many of her mid-19th-century contemporaries.[3]

Another well-known 19th-century teacher, Mary Swift, entered the first class of the nation's first public normal school, which met in Lexington, Massachusetts, in the fall of 1839. Horace Mann had recently hired Cyrus Peirce to open the first of his projected network of Massachusetts normal schools in that city. Swift was 17 when she left Nantucket Island to attend school in Lexington, the same age that Forten was when she began studying at Salem some 15 years later.

After completing the yearlong course, Swift went on to teach at the Perkins Institution for blind and deaf students in Boston—she was one of Helen Keller's first teachers—then led an academy, administered the Hartford Institute for the National Board, and later served on the school committee. At Lexington she kept a careful diary. Peirce, she wrote, was intent on making his students understand the importance of the experiment of which they were a part. As Swift transcribed it, he had said:

> To us, therefore, all the friends of Education, turn, anxious for the success of the first effort to establish such schools. For this success, we shall depend, chiefly, on three particulars: 1st on interesting you in the studies to which you attend & in the daily remarks; 2nd on the course of lectures to be given & 3rd on the Model School.[4]

In 1 year students, many of them fresh out of their own district school, would learn a range of academic subjects, would be given lectures about teaching, and would practice their profession in a model school.

Swift's journal of her year at Lexington reflects many of the same subjects that her sisters at female seminaries were studying. She prepared for and heard lectures in natural philosophy, physiology, and natural history—which meant the sciences and political economy, as well as lectures on pronunciation and orthography (spelling). As much, or perhaps more, than at the female seminaries, students at Lexington were also reminded of the high calling of teaching and given regular lectures by Peirce on "the motives, qualifications and responsibilities of a teacher." Again and again, according to Swift's journal, Peirce told them to "remember that you are to influence the character, the future standing of the ten, fifty, or an hundred children who are committed to your care. Imagine each in his course through the world, and that your work will shape all their feelings, and the influence which they will exert through life. This will be imparted to those who are placed under their care, and thus your influence, instead of being confined to the hundred under your eye, will extend to thousands." There was no missing the "high responsibility" to which Peirce believed a teacher was called.[5]

CREATING A NEW INSTITUTION: THE STATE NORMAL SCHOOL

The schools that Forten and Swift and ultimately thousands of their sisters—and some brothers—attended in the century between 1839 and 1939 were first founded in Massachusetts as something of an afterthought as part of a larger reform effort. And yet the structure and the state control of these institutions fit almost perfectly with the other aspects of what was known as the common school campaign—the effort by a group of reformers led by Horace Mann in Massachusetts, Henry Barnard in Connecticut, and other allies to improve the education offered to the youth of their communities by centralizing the public school systems of the states with state boards of education, state mandates in curriculum and teaching, and the earliest beginnings of state bureaucracies with the creation of the positions of chief state school officers.

In the case of Massachusetts, where the normal schools began, they were a direct outgrowth of the same reforms that led to the creation of the state Board of Education in 1837 and Horace Mann's election as its secretary—and only paid staff person—a few weeks later. In the spring legislative session of that year the Whig governor Edward Everett, who had observed the Prussian school system while a student at the University of Gottingën, urged the legislature to establish a state Board of Education in order to bring order to what he saw as a chaotic system of local control of the schools in the districts, towns, and cities of the Commonwealth. At that point, Horace Mann was a 10-year veteran of the state legislature, recently elevated to the State Senate, and seen as a likely prospect to eventually succeed Everett as governor. Mann had supported Everett's efforts; indeed, he had also hoped to do more than Everett in terms of channeling state funds to the schools.[6]

Having created the board, Governor Everett and his prime advisor, the prosperous manufacturer and philanthropist Edmund Dwight, decided to use the one paid position allowed to the board to bring it status and skill. Instead of turning to some of the logical candidates among Massachusetts' small pool of well-respected educators, they turned to a political leader, the rising star in the State Senate, Horace Mann. To the surprise of almost everyone, Mann accepted, turning his back on a promising political career to devote himself to the cause of education reform.[7]

While much has been written about the personal soul-searching that led Mann to make this unusual move from politician to educator, the larger political agenda of Mann, Dwight, Everett, and their allies, all Whig politicians, was quite clear. As Carl Kaestle has aptly described it, the Whig goal for education was to mold good citizens through concerted state action. "The survival of the American republic depended upon the morality of its people," Kaestle wrote, "—not in armies or constitutions or inspired leadership—but in the virtue of the propertied, industrious, and intelligent American yeoman." And the means of ensuring the proper education of the next generation of yeomen and women could not be left to happenstance or local action. Democrats might trust farmers and farm communities. Whigs believed that an educated elite needed to use state governments to accomplish their goals, and that included a quite specific approach to systematizing education. Thus:

> [Whig] Essayists, state superintendents, and local school committees continually coupled their specific reform proposals with a repetition of the unassailable social functions of common schooling. The rhetorical effect was to imply that if one was against centralization, supervision, new schoolhouses, teacher training, or graded schools, one must also be against morality, good order, intelligent citizenship, economic prosperity, fair opportunity, and a common American culture.[8]

And after 1839, if one supported teacher training, one was expected to support a specific form of that training—the state normal school.

Writing about the campaign led by Horace Mann and Henry Barnard to bring order to the preparation of teachers, and, indeed, to all aspects of the common schools, Jurgen Herbst has summarized their essentially Whig values, "a middle-class morality, centering on a sense of human decency and on what has become known as the Protestant work ethic, a bourgeois conception of economic security based on a commitment to hard work and the ownership of private property. Civil order, security of property, decency and gentility in interpersonal relationships among the members of a white, middle class, and overwhelmingly Protestant citizenry," these were the ways to avoid the anarchy of class struggle or the dissension caused by an overly privileged elite. Herbst also goes on to note that common institutions, like the common schools and normal schools, were part of an even larger campaign to strengthen national unity through a common language—an Americanized English—and a common religion in "a common-core or nonsectarian Protestant Christianity." And it was the role of government, a government led by Whigs like Mann and Barnard and their political allies, to enforce these common, unifying threads. "A common language and a common faith," Herbst continues, "however, were not enough. Discipline to enforce, if need be, adherence to common values and standards of behavior was required as well. Public education was to be promoted not only as opportunity and right but as obligation and duty as well." And in order to fulfill their role, teachers needed the knowledge, the skills, and the values to accomplish their high and essential calling through a common experience of preparation.[9]

At the beginning of his tenure as secretary to the state board, Mann outlined what he meant by the need for what he always called systematization:

> In this Commonwealth there are about three thousand public schools, in all of which the rudiments of knowledge are taught. These schools, at the present time, are so many distinct, independent communities; each being governed by is own habits, traditions, and local customs. There is no common, superintending power over them; there is no bond of brotherhood or family between them.[10]

As Lawrence Cremin observed of Mann, "Systematization, he would have argued, meant rationality, not uniformity. Still, the call for uniformity also sounded through his reports—uniformity of textbooks, uniformity of curricula, uniformity of library collections, uniformity of methods, and uniformity of discipline." And, one might easily add, uniformity of teachers and teacher preparation; like all aspects of the uniformity under the wise and benevolent, but tight, control of Mann and his board.[11] In that context, gaining state control over the preparation of teachers was an essential element. If the structures for the normal school came to them by accident, the purposes of a state school were far from accidental; indeed, they were an absolutely essential part of the Whig agenda for education and the still new American nation.

In evaluating the efforts by Mann and his allies to seize control of the state system of public education, it is important to note just how much the schools of Massachusetts and the nation needed reform in the 1830s. Christine Ogren has aptly described the situation in the early decades of the 19th century:

> Whether virtuous or scoundrels, teachers before the antebellum period had no specialized training. They were usually hired by town elders or some sort of community group, who attempted to test applicants' subject matter and pedagogical knowledge, as well as character and religion. In some towns, the ignorance of the hiring committee or lack of applicants made the interview process a bit of a farce; other committees forwent the interview to hire their relatives. Disturbed by such trends, school reformers called for a wider pool of better-prepared applicants as a step toward the professionalization of teaching.[12]

Reform of some sort, it seemed, was badly needed.

At the same time, the specific reforms Mann advocated were hardly the only possible vehicles to improve the schools and the quality and quantity of available teachers. As the previous chapter has shown, beginning in the second decade of the 19th century, Emma Willard had begun her one-woman crusade to improve teaching by recruiting and preparing women to be both deeply committed and well-prepared for the classroom. Willard's efforts represented the beginning of a grass-roots campaign to create female seminaries around the country that would serve the same mission. At about the same time, others, like Samuel Read Hall, were starting teacher preparation programs in existing academies like Andover and writing textbooks that would also improve teaching. After a frustratingly slow start, New York State had appropriated significant funds to help the academies in their teacher preparation mission. And a generation of women like Catharine Beecher were recruiting women by the hundreds and offering their own institutes to these new teachers.

Mann would happily use techniques first developed by Willard and Hall. He followed New York in making the appeal for state money, and he enthusiastically included the women Beecher and her allies recruited in his plans. But for him, and for his nearly all-male allies across the country, there was a significant difference. No grass-roots campaign would do. Funding academies poured state dollars into the hands of institutions that were beyond the control of the funders. He would have nothing to do with creating schools for teachers that mirrored the schools for children as "distinct, independent communities; each being governed by is own habits, traditions, and local customs." He wanted a "common, superintending power over them," and he wanted it to be him and his board, or similar Whig leaders with similar boards in other states.

Multiple sources have claimed—or been given—the credit for first coming up with the idea of the normal school. In the summer of 1837, during his first days in his new position as secretary to the state board, Mann attended the Worcester, Massachusetts, Convention of the American Institute of Instruction, then one of the most powerful lobbying groups for education in the country. Among those who sought the ear of the new secretary was Reverend Charles Brooks of Hingham, who had become obsessed with the idea of creating a network of state-controlled "teachers seminaries," following a shipboard conversation with Heinrich Julius of Prussia in 1835. Brooks had spent the two years between 1835 and 1837 attempting to convince anyone he could reach that the Prussian system of state control and state uniformity in the preparation of teachers was just what the United States needed, starting with Massachusetts. Mann, it seems, was convinced.[13]

Early the following year Mann's former colleagues in the Massachusetts state legislature invited him to address the body, and he used the occasion to lobby for state intervention to improve the quality of the teachers in Massachusetts. Two weeks later, Brooks was back in Boston again pushing his idea for a Prussian system of state teacher seminaries. More important than either Mann or the legislature, Edmund Dwight, the most powerful member of the state board, was convinced of the need for a specialized and state-controlled program to prepare teachers. And Dwight had the resources to back his convictions. He offered Mann $10,000 to launch the institutions if the legislature would match the amount. The legislature quickly complied, and by April 1838 the state board had the funds in hand to begin their new venture in teacher preparation.[14]

In reality, while Brooks later claimed most of the credit for the idea, some form of the normal school model had been floating around among Massachusetts's educators for more than a decade. In 1825, three of the nation's leading educators all published remarkably similar essays calling for state "institutions" or "seminaries" specifically devoted to the preparation of teachers. Thomas H. Gallaudet of Connecticut, best known for his work in fostering the education of the deaf but in his own lifetime a reformer of many interests, Walter R. Johnson of Pennsylvania, and James G. Carter of Massachusetts all published essays on the topic with quite similar recommendations. Historians have speculated about the degree of collaboration among the three, but clearly something was in the air. Many besides Brooks knew the Prussian school law of 1819, with its provision for state institutions for teachers. And the need in a new democratic nation for better schools with better teachers was widely felt in the first decades of the 19th century.[15]

Of the three reformers, James G. Carter was probably the best known. Only 5 years after his graduation from Harvard College, Carter was an experienced teacher who had taught to earn his way through academy and college. His essay, first published in the *Boston Patriot* in February 1825, outlined with great foresight the purposes of the state normal schools. Carter began by insisting that "it will do but little good for the Legislature of the State to make large appropriations directly for the support of the schools . . . [or] constitute an independent tribunal to decide on the qualifications of teachers, while they have not had the opportunities necessary for coming up to the proper standard." Reform thus needed to begin, not end, with teacher preparation. And, Carter continued—anticipating many debates a century and a half later—teacher preparation was a complex task, involving both content knowledge and pedagogical knowledge, or, as he said, "Though a teacher cannot communicate more knowledge than he possesses, yet he may possess much, and still be able to impart little."

The solution, Carter was clear, was a new institution specifically dedicated by the state to the preparation of teachers who would learn both what to teach and how to teach in the service of an expanding country. He wrote:

> An institution for the education of teachers, as has been before intimated, would form a part, and a very important part, of the free-school system. It would be, moreover, precisely that portion of the system, which should be under the direction of the State, whether, the others are or not. Because we should thus secure at once, a uniform, intelligent, and independent tribunal for decisions on

the qualifications of teachers. . . . An institution for this purpose would become, by its influence on society, and particularly on the young, an engine to sway the pubic sentiment, the public morals, and the public religion, more powerful than any other in the possession of government. . . . It should be emphatically the State's institution.[16]

Here Carter outlined the need for special emphasis on teacher preparation as a key to the larger reform efforts and the reasons why this aspect, above all others, needed to be in the hands of the state government.

It is important to note, in this context, that until 1830 the Congregational church was the established state church in Massachusetts and the clergy were often called on to examine teachers as part of their duties as civil servants. Perhaps anticipating disestablishment, Carter wanted to move that responsibility to others whom he deemed more appropriate, the new generation of educators like himself who would lead the new institutions and the new reform efforts.

In spite of the powerful pleas of Carter, Gallaudet, and Johnson, no state action was immediately forthcoming. Carter opened his own teacher seminary in Lancaster, Massachusetts, with private funding in 1827 and then appealed to the legislature for aid. Samuel Read Hall, who had opened one of the first specialized schools for teacher preparation in Concord, Vermont, in 1823 and then moved himself and his school to Phillips Academy in Andover, Massachusetts, in 1830, wrote in the preface to his popular *Lectures on School-Keeping* in 1829 that "institutions should be established for educating teachers, where they should be taught not only the necessary branches of literature, but, be made acquainted with the science of *teaching* and the mode of *governing* a school with success." Henry E. Dwight's *Travels in the North of Germany in the Years 1825 and 1826*, published in 1829, also praised the Prussian government's teacher training institutions, and in 1828 William Channing Woodbridge noted that the Prussian institutions were for men only while both Prussia and the United States needed schools for women. Finally, the French philosopher Victor Cousin also visited Prussia and recommended their system to France in a report that was published in English in the United States in 1835, leading to the use of the term "normal school," a translation of the French *école normale*. Almost a century later, in 1923, G. E. Maxwell, president of Winona State Teachers College in Minnesota, captured the early history with his tongue-in-cheek description of "These institutions, the adaptation of a German idea, tagged with a French name, and developed in a new continent . . ."[17] Clearly, the normal school idea was in the air, though it took Edmund Dwight's money and Horace Mann's political ability to pluck it out of the air and make it real on the ground of several Massachusetts towns at the end of the 1830s.[18]

OPENING THE MASSACHUSETTS NORMAL SCHOOLS

With $20,000 in hand from the Dwight gift and the legislative appropriation, the state board, under Mann's leadership, made a number of key decisions about how to proceed. First, as noted above, they decided not to follow the New York model and provide grants to existing academies that agreed to add teacher preparation departments or to support private schools. Rather, they wanted state-managed schools dedicated specifically to the preparation of teachers, for, as Mann argued, "the course of instruction, proper to qualify teachers, must be essentially different from a common academical course." Second, in order to engage and serve the widest population possible, they decided to spread their resources thin and open three schools in three different parts of the state. And finally, they decided to seek bids from the various towns that might want a school. The new institutions would go to the towns that promised to cover the cost of "suitable buildings, fixtures and furniture, together with the means of carrying on such school (exclusive of the compensation of the teachers of the school)." The curriculum was to prepare students in all the subjects taught in the state's common schools and was to last 1 year. To be admitted, males should be at least 17 and females 16, must demonstrate academic skill, and "must declare it to be their intention to qualify themselves to become school teachers." And the purpose of the institutions was clear. "We want," Mann wrote, "improved teachers for the Common Schools, where the mass of the children must look for all the aids of education, they will ever enjoy."[19]

The happy result of the decision to ask the towns to pick up the cost of land and buildings was a bit of a bidding war that was ultimately resolved when a bid from Lexington was accepted by the board in December 1838, with the provision that it be exclusively for women; followed by another from Barre in 1839, which was to be open to men as well as women; and a third from Bridgewater in 1840, open to men and women. Much later, in 1854 a fourth school, like Lexington for women only, was added in Salem, with others following in the 1870s to 1890s. In fact, the first two schools had quite rocky starts. The school at Lexington moved to West Newton in 1844 and then in 1853 to a permanent home in Framingham. The Barre school was closed for a time and then reopened in Westfield. Only Bridgewater and Salem stayed in their original locations.[20]

Jonathan Messerli describes the inauspicious opening of the first public normal school in the United States at Lexington, Massachusetts, on July 3, 1839: "It rained all day and only three applicants appeared." Mann wrote in his journal, "In point of numbers, this is not a promising commencement." With such a beginning, things could only go uphill, and they did. More students enrolled, and the school was launched. Mann's wise choice for the principal of this first school was Cyrus Peirce, who had previously been a successful teacher in Nantucket. Peirce literally wore himself out teaching all the courses at the normal school, teaching at the model school in which the normal students were to practice, and generally maintaining the whole operation. In January 1841 he wrote to Henry Barnard describing the large building that housed the normal school classes as well as the model school for children. After 18 months of operation the school had taught 41 students, with the largest number at one time being 34. Normal students studied "all the common branches," that is, what was taught in common school, specifically composition, geometry, algebra, physiology, natural, intellectual, and moral philosophy, natural history, botany, political economy, bookkeeping, vocal music, and the "*art of teaching*"; all taught by Peirce.[21]

THE CURRICULUM: WHAT WAS TAUGHT AT
THE MASSACHUSETTS NORMAL SCHOOLS

Primarily because of Peirce's indefatigable work, the first normal school at Lexington was a success. Nevertheless, Mann wanted a more auspicious start when the second school opened at Barre 3 months later. Mann could not control the weather, but he did make sure that the opening was well advertised, and he persuaded Governor Everett to give the opening oration. Twelve women and eight men passed the entrance examinations and were on hand, along with many citizens of the town and dignitaries from across the state, when Everett spoke on September 3, 1839.[22]

Everett, who had been among the most important backers of centralization, the creation of the state board, the appointment of Mann, and the launch of the normal schools, used his speech to outline just what he thought the new institutions should accomplish. He saw four core elements in their program of instruction. As Christine Ogren has noted, "Everett was either insightful or prophetic, for he described the approach of state normal schools throughout the United States for decades to come."[23]

First, Everett, like Peirce, insisted that the future teachers needed to acquire a high level of content knowledge in their year of normal study. So, he said, the schools should offer "careful review of the branches of knowledge required to be taught in our common schools; it being, of course, the first requisite of a teacher that he should himself know well that which he is to aid others in learning." Peirce and others would come to complain that this aspect dominated the work of the normal schools more than they might have wanted, for the applicants turned out to be far less well prepared than they had initially hoped. While he had expected a more solid preparation of his students that would allow him to focus on how to teach, Peirce regularly complained that they had "come to learn the Common Branches rather than to learn to *teach* them." But from the beginning, a solid foundation in content knowledge was to be part of the normal curriculum. The content–pedagogy split would not be tolerated.

However, content knowledge was not enough. Everett also insisted that "the art of teaching" needed to be given equal weight with the content of the curriculum. A decade earlier, James Carter had insisted that the teacher seminaries would be different from other schools because they would teach their students to "establish an intelligible language of communication between the instructor and his pupil, and enable the former to open his head and his heart, and infuse into the other some of the thoughts and feelings which lie hid there." So now Everett was saying that "there are peculiar methods, applicable to teach each branch of knowledge, which should be unfolded in the instructions of a Normal School." This part of the assignment was far more difficult than the first, for as Ogren and others have noted, the state of knowledge about pedagogy then in existence was very limited. There were a few textbooks, like Hall's 1829 *Lectures on School-Keeping* and later David Page's 1847 *Theory and Practice of Teaching*, but in general this aspect of the curriculum—so important to Mann and others—was the least developed. Peirce and his fellow normal school principals had been selected because of their recognized expertise in teaching and they generally drew on their experiences, so that one student would later recall that at Bridgewater in the early years, where Nicholas Tillinghast was the principal, "Mr. Tillinghast was our textbook in theory and Art of Teaching." It would be well after the Civil War before research in child development and psychology would make it possible to study pedagogy in greater depth with more than autobiographical information from experts and anecdotal stories.[24]

Third, as Ogren recounts the speech and its impact, Everett saw the normal schools preparing future teachers to be expert in "the government of the school," including how to become a moral influence in the community around the school while also mastering the practical aspects of how to maintain order in classroom. In her detailed journal of the first year at Lexington, Mary Swift recorded numerous lectures by Peirce on school governance. On August 31 she recorded, "After these remarks, he proceeded to deliver his lecture, which was upon the subject of School Order. He commenced by calling our attention to the importance of the office of the teacher, with how many & various & invaluable interests it may connect us; if we are faithful how many will be rendered more happy by our instructions." But for Peirce order was the key to this happiness. "A good school must be orderly; whatever its object or title, or whoever its teacher may be. . . . The work of Education is a work of order." Later in the fall, Peirce elaborated on his commitment to school order in language with which many a teacher could identify. "When you go into a new school, and there meet those, for whom you have never done anything & who are, therefore, under no obligation to you & feel no gratitude to you, there must be an expression of authority and rebuke, as well as of love. The look of the eye must threaten rebuke, and there are few so hardened as to withstand it."

Finally, the fourth aspect of the normal experience, as Everett envisioned it, was the opportunity to observe and practice good teaching. He insisted that as part of every normal school, "there is to be established a common or district school, as a school of practice, in which, under the direction of the principal of the Normal School, the young teacher may have the benefit of actual exercise in the business of instruction." Administering both the normal school and, in the same building, the district school that was to be the normal school students' practice school may have exhausted Peirce, and ultimately have broken his health, but he and his colleagues and successors all believed that direct school practice, under careful supervision, was the key to the success of the whole venture. When the practice schools were disrupted because of space problems or conflicts with parents, "who did not want their children experimented upon," the normal school leaders worked quickly to restore the arrangements. When the links to the practice schools could not be restored quickly enough, normal school leaders arranged for the normalites to practice teaching on each other, but everyone agreed that pseudo-teaching was a much less desirable arrangement. And when the links between the normal schools and their practice schools were in place, the opportunities for practice teaching were the pride and joy of the normal faculty.

In 1865, Richard Edwards, principal of the Normal School at Normal, Illinois, insisted, "It is said that more skill is necessary to teach a class of adults personating children, than to teach an equal number of actual little ones, and that, therefore, this practice is of more value than the other. . . . But this assumption is not true." Teaching real children was much better preparation for a teacher, Edwards insisted, because "There is no make-believe." Teaching under supervision, receiving immediate critique, and teaching again, Edwards believed, was "an opportunity for improvement in the art of teaching such as offered by no other instrumentality." At a time in American history when most future lawyers read law books in the home of a distinguished lawyer, future ministers read divinity or attended the academic program at one of the new theological seminaries, and future doctors were apprenticed, often at a very early age, to another doctor, this opportunity to move between theory and practice, and in the practice to receive immediate feedback from those who taught the theory, represented a new and important breakthrough in the structuring of professional education. Student teaching, as part of the preprofessional curriculum, is a legacy of the early normal schools to a wide range of institutions that succeeded them.[25]

To greater or lesser degrees the antebellum normal schools, in Massachusetts and beyond, did continue to follow Everett's mandate. They offered instruction in the liberal arts beyond the common school curriculum to students who had no other opportunities to study in high school, academy, or college.

They offered practical advice about instruction and about classroom management, advice that was based more on the craft knowledge of acknowledged experts than on more advanced research about learning, but significant advice nonetheless. And they offered the opportunity not only to teach, something that many of the normal students had already done before enrolling, but to teach under observation and with immediate feedback that no doubt improved the teaching ability of the novice teachers who studied there.

Most of all, however, the early normal schools were imbued with a spirit of commitment to teaching and a sense of the value of the enterprise. As the 1844 catalogue of the second Massachusetts normal school, now resettled from Barre to Westfield, stated:

> In the Normal School one object is kept in view, and the members of it are surrounded by a Common School atmosphere; they inhale it, and are invigorated by it. Such an atmosphere cannot be created in other Schools in which the preparation of School teachers is only incidental.[26]

In spite of always limited funds and limited time, in spite of students who wanted to use the schools for their own ends, and in spite of community and political resistance, creating a new set of institutions where prospective teachers were "surrounded by a Common School atmosphere," and had no choice but to "inhale it," was the goal of the normal schools' founders. When Marshall Conant, principal of the Massachusetts State Normal School at Bridgewater in the 1850s, wrote, "have sought to awaken the conscience to feel the responsibilities and duties that devolve upon the teacher," he spoke for a generation of early normal school faculty.[27]

AN ALTERNATIVE VISION

The Massachusetts normal schools, destined to be a national model, were almost closed before they had gotten started. Only a few months after the schools at Lexington and Barre had opened, in November 1839, Edward Everett was defeated for reelection by the Democratic candidate, Marcus Morton, and a Democratic majority was elected in the legislature. These Democrats saw the common school crusade as a Whig venture as much as later generations of historians would.

In March 1840 the majority of the Committee on Education of the Massachusetts House recommended abolishing the state board of education, the office of secretary, and the two normal schools that had been opened at that point. They saw Mann's centralization efforts as essentially as an antidemocratic movement away from local control. And they certainly saw no reason why the educational system of Prussia, one of the least democratic nations of

Europe, should be a model for democratic America. Thus they prefaced the rest of their report by saying:

> After all that has been said about the French and Prussian systems, they appear to your Committee to be much more admirable, as a means of political influence, and of strengthening the hands of the government, than as a mere means for the diffusion of knowledge. For the latter purpose, the system of public Common Schools, under the control of persons most interested in their flourishing condition, who pay taxes to support them, appears to your Committee much superior. The establishment of the Board of Education seems to be the commencement of a system of centralization and of monopoly power in a few hands, contrary, in every respect, to the true spirit of our democratical institutions; and which, unless speedily checked, may lead to unlooked for and dangerous results.

Results these Democrats were determined to avoid.

Having recommended abolishing the board and the office of secretary, the legislative committee turned specifically to the normal schools. Noting that half of the funds appropriated to launch the experiment were a private gift, and that the schools were but a few months old, the committee nevertheless argued that since they were a bad idea, the state would best be served by returning the funds to the donor and moving in a different direction. A more decentralized system of teacher preparation seemed much preferable; after all, "Academies and high schools cost the Commonwealth nothing; and they are fully adequate, in the opinion of your Committee, to furnish a component supply of teachers." Indeed, not only did allowing academies and high schools to flourish cost less, but "There is a high degree of competition existing between these academies, which is the best guaranty for excellence." While the state board might argue "that the art of teaching is a peculiar art, which is particularly and exclusively taught at Normal Schools," the committee believed that "every person, who has himself undergone a process of instruction, must acquire, by that very process, the art of instructing others." And they wondered if specialized professional training for teachers was desirable, since "it is obviously impossible, and perhaps it is not desirable, that the business of keeping these schools, should become a distinct and separate profession, which the establishment of Normal Schools seems to anticipate." The cause of poor-quality teaching, they argued, was poor compensation, not poor training, though they did not offer to do anything to supplement town budgets to redress that wrong.

In the end, the committee, believing that the normal schools, like the board and secretary that had launched them, represented "a great departure from the uniform spirit of our institutions, a dangerous precedent, and an interference with a matter more properly belonging to those hands, to which our ancestors wisely intrusted it," i.e., the individual towns and school districts that were closest to those who paid the taxes and wanted the control of their children's education. When the bill came to a vote in the full House of Representatives, the committee report was rejected and Mann's job, his board, and his normal schools were spared, but it had been a close call. From a later perspective, here in the 1st year of the existence of this new institution, some of the most important battles to roil teacher education throughout the nation's history were played out. Mann believed that centralized control was the key to high standards; his opponents thought excellence would be achieved through competition and the powers of democratic localism. Mann believed that he had found the best way to prepare teachers; his opponents insisted that multiple routes—alternative routes in later discourse—represented the key to a well-prepared teacher corps. Mann believed that one needed to learn the art of pedagogy; his opponents believed that if one knew a subject, one could teach it. Mann wanted to create a profession with high standards; his opponents wondered if teaching really was or should be a profession, as opposed to a public service that many might offer for a short period of time. Mann may have won this battle, but the war that is represented in the committee's report would continue to rage, on and off, to the present.[28]

THE SLOW SPREAD OF THE NORMAL SCHOOL
MODEL BEFORE THE CIVIL WAR

Having survived the battle with the Massachusetts legislature, the new Massachusetts-minted institution spread to several other states around the country. State leaders in Pennsylvania, Missouri, and Wisconsin all read the reports coming from Massachusetts—Mann was, after all, a first-rate publicist—and pleaded, as Wisconsin's did, that "Until we have an institution of this kind, we cannot reasonably expect the character of our schools to be satisfactory."

New York, whose earlier model of supporting a wide range of academies Mann had specifically rejected, opened its first normal school in Albany in 1844 with the provision that it be a 5-year experiment. In 1849, Connecticut, where Mann's closest ally, Henry Barnard, sometimes held a similar office, authorized a normal school and it was opened in New Britain. Michigan opened one in Ypsilanti. New Jersey's first state normal school was opened in Trenton in 1855, and Illinois opened one in a town named after its school, Normal, Illinois, in 1857. Pennsylvania authorized a school in Millersville in 1859 and Minnesota, one in Winona in 1860. Even during the Civil War, other state normal schools were established in San Francisco, California, in 1862, Farmington, Maine, in 1864, and Emporia, Kansas, in 1865. By the end of the 1860s there were 35 state normal schools in 16 different states.

Most of the normal schools followed the Massachusetts model. The legislation authorizing the school in Michigan specified that "a Normal School be established, the exclusive purpose of which shall be the instruction of persons both male and female in the art of teaching, and in all the various branches that pertain to a good common school education," and reinforced the stated purpose of the school by requiring students, once admitted, to sign a declaration "of intention to follow the business of teaching primary schools in this State."[29]

Christine Ogren has summarized the early years of the normal school experiment: "During their first three decades of existence, state normal schools were on shaky ground. They struggled against public skepticism and scrutiny, limited state funding, and the popularity of other types of institutions. Making only small advances toward developing and teaching educational theory, normals were successful in fulfilling their intention to instill their students with a sense of teaching as a calling." It was not just the Massachusetts legislature that challenged the schools. Indeed, Massachusetts was more generous than many states. The Connecticut legislature cut off funds for the New Britain school in 1867, and it was closed for 2 years. For decades Pennsylvania simply authorized the normal schools, assuming that someone else would pay the bills. Schools in most other states always struggled both with hostile legislatures and with the tendency of state universities to absorb all available funds. Nevertheless the new model survived, thrived in some cases, and after 1870 would blossom into what would be, for a few decades at the end of the 19th and beginning of the 20th centuries, a prime means of preparing teachers for the schools of the United States.[30]

SO DID THE NORMAL SCHOOLS PREPARE TEACHERS?

Historians have long debated the degree to which the early normal schools operated as their founders expected. For all of the efforts of the state legislatures like Michigan's to insist that the schools were strictly for the preparation of teachers through requirements such as the oath that the students signed, "of intention to follow the business of teaching primary schools in this State," students used the schools in a wide variety of ways.[31] What Jurgen Herbst has noted for Massachusetts was true in many places: "For men in the rural hinterlands the normal school offered a second chance. It brought them educational opportunity. Many of the graduates would subsequently leave teaching to pursue further studies or enter upon different careers. For both the opponents and some friends of the normal schools, that constituted one of the major grievances. A public institution was being abused for private gain. Others argued that these graduates were only practicing the time-honored American way of trying to get ahead in life and to climb the ladder of social mobility." But while the civic leaders and taxpayers debated, the students used the normal schools for their own purposes.[32]

While nearly all the normal schools required a fixed curriculum, initially 1 year and soon expanding to 2 or even 3 years, students dropped in and out of the schools as the institutions served their needs and interests. Beginning in 1844, the principals at Westfield Normal School in Massachusetts began recording important details about their students, details that have served historians well in succeeding years. That September 1844 class included 49 students, 32 of whom were the children of farmers, reflecting a national pattern among normal schools; they served the youth of rural areas as their students and expected to send their graduates to teach in rural schools. In that same year, the record showed that 31 of the 49 students had also taught for some period of time in the district schools prior to enrolling. Thus at Westfield, as at many schools in the middle decades of the century, the normal schools were not truly a preservice institution, in the 21st century use of that term, as much as part of the continuing education of many teachers, many of whom taught for a period of time, enrolled in normal school for a season or two, and then returned to teaching or moved on to other careers without much worry about whether they had received the certificate that was generally issued to those who had completed the full curriculum.[33]

Normal students left in midcourse for many reasons. George Minns of the San Francisco State Normal School reported that, after all, "it was absolutely necessary for them to do something to support themselves."[34] Perhaps more troubling to those who believed that the state-funded and state-controlled normal schools were to prepare teachers for the state's schools was the fact that so many of the institution's graduates did not teach. In the case of Westfield, between 1844 and 1857 a total of 927 students—275 males and 652 females— enrolled for some period of time. While slightly more than half had taught in the common schools before enrolling at Westfield, follow-up records indicated that almost half of those who had studied at Westfield—126 males and 328 females—never taught again.[35] As Herbst recognized, the normal schools did not so much help to provide teachers for rural schools, their intended goal, as help students and teachers from those schools escape from the countryside to a world of larger opportunities elsewhere. "The normalites were on the move both socially and geographically," Herbst concluded, "and only few stayed or returned to play the role of country schoolmaster or schoolmistress."[36]

Nevertheless, something very important had happened to the preparation of teachers in the United States with the launch of the normal schools in the decades of the 1840s, 1850s, and 1860s. While two of the first four Massachusetts normal schools were for women only, the two coeducational schools also reflected the growing feminization of teaching. In 1844, the 1st year for which detailed records are available, Westfield's student body was 57 percent female while the whole teacher corps of the state was 64 percent female. However, 5 years later, in 1849, Westfield had moved to 72 percent female while the state's teachers were 70 percent female. The normal school would continue to reflect, and stay slightly ahead of, the statewide trend, until in 1870 both the Westfield enrollment and the state's total count of teachers stood at 88 percent women. The movement, begun through private initiatives by women like Emma Willard and Catharine Beecher to claim teaching, especially teaching in the common schools, as "women's true profession," had succeeded in the public normal schools, at least on the East Coast.[37]

Certainly the launch of tax-supported and essentially tuition-free institutions that offered an education beyond the common school opened opportunities for many who might not have otherwise had them. Ogren is right that "the provision of post-common school education at little or no cost was an unintended yet profound change in educational opportunity." These generally rural students were, most for the first time in their lives, living in a town, away from a farm and family supervision. "They seized opportunities to learn about and venture into the larger world, lightly brushing class and gender boundaries." And in the process, many—though not a majority—became teachers, some for shorter periods of time and some as a lifetime career.[38] The preparation of teachers had a new model that would eventually impact all other approaches to the professional preparation of educators, though it never prepared the majority of those who worked in the nation's classrooms.

4

Teachers' Institutes

1830–1920

In 1919 J. H. Minnick, then dean of the School of Education at the University of Pennsylvania, recalled a time, much earlier in his career, when as a rural schoolteacher he, like most teachers in the United States between the Civil War and World War I, had been required to attend the teachers' institute for his county. To the question, "in your experience with County Teachers' Institutes, have you found they actually contribute to the professional training of teachers?" he responded, "Only in a very small way. My only experience was as a county school teacher. The institutes were very poor. The most I got out of them was association with other teachers."

By 1919 Minnick was hardly alone. Indeed, his response was part of a growing chorus of complaints from educators—classroom teachers and superintendents—insisting that the teachers' institutes had served their purposes, that in the 20th century there were better ways of preparing teachers and keeping them professionally engaged throughout their careers and that, in the words of New York state's commissioner of education, the "inspirational address" that was the centerpiece of many institutes was "simply a disguise for 'hot air.'"[1] Such responses had not always been the case. In their heyday, teachers' institutes had been seen as a significant advance in the professional preparation of the nation's schoolteachers.

THE ORIGINS OF TEACHERS' INSTITUTES

The origins of one of the first—if not the first—teachers' institute in the United States tells a lot about the purposes of the institutes. In October 1839, Henry Barnard, perhaps Horace Mann's closest ally and at that time the secretary to the State Board of Education in Connecticut, "assembled twenty-six young men together and formed them into a class. They were taught for six weeks by able lecturers and teachers and had the advantage of observation in the public schools of Hartford." Since at this point young men generally taught school during the winter term, while summer-term schools were already being taught by women, one may presume that Barnard wanted to have these 26 men ready for the term that would open across Connecticut early in 1840.[2]

Barnard was also clear from the beginning that the institute—though at that point he simply called it a "Teachers' Class"—was his second choice. He would have preferred a normal school like the ones Mann was just then launching across the state line to the north, but he could not get the Connecticut legislature to support him financially. Indeed, it would take a decade before, in 1849, Connecticut's legislature authorized that state's first normal school at New Britain, and for many decades after that only a small proportion of the state's teachers graduated from, or even attended, the normal school. In the meantime, after he had tried and failed to persuade the legislature to create a more permanent institution, Barnard turned to the institute idea. Each year after what he considered an encouraging start in 1839, he organized a 4-to-6-week program that included lectures and "a traveling model school, to give demonstration lessons in the art of teaching."

Barnard was clear on the purpose of this new experiment he was launching. It was "to show the practicability of making some provision for the better qualification of common school teachers, by giving them the opportunity to revise and extend their knowledge of the studies usually pursued in the District Schools, and of the best methods of school arrangements, instruction, and government, under the recitations and lectures of experienced and well known teachers and educators." He came to believe that attending these classes twice a year for 3 years was the equivalent of a normal school preparation, and given the fact that the normals schools then lasted 1 year and that many students did not stay for the full term, he was probably right. In the process he had also launched what would continue to be, for most of the next century, one of the prime institutional structures for teacher preparation.[3]

A few years after Barnard launched his class in Hartford, J. S. Denman, the County Superintendent of Tompkins County, New York, organized a 2-week institute in Ithaca, New York, for April 1843 that served 28 teachers. As Denman described the program, it included "the best modes of governing and teaching the various common branches which necessarily included a critical review of those branches . . ." Denman was not modest as to the results. He reported, "Having previously visited the schools of those present at the institute, it gives me great pleasure to be able to state that their schools during the past summer have been conducted from 50 to 100% better than formerly." Denman may have been the first to use the term "institute" to describe his program for teachers, and thus Horace Mann and some later historians have given him the credit for offering the first teachers' institute in the country. Be that as it may, the idea of a short 2-to-6-week course for teachers, offered once or twice a year, caught hold quickly. In his 1845 report to the Massachusetts board, Horace Mann reported that only a few years after the first ones had been offered, more than half the counties of New York and the states of Ohio, Pennsylvania, New Hampshire, Rhode Island, and his own Massachusetts were all offering teachers' institutes.[4]

In a 1922 study of the teachers' institutes of Pennsylvania, Carmon Ross places the institutes in their proper historical context. They were founded as part of the same reform movement as that which led to the founding of normal schools, and often by the same people. Both the normal schools and the teachers' institutes were a response to the perceived crisis in the nation's schools in the 1830s, that, as an 1837 American Institute of Instruction petition said, "whenever, in any town, exertion has been made to improve these schools, it has been met and baffled by the want of good teachers." The need was greatest in the rural district schools, though it could be felt everywhere. Too often, according to the American Institute of Instruction, classrooms were filled "by persons exceedingly incompetent, in many respects," and only a uniform system of preparation for professionals could change the situation. Where possible that system would be led by normal schools, permanent institutions offering at least a 1-year curriculum, but when such arrangements were not possible, either because, as in Connecticut, the legislature would not fund the normal schools or because, as in Massachusetts, only a small minority of novice teachers were willing to take the time and spend the money to attend them, then shorter courses covering much of the same curriculum, and with the same emotional intensity, were needed, the reformers argued. The teachers' institutes would fill the need until political pressure and economic prosperity would allow the higher standard for everyone.[5]

It is not surprising that, especially in the early years, there was great confusion about just what constituted a teachers' institute. Barnard was slow to adopt the term, though he did eventually, leading to the struggle for pride of origin between his Hartford program and that offered in Ithaca, New York. More confusing was the fact that many different programs for educators were called at various times *institutes, conferences, associations,* and other names, and in the early years, not only were the names interchangeable, but *institutes* referred to many different kinds of programs and organizations, some of which were not focused on teachers at all.

The American Institute of Instruction, founded in 1830 and perhaps the most venerable and powerful educational organization in the United States in the 19th century, to give one example, was not a teachers' institute at all. Early in its history the American Institute of Instruction was dominated by "friends of education," who, as Paul Mattingly wrote of them, were "learned, affluent and oriented toward Boston and the Boston intellectual establishment." It was an organization of college professors and presidents, later joined by school superintendents and an occasional teacher, though it used the name *institute.* But the American Institute was a long way from—and nothing to be confused with—the week or 2-week-long institutes organized specifically around the needs of new and continuing teachers that were what the term *teachers' institute* came to mean in the United States in the course of the 19th century.[6]

Another organization that used the institute name, Cincinnati's Western Literary Institute and College of Professional Teachers, did include teachers, but only males who were the leaders of the profession. Incorporated in 1834 by a group of leading educators and clergy in Cincinnati, though it had been meeting under various names since 1829, the Western Institute was an organization of male leaders in southern Ohio who lobbied strongly and effectively to spread public schools in the region and to be sure that these schools reflected the middle-class Protestant values of the institute's leaders. Its annual fall meetings throughout the 1830s included papers and discussions on some of the major educational issues of the day. Women were not allowed to speak at Western Literary Institute meetings, so even Catharine Beecher had to arrange for her father, the Presbyterian minister Lyman Beecher, who was one of the organization's founders, to read her remarks on the education of women teachers. But like the American Institute, with which it has often been compared, for all of its effectiveness, the Western Institute, was not dedicated to the immediate professional needs of common-school classroom teachers.[7]

On the other hand, at least as early as 1800, a grass-roots movement of teachers' conventions or associations had emerged among teachers in different parts of the United States. Starting with private school teachers, many of these associations started out as simply social organizations aimed at teacher self-improvement, but expanded into organizations that advocated for support for schools and for protecting teachers. The Massachusetts Teachers Association, forerunner of the 21st-century state affiliate of the National Education Association, now the nation's largest teachers' union, did not, in its earliest antebellum years, admit women teachers to its ranks. These and many other similar organizations were part of the educational atmosphere of the United States between the Revolution and the Civil War, but none of these organizations were teachers' institutes as the term came to be known, though in some cases the county institutes did displace earlier, more informal—and more teacher-controlled—township and county teachers' associations.[8]

By the early 1840s, however, and continuing into the 1920s, there were some fairly clear defining characteristics of teachers' institutes, at least as the term is used in this volume and in most discussions of the history of teacher preparation in the United States. Henry Barnard himself provided a useful definition when in 1844, having moved from Connecticut to Rhode Island, he proposed a new school law that called for them. In Barnard's words:

> It is an organization of the teachers of a town, county, or state for improvement in their profession, by meeting for a longer or shorter time for a thorough review of the studies of the public schools, under teachers of acknowledged reputation,

as well as for lectures, discussions, and essays on various methods of school discipline and instruction . . .

Two years later, in 1846, the *American Journal of Education*, with Barnard's blessing, carried a description of them that expanded slightly on Barnard's Rhode Island recommendations:

> They are conventions for mutual improvement and excitement. . . . Here raw and timid teachers are initiated into their new business; older teachers receive valuable suggestions and—apply them. An enthusiasm in their business is excited. . . . These institutes differ from ordinary conventions, in that they furnish definite business, and are spent in gaining real knowledge.

In addition to including the same general curriculum as the normal schools—both content knowledge and pedagogical skills—the institutes as they emerged in the 1830s also mirrored one other aspect of the normal schools—they were state- or district-controlled. They were not private institutions, and the teachers themselves did not control them.[9]

Normal school advocates like Edward Everett, Horace Mann, and Cyrus Peirce would all have been in full agreement with Barnard's goals. The teachers' institutes were normal schools writ small. Or as Peirce himself said, in describing his normal school, it was a "kind of standing Teachers' Institute,"[10] that is, a teachers' institute institutionalized in a permanent place with a longer program. Both the normal school and the teachers' institute had the same curriculum and the same purposes. Improving the preparation of the teachers of the common schools, educating the men and the increasing numbers of women who were quickly becoming the vast majority of the teachers, required that the teachers be given greater expertise in the content of the curriculum, the "common branches" of learning that they should have learned themselves in common school but in which they needed greater depth. It also meant instruction in the art of teaching and managing a classroom so that the novice teachers would be expert in pedagogy. And finally, it meant creating a sense of commitment, reminding teachers of their high calling and expanding the sense of "excitement" about their work.

Excitement about the work of teaching in the antebellum era meant much more than simply expanding the emotional energy level of teachers. Teachers' institutes, like many of the reforms that emanated from the common school movement, were closely tied to the revivals of Protestant evangelical Christianity that were sweeping the country in the post-Revolutionary religious movement known as the Second Great Awakening. And before the Civil War the walls between Protestant religious revivalism and school reform were highly permeable. Paul Mattingly has well summarized the quasi-religious atmosphere of an institute: "For the first generation of professional educators this institution made explicit, more than any other educational agency, how determined

schoolmen were to equate professionalization with 'awakening' of moral character rather than with training in communicable skills and the standard techniques of teaching. 'Awakening' arranged the inspiration of the inner man . . ."
Clergy were regularly called on to lead not only the opening devotions but other aspects of the program throughout the institute day, so that Samuel Bates's 1862 recommendations for an institute included the suggestion that one of the clergy "who usually take sufficient interest in public education to be present without special invitation" should be called on to lead the devotions with which an institute always began its day.[11]

In a more secular day, it is important to understand that in much of the United States, especially in the rural areas where the majority of people lived and sent their children to schools led by teachers prepared and "awakened" at county teachers' institutes, the dividing line between church and state was between different denominations and the larger public realm, which was also expected to be religious. Most people throughout the 19th century were confident that they could send their children to public schools that, as Robert W. Lynn has written, reflected "the inherent and inevitable harmony of public education and the Protestant cause." Such "inevitable harmony" would begin to disappear after the Civil War, first of all in the more religiously diverse cities, but also as the professions of minister and teacher or educational leader became more and more differentiated, but in the early days, the inspiration that one gained at a teachers' institute smacked strongly of Protestant Christianity.[12]

While the basic structure of a teachers' institute was fairly well stabilized by the 1840s, the occasional nature of the institutes meant that more than at the permanent and well-structured normal schools, a great deal of the strengths or weaknesses of any one institute depended on who was leading it. Emma Willard, who after her years at Troy Seminary came to work closely with Henry Barnard in the development of teacher institutes, wrote that if "no other person but myself could put in practice the plan to be proposed," she would not defend it. After all, even the temporary institutes needed to be replicated far beyond the power of any one person. On the other hand, she also said, "Yet I would not hold myself responsible for its success in any other hands." Replication of the model was essential for Willard, but she did not want to be personally accountable for any but those she personally led. For Willard, at whose academy the capstone course was her own in moral philosophy, it was not a stretch to lead an institute that was supportive to teachers regarding both content and pedagogical knowledge but that, most of all, focused on a teacher's personal morality and their moral commitment to their calling.[13]

While he was in Rhode Island, Barnard sent out an "Institute Circular Letter" to county superintendents and those who would be in charge of that state's teachers' institutes summarizing what should be included:

1. A review of the studies usually taught in the public schools of this state with the exemplification of the best methods of instruction in each branch, and with special attention to difficulties as any member of the Institute may have encountered teaching the same;

2. Familiar lectures and discussions among members in the organization of schools, the classification of pupils, and the theory and practice of teaching;

3. Public lectures and discussions in the evening, on topics calculated to interest parents and the community generally, in the subject of education, and the organization, administration, and improvement of public schools.[14]

With surprisingly modest changes, this remained the curriculum of the institutes for the next 80 years.

THE HEYDAY OF THE TEACHERS' INSTITUTE

As public schools spread throughout the United States, and as the demand for teachers always outpaced the numbers produced by normal schools, academies, and colleges, teachers' institutes grew rapidly in popularity. The fallback position of Henry Barnard and a few colleagues in Connecticut, Rhode Island, New York, and Massachusetts in the late 1830s became, after the Civil War, a very large enterprise, indeed. Before the war, in 1860, 8 institutes were held in Michigan serving 1,251 teachers. A decade later the number grew to 16 institutes serving 2,005 teachers. And by 1880 Michigan reported 65 institutes with a total attendance of 4,482. Other states reported similar statistics. In Ohio, 1,294 teachers had attended institutes in 1860, 10,972 in 1880. In only 8 years, between 1869 and 1877, the state of Illinois reported an increase from 4,651 teachers to 8,010 teachers participating in institutes. For the year 1886–1887 the United States Commissioner of Education reported that across the country a total of 2,003 institutes had served an astounding 138,946 teachers, almost half of the 363,992 teachers that the U.S. Office of Education would report for the nation in 1890.[15] These numbers reflect not only the success of the institutes but a fundamental shift in their purpose from the original model that Barnard and others had developed for the preparation of those about to begin teaching careers to a more or less permanent fixture of continuing teacher education. In the language of the 21st century, the institutes had moved from preservice to inservice for most of their participants in the decades after the Civil War, although in some cases, especially when they were designed to help aspiring teachers pass licensing examinations, they were a route into teaching well into the 20th century.

For the generation who succeeded Mann and Barnard, the teachers' institute was an institution that they wanted to expand as quickly and as widely as possible even as they also secularized its evangelical zeal, but not its focus on a more generalized but still strong inspirational message. In 1848, William Russell, editor of the *American Journal of Education*, published his *Suggestions on Teachers' Institutes*. Reflecting the institutes' changing role, Russell saw the institutes as coexisting alongside the normal schools rather than as a stopgap measure. As strongly as he advocated for the institutes, he also insisted that they should never be substitutes for normal schools, for they could never "serve all the purposes of an adequate education of teachers." And at the same time, he hoped that the spread of normal schools and academies would not undermine the institutes, for although the institutes should not "interfere with the usefulness of such institutions," they could be a valuable addition to the whole configuration of teacher preparation. So Russell insisted, "The institute which is most useful to the interests of education, is uniformly, that at which are assembled the largest number of students who have been trained at a normal school." Unfortunately, he could point to few cases where this ideal was achieved. He hoped that while "Institutes are properly the pioneers of such schools [permanent normal schools]," and might in time inspire legislatures to fund permanent normal schools, he also saw that the institutes "are efficient temporary substitutes for such professional seminaries," though the reality would be that in many places the temporary expedient would continue to be the sole option offered to many teachers well into the 20th century.[16]

Russell was one of a host of authors who not only advocated for teachers' institutes but also outlined what should be done at the institutes in great detail. By the middle of the century, institutes had generally been shortened to 1-week affairs. Writing in 1862, Pennsylvania's Samuel Bates insisted, "An Institute should not convene for a less time than one week, when suitable Instructors can be secured for conducting it; nor is it advisable to have it continue longer than a week or ten days." Less time meant more time and trouble in travel than the actual institute warranted and a longer time meant losing too many people. In addition, the best time of year for an institute was "immediately preceding the opening of schools for the season." Since in many rural areas school only convened during a few months in midsummer and midwinter, institute time could be late spring or just before or just after the Christmas holidays. In towns and cities with a longer school year, late summer or another convenient time seemed best.[17]

Russell and Barnes, like others, also advocated for what came to be a fairly standard institute day that included morning, afternoon, and evening sessions. The morning session usually began with a ceremonial opening, followed by a mix of instruction to the teachers and time for discussion and debate among them. The afternoon was similar, if a bit shorter, but the evening session was different. For one thing, the evening sessions were often open to the general public and, in fact, were calculated to engage parents and other citizens in a greater interest in education. Evening sessions also often included an extended lecture by some well-known authority on some aspect of education or on one of the fields covered in the curriculum. Finally, evening sessions became an opportunity for teachers to debate some of the vital topics of the day. In 1846 the teachers at the Chenango County (New York) Institute used their evening session to discuss a major issue in their professional lives and resolved that:

> Whereas, The education of a lady is obtained at no less expense than that of a gentleman, and as it is generally admitted that they can impart instruction with equal facility and success, therefore,
>   Resolved, That ladies and gentlemen of equal qualifications, should receive equal compensation.

This almost 80 years before "equal pay for equal work" became a national reality. But consideration of this sort of resolution was every bit as much a part of a teachers' institute as the daylong meetings organized to instruct teachers in the latest emerging content knowledge and pedagogical skill.[18]

In spite of the shortened time span and the desire, when possible, to coexist with normal schools, the core business of teachers' institutes remained quite consistent. When Samuel Bates, for example, outlined the objects of the institute, they included introducing all teachers to a scientific approach to pedagogy so that the teachers would not merely "follow on in the beaten track, and adopt the plans pursued by those who taught them," but rather "develop the elements of science" for themselves. Bates gave less emphasis to the common core subject matter, preferring that teachers establish that foundation earlier in their careers, but he prized the opportunities that the institutes allowed for a teacher to have "direct intercourse with his professional brethren," and "to measure himself intellectually and professionally with others." A little competition seemed to him to be a good thing, especially when mixed with "esprit de corps, a professional pride, a feeling which is an element of success in every calling." By the time Bates wrote in 1862 he also insisted that institutes should serve a range of teachers, for they were "an excellent school for young teachers to learn to express their thoughts in public," but equally an opportunity "of readily introducing into the practice of the profession such new improvements as are made in the science and art of teaching." Preservice and in-service education melded well in the institute that Bates wanted.[19]

At their core, however, teachers' institutes were a revival agency for teachers. At a time when the core of much of American Protestantism was evangelical revivalism, teachers were expected to have their own revivals and to make their own quasi-religious commitment to their profession. State superintendents were clear that while the institutes were very important agencies—and at midcentury often the only agency—that taught teachers content and pedagogy, they were also expected to provide, as Illinois's superintendent said in 1858, the equiva-lent of the Muslim's pilgrimage to Mecca, "the source whence he renews the spirit and life of his existence," or as West Virginia's superintendent said of that state's institutes in 1870, "It inspires him with an unwonted enthusi-asm, caught by contact with superior and sympathetic hearts; and carries him back to his school room with new impulses and higher aspirations, to work out better results." Like the religious revival, the revivals that took place at the teachers' institutes were expected to lead to changes in the actions and commitments of the teachers when they returned to their classrooms. No wonder Barnard himself was so clear that they were an "educational revival agency."[20]

TEACHERS' INSTITUTES, EXAMINATIONS, AND CERTIFICATION: A CASE STUDY

In summing up the role of teachers' institutes, Paul Mattingly has written that "By the late 1840s institutes were the most prevalent teacher preparatory agency in America and touched the lives of more teachers than any other educational institution."[21] If one reads the reports from virtually any state or studies the biographies of many teachers, Mattingly's conclusion seems accurate and would continue to be so for decades. A detailed look at one part of the nation—one not usually the primary focus of educational history—reveals both the truth and the complexity of Mattingly's assertion. A case study fo-cused on the Territory of New Mexico not only confirms Mattingly's analysis but, in fact, leads one to believe that, at least for rural teachers in more sparsely settled parts of the United States, the same generalization continued to be true well into the 20th century.

In 1910, 2 years before it was admitted to statehood, New Mexico's Ter-ritorial Superintendent of Public Instruction described the educational in-stitutions of the state. While New Mexico is hardly representative of the whole of the United States, it provides a useful case study for a number of reasons. New Mexico was predominantly rural, as was most of the nation into the first quarter of the 20th century; it kept especially clear records in part because as a territory it was under direct federal control for so long; and it offers a use-ful antidote to the tendency to write American history from the Northeast westward.

In 1910 there were nine public institutions of higher education, all very small in their enrollments, including the University of New Mexico at Albu-querque, New Mexico College of Agriculture and Mechanic Arts at Las Cruces, New Mexico Normal School at Silver City, New Mexico Spanish-American Normal School at El Rita, New Mexico Normal University at Las Vegas, and New Mexico School of Mines at Socorro, as well as the New Mexico Military

Institute, the Institute for Deaf and Dumb, and the Institute for the Blind at Santa Fe. Of these institutions, four prepared teachers—the state university and the three normal schools—although graduates of the colleges of agriculture and of the school of mines were considered qualified to teach if they had also taken some education courses. However, these institutions, taken together, prepared only a tiny proportion of the territory's teachers.

New Mexico had 1,200 tax-supported public schools with an enrollment of 56,000, 20,000 of whom, or a little over one-third, were "Spanish-Americans," often taught in separate Spanish-speaking schools. There were also about 100 African-American students, some of whom were, in spite of their very small numbers, in segregated schools or classes in 1910. In that year, there were 1,496 teachers in these schools, of whom 1,342 were in rural areas and 154 in the seven incorporated cities, none of which itself constituted a large urban area. Of the teachers who reported their gender, 554 were men and 778 women.[22]

In this relatively small soon-to-be a state system there were a bewildering array of routes into teaching, forms of teacher licensure, and requirements for different teacher certificates. While it was illegal for any county or town to employ a nonlicensed teacher, it was relatively easy for a teacher to gain an approved license. According to the 1905 school laws, there were five basic levels of teacher licenses. There were 1st-, 2nd-, or 3rd-grade county certificates. The grades did not refer to the level taught but to the score achieved on a teacher examination. All county licenses were achieved by examination with no prior education of a specific kind required, though, as we will see, the teachers' institutes specifically prepared one for these exams. Higher grades on the examinations yielded the 1st-grade county certificate, good for 3 years; lower grades led to the 2nd-grade, 2-year certificate or the 3rd-grade, 1-year certificate. Graduation from any state university also led, automatically, to a 1st-grade certificate. In addition, there were two levels of territorial certificates, one for 5 years and the other a lifetime certificate. Normal school graduates were automatically eligible for the territorial 5-year certificate, and after the first 5 years they would usually be eligible for life certificates. There were other routes into teaching and to achieving any of these levels, including a provision that any county superintendent could grant an emergency 1-year certificate and that "Each city is a law unto itself in the matter of certificating its teachers," but the general five-level certificate arrangement applied to most teachers.[23]

Given these requirements for teacher licensure, the actual numbers of teachers holding the various certificates gives a pretty clear picture of the forms of preparation that were most common in New Mexico and most probably in many rural areas in this first decade of the 20th century. In 1910, 450 teachers held 3rd-grade certificates, 361 2nd-grade, 292 1st-grade, and 61 professional or territorial certificates. While these numbers do not account for quite all of the state's teachers, it is very clear that the vast majority—all of the 3rd-grade and 2nd-grade certificate holders, and probably a significant majority of the

1st-grade holders—had all achieved their certificates by examination, probably based on having attended a 2-week institute to prepare for these exams. Sixty-one teachers in the state, or something like 4 percent of the teachers, held the higher-level certificates that were the reward for graduation from one of the normal schools or an equivalent institution in another state. On the other hand, between 90 and 95 percent of the territory's teachers were products of the county institutes that prepared them for the exams that got them the 1st-, 2nd-, and 3rd-grade county certificates.[24]

When Carmon Ross criticized the Carnegie Foundation for the Advancement of Teaching for ignoring teachers' institutes in favor of a study focused exclusively on normal schools, he certainly had a point in terms of where the nation's teachers were actually being prepared. New York State, with its wide range of normal schools, colleges, and urban-based professional development programs, abolished its state-sponsored county institutes in 1911, but not only in the rural Midwest and far west but in such major industrialized states as Pennsylvania and Illinois, teachers' institutes remained a primary means of preparing teachers—probably the primary means outside the major metropolitan areas—well into the third decade of the 20th century.[25]

In New Mexico teachers' institutes developed as the primary state-sponsored means to improve the education of teachers for the far-flung cities, towns, and pueblos of this part of the Southwest. New Mexico became a territory of the United States by the treaty ending the U.S. war with Mexico in 1848. Previous Spanish and then Republic of Mexico governments had supported schools—the Spanish led by Franciscan missionaries and those of independent Mexico by secular teachers—but the system was undeveloped and, of course, those informal schools that then existed offered instruction in Spanish in what was suddenly a territory of an English-speaking nation. While the Catholic bishop of the territory, Jean Lamy, began some schools as early as 1851, and some Protestant mission schools soon followed, it was well into the 1880s before anything like a state system of public education began. The first state law regarding teachers, passed in 1889, simply required that "anyone who cannot read and write sufficiently to keep his own records in Spanish or English shall not be employed as a teacher." Given that some territorial records showed documents of the time in which a teacher signed with an x, this was an important first step.[26]

Amando Chaves, the first territorial superintendent, appointed in 1891, and his successors, working with the county superintendents who had begun to be elected in the 1880s, began a campaign to expand public support for the schools and systematize the operation of the schools across the vast territory in which different schools served English-speaking newcomers, Spanish-speaking families who had been in the area for generations, and various tribes of Indians, especially Navajo, Pueblo, and Apache.[27]

From the moment he assumed office, Chaves made ensuring a steady supply of good teachers a high priority, and he insisted that every teacher pass at least an oral examination by county leaders before receiving a certificate. While he and his allies in the territorial legislature moved quickly to create a system of normal schools—the first opened at Silver City in 1894, a second at Las Vegas in 1898, and a third for Spanish-speaking teachers at El Rita in 1913—these institutions provided only a small number of the teachers needed for New Mexico. The primary means used was to create a teachers' institute in every county and then, quite specifically, to tie these institute, to the preparation of prospective teachers for the examinations that provided a minimal floor of expertise for those who would teach throughout the territory. At the end of 1893, two years into his term, Chaves proudly reported that the legislature had mandated teachers' institutes and that teachers were already actively participating in them, even while plans were being made for the first two normal schools. As in New England more than half a century earlier, the institutes and the normal schools were part of a single package for Chaves, as they had been for Mann and Barnard.[28]

In his annual report for 1909–1910, Chaves's successor, Hiram Hadley, described the link between the institutes and the examinations and the need to tighten it further. After reviewing a number of issues, including school finances and schoolhouse construction, Hadley turned to the preparation of teachers, writing, "Another very serious handicap of the rural school is the unprepared teacher. In large measure the preparation of the teacher is shown by the grade of her certificate. . . . only nine counties having over fifty percent of their teachers holding county licenses of the first and second grade [which require a higher test score than the third grade license] . . . Only four counties have holders of professional licenses engaged in their rural school work." The implications of these statistics were obvious. The majority of New Mexico's rural counties had no normal school graduates teaching in their schools, while in most counties the majority of teachers had barely passed the basic licensing examination.[29]

The county superintendents echoed the same complaint. One 1910 county report concluded, "The principal need of the schools in Grant County [New Mexico] is more good teachers, teachers who are interested in their work and expect to make the same a profession." Guadalupe County's leader agreed, writing that "the difficulties as I have found are that some of the teachers do not prepare themselves before coming to the school room . . . The chief needs in our public schools are teachers of more experience." In New Mexico in 1910, the call for a more thorough preparation of teachers was not just a state-level call with which local leaders might disagree.[30]

Hadley also believed that "Conditions are such that we cannot successfully import teachers for these rural schools, but we must improve the preparation of the teachers in the service." In 1910 a teacher who moved to New Mexico from elsewhere usually wanted to teach in Santa Fe or Albuquerque, not in an isolated rural school. But there was a solution, if only temporary and partial, that Hadley advocated: "We could do no less than insist strictly upon attendance at institutes and secure legislation providing for practically all expenses of such teachers upon a long institute of four weeks, then place in charge of these institutes the most competent instructors possible to secure."[31]

The good news that Hadley's report also included was that teachers were responding to the opportunities that the institutes offered and districts were enforcing the requirement that every teacher attend one. In the summer of 1910, 1,331 teachers attended 2-week county institutes, 189 4-week county programs, and "nearly as many" 8-week summer schools offered by the state's normal schools. That meant that virtually every teacher in New Mexico (actually, Hadley's numbers add up to more than the 1,496 teachers employed in the state at least partially because every year some prospective teachers did attend the institutes but failed to receive a test score for even a 3rd-grade certificate) attended a teachers' institute in 1910. While exact statistics are not the strength of these early reports, the importance of New Mexico's institutes at improving the skills of the teachers is quite clear.[32]

The curriculum for the New Mexico teachers' institutes was published annually and reflected what the state's leaders believed every teacher needed to know and every New Mexico student needed to learn. By 1901 the oral examinations had been replaced by a single territorial written examination that was offered in every county on the last Fridays of August and November of each year. With written examinations across the territory and a course of study tied to the same set of expectations, New Mexico was well on its way to what, a century later, might have been called a single set of state standards for the curriculum and for the teachers who would deliver it. As the territorial superintendent said at the time, the "law governing the examination of teachers and the conduct of teachers institutes, on the whole appears to be working very satisfactorily, and have had the effect of very decidedly raising the standard of school work."[33]

The Introduction to New Mexico's 1907 Course of Study made it clear that "The sole purpose of all institute work is to bring about better teaching." In order to accomplish this goal, institute leaders needed to adjust the institute to the teachers and prospective teachers who appeared before them. "If the teachers of one county are more in need of method than of matter," the course of study recommended, "then let the conductor emphasize the method; if the teachers of another county are not well prepared on the subject matter, let the time of the institute be placed upon the study of essentials in the elementary branches." While the curriculum covered both pedagogy and the content of the elementary curriculum—and teachers would be tested on both at the end of the institute—institute leaders were given wide leeway in their day-to-day activities, depending on the needs of their immediate audience.

The course of study itself was thorough. "School Management" received significant attention, with reminders to "Teach that only which you know. Knowledge of a subject gives a teacher confidence in herself, and gains the confidence of her pupils." More immediate advice was also included, such as, "Lower windows from the top. Not enough to cause a draft on the heads of the pupils," and "Appeal to the pride of the pupil by telling how much better he looks when he sits straight." Discipline was key, as teachers were reminded: "Her word must be good. If she promises a treat, she should be sure to give it. And also, if she promises a whipping, she should be sure to give it." "If pupils do well, tell them so." But on the other hand, "Use corporal punishment as a last resort. But if it is necessary, do it; it may be "the makin' of the boy."

At the same time, teachers received a thorough review of arithmetic, "Add and explain the following exercises: 2576 plus 349 plus 7865 plus 8345"; geography, including "that portion of the earth of greatest interest in current history"; English literature; New Mexico, United States, and world history; and other disciplines.[34]

How effective were the institutes in addressing the oft-repeated plea for better-qualified teachers? From the distance of 100 years this is difficult to assess, just as, in reality, it is difficult to assess the impact on actual student learning from the experience of other teachers in normal schools or academies or colleges. Certainly it was the case that nearly all of New Mexico's teachers were engaged for some period of time, often 2 to 8 weeks, in study and preparation for teaching with other teachers from their part of the territory almost every year. Even those few teachers with 5-year or lifetime certificates were expected to attend the annual institutes in their county, and most teachers needed to review the institute material in order to pass the annual examination in order to keep their 3rd-grade—annual—certificate. What is absolutely clear from a careful look at the historical record is that historians of education have overlooked these institutes, which were the primary means of preparing rural teachers—the majority of the nation's teachers throughout the 19th century and beyond.

AN INSTITUTION THAT WOULD NOT DIE

In his classic 1939 study of teacher preparation in the United States, Willard S. Elsbree said of the teachers' institutes:

> It was becoming increasingly apparent, with the development of expert supervision, summer schools, and municipal normal schools, that the old type of institute was no longer needed to advance the professional status of city teachers . . .

although, in some states, the institute "craze" was so widespread that no amount of logic could remove the legislation which imposed this agency upon districts regardless of need. . . .

Twenty years earlier, Carmon Ross's detailed 1919 state-by-state survey of teachers' institutes found that in that year 35 of the 48 states still held county teachers' institutes in a relatively traditional form, while 5 states had formally abolished them and 8 others had substantially modified them. Elsbree found that in 1922 44 states were using some form of institute, and "in thirty of these states it was maintained by law." He also reported that "as late as 1933 twenty-six of the forty-eight states were still holding institutes on school time." Writing in 1939, Elsbree concluded that it seemed certain that the institutes "are doomed to extinction," since the reasons for their establishment had passed, but he wisely refused to predict when that might happen or in what form they might reappear.[35]

Long before Elsbree wrote, teachers' institutes had, in many places, become a permanent fixture in the continuing education of teachers but not a means of entry into the profession. Certainly this was true in the nation's major cities, even if they continued to constitute preservice teacher education in rural areas. In 1896–1897 the Chicago superintendent of schools reported that the city had offered five different 5-day institutes the week of August 30–September 3, 1897, in preparation for the new school year. Thirty-five hundred Chicago teachers, the majority of the city's teaching corps, contributed one dollar each to help cover the expenses of programs like the one led by Assistant Superintendent Ella Flagg Young at the Forestville School building, which included lectures by Professor James R. Angell of the University of Chicago on the "Nature and Scope of Psychological Problems" and "The General Conception of the Structure and Function of the Mind in the Light of Experimental Psychology," as well as others by Professor S. H. Clark, also of the University of Chicago, on "The Psychology of Oral Reading." Given the leaders, this may have been relatively sophisticated material. In the 1920s, Pennsylvania mandated at least 5 days of similar institutes, either prior to the school year or in half-days throughout the year. In Philadelphia and Pittsburgh the city conducted these institutes, while across the state Pennsylvania State College took the lead in offering 30 to 40 institutes a year, with the University of Pittsburgh, Bucknell University, and others also offering opportunities for teachers to continue and expand their professional learning.[36]

Given the degree to which teachers' institutes have been understudied, it is hard to reach clear conclusions as to their demise. In reality, teachers' institutes did not die as much as they were transformed—much as Elsbree predicted—into other opportunities for teachers' continuing education, including summer school programs, afterschool graduate courses, and the in-service professional development that has been part of most school districts for most of the decades since teachers' institutes—by that name—disappeared.

At least two 20th-century developments did lead to the disappearance of the teachers' institutes as Barnard and others had envisioned them in the 1830s and 1840s or as states as diverse as Pennsylvania and New Mexico continued to implement them in the 1910s and 1920s. The first was the growing chorus of complaint that the institutes had become rigid and inflexible. In his exhaustive study of Pennsylvania's institutes in 1922, Carmon Ross reported the growth of criticism across the country, such as the 1907 judgment of John F. Carr, county superintendent for Marion County, Indiana:

> The County Teachers' Institute in Indiana remains practically unchanged from what it was at its origin. Surely, it did not leap into existence fully developed and perfected. On the contrary, it is full of defects, and if it were not for an indifferent legislature that has control of it, it would long ago have abolished itself or have made radical reforms.

Ross also reported many defenders, from experts who said that the continuing lack of formal preparation that most rural teachers brought to the job meant "the necessity of supporting and maintaining teachers' institutes in addition to Normal Schools," to the more enthusiastic endorsement of one person who in 1911 said of the Pennsylvania institutes, "It is still the most helpful means of reaching and influencing the mass of teachers . . ." Nevertheless, the anonymous reports of those county superintendents who responded to one of Ross's questionnaires seem to represent a growing consensus that "Institutes as now conducted in our counties are a farce—oriental, dead, lack definiteness, are a conglomeration of nothingness." Or as another said, "They have outlived their original purpose. The reformer is needed."[37]

The second reason that teachers' institutes as such disappeared in the 1930s was, as we will see later, the impact of the Great Depression. No other single event in the nation's history had such a startling impact on the qualifications of teachers. For a country that for most of its history had a shortage of teachers and that, therefore, depended on programs like the teachers' institutes to help expand the knowledge and skills of young teachers, many of whom were barely out of the elementary grades themselves, suddenly there was a surplus of well-educated prospective teachers. Teachers colleges and university education programs had been preparing more teachers than were needed by the schools even in the 1920s, and then, given the massive unemployment of the Great Depression, college graduates, normal school graduates who had turned to other forms of work, and many more without a degree but with significant post-high school education were suddenly desperate for a job. The decade between 1929 and 1939 saw the fastest increase in teacher qualifications of any in the nation's history. School boards and superintendents could pick and choose as never before. And the traditional teachers' institute was one of the casualties.

Perhaps the institutes' greatest strength was also its greatest weakness. It changed very little between 1840 and 1920. And when it did change, its name changed also. With higher—or at least more formal and structured—standards for entrance into teaching, the distinctions between preservice and in-service education became greater and greater. Institutions of higher education took on more and more of the preservice role, while schools and school districts, along with colleges and universities, conducted in-service programs. And the teachers' institutes, though now long forgotten, live on in the summer school, afterschool, weekend, and released-time programs offered to teachers in the 21st century.

5

High Schools and City Normal Schools

1830–1920

In 1891 the Chicago Board of Education elected a new superintendent, long-time Chicago veteran Albert G. Lane, to replace George Howland, who was retiring after a total of 33 years of service in the city's schools. Lane was a widely respected educator who had already served a term as president of the National Education Association. There was nothing particularly unusual about Lane's election as superintendent. Urban school systems tended to elect veteran insiders, and in the 1890s they always elected men. Another thing that was not unusual about Lane was his formal preparation for a career in education. He had attended grammar school in Chicago, and he had then joined the first entering class at the new Chicago High School in 1856, where he completed the 2-year high school normal course outlined for those who wanted to teach in the Chicago schools.[1] And that was the end of his formal professional preparation. For Lane and for hundreds of other Chicago teachers and thousands of other teachers in urban centers across the country, a high school diploma was more than sufficient preparation for a career in teaching. Lane did not attend a state normal school. He did not go to college. He did not earn an academic degree. He attended high school and became a teacher and remained a teacher. And so did many, many others.

A FRESH LOOK AT THE NINETEENTH-CENTURY HIGH SCHOOL

High schools were a relatively new invention in early- to mid-19th-century America. Boston likes to claim credit for the first American high school with the opening of the English Classical High School in 1821, though the distinction between "English" and "Latin" (the Boston Latin School was founded in 1635) is sometimes less clear than it first appears. In fact, the English Classical High School was created to allow Boston's boys an alternative to the college preparatory and classically oriented Latin school that had been available in their city for almost 200 years. By the 1820s, some sort of advanced—that is, beyond primary and grammar school—education that would prepare students for the world of work was becoming more and more desirable. Rather than modify the Latin curriculum, Bostonians created a completely new institution. Boston's English Classical High School, which is generally recognized as the nation's first high school, was, as William Reese notes, not as much of a national model as it likes to claim. English Classical was really far more English than it was classical. The venerable Latin school took care of the classics. What the new school really offered was an English—and practical—education for boys as opposed to the Latin school that was the college preparation institution, also for boys. Massachusetts did continue to lead the high school movement for some time, with 26 high schools in place in different parts of the state by 1840, though unlike most of the nation, Massachusetts towns often limited its high schools to boys.

Other urban areas across the country also followed quickly in creating the new institutions. Unlike Boston, which continued the separate Latin school for college preparation from the English school for those planning to enter the world of work after high school, most of the new high schools mixed college preparation and "practical" preparation (and teaching definitely fell on the practical side). And in most of the rest of the country beyond the Atlantic (and to some extent the Pacific) seaboards, not only were the different programs housed in one place but so were the sexes, as boys and girls learned together.[2]

Philadelphia authorized its first high school in 1836 and opened Central High School in 1838 for boys and followed this a decade later—and much more quickly than Boston—with Girls High School, opened in 1848.[3] High schools spread to the other major urban centers of the country fairly rapidly, and beyond the East Coast they were generally coeducational institutions from the beginning. It was simply not economical to contemplate two separate schools, and limiting enrollment to boys alone seldom produced a class of even modest size. Central High School opened in Cleveland in 1846. Cincinnati organized its first high school in 1847. And many other cities and towns in Ohio—and the nation—followed suit.[4]

Many schools claim to be the first high school in their city, state, or region. The reality is that until at least the Civil War, and much later in some areas, the term *high school* joined the ranks of other institutional names like *academy, normal school,* and *college*—or *collegiate institute* or *seminary,* to include some of the then-popular terms—in an imprecise set of names for schools that served students who had completed the common school or primary and grammar curriculum. The level of education offered at educational institutions carrying any of these names, at least until the 1890s, is hard to gauge. Some offered 1- or 2-year programs; others began with what later became the common model—a 4-year curriculum leading to a diploma for those who successfully completed the whole program—though it would be a long time before those who took a shorter high school course were considered "dropouts." As William Reese wisely wrote, "The imprecise terminology so common in the 1820s and 1830s frustrated those who wanted uniform public schools and a common educational vocabulary."[5] It frustrated many contemporaries for the rest of the century, and it frustrates historians today.

Nevertheless, beginning in the 1820s and expanding rapidly in the 1830s and 1840s, a new educational institution was born in the United States, building on the work of the primary and grammar schools, offering many citizens a more advanced formal education than had previously been possible, inserting itself between the grammar school and the college, and in many areas replacing the older private academies, all at public expense. However imprecise the early definitions, by the end of the Civil War, the term *high school* began to take on some of its modern meaning.

Thanks to the work of several historians, the general outline of the emergence of the high school in the United States in the 19th century is fairly well known. However, one of the key aspects of the 19th-century high school story has virtually been ignored. High schools prepared some for college and many more for more advanced places in the world of work in an increasingly industrial and commercial society. They were very popular with middle-class parents, who saw in them the opportunities for an academy-like education at public expense. And, in addition, as one of their key components, high schools prepared teachers. Often there was a separate normal course of study that in 1 or 2 years took a graduate of the common schools and shaped her or him into a teacher, ready for a career in those same schools, or even in one of the emerging high schools themselves. Sometimes the normal curriculum was limited to girls, and in many schools in the early years it was the only secondary program open to girls. But it was an essential part of many high schools in all parts of the United States.

There have been many first-rate studies of the history of secondary education in the United States. There is, of course, Edward A. Krug's now dated but still in many ways definitive, two-volume *The Shaping of the American High School.* More recently, two studies of the early history of the high schools dramatically recast our understanding of the history of secondary education in the United States. David F. Labaree's *The Making of an American High School: The Credentials Market & the Central High School of Philadelphia, 1838–1939* focused in depth on one school in one city, while William J. Reese offered a wide-ranging overview in *The Origins of the American High School.*[6] Valuable as these studies are, however, all three seriously understate the role of the 19th-century high school as a teacher preparation institution, which it assuredly was.

Labaree notes that Philadelphia's all-male Central High School did not have a normal school curriculum like Chicago's high school. However, Labaree points out that Philadelphia's school did engage the issues of teacher education in several tangential but significant ways. While they did not have any direct power, "the principal and faculty of Central High School acted like the members of the superintendent's staff, offering informal guidance to local boards about selecting teachers." Until 1856 this informal guidance was the only check on the ward leader's selection of elementary teachers, and it continued to be important well beyond that date. John Hart, one of Central's leaders, also "operated a voluntary Saturday normal school for female elementary-school teachers from 1844 until 1851, when the opening of the Girls Normal School made it redundant." Redundant, of course, because the school for girls did offer a normal, or teacher preparation, program. And finally, Central High School itself, though it did not have a normal curriculum, still produced the majority of the male teachers in the grammar schools, who, given the culture of the times, became respected leaders in spite of their limited numbers and lack of formal pedagogical preparation. Indeed, the most successful of these male grammar school teachers became the nucleus of the faculty of Central High School itself, often without further formal preparation, although as the century wore on more and more also earned some advanced academic degree, interestingly more often an M.D. than a B.A.[7]

William Reese also explores the way in which female high schools often emerged on the coasts and in the South years and sometimes decades after the male schools and even then offered women an abbreviated curriculum aimed at preparation for teaching, not for the commercial world or for college, even though more and more colleges began to open their doors to women after the Civil War. Still, in many of the places that Reese studied, "Enrollments in female high schools boomed when job opening for elementary teachers were plentiful, but girls in separate facilities occasionally complained that their normal-high schools lacked the full academic orientation of male secondary schools. Women who did not want to become teachers felt slighted." Presumably those who did want to teach were much more content with the arrangements.[8]

It is not fair to critique Krug, Labaree, and Reese for not looking more carefully at the normal curriculum within the high schools. Their interests lie elsewhere. But the lack of attention to the teacher preparation role of the 19th-century high school does represent a significant gap in the literature. High schools did for cities what normal schools were supposed to do for whole states. For most of the 19th century they became the preferred means of preparing teachers, large numbers of them young women who often found the normal curriculum the only one available to them in their local high schools, but also smaller numbers of men who choose that option. They responded to a need voiced by Chicago's first superintendent, William Harvey Wells, in 1859 that "It is to be regretted that so few of our Primary teachers receive any special training before entering upon the peculiar duties of their office." In Chicago and elsewhere there was the hope "that in the Normal Department of our High School" this needed training would be provided and that, indeed, "a majority of our female teachers will be furnished by our own Normal School." This aspect of the history of urban high schools deserves far more attention than it has received to date.[9]

In terms of hard numbers (something very difficult to get, given the mobility of the profession), there is good reason to believe that high schools prepared, in total, more teachers for the United States than all of the nation's normal schools combined. Certainly that was true in the big cities. Early in the 20th century, high schools were still preparing the bulk of the nation's urban teachers. A 1912 study by the U.S. Bureau of Education reported 711 high schools in the United States that offered "training courses for teachers," and at these schools the teacher preparation curriculum enrolled 2,103 boys and 12,577 girls, an extraordinary enrollment for an institution that still served only a small segment of the high school age population.[10] The founders of the early high schools knew exactly what they were up to. And among other things, they meant to prepare common school teachers. No study of the history of teacher preparation is complete without attention to this important route into the profession.

THE HIGH SCHOOL NORMAL CURRICULUM— PREPARING CITY TEACHERS

When Chicago, barely 20 years old as a city, opened its new—first—high school in 1856 it enrolled 169 students, boys and girls, and it quickly doubled in size. Students at Chicago High School elected one of three programs of study: the classical program, based on Latin and Greek, that (following the mold of Boston Latin and other similar schools) prepared students for admission to college. Or a student could take the English program, which through an extraordinary range of 16 subjects prepared them for a career in the rapidly expanding city's commercial institutions. And third, equal among the options from the beginning, was a 2-year normal training course for teachers. The result was that beginning in 1858, the first graduates of this program, including future superintendent Lane, were entering the small corps of teachers who served the 14,000 children, most of them in the earliest primary grades, then enrolled in the public schools of the burgeoning city.[11]

The normal curriculum at Chicago's high school was closely supervised by the then-superintendent, William Harvey Wells. In 1859 Luther Haven, the president of the Board of Education, recommended tightening this link further; moving the supervision of the normal school from the high school principal directly to the superintendent. But whether directly or indirectly, Wells meant to be in charge of the preparation of his teachers. Wells had come to Chicago from a very successful 2-year term as the principal of the Massachusetts state normal school at Westfield, so he was certainly familiar with teacher preparation and the Massachusetts model of a normal curriculum. Although he did not have a college degree, Wells's life story linked most of the antebel-lum forms of teacher preparation. He had studied at Samuel Read Hall's teach-ers' seminary at Andover Academy and had been an assistant to Henry Barnard as well as a teacher at the teacher seminary in East Hartford, Connecticut, prior to assuming the leadership of Westfield in 1854. What he had done for the preparation of rural teachers in western Massachusetts between 1854 and 1856, Wells was going to do for urban teachers in Chicago.[12]

Superintendent Wells was deeply frustrated about the lack of training of the primary school teachers. He worried that so many "applicants seem wholly unconscious that there is any necessary connection between their familiarity with the rudiments of learning and their fitness to teach a Primary school." He used the high school's teacher education program to introduce new teach-ers to the notion of graded classrooms, while he was bent on reorganizing Chicago along similar lines. Moving from the nongraded one-room school to a graded school to a tightly organized hierarchical school with students grouped by age and general levels of achievement was both the foundation on which the 19th-century high school movement was built and an essential goal of the reformers who succeeded Mann and Barnard in the 1850s. In Chicago, Wells was the agent of this movement. And by 1859 he was happy to say "that in the Normal department of our High School, these first principles are thoroughly taught, and I trust the time will come, when a majority of our female teachers will be furnished by our own Normal School."[13]

Superintendent Wells also focused on new means of "oral instruction" so that the novice teachers would understand their responsibility to maintain the interest of the children by linking the lessons and reading and arithmetic to the world around them. He wanted to be sure that teachers understood their responsibility to "cultivate observation and secure accurate use of language" by helping children understand their world as well as memorize facts. While hardly a full-blown progressive education, here—almost half a century before John Dewey and Ella Flagg Young, though perhaps with some substantial in-fluence from Pestalozzi—was a course designed to dramatically improve the quality of preparation and of teaching in the schools of this new city. And the Normal Department of the high school was at the center of the reform effort. So in 1861 Wells proudly wrote, "I am happy to be able to say of this impor-tant branch of our school system, that its condition could hardly be improved. Most of the graduates of the school are now among the best teachers of the city, and the average attainments and qualifications of the present members are higher than those of any previous class since the opening of the school. I would respectfully recommend that early measures be taken to enlarge this department of the High School, so that we may hereafter be able to educate most of our own female teachers."[14]

Philadelphia, whose Central High School, launched in 1838, gives it claim to having one of the nation's first high schools, may also make a claim to having offered one of the earliest municipal programs for the preparation of teachers. In 1818 the Philadelphia Model School was established under the control of the city's Board of Controllers "in order to qualify teachers for the sectional schools and for schools in other parts of the State." At that time, Philadelphia's common schools operated on the widely popular and tightly structured Lancasterian system—which moved large numbers of students through a lock-step education—and the city meant to prepare its own Lancasterian teachers. Indeed, for a period of time Joseph Lancaster himself came from London to lead the Model School and to prepare teachers for Philadelphia as well as for other parts of the state that were willing to pay. An 1834 report spoke proudly of the Model School's success in helping prospective teachers in "the acquirement of practical skill in conducting these schools," so that several were now "competent to take charge of similar establishments."

During the decade between 1838 and 1848, when Philadelphia offered secondary education only to boys, and when at the same time the Lancasterian model was losing favor, the Model School was briefly transferred to the boys' Central High School where the Board of Controllers reported in 1842 that "the High School will serve essentially as a Normal School for the education of male teachers; ten of the class who are to leave the school in July intending to become teachers." However, Philadelphia's boys generally sought professions other than teaching, and so the Model School again became independent, offering Saturday classes for girls from the grammar schools.

Finally, in 1848, the Model School became part of the core of the new high school for girls that opened in that year and continued to provide high school–educated teachers for the lower grades of Philadelphia's schools throughout most of the rest of the 19th century. In 1859 the school briefly dropped the word *Normal* from its name to become simply the Public High School for Girls, but continued special instruction for girls who wanted to teach. Only a year later it changed back to being the Girls' High and Normal School, with participation in the senior class reserved for those girls who wanted to teach. After the Civil War the focus on teacher preparation was strengthened, leading to another name change as it became simply the Girls' Normal School of Philadelphia. A magnificent new building that opened in 1876 testified to the importance that city placed on preparing its own young women to teach in the city's burgeoning common schools.[15]

Efforts to launch a high school in San Francisco began in 1853 when the Board of Education adopted "The Rules and Regulations of the San Francisco High School and Ladies' Seminary." It took 3 more years before these rules applied to anyone, for actually opening a school was much more expensive than writing its rules, but in 1856 San Francisco had a secondary school first called the Union Grammar School and then in 1858 the San Francisco High School. Decades, and several name changes, later this school would in 1894 become San

Francisco's famous Lowell High School. But in the late 1850s San Francisco's superintendent, Henry James, saw the value of the new institution and commented in his annual report for 1858 that "This grade of public school has elsewhere been regarded as exerting a salutary influence upon the lower grades, and our experience justifies such a conclusion. The San Francisco High School has acquired a reputation that commands the respect and favor of all our citizens." Whether all of the citizens agreed, the school's impact on the lower grades—both by creating a standard which the graduates should seek to attain and by providing teachers for those lower grades—could be seen quickly.

The first graduating class in December 1859—the school offered only a 1-year curriculum—included seven boys and four girls. When they had begun their studies, however, the class had included 22 boys and 13 girls. Four of the girls had left before completing the program to become teachers in San Francisco. If the national pattern was followed, at least two of the four graduates would follow them, and the same numbers would hold for subsequent classes. And the classes were growing. Already in December 1859 the school reported an enrollment of 139 and an average attendance of 97. In addition, the school department conducted weekly meetings at the Normal Department for other teachers who wanted further instruction.[16]

In 1864 San Francisco split its high school offerings for girls and boys, and the academic coursework for girls was reduced in favor of an expanded normal program. The girls were moved out of the new high school building that had been opened, with great celebrations, in 1860 and assigned to an older brick school building. Three years later, in 1867, the Girls High School became the Girls' High and Normal School, with the emphasis, apparently, on the latter. This had the advantage of offering the girls who would soon take up teaching positions in San Francisco a more focused education, but it appropriately drew substantial complaints, as did other similar moves across the country, that girls were being given a second-rate education. In San Francisco, as elsewhere, "separate but equal" nearly always meant "separate and unequal."[17]

The normal program at Chicago's, Philadelphia's and San Francisco's first high schools may have been more carefully developed than some, but they were hardly isolated examples. High schools, those that mixed girls and boys and those that were for girls only, had similar curricula across the United States. David Tyack has found evidence of normal departments in 21 cities in the United States by 1885, though his research also seems to indicate that Chicago's Albert Lane was unusual, as almost no boys were enrolled in these departments even when they existed in coeducational high schools. Indeed, the normal course came more and more to be a girls' ghetto, sometimes a very large ghetto within the budding comprehensive high school.[18]

HIGH SCHOOLS, GENDER, AND THE ROAD
TO WOMEN'S TRUE PROFESSION

In St. Louis, Missouri, in 1882 the president of the Board of Education defended that city's high schools from the usual complaints that such schools were elitist and expensive by writing, "the advanced general education of the teachers of our schools is itself a work, which, in my opinion, justifies the existence of a high school as part of our public school system, irrespective of other questions." There might be many reasons for a city like St. Louis to launch and maintain high schools, but clearly the preparation of teachers was very high on the list of reasons for doing so. A decade earlier, in 1871, Detroit's school board president had made a very similar argument. The public high school in Detroit was essential because it "affords us a supply of well trained teachers always ready and available to fill the vacancies constantly occurring." While neither board president said so directly, they also meant that their high schools were essential because they were preparing women, for by this time it was women who taught in the common schools of their respective cities. An 1873 survey of the Saint Louis high school alumni showed that over 90 percent of the school's graduates who became teachers were women and that over half of the more than 700 women graduates who responded to the survey had, in fact, become teachers for some period of time. A similar survey in Detroit indicated that between 1860 and 1882 95 percent of that school's graduates who taught were women. High schools might, in most cities, open their doors to women and men and offer a coeducational experience in their classes. But when the students graduated, the women and men went in different directions. The women taught.[19]

In their thorough study of coeducation in American public education, David Tyack and Elisabeth Hansot note that for the most part, high schools were coeducational from the start. There were exceptions, especially in some of the largest East and West Coast cities that had both the financial resources and strong conservative traditions, that led to separate schools for boys and girls. But as Bryn Mawr College's feminist president M. Carey Thomas said, it had been "a fortunate circumstance" for girls that the country was "sparsely settled; in most neighborhoods it was so difficult to establish and secure pupils for even one . . . high school that girls were admitted from the first." And they were. In 1882 only 19 of 196 cities reported separate-sex high schools, and by century's end only 12 out of 628 cities reported any single-sex high schools.[20]

While in most cases boys and girls attended school together from the beginning, however, boys and girls had very different experiences in high school throughout the 19th century and beyond. For boys, there was always the question, "Why am I here?" For those boys who did not plan to attend college, the value of entering, much less graduating from, high school seemed quite limited if not irrelevant. Until well into the 20th century, not only blue-collar but white-collar jobs were open to anyone with the right connections and skills, without any value added from a high school diploma. For girls, however, the situation was different. As Tyack and Hansot note, for native-born middle-class girls, high school was seen as a safe place to spend one's adolescence, a way station between childhood and marriage. But for a substantial number of females, "high school was a gateway for many young women into teaching careers, one of the few white-collar jobs open to women at the time."[21]

Writing in 1898, Edward G. Halle, the president of Chicago's Board of Education, understood exactly what the problem was. "It is to be regretted that the number of girls far exceeds that of the boys in the high schools," he said. "It may be that the commercial spirit of the age entices the boys early to engage in business pursuits." And he recommended expanding the manual training program and establishing a commercial high school to keep the boys. On the other hand, the girls not only constituted a majority of the city's high school enrollment, they knew why they were staying, just as, Halle thought, the boys knew why they were leaving. So he reported that "about sixty percent of our 1175 high school graduates this year sought admission to the Normal School, desiring to become teachers." By 1898 normal training had been expanded to a 1-year program after high school, and Chicago's girls wanted the additional year of education and the license to teach that it brought.[22]

As a result of this strong link for girls between a high school education and the opportunity of a career—of whatever length—in teaching, high schools became enormously popular with young women. Although high schools admitted women and men on something close to terms of equality, they did not attend or graduate in equal terms. In 1890 girls represented 57 percent of the high school students and 65 percent of the graduates, and in the largest cities the percentages were higher. The U.S. Commissioner of Education estimated that in 1889 only one-fourth of high school students in the nation's 10 largest cities were boys. By this time teaching had been fairly thoroughly feminized, and a high school diploma gave girls a substantial leg up in entering one of the few professions open to them even as it offered boys far less advantage in the commercial and industrial worlds.[23]

RURAL HIGH SCHOOLS FOR RURAL TEACHERS

Writing about the Scopes trial, that grand battle about the teaching of evolution that rocked Dayton, Tennessee, and the nation in 1925, Edward J. Larson has noted that one of the many reasons the battle took place then, and not in earlier generations, is that high schools had simply not existed in towns like Dayton, Tennessee, in earlier years, and without high schools there was not likely to be a battle about what should be taught in their biology classes or elsewhere in their curriculum. High schools had begun as the capstone of the educational system in big cities early in the 19th century. Until very late in that century, they did not exist much of anywhere else. But in the early years of the 20th century, high schools spread rapidly across the country, to small towns like Dayton, and even to rural areas. Where in 1890 200,000 students had been enrolled in high school, in 1920 enrollment stood at almost 2 million.[24]

The movement of high schools into small towns and rural areas naturally opened battles about what should be taught in these schools—such as whether to teach about evolution—but the schools also opened up the possibility of much better preparation for small-town and rural teachers. While since the 1840s normal schools had been designed to prepare teachers for these more isolated schools, in practice they seldom produced nearly enough teachers. Because their graduates were among the elite of American teachers, normal school graduates often sought higher-paying jobs in cities, in the new high schools, or in school administration. The teachers of the rural one-room schoolhouses were seldom normal school graduates; at most they might have had a few weeks or a semester of study in one of them. The spread of high schools, however, opened the possibility that these much more local institutions could fill the gap.

Between 1910 and 1925 24 states specifically launched some kind of rural high school program for the preparation of rural teachers. In Kansas, for example, prospective teachers studied what were still known as the "common branches," that is, the content of the elementary school, or common school, curriculum. They also had classes in classroom management but did not have any hands-on experience in common school classrooms. Other states offered more. In a program that received high praise, Minnesota offered not only advanced instruction in the common branches, but specific courses related to rural teaching and a requirement that high school students in the normal program spend from 120 to 180 hours in observation and practice teaching. While New York's secondary rural teaching program did not involve student teaching, it did include a more detailed curriculum in rural sociology and rural life.

From the beginning the normal courses at rural high schools were seen as a temporary stopgap until more advanced preparation could be offered for rural teachers—though they were often a long-lasting stopgap. Nevertheless, by the early 1920s several states had added a 5th year to the high school curriculum so that there was time for more professional preparation. By 1924 five states had a stated mandated departmentalized program that brought a normal school instructor to the rural high schools for teaching and supervision. As with many other stopgap measures, the rural high school programs for preparing teachers generally disappeared after 1929, and by 1933 only seven states still had any specific programs of this sort. The transition from an almost totally informal preparation of teachers, if anything beyond the common school itself was expected, to high school preparation, to more advanced preparation took place much faster in rural areas than it did in cities where a high school diploma was long the key to teaching, though in both situations, the high school did play its role.[25]

In the rural South, a specialized high school for African American teachers also emerged very quickly in the early years of the 20th century. In 1910 James Dillard, the general agent of the John F. Slater Fund, one of the major northern philanthropies designed to support, and shape, the education offered to Southern blacks, decided that a key step to improving the teaching in the segregated schools was to create county training schools, rural—and occasionally urban—secondary schools specifically designed to give more advanced education to a cadre of young African Americans who would return to their own communities as teachers in the often-one-teacher schools that were the norm in rural areas whatever the race of the students and teachers. Because the Slater Fund had considerable resources to put behind its agenda, county training schools spread rapidly, and during the next 22 years 612 schools in 517 different counties across 15 Southern states were founded and in operation. The story of these county training schools will be told in the next chapter, focusing on the unique experience of African-American teachers, but they too were a substantial part of the early-20th-century rural high school teacher preparation movement.[26]

BEYOND HIGH SCHOOL: FROM CITY HIGH SCHOOLS TO CITY NORMAL SCHOOLS AND COLLEGES

In 1852, 31 years after becoming a national leader with the opening of the English Classical High School for boys, Boston finally caught up with many other cities and also opened a permanent high school for girls. In fact, Boston had opened its first high school for girls in 1826, only 5 years after the English High School for boys. But this first school, which offered a classical curriculum, was short-lived. The problem was that too many girls wanted to attend. Of the 133 students admitted in the first entering class at the girls' high school, no one dropped out. With a curriculum projected to last over 3 years, the High School for Girls would quickly outpace the English school in size and cost, though the per-pupil costs were kept much lower in the girls' school. As Boston's Mayor Josiah Quincy famously complained, the majority of boys dropped out of high school and thus kept the cost down. Girls did not leave and therefore the whole enterprise was far too expensive. The school was closed after only 18 months.[27]

Circumstances in a much larger and much more diverse Boston were very different in the 1850s than they had been in the 1820s. The Irish immigration had more than doubled the city's population. In 1851 Nathan Bishop, the first superintendent of the city's schools, wrote that "Every year, between forty and fifty well-qualified female teachers will be wanted to fill vacancies which are occurring in the places of teachers. If these places are filled by persons of very high qualifications, the schools will be greatly improved without any increased expense." And the key to creating this pool of female "persons of very high qualifications" was to prepare them within the schools themselves. Unlike the experiment of the 1820s, in 1852 the Boston School Committee admitted 100 young women to the Boston Normal School, renamed the Girls High and Normal School in 1854. From the beginning the curriculum at this school focused on teacher preparation and included a link to a practice school where students could observe and practice under supervision.[28]

As the 1854 name change indicated, Boston's Girls High and Normal School offered several high school–level options to girls, as was the case in Chicago and other places, but among several options at Girls High School (though it had not been one at the boys-only English school) was a normal curriculum designed to prepare grammar school graduates to return to those places as teachers. For 20 years, the normal course of study at Boston's Girls High and Normal was a good illustration of the high school–based teacher preparation program, and the primary source of Boston's elementary teachers.

Beginning in 1872, however, Girls High was split into two separate institutions and the Boston Normal School slowly expanded beyond its high school status into a post–high school program for teachers. Also following a national pattern for both state and municipal schools, the institution changed its name to the Teachers College of the City of Boston in 1924 and then to the State Teachers College at Boston in 1952, when control and responsibility moved from the city to the state. In 1960 the institution became the all-purpose Boston State College. Finally, in 1982, the institution was merged with the University of Massachusetts at Boston and its education programs became the nucleus of the Graduate School of Education at the state university.[29]

A similar pattern, although an even more circuitous road, was followed in Chicago. The Normal Department that had been an essential element in Chicago's new Central High School in 1856 continued for 15 years. An 1859 report described the two-year curriculum as including, among other subjects, arithmetic, political geography & map drawing, grammar, algebra, botany, chemistry, astronomy, English literature, the Constitution of the United States and principles of government, and the history of the United States and "general history," the so-called "common branches" that were taught in the primary grades, as well as two terms of Theory of Teaching and practice teaching throughout the program. In 1865 a young Ella Flagg, who 40 years later would lead the school in a different incarnation, took over supervision of the practice teaching. In 1871 the Normal Department became an independent school, the Chicago Normal School, but in 1876 that school was closed because Chicago had more teachers than were needed.

As we will see in chapter 9, however, even before the Chicago Normal School was closed, Cook County Normal School had been established at the county level in 1867 in Blue Island, Illinois, at a time when the state of Illinois was encouraging county-level programs for teacher preparation. In 1897 the city of Chicago board of education acquired Cook County Normal, merged it with an apprenticelike cadet system that had been operating in the place of the Normal School, and christened the school Chicago Normal School. Students interested in teaching in Chicago or the rest of Cook County were expected to complete 4 years of high school and then study at the Normal School for a single 5th year of intensive study of pedagogy. Following that year they were expected to "cadet" for 4 months, during which they "have an opportunity of observing the methods of teaching, the details of school management, and to put in practice the theories learned at the Normal School." After this they were ready for placement in a school. In the last decades of the 19th and first decades of the 20th century, Cook County, later renamed Chicago Normal School, emerged from its high school status to offer college-level instruction and eventually to become a fully college-level institution now known as Chicago State University. In the Progressive Era it was also one of the best-known centers of progressive educational ideas in the United States, but that is a story for chapter 9.[30]

Boston and Chicago were hardly alone in creating a high school program for future teachers, sometimes in a gender-segregated girls school, sometimes in a coeducational one. And Boston and Chicago were also hardly alone in slowly elevating these programs from one option within the high school to a post–high school program of 1 or 2 years to a full-fledged 4-year postsecondary program, often one that granted the baccalaureate degree as well as the perhaps more prized teaching credential. By 1914 virtually every city in the United States with a population of 300,000 or more and 80 percent of those over 100,000 maintained its own teacher preparation program as part of the public school system. The specific time line varied with the political climate and financial resources of each city, but most of these city systems also evolved in a trajectory similar to Boston's and Chicago's. As the programs became less like high schools and more like colleges, there was pressure to move them out from municipal control and into some part of the state system of higher education or, in other cases, to let existing state institutions fill the need and simply close the municipal ones. By 1930–1931 only one-fifth of the 94 cities still supported municipal schools for teachers. With rare exceptions, the future would be elsewhere.

At the same time as the urban high school's normal programs were either disappearing or being transformed into city college programs of one sort or another, states were beginning to raise the standards for entry into teaching. Where these issues had previously been left to individual school districts, in the second and third decade of the 20th century state departments of education, with the backing of state legislatures, were setting new standards. Often these standards were simply the requirement of a high school diploma, first mandated in Indiana in 1907. However, with the never-ending American pressure to improve the schools and the quality of teaching, and especially with the growth of the applicant pool in the 1920s and during the Great Depression, states moved quickly to add more advanced requirements. California was one of the first states to move in this direction with a new 5-year and then 6-year program for elementary teachers—that is, 4 years of high school plus first 1 year and then 2 years of a college or normal school program beyond high school becoming the minimum for teaching in that state. At the same time, California formalized a requirement that had been something of a universal norm already—high school teachers needed to be college graduates and perhaps even have some graduate study before entering the classroom.[31]

Table 5.1 outlines the changes in state requirements for teachers in the then 48 states during the 1920s and 1930s. Several things stand out in this table. While at the end of World War I, in 1921, 30 of the 48 states had no minimal requirements and only 4 required more than a high school diploma, by 1937, 41 of the states required at least a high school diploma, and the majority of the states—35 out of 48—required this and some college or normal school education beyond high school. Clearly standards, at least standards in terms of years of schooling prior to entering the classroom as a teacher, were rising. Nevertheless, in spite of the dramatic changes in these 2 decades, in 1937 the high school diploma was still the core requirement. Only five states required 4 years beyond high school, and even among those a college degree was not necessarily essential.[32]

With the Depression-era surplus of teachers and the concomitant pressures on city resources, most of the remaining city programs were either transformed to state ones or disappeared. And, as chapter 10 will show, the standards just kept rising as teachers were expected to have more and more postsecondary education and as specific professional preparation moved increasingly to the postsecondary level. Today few people remember that high schools, now an almost universal part of American education, were often founded because of the need for an institution to prepare teachers and that those high schools were

Table 5.1. State Requirements for Teachers, 1920s–1930s

Minimum Requirement	1921	1926	1937
No specific requirement	30 states	15 states	7 states
High school diploma	14 states	6 states	6 states
High school plus minimal training	4 states	14 states	2 states
High school plus 1 year	0 states	9 states	8 states
High school plus 2 years	0 states	4 states	11 states
High school plus 3 years	0 states	0 states	9 states
High school plus 4 years	0 states	0 states	5 states

also once the nation's primary resource for the preparation of teachers. As late as the early decades of the 20th century any but the most elite schools and districts would be proud if they could place a high school graduate in every elementary classroom. For a century these high school normal programs were a very important part of the American configuration of teacher preparation, especially in cities but in time even in the smaller towns.[33]

6

Normal Institutes, Missionary Colleges, and County Training Schools: Preparing African American Teachers in the Segregated South

1860–1940

In 1909, more than half a century after Charlotte Forten had gone to the Georgia Sea Islands to teach newly freed slaves, Mamie Garvin Fields assumed her duties as a teacher on St. John's Island, South Carolina. She recalled the day when "The children took me through the woods and the bushes to Humbert Wood School, a two-room, darkly painted school in a thick wood. . . . And what a poor place!" Michael Fultz has aptly described the situation faced by Fields and hundreds of other African American teachers across the racially segregated South between the Civil War and World War II. "Into these ramshackle, undersupplied facilities," Fultz wrote, "poured African American children, their numbers increasing over the years. Black teachers in the South during this period had substantially higher teacher-pupil ratios than did their white southern (or northern) counterparts and confronted potentially chaotic classrooms." Given the conditions, Ambrose Caliver, the author of a Depression-era federal report on the preparation of African American teachers, said, with considerable understatement, that they might "tax the ingenuity of the best trained teachers."[1]

Mamie Garvin Fields, then Mamie Garvin, was 21 years old and had already taught for 1 year when she took the job on St. John's Island. Her own education as a teacher was certainly more advanced than that of many, black or white, who taught in the rural schools of the United States in 1909. In her autobiography she wrote, "I always wanted to become a teacher," and she had prepared herself accordingly. Garvin had attended a segregated school in her hometown of Charleston, South Carolina, and graduated at the top of her 8th-grade class. At the time South Carolina did not offer any public secondary schooling for African Americans, but her family considered three different secondary schools for her—Aver Institute, the Browning Home, and Claflin University, all essentially secondary schools. She chose Claflin.

Claflin had been founded by Methodists in 1869 to prepare African American ministers but quickly expanded its curriculum. As with many schools that used the name *university*, its students clearly understood that it was primarily a high school. A decade after Garvin had graduated, a 1917 federal report listed Claflin as a combined secondary school and college and noted that in most such schools 90 percent of the students were in the secondary program. Fields remembered the requirements she had to meet: "Those in training to be teachers had to take pedagogy, the arts of teaching, as well as all the regular high school subjects—English, history, math, music, sciences, and of course the Bible." She liked all of her subjects and she liked the religious atmosphere that Claflin offered, but she was especially proud of her work in pedagogy. She recalled:

> As a senior at Claflin, my most important class was pedagogy, which consisted of both class work and practice teaching. The practice teaching was the bigger part, because through it we learned exactly what to expect in our schools. A critic teacher always went along with a group of us, to a particular school. She would observe what we were doing and tell us what was what afterwards.

In some ways the Claflin curriculum was very similar to that offered in the pedagogy programs of the white public high schools of the North whether in large cities in the 1860s and 1870s or the rural high schools of the early 20th century. In the South of the late 19th century, African Americans could get such a curriculum only in private schools, and only a very small number of African American teachers received such an advanced level of preparation. Hostility from the white community and limited resources kept the options extremely limited.[2]

There were other ways in which Claflin's curriculum was different from its public high school counterparts. Garvin's teachers knew the schools their own students were likely to find. The students might study what others considered a more ideal school, but they also studied how to adapt their work to the dilapidated one-room rural schoolhouses where most of them would find their actual work. They were taught that their work was much more than teaching skills. They were there to uplift a race.

> Since we were being taught, above all, how to be a good influence on the children, much of the classroom work was about how to discipline ourselves to be able to make do with whatever we had, wherever we went—what to do with 125 children, by yourself, in a one-room school, for example; how to divide that crowd into groups and supervise all at one time; how to make the schoolroom attractive for the pupils, no matter what the conditions were. Our teachers knew that most of us would never be in ideal schools, and they prepared us accordingly.

Giving aspiring teachers excuses for future failures because they lacked time or resources was not part of the Claflin curriculum. Mamie Garvin Fields taught for most of the next 35 years, retiring in 1943 and continuing to devote herself to civil rights, women's federation, and local day care activities until well into her 90s. In an era when most European American women taught for only a year or two, and in which most teachers of all races had very limited preparation for their work, her opportunity to study at Claflin and her 35-year career were unusual. But as an African American woman preparing herself for a career in teaching in the most dangerous and difficult years of the Jim Crow South, her story is illustrative of the preparation of one small but very significant subset of her contemporaries, and the value she placed on her work was shared by many.[3]

INFORMAL PREPARATION IN SLAVERY AND FREEDOM

In 1865, as slavery finally came to an end in the United States, somewhere between 5 and 10 percent of the former slaves were able to read and write. The 90 to 95 percent who were illiterate had been kept that way by the laws of nearly every Southern state.[4] Some slaves learned to read and write in spite of the laws. Frederick Douglass, having learned to read by convincing some white boys to teach him, then found himself wanting "a Sabbath-school in which to exercise my gifts and to impart to my brother-slaves the little knowledge I possessed." Douglass found aspiring students and he "was not long in bringing around me twenty or thirty young men, who enrolled themselves gladly in my Sabbath-school," and who kept their school a secret from prying whites. After the Civil War, another ex-slave, Will Cappers, said that there had long been a school on St. Helena Island and that he had "conducted a secret night school for men during plantation days."[5]

Carter G. Woodson has noted that occasionally there was "much winking at the violation of the reactionary laws," and at other times great success in keeping schools secret. When Sherman's army marched through Georgia they discovered that "a colored woman by the name of Deveaux had for thirty years conducted a Negro school in the city of Savannah." When Sherman's army arrived, Deveaux simply expanded her efforts. Jane Deveaux was the daughter of a slave and a free black woman from Antigua who had secretly taught her and other black children to read the Bible. When John Alvord met her after the Civil War he wrote, "Although quite advanced in life, she labors with earnestness and zeal. It is especially interesting to hear her relate how her work was carried on in secret, eluding, for more than a quarter of a century the most lynx-eyed vigilance of the slaveholders of her native city."[6]

In the immediate aftermath of the Civil War, schools burst forth across the South. Booker T. Washington spoke of "a whole race trying to go to school."

James Anderson has also reminded us that the recently freed slaves were not only going to school, they were teaching school. In July 1868 John W. Alvord, general superintendent of schools for the Freedmen's Bureau, reported a total of 8,004 teachers in schools for blacks across the South, of which the majority, 4,213, were black. The white missionaries were important, but they were never the majority of teachers for the freedmen. Literacy and freedom were intrinsically linked, and this made teaching essential work.[7] The teachers of these first schools for freedmen, like the teachers among the slaves in the time of slavery, and the teachers in many a one-room schoolhouse for whites in the same years, had themselves received no formal preparation for their tasks. One way or another, they had learned to read and write. And one way or another, they taught others.

Nevertheless, in the South of the Reconstruction and post-Reconstruction eras, several more formal means of teacher preparation would emerge for African American teachers beginning in the 1870s. It is essential to note how slowly the more formal patterns of preparation emerged. As late as 1917 the U.S. Bureau of Education found that "In Georgia and Alabama, for example, 70 per cent of the colored teachers have temporary or emergency certificates representing a schooling of less than eight elementary grades." It was well into the 1930s before the combined work of competing normal institutes, missionary colleges, and county training schools would impact the majority of Southern black teachers.[8]

THE HAMPTON-TUSKEGEE MODEL: NORMAL AND AGRICULTURAL INSTITUTES

One of the best-known efforts at the formal preparation of African American teachers began when Samuel Chapman Armstrong, a European American, founded Hampton Normal and Agricultural Institute in Hampton, Virginia, in April 1868. Thirteen years later, Armstrong's star pupil, Booker T. Washington, who had himself grown up in slavery, was recommended by Armstrong to lead Tuskegee Normal and Industrial Institute in Alabama. Between the two schools and the two educators, a new model of teacher preparation was inaugurated. The Chapman-Washington model focused on reshaping the lives of recently freed slaves by preparing a generation of African American teachers for segregated common schools for African American youth.

James Anderson has noted that although many have looked at the industrial side of Hampton and Tuskegee, such a view misses their central purpose. "The traditional emphasis on Hampton [and Tuskegee] as a trade or technical school," Anderson writes, "has obscured the fact that it was founded and maintained as a normal school and that its mission was the training of common school teachers for the South's black educational system. The Hampton-Tuskegee curriculum was not centered on trade or agricultural training; it was centered on the training of teachers." In order to be admitted to Hampton, a prospective student had to promise "to remain through the whole course and become a teacher." And the vast majority did just that. Some 84 percent of the 723 graduates of Hampton in its first 20 years became teachers.

The Hampton-Tuskegee model had a clear purpose. In Anderson's view, Armstrong and Washington "represented a social class, ideology, and world outlook that was fundamentally different from and opposed to the interests of the freedmen." Where the teachers that Alvord had found opening schools where no white had ever been reflected a passion for learning and liberty, the teachers who emerged from the normal programs at Hampton and Tuskegee were expected to represent the famous Atlanta compromise espoused by Washington in which a black laboring class would "buy your surplus land, make blossom the waste places in your fields, and run your factories," while representing "the most patient, faithful, law-abiding, and unresentful people that the world has seen."

For Anderson the differences were stark:

> The ex-slaves struggled to develop a social and educational ideology singularly appropriate to their defense of emancipation and one that challenged the social power of the planter regime. Armstrong developed a pedagogy and ideology designed to avoid such confrontations and to maintain within the South a social consensus that did not challenge traditional inequalities of wealth and power.

No wonder so many were critical of these schools and their founders.[9]

If one looks carefully at the Hampton curriculum—and the one Tuskegee adopted after its founding in 1881—one sees many elements similar to what was offered at white normal schools. Prospective teachers came to Hampton and Tuskegee with at most a common school education, and many did not have that. Few, if any, of the students in the early years had studied at high school prior to attending these normal institutes. Anderson has estimated that the average Hampton-Tuskegee graduate had achieved a 10th-grade education, about the same education as the graduates of many other 19th-century normal schools or the normal course at most urban high schools. In their 2 or 3 years at Hampton or Tuskegee, students studied both academic subjects and pedagogy and prepared themselves to qualify for an elementary teaching certificate. When Anderson says, "Normal school students tended to be much less educated, older, and more economically disadvantaged than college students. . . . normal school students sought professional education courses to achieve their major goal of becoming elementary school teachers," he describes a student body who, except for their race, could have been their contemporary white students.[10]

There were two ways—in addition to the all-important issue of race—in which Hampton and Tuskegee differed from most other 19th-century normal schools. Hampton and Tuskegee were both manual labor schools. The women and men who attended these schools were expected to work, and work hard, in the fields, the kitchens, and the shops of the institutes. Although observers who saw this work going on thought the students were enrolled in a trade program, this was not the case. As late as 1900 only 45 of Hampton's 656 students were enrolled in the trade division and only 4 in agriculture. A 1903 study of Tuskegee's industrial training program found that "there were only a dozen students in the school capable of doing a fair job as joiners. There were only fifteen boys who could lay brick." But this did not worry the school's leaders. On the contrary, the goal was to teach future teachers "steady work habits, practical knowledge, and Christian morals." As Hampton supporter Atticus G. Haygood, General Agent of the John F. Slater Fund, wrote in 1888, the manual labor programs were designed to foster moral discipline for "those who are to be teachers and guides of their people." If the graduates were going to teach in common schools across the South—especially the rural South—and inculcate a generation of African Americans in the values of hard labor, they needed to know how to work hard, and uncomplainingly, themselves. They did not need to develop their own skills as joiners or bricklayers.[11]

Hampton and Tuskegee also differed from Northern normal schools in terms of ideology. Students at Hampton, Tuskegee, and the schools that followed after them were taught to teach their own students to find their place in the segregated world of the post-Reconstruction South. In the political economy courses, future teachers learned that they had to respect the rights of capital and labor and that their students should fit uncomplainingly into a political system that disenfranchised them and an economy that needed their labor but required them to stay at the bottom of the economic ladder. It was an ethic that, as Anderson say, "was deliberately teaching prospective black leaders and educators economic values that were detrimental to the objective interests of black workers."[12]

While the primary focus of those who sponsored Hampton and Tuskegee was the education of African Americans, there was another group of Americans who were deeply affected by Armstrong and Washington and their successors. In 1878 Army lieutenant Richard Henry Pratt asked that he be allowed to bring a group of American Indian prisoners to Hampton, and Armstrong agreed. As with the African American students, Pratt and Chapman wanted to use the manual labor system at Hampton to induct Indians into a culture of hard work and traditional European values, and to assimilate them so thoroughly that they could then take the new culture they had learned at Hampton back to their tribes. Unlike the African American students, these first American Indian students at Hampton were military prisoners. They had no choice but to stay where the government, as represented by Lieutenant Pratt, put them.

Pratt himself moved on quickly from Hampton to found his own Carlisle Indian Industrial School along the lines laid down by Chapman, but Hampton itself continued to educate generations of American Indians, 1,388 Indians from 65 different tribes between 1878 and 1923. When Pratt was able to open his own Indian-only school at Carlisle, Pennsylvania, the model was Hampton, though with a strong emphasis on ensuring that Indians learned English, that they were thoroughly assimilated into European American culture and removed from their tribal culture, and that they would take their new culture home when and if they returned to their tribes. On the one hand, Pratt fought long and hard with many because he argued that Indians were able to benefit from the same education as whites. On the other hand, his assimilationist policy could not have been clearer. In 1921, long after his 1904 departure from Carlisle, Pratt wrote, "Every church effort . . . and all government education except . . . by a very few non-reservation schools, had the same tendency—to strengthen and build up the tribes, as such." Pratt's goal was the opposite, to prepare a generation of Indians who would weaken the tribes and teach individual Indians in an individualist model.

Hampton's and Carlisle's influence was seen when President William McKinley appointed Estelle Reel superintendent of Indian schools in 1898. She served until 1910. Reel's views reflected those of many white progressives of her era. As state superintendent of public instruction in Wyoming from 1894 to 1898 she promoted equal pay for women teachers. As superintendent of Indian schools she insisted on visiting most of the 252 schools with their 2,000 teachers and 20,000 students around the country. She also created the Uniform Course of Study for Indian Schools, which reflected both her progressive values and the Hampton approach. In the curriculum, she asserted,

> The child learns to speak the English language through doing the work that must be accomplished in any well regulated home, and at the same time is being trained in habits of industry, cleanliness and system. He learns to read by telling of his daily interests and work with the chalk on the blackboard. In keeping count of his poultry and in measuring his garden, he becomes familiar with numbers in such a practical way he knows how to use them in daily life, as well as on the blackboard in the schoolroom. . . .

Both John Dewey and Samuel Chapman Armstrong would have applauded this approach, but a contemporary news release probably got it right in describing Reel's curriculum: "She believes in what Booker T. Washington is doing for the negro, and has adopted many of the Tuskegee methods for Indian schools."[13]

In the last decades of the 19th and first decades of the 20th centuries, there was extraordinary money and power behind the Hampton-Tuskegee model; indeed, far more money and power than actual students. While early philanthropic supporters, especially the John F. Slater Fund and the Peabody Education Fund, conditioned gifts to other schools across the South on their emulation of the same model, the dollars grew exponentially after 1900. In 1902 John D. Rockefeller Sr. donated $1 million to create the General Education Board, adding $53 million in 1909 and $129 million in 1921. The earlier Slater and Peabody Funds became closely linked with the General Education Board and the newer Anna T. Jeans Foundation and the Phelps-Stokes Fund to create a "virtual monopolistic control of educational philanthropy for the South and the Negro," as one critic noted.

James Anderson's case study of Georgia's Fort Valley High and Industrial School illustrates the spread of the Hampton-Tuskegee model. Fort Valley was founded by Atlanta University graduate John W. Davison in 1890. Though it received a public charter in 1895, it received no funds from the state of Georgia or the federal government. In its early years under Davison's leadership, Fort Valley relied primarily on the support of the black community in Georgia. The school was only able to offer a four-month curriculum to about 100 pupils at a time, although it was in the midst of Georgia's black belt and 500,000 blacks lived within a 100-mile radius.

Between 1900 and 1904, however, Fort Valley's financial prospects changed dramatically as a number of Northern philanthropists, led by George Foster Peabody, joined its board and connected the school to the Rockefeller-funded General Education Board. The new board soon clashed with Davison, who, Anderson notes, "was concentrating mainly on the development of a good liberal arts secondary and normal school for the training of black teachers," along the lines of his alma mater, Atlanta University. Peabody, other Northern white trustees, and the General Education Board wanted an industrial school in the Hampton-Tuskegee mold. By June 1903 they had forced Davison out of office and begun a search for "some colored man from the South who has industrial training and is 'chuck full' of common sense," meaning that he was committed without reservations to the Hampton-Tuskegee model. They also managed to oust most of the black trustees who supported Davison and replace them with others who accepted their model. Under the leadership of the new trustee's choice for the school's presidency, Henry A. Hunt, Fort Valley prospered with generous donations, including $100,000 in 1928 for buildings and equipment.

At first Hunt's appointment led to a dramatic drop in enrollment, but in time the financial resources and the lack of alternative opportunities led to a student body of 500. The students were immersed in a work regimen, laundering, cooking, and most of all agriculture. As Anderson concluded, "Fort Valley's student teachers were being prepared to socialize their prospective pupils for the role of common laborer for white landowners." In 1932 Fort Valley dropped its high school designation, becoming Fort Valley Normal and Industrial School and in 1939 simply Fort Valley State College. By then much of the push for the Hampton-Tuskegee model had disappeared and the school had joined the growing list of other segregated public state teachers' colleges.[14]

While these philanthropists and the institutions they supported fostered only the most limited education for blacks, it is important to note that they were also attacked at the time by the archsegregationists of the South as offering far too much educational opportunity to the African American community. Governor Allen D. Candler of Georgia informed the philanthropists that "we can attend to the education of the darky in the South without the aid of these Yankees," while the *Memphis Commercial Appeal* responded to the growth of the funds, "All that the South asks is that the North will mind its own business and keep its missions to itself." The alternative to the Hampton-Tuskegee model was not necessarily the expanded education for teachers and others that was advocated by the founders of the missionary colleges or later by W.E.B. Du Bois. There were many forces in the white South opposed to virtually any education for African Americans, and there have been many who argued that if it had not been for the educational compromises proffered by Hampton and Tuskegee the progress that did happen would have been blocked. Whether Booker T. Washington, Henry A. Hunt, and hundred of other like-minded educators truly believed the ideology of segregation that they promulgated or were simply making the best of an intolerably bad situation is beyond knowing.[15]

What is clear is the fact that Hampton, Tuskegee, and the other schools that were influenced by them prepared quite a number of African American teachers as well as a few American Indian teachers between 1870 and 1920. Whether the teachers who graduated from these schools accepted all the values that they were taught, and whether they performed in their own classrooms the way that they had been taught to perform, was, however, a very different question. As early as 1878 Hampton's Alumni Association was complaining that at commencement they had been "wounded most grievously by being barred from some of the privileges that ordinary white visitors enjoyed." In light of such experiences, it is certainly likely that many of the alumni took the morality that they had been taught, and taught to teach others, with a very large grain of salt. Much to the frustration of teacher educators in every generation, students often seem to take the knowledge and the skills that they have been offered without accepting the values that are supposed to be linked to them. In the case of many African American teachers in the South between 1870 and 1920, this was a very good thing.[16]

MISSIONARY COLLEGES AND NORMAL SCHOOLS

In spite of the positive press reports about Hampton and Tuskegee, and in spite of the considerable pressure to conform to the model that was brought to bear on other schools that sought to prepare African American teachers by Northern philanthropies, a wide range of missionary colleges and normal schools, some controlled and led by Northern whites and others by Southern blacks, resisted the Hampton-Tuskegee model in ways both overt and covert.[17]

Almost immediately after the Civil War, a number of secondary schools and colleges were opened across the South, created for the most part by missionary organizations of either Northern white denominations or Southern black ones. The American Missionary Association (Congregational), the Freedmen's Aid Society of the Methodist Episcopal Church, the American Baptist Home Mission Society, and the Board of Missions for the Freedmen of the Presbyterian Church—four major white Protestant bodies—took the lead in college founding. However, a number of secondary schools and colleges—the distinction between a high school and a college was often, as we have seen, vague—were also founded by black denominations, including the African Methodist Episcopal Church, the Colored Methodist Episcopal Church, and the African Methodist Episcopal Zion Church. These religious bodies, and the schools that they founded, went in a very different direction from Hampton and Tuskegee. Anderson concludes that "Teacher training in the missionary schools focused on the classical liberal tradition," and it was not a curriculum that prepared teachers who would encourage those who had recently been slaves to accept political and economic disenfranchisement.

In 1895 Thomas J. Morgan and William Hayes Ward of the American Missionary Association attacked the "reviving Negrophobia" that they saw in the post-Reconstruction era, and they linked it to support for Hampton-Tuskegee–style industrial education, which they believed was based on a widespread belief "that all the Negro needs to know is how to work. This proceeds upon the assumption that the race is doomed to servitude." Ward protested "vehemently against any philosophy of education which will restrict the Negro schools to industrial training, or to rudimentary education." He warned his colleagues that they must "never forget that it is your work to educate leaders" who would fight for political and economic rights. A year later, Morgan responded to a pro-Hampton-Tuskegee presentation by insisting that "no form of industrial training yet devised can take the place of a college curriculum in giving breadth of knowledge, catholicity of sympathy, power of thought, constructive ability and fitness for leadership." Long before W.E.B. DuBois's critique of Washington, James Anderson tells us of others who advocated a very different model of appropriate education for African American leaders, including teachers, than the Hampton-Tuskegee option.[18]

Prior to the Civil War, the American Missionary Association, perhaps the largest but far from the only Northern religious organization to become devoted to Southern education, had focused on sending religiously motivated abolitionist agents across the North and into the boarder states. Joe M. Richardson reports that when the war came the AMA's leaders were ready to move further south. Thus, while war still raged, people within the AMA became convinced that their next major task was "to teach the teachers" of the soon to be freed slaves. In 1863, Louisa A. Woodbury wrote from Virginia, "I am very sure that our great work just now is to teach these freedmen, & women & children to teach each other—& thus hasten their mental growth & development." The AMA's leaders quickly learned from what they saw in the schools that were emerging among the freedmen and women themselves.

In September 1861, Lewis Lockwood, a white AMA agent, was sent to Fortress Monroe in Hampton, Virginia, close behind the Union Army's conquest of the town. There he met Mary S. Peake, a free black who had been teaching in Hampton for years. Peake's parents, a free black mother and a white father, had avoided Virginia's laws against education for any blacks by sending her to "a select colored school" in Alexandria, then part of the District of Columbia. When she returned to Virginia, Peake violated the Virginia laws and taught a clandestine school first in Norfolk and later in Hampton. With the arrival of the Union Army, Peake, like many others, simply expanded her work, teaching day and night in the front room of her house. As Heather Williams notes, "Formerly enslaved children and their parents now had direct access to Mary Peake and her education. She in turn could openly teach them in front of white men." Lockwood saw Peake as a model, alternatively holding her up and trying to claim some credit for her efforts, though Peake had been at work long before the AMA missionary arrived. When Peake died in February 1862 she became something of an AMA saint, and the missionary organizations, white and black, like the AMA wanted to build on and support the education movement that she represented.[19]

The AMA's goal quickly became to establish a "school of high grade," or a normal school, in every major population center of the former Confederacy, schools that would prepare a whole generation of Mary Peakes. The AMA's leaders understood that for all the good that white teachers who went South might do, the region and its African American population needed African American teachers. There would never be enough white teachers, and besides, they believed that it was not right for one race to depend on another for the majority of its teachers. William H. Woodbury wrote from Virginia in 1862 that though freedmen were happy to respect the white teachers, "let a colored man . . . come before them & he has a power in his race & color, which no white person with the same talents can command." The goal for the AMA was to prepare these teachers of color.[20]

By 1867, Richardson reports, the AMA was operating normal schools in Nashville, Hampton, Charleston, Talladega, and Atlanta. And by 1871 it was operating 21 normal and secondary schools with 110 teachers and 6,477 students. The size and quality of these 21 schools varied greatly, and the AMA was always underfunded in its efforts. But their impact was significant.

Francis L. Cardozo, son of a Jewish businessman father and a free black mother, had been born in Charleston, South Carolina, the very heart of the Confederacy, and had received an early education in Charleston schools before studying for the ministry in Scotland at the University of Glasgow, where he won honors in Latin and Greek. In 1865 he resigned as minister of the

Temple Street Congregational Church in New Haven, Connecticut, to offer his services to the AMA. By November 1865 Cardozo had established a normal school, Avery Normal Institute, in his old home of Charleston that had 1,000 students in 19 classes. The faculty included an equal number of white and black teachers, some of the blacks having come south with Cardozo and others from the Charleston community. Though Cardozo left to enter elective politics in South Carolina, Avery Institute continued well into the next century as a major center of teacher preparation.

Mary F. Wells, a white Mount Holyoke graduate, Civil War army nurse, and former Michigan schoolteacher, organized Trinity School in Athens, Alabama, in 1865. Though threatened by the white community, Wells stayed in Athens for 30 years, teaching students from basic reading through a high school curriculum and preparing the majority of African American teachers in the region through the end of the century. It was far from the only example of the AMA's impact. As late as 1890 approximately one-third of Southern black normal students were in AMA schools. In 1888 there were approximately 15,000 black teachers in the South, and almost 7,000 of these had been prepared in AMA schools. Though its normal schools received far less attention, and far less financial support, the AMA's schools produced far more teachers than Hampton, Tuskegee, and their successors.[21]

Because they had a very different sense of the purposes of their schools, the AMA's white leaders, though often caught in their own moments of prejudice and condescension, did not place the limits on the uppermost reaches of their efforts that were an inherent part of the Hampton-Tuskegee model. The AMA was committed to founding not only secondary schools and normal schools but also colleges and universities. In January 1866, less than a year after the defeat of the Confederacy, AMA agents opened the Fisk School in Nashville in an abandoned Union hospital building. They proposed a graded school based on a "broad Christian foundation," a normal school for desperately needed black teachers, and on top of that a first-class college. Fisk was an immediate success in Nashville's black community. By the end of the first year Fisk had an average daily attendance of 1,000 students, ranging from many who were just learning to read to more advanced students. Its first principal, John Ogden, a former Union Army officer and one-time Confederate prisoner, believed that Fisk should be in the "business of making teachers," but when the school was incorporated in August 1867 it took the name Fisk University, and its new board of trustees was authorized to confer all such degrees and honors as were granted by universities in the United States. Fisk did not have any college students until 1871, and for many years the college department was a tiny unit of an educational institution that focused on secondary and normal education, though the secondary and normal programs did send some of their best students on to the college level program.

By 1869 the AMA had chartered seven colleges, including Fisk in Tennessee, Talladega in Alabama, and Straight (now Dillard) in New Orleans, Louisiana, the latter with not only normal and college departments but a law and a medical school. In addition there was Atlanta University in Georgia, Tougaloo in Mississippi, Berea in Kentucky, and of course Samuel Chapman Armstrong's Hampton Institute in Virginia. While Armstrong had been dependent on the AMA in founding his school, he clearly went a very different direction than the majority of the association's schools, and while the association supported both industrial and classically oriented schools, the majority of its presidents and its benefactors supported the classical approach.[22]

The AMA's colleges, like other denominational colleges that were founded across the South to serve African Americans in the decades after the Civil War, responded to some of the highest ideals in American education. They were based on a belief, as the AMA's secretary said in 1890, it was "too late in the history of civilization to impose any repression upon any class of people." But there were several problems with the model. There was the never-ending shortage of money and of students ready for college-level studies. In their enthusiasm for their work, the missionaries built too quickly and spread their energy far beyond the resources that could follow. In all parts of the United States, many colleges also sponsored their own secondary schools, and some elementary schools, offering 8, even 16 years of education on their campus. Of course, as Joe Richardson, the historian of the AMA's efforts, notes, while the schools were not comparable to major universities, "neither were scores of white colleges. Limited faculties and scarce equipment were not peculiar to black or even southern schools." All of these problems were more severe in the segregated South, however. In 1917, a major federal study found that of 12,726 students in historically black colleges in the South, "only 1,643 are studying college subjects and 994 are in professional classes. The remaining 10,089 are in the elementary and secondary grades."[23]

It was also true, as Richardson also noted, that "the association sometimes failed to live up to its own lofty ideals. It failed to recognize the richness and vitality of black culture and institutions and only belatedly to comprehend black insistence on self-determination. Paternalism and racial prejudice were too often present in its agents." The AMA, after all, was a white-led organization in a deeply racist white nation. The fact that it offered far more than some others did not change this basic reality.[24]

But there was another problem in the AMA's focus on offering the most advanced forms of higher education to the nation's African American communities: There was in the 19th century, as in the 21st, a tendency to separate advanced learning from teacher preparation. As schools like Fisk turned to more advanced programs, they tended to turn away from their first role as teacher preparation schools. Of course a diverse curriculum, offering students a wide range of intellectual opportunities and career options, is a good thing. But it was unfortunate that the move to higher learning and higher culture was often seen as a move away from preparing teachers.

Symbolically at Fisk, an important change came when its first principal, John Ogden, left for what was then the Ohio State Normal School. His successor, Adam K. Spence, professor of Greek at the University of Michigan, was expected to build up the college department. He did just that, building programs in Latin and Greek and in the sciences. Spence also supported the move by the school's music director, George L. White, to launch the Fisk Jubilee Singers, who gave the school both an international reputation and, for the first time, a sound financial base. But Spence did not attend much to teacher preparation. The split between the lower-level normal school for teachers and higher-level education for lawyers, doctors, and political leaders would bedevil the teaching profession, North and South, black and white, for a long time.[25]

While Fisk in Nashville and the federal government–supported Howard University in Washington, D.C., were, by far, the most well-established black colleges of the post–Civil War era, they were far from alone. The U.S. Bureau of Education 1917 study of black higher education listed Fisk and Howard as the leaders but 15 other schools that offered both a secondary and college level curriculum, even if most of the students were enrolled in the secondary program, and a long list of additional schools that offered some college subjects. Independent Atlanta University was by far the largest of the combined secondary and college-level schools, but the list also included Baptist-sponsored Benedict and Bishop Colleges, Methodist Claflin, Presbyterian Knoxville and Lincoln, African Methodist Episcopal Wilberforce and Morris Brown Universities, Colored Methodist Episcopal Lane College, and African Methodist Episcopal Zion's Livingston College.[26]

W.E.B. DuBois summarized the contribution of these missionary schools to the education of teachers and other leaders. He saw their missionary founders as "men radical in their belief in Negro possibility." And he noted that between 1865 and 1900 these schools had "trained in Greek and Latin and mathematics, 2,000 men; and these men trained fully 50,000 others in morals and manners, and they in turn taught the alphabet to nine millions of men." While DuBois recognized the problems—the lack of resources and the limited academic offerings of many of the schools—he had no patience with the "sneers of critics," for above all there was "one crushing rejoinder; in a single generation they put thirty thousand black teachers in the South" and "wiped out the illiteracy of the majority of black people in the land."[27] DuBois was not engaging in hyperbole. In 1865 95 percent of African Americans were illiterate, while by 1930 the black illiteracy rate was 16 percent. In 1865 approximately 2 percent of African Americans of elementary school age were enrolled in formal schools, while by 1930 the number was 78 percent. Distressing as the 1930 numbers are, some very important teaching had been going on in the inter-vening 65 years.[28]

COUNTY TRAINING SCHOOLS

Early in the 20th century, a new institution for the preparation of African American teachers emerged and spread quickly across the South, the county training school. The author of a major study of these schools conducted in the 1930s defined these schools. The county training schools "were to be centrally located schools open to all Negro children in a county." They were expected to supply the rural elementary schools with better-trained teachers than were generally available when the schools were started and they were encouraged to offer "industrial training, laying particular emphasis upon subjects pertaining to home and farm." In other words, they were like the white rural high schools that were emerging at the same time, supposed to offer a specialized second-ary education focused on fostering a new generation of teachers and farmers. And unlike other rural high schools, the county training schools were explic-itly racially segregated and were expected to extend the Hampton-Tuskegee ethic of schooling for disenfranchised second-class citizenship and do so at public expense.[29]

The idea for county training schools originated in 1910 with James Hardy Dillard, who was the general agent of the John F. Slater Fund. The Slater Fund, which had been active in support of African American education in the South, mostly in the Hampton-Tuskegee model, was by 1910 interested in shifting substantial resources into the development of public black secondary schools. It was a fertile field. High schools were growing in importance in other parts of the country, often replacing private academies. As N. C. Newbold, State Supervisor of Rural Elementary Schools—which meant supervisor of black schools—for North Carolina, wrote, "in 1911 when County Training Schools were first established there were no rural high schools for Negroes in the South and very few in cities." Indeed, as late as 1916 there were 64 public high schools for blacks across the whole of the South, of which only 45 offered a 4-year course. The county training schools changed that. With Slater Fund support, beginning with the Tangipahoa Parish Training School in Louisiana in 1911, 612 county training schools in 517 counties were established between 1911 and 1935, constituting more than half of all of the public high schools available to African Americans in 1935.[30]

From the beginning of its efforts in 1910–1911, the Slater Fund placed sev-eral conditions on the support it gave for the development of new secondary schools for blacks. First, the Slater Fund, consistent with its longstanding policy, would never provide all of the funds. Local governments and community groups needed to contribute the major share. And, indeed, though white-controlled county school boards did contribute, various organizations within the local black communities also contributed funds to all of the early county training schools. The schools were also expected to be part of the public school system, and the county superintendents and boards needed to authorize them. Some of the first such schools were actually private schools that were deeded to the county to make them eligible for the additional funding. The Slater Fund did allow flexibility to meet local conditions, but there were also some nonnegotiable terms. As a 1915 bulletin distributed by James Dillard stated the conditions, they included:

> First, that the school property shall belong to the State or county, thus fixing the school as a part of the public school system;
>
> Second, that there shall be an appropriation of at least $750 from the public funds for maintenance;
>
> Third, that the teaching shall be carried strictly and honestly through at least the eighth grade, including industrial work, and in the last year some training, however elementary, for the work of teaching.

While the model was new, there were some quite easily recognizable features for anyone who was familiar with what had been going on at Hampton and Tuskegee for decades. And the Slater Fund leaders were certainly familiar.[31]

While the goal of the county training school movement was ultimately to set the stage for the development of all-purpose rural public high schools, the schools also had, as one of their most immediate assignments, the preparation of teachers, especially for the rural elementary schools that were expected to serve the African American community. As Edward Redcay noted in a 1935 report, "It, also, was recognized that trained teachers could not be had for the meager salaries paid rural Negro teachers in the primitive elementary schools. Through this superior county school, each of these superintendents hoped to get a regular and fairly good supply of teachers trained to do the work needed in their respective counties." Raising the salaries or improving the working conditions for teachers in the segregated black schools was not on the agenda. But perhaps offering an intermediate local institution would allow local young people to enter the teaching profession and fill the immediate need could be.[32]

In 1917, while county training schools were still emerging, a group of Slater Fund–sponsored leaders recommended that every school include at least three elements in their teacher preparation curriculum:

1. Observation and Practice Teaching (60-minute period daily)
2. Elementary Principles of Teaching (30-minute period daily, one-half year)
3. School Management (30-minute period daily, one-half year)

Apparently only a minority of the county training schools adopted this curriculum, but its wide distribution and the imprimatur of the Slater Fund must have had some impact on what was offered in these schools.[33]

One of the great hallmarks of Southern African American education, especially in the era of segregation, was the way in which covert resistance dramatically changed the actual practice of schooling for African American students. Joan Malczewski has tracked information from two North Carolina county training schools that indicates the nature of local resistance to the imposed Hampton-Tuskegee model based on observations of what was actually done in the schools. In the Method Training School in Wake County and the Smithfield Training School in Johnston County the daily programs of study did not conform to the industrial model that the Slater Fund expected. Students in the Wake and Johnston County schools attended for about 5 hours a day or 25 hours per week. At the Method School in Wake County, the most time that girls spent on industrial training was 5.25 hours per week for grade 3 and only 1.75 hours for grade 6. Boys spent less time, 1.75 hours in one time slot on Fridays during 3rd grade. In the case of Smithfield, the reports are less specific in terms of the specific number of hours, but again relatively little time seems to have been spent in actual industrial education. Thus Malczewski concludes, "In both of these schools, the actual classroom curriculum focused not on industrial education, but rather on traditional academic subject matter (such as reading, writing, and arithmetic). This information, juxtaposed against the reports of the teachers, indicates that there was only limited time devoted to industrial training during school hours. This provides evidence that reports were framed to generate support for southern education reforms, regardless of what actually was occurring." At least in the case of these two schools, and probably in the cases of the majority of their counterparts, the teachers who emerged from this curriculum to return to the rural schools had a far richer academic experience than their white sponsors in either the local county government or the Washington and New York–based foundations anticipated or wanted.[34]

The Slater Fund's James Dillard and other organizers of the county training schools did understand that their mandates were not always being followed. One visitor at the Haywood County, Tennessee, training school in 1914 found black teachers "attempting to teach four years of Latin, and neglecting a great deal of the [industrial] school work." A year later, Dillard himself discovered that at the Ben Hill County Training School in Georgia the school taught Greek, German, psychology, ethics, moral philosophy, economics, and evidences of Christianity. Dillard asked the state supervisor to cut out the "objectionable parts of this course." In October 1915 Abraham Flexner, author of the 1910 report on that had already begun to transform medical education in the United States, called for a meeting in New York "in order to agree upon a program for the development of the county training schools," and by 1917 a *Suggested*

Course for County Training Schools that followed the Hampton-Tuskegee line was issued by the Slater Fund. But for all of their efforts, unlike the case with medical schools, asserting control of widely dispersed schools for teacher preparation was difficult. Unlike Hampton and Tuskegee, where the advocates of an academically limited model of industrial training actually ran the schools, the teachers who did the day-to-day work in the county training schools were many miles from those who sought to assert ideological and financial controls. They used their distance and the freedom that it brought them well.[35]

When Edward Redcay set out to write his major Slater Fund study of the county training schools, their mission had already begun to change substantially. In the beginning, Redcay noted, those who sponsored this model of schooling "were entirely cognizant of the practical opportunities the schools offered for giving Negroes a simple preparation for teaching in the rural schools of the county wherein the Training School was located."

By the 1930s, however, Redcay reported that "the teacher-training function discharged by County Training Schools is no longer of primary importance." Two factors were bringing about that change. On the one hand, segregated schools for Southern blacks were being impacted by the Great Depression, as were all other schools. State authorities were using the first-ever surplus of teachers to raise the standards for teacher licensure and to push teacher preparation programs out of the high schools and into institutions that offered at least the first 2 years of a college-level program. At the same time, the county schools were being transformed into local black high schools, part of the county system of schooling that across the South ran a dual system that demanded at least the pretense of equal to maintain separate but equal. Redcay, among many others, was clear that while the high schools for blacks—often very small schools offering only a 1- or 2-year curriculum—were becoming a fixture of Southern education by the 1930s, in terms of resources, materials, and buildings they were far from equal. So he concluded that finally "one must bear in mind the fact that in the allocation of public monies for educational purposes, a discrimination is practiced to the disadvantage of the Negro, which is exceedingly adroit, if not downright dishonest."[36]

In the end, James Anderson's analysis of the difficulties faced by the black state colleges, as well as the private colleges and the county training schools that were all struggling to prepare teachers and an expanded leadership class during the first three decades of the 20th century, is worth citing in detail.

> Black college educators had to steer between two equally critical courses. On one hand, they were dependent on the benevolence of industrial philanthropists for the very survival of the private black colleges that formed the backbone of black higher education. On the other hand, it was their mission to represent the struggles and aspirations of black people and to articulate the very source of the masses' discomfort and oppression. . . . Black college educators had no noble path out of

this contradiction . . . [and] . . . could do little more than succeed in keeping their institutions together while maintaining themselves and their students with as great a sense of dignity as was possible. When their students helped launch the civil rights movement of the 1960s, the hard work of these educators seemed far more heroic in the hour of harvest than it did during the years of cultivation.[37]

Certainly time would confirm the truth of that conclusion.

If one looks at teacher education as a field that always involves questions of moral values and commitments as well as content knowledge and professional pedagogical skills, then in the end, these schools did something in the arena of values that few other educational endeavors could match.

7

The Heyday of the Normal School

1870–1920

Corinne Seeds attended the Los Angeles Normal School between 1908 and 1910. After completing her program, Seeds began teaching 6th grade in the Los Angeles Public Schools. After 9 years teaching and leading the night school at the Avenue 21 School, Seeds left for New York, where, between 1919 and 1921 she earned her baccalaureate degree from Teachers College, Columbia University. (Teachers College had an undergraduate program until 1926.) She then returned to Los Angeles and taught at the lab school of the successor institution to the normal school she herself had attended.

The Los Angeles State Normal School was discontinued by the state legislature in 1919 just as Seeds went to New York, but it became the core of the education program of the new University of California Branch Campus that opened that same year, a campus that later became the University of California at Los Angeles in 1927. Seeds remained on the UCLA faculty from the time she returned to the West Coast in 1921 until her retirement in 1957, the last 32 years as director of the lab school. In the half-century between 1900 and 1950 it was not so unusual for a person like Seeds to be part of a university education faculty without a graduate degree, just as it had been normal for her to have a successful teaching career in Los Angeles without a baccalaureate degree.

Seeds may not have been typical in either her length of teaching service or her level of academic success, but her career as a very successful early-20th-century educator clearly illustrates the fact that prior to World War II, the lack of a college degree was not a hindrance to success in teaching. A 2- or 3-year normal school curriculum, usually now taken after high school (instead of in place of high school, as it had been in the 19th century) was considered ample preparation for teaching.[1]

JUST WHAT WAS A NORMAL SCHOOL?

Few institutions in American education have been subject to so many assumptions, many of them inaccurate, as the normal schools. Reading any number of histories one might quickly assume that in the 19th century the majority of teachers were prepared in normal schools just as in the late 20th century they attended college- or university-based education schools or departments. But at no time did the normal schools prepare the majority of the nation's teachers, and they certainly did not have the monopoly position that was held by university-based programs between 1960 and 1990.[2]

Perhaps even more confusing, a normal school could be a 1, 2, 3, 4, or occasionally a 5-year program. A normal school could be a state school, a municipal school (at one point most large cities had their own normal school), or a private school, as happened especially with the missionary schools of the South, but also across the country. It could be the equivalent of high school, requiring at most completion of a common school curriculum for admission, or it could require a high school diploma for admission and offer courses that were the equivalent of those at most of the nation's colleges. Occasionally in their later years a few normal schools even granted baccalaureate and even graduate degrees. It could limit admission to women or offer coeducational programs, though there do not appear to have been any all-male normal schools; it could be limited almost exclusively to students preparing to be elementary-level teachers or it could move its focus to the preparation of high school teachers, principals, and other educational leaders; or it could serve primarily students with little interest in teaching in any form who wanted to take advantage of its relatively open admission policies and cheap cost. Indeed, it was often their very flexibility that made normal schools so important to students and so attractive to state legislatures. They played many different roles for many different people and groups in their century of existence. No wonder the history of these institutions has been subject to so much confusion and debate. And yet, of course, there is much that can be said about the normal schools that developed in the United States beginning in the 1830s and that had largely disappeared by the 1930s.

Increasingly the state normal school became the standard, and today most people use the words *normal school* and *state normal school* interchangeably. It was not always so. As chapter 5 illustrated, many city high schools offered a normal curriculum, which was often eventually moved out of the high school into a separate and more advanced municipal normal school that prepared teachers for its city as part of the public school system of the city. Chapter 6 tells the story of private missionary normal schools for the South. In the North many states, Pennsylvania being but one clear example, also fostered private normal schools long before they developed any state or public ones. Nevertheless, by the time of World War I, both private and municipal normal schools were well on their way to oblivion, though they had served an important purpose, and had a large constituency, in the years before World War I.

As discussed in chapter 3, state normal schools were part of the common school movement, associated with leaders such as Horace Mann and Henry

Barnard. They borrowed from what they saw in both the German teacher seminary and the French *école normale* and created something new: their own state-supported school for the preparation of public school teachers.

For all of their diversity, some elements of the earliest incarnations of the normal schools continued to be part of nearly all of the successor institutions, state, municipal, and private. First, normal schools were never simply focused on pedagogy, on how to teach. The leaders of the movement knew that their students might well be deficient in the "common branches" of knowledge that common schools were expected to convey, and besides, they believed that teachers should know their subject much better than their students. Thus normal schools were always academic institutions committed to imparting a broad academic content to their students along with skills in pedagogy.

Normal schools were also focused on giving teachers, especially elementary teachers, the skills needed to teach. Normal schools virtually without exception were concerned with how to teach as well as what to teach, with offering their students a practical preparation for future teaching. The experience of student teaching was essentially invented in the first normal schools, and most of the time these institutions offered supervised practice teaching in their own lab school or a nearby school, with time for reflection on successes and failures for their students.

Finally, normal schools were places where commitment was not a frightening or nonacademic term. As Mary Swift recalled the lectures she heard from Cyrus Peirce during her first year of study in the nation's first normal school, she and her classmates were told to "remember that you are to influence the character, the future standing of the ten, fifty, or an hundred children who are committed to your care. . . . in stepping over the threshold of your schoolroom, you have stepped into a very great responsibility." Commitment, as well as skill and knowledge, would be needed in order to meet that responsibility. Students who moved through a normal school had the opportunity to expand their knowledge, their skills, and their commitment to the practice of teaching whether like Swift they did so for 1 year that was essentially the 1st year of high school or a century later, like Seeds, in a 2-year post-high school college course.[3]

AN INSTITUTION WHOSE TIME HAD COME— GROWTH BETWEEN 1870 AND 1920

Once established in the 1830s, normal schools spread relatively slowly until the Civil War. Then, as Christine A. Ogren tells their story in *The American State Normal School: "An Instrument of Great Good,"* suddenly they spread very rapidly to almost every part of the Union, becoming one of the dominant forms of teacher preparation—and probably the most respected—before the beginning of the 20th century. As normal schools became more popular, more states wanted to have one of their own. In the South, the Reconstruction era also saw the rise of segregated state normal schools for both black and white future teachers. Maryland and West Virginia were the first states south of the Mason-Dixon line to start white normal schools. Maryland opened a State Normal School in Baltimore in 1866 that later moved to Towson, though it did not open the Maryland Normal and Industrial School for African-American students at Bowie until 1914, when federal funds through the second Morrill Act required equal resources for whites and blacks. West Virginia opened the State Normal School at Fairmont in 1867 and the first school for blacks at Institute in 1891 (a school that in 2004 became West Virginia State University). Alabama opened a white normal school in 1873 in Florence when the state was deeded the land and buildings of the former Methodist Florence Wesleyan University, and in the same year they took over the campus and resources of the Lincoln Normal School, which had been created by the black residents of Perry County, Alabama in 1867, creating the Lincoln Normal University that later moved to Montgomery. The first state-supported normal school for blacks opened in Holly Springs, Mississippi, in 1871, and only in 1912 was the white Mississippi Normal School opened at Hattiesburg.

In 1875, Iowa's state superintendent of public instruction told the legislature that there was "no good reason why Iowa should continue to be an exception to the general rule." Not wanting to be left out, and having land and buildings in Cedar Falls, the Iowa legislature established the State Normal School at Cedar Falls in 1876. California's first state normal school opened in San Francisco in 1862 and moved to San Jose in 1871. New Mexico opened normal schools—at Silver City in 1894 and Las Vegas in 1898—while it was still a territory and then added a third Spanish-American Normal School for Spanish speaking teachers at El Rita in 1913. Oklahoma also opened a Territorial Normal School at Edmond in 1891 and added a Colored Agricultural and Normal University at Langston in 1897 and a school for Indians aspiring to be teachers at Tahlequah in 1909. And so the story went.

In 1869, 30 years after the first normal school opened, Ogren reports 35 state normal schools in the United States. A decade later, in 1879, she found 69 such schools in 26 states. By 1889 28 more state normal schools opened and 33 of the states had them, and by 1900 43 states operated a total of 139 normal schools, according to her tracking of their development. The number would peak in 1927 when almost 200 state normal schools operated in 46 of the then 48 states.

Enrollments in state normal schools also climbed rapidly. For the 1874–1875 school year the U.S. Commissioner of Education reported a total enrollment in all normal schools—state, city, and private—of 29,100 students. By the last academic year of the 19th century enrollment in all normal schools had risen almost fourfold to 116,600, of which 60,300 were in state normal schools and 48,700 in the still popular private normal schools, presumably with the remaining 7,600 in city normal schools. By 1914–1915 the total normal school population had increased only slightly more, and had actually dropped since its high in 1910, but in the 1914–1915 report out of a total of 119,000 students 102,700 were in state schools and only 8,200 in the fast-disappearing private normal schools, while 8,100 were in the municipal schools. Some of the larger state normal schools, such as those at Genesco, New York, Oshkosh, Wisconsin or San Jose, California, had enrollments in the 500 to 600 range between 1890 and 1915, while other schools in Ogren's inclusive sample were much smaller.[4]

CHANGING ADMISSIONS, CHANGING CURRICULUM, CHANGING STANDARDS

One of the most difficult things to classify about normal schools, in all but the last decades of their century-long life, was the question of just what level of education they offered. The fact that they gave courses in a subject like history or mathematics or the methods of teaching hardly tells one how elementary or how advanced the instruction was. Given the tendency of all institutions to burnish their self-image, many of the catalogs and other materials offered by the normal schools can be misleading. Admission requirements, while hardly definitive, offer a better guide to the relative level of these schools than most other indicators. And admission requirements were fluid, as they were in colleges and other sorts of educational institutions.

It was certainly the case that in the early decades, most students attended normal school with at best a solid common school or elementary school experience. Since the first normal schools also offered a 1-year curriculum, it may be considered the equivalent of the 1st year of today's high school level instruction, but then many of the early high schools were themselves only 1- or 2-year programs. Since at that point most of the nation's teachers were simply returning to the common schools from which they had just graduated, a year at Lexington or Barre, studying both academic subjects and pedagogy, was a very important advancement in their education even if it would be seen as terribly deficient by later standards.

For purposes of comparison it is useful to look at medical education in the same era. While late-20th- and early-21st-century teacher educators grow used to being compared—always unfavorably—with medical educators, in the 19th century the comparisons might not have been so unfavorable. As Kenneth M. Ludmerer, historian of medical education, wrote in 1985, "A century ago [1885], being a medical student in America was easy. No one worried about admission, for entrance requirements were lower than they were for a good high school." The problem was a severe one, at least until the major reforms of the 1890s took place. So:

In the immediate post-Civil War years medical education was hampered by another severe problem: a preponderance of poorly prepared students. Throughout the country's medical schools the most stringent entrance requirement was the ability to read and write, and many schools accepted less if the students could afford the fees. President Angell of Michigan wrote in 1873 that, "the most we can at present easily do . . . is ask for a substantial knowledge of the fundamental elements of an English education [that is a common school education]."

Linked to the fact that with only three or four institutional exceptions, medical education lasted less than a full year, one understands why so many hesitated to see a doctor. And in comparison, normal school programs and admission standards start to look quite impressive.[5]

The admission standards at many normal schools continued to be quite minimal, not only in the early years, but well into the 20th century. Christine Ogren has concluded that throughout these decades, the standards for admission generally rose in tandem with the "growth of public education in the area in which it was located." Thus while by 1880 two-thirds of the students admitted to Bridgewater were high school graduates—thus moving it closer to a collegiate level—very few of the students who attended the more isolated and rural Westfield State College in the same state had any high school or academy experience but came instead, as its principal said, "from country schools many of whose teachers possess limited qualifications." A similar pattern of persisted across the country. The state normal school at Winona, Minnesota, saw an extraordinary jump from 8 percent high school diplomas in the entering class of 1885 to 83 percent in the class that entered in 1900. In the first decade of the 20th century leaders in Kentucky agreed that it would be futile to require a high school diploma to attend that state's normal schools, while the white state school at Florence, Alabama, only moved to require a high school diploma in 1925, and the white normal school at San Marcos, Texas, still allowed non-high school graduates into the 1930s.

Slowly, as high schools spread across the nation, state legislatures and normal school authorities started to require a high school diploma for admission, although the requirement was often waived as often as it was enforced. In 1894 Massachusetts required a high school diploma or the equivalent to attend any of its normal schools, though not every normal school in that state held firm to the new requirement. San Jose State Normal School began requiring a high school diploma for admission in 1901, but other normal schools in California did not immediately follow its example. But full collegiate status— in terms of admission requirements as well as the extent of the curriculum— would only be achieved at most schools in the 1920s, by which time they were prepared to shed the normal school name and claim a collegiate title.

A report of the National Bureau of Education reviewed admission requirements for 1920 and found that the 38 schools that called themselves teachers colleges all reported that they required a high school diploma for admission. Of those still called normal schools, one required 2 years of college for admission, 114 required 4 years of high school, 7 required 2 years of high school work, 8 required completion of 8th grade and one of 7th grade. By 1920 those places that did not require a high school diploma were in the minority. But that was a recent development. For most of the time between 1870 and 1920, most of the 200 normal schools in the United States admitted students who had previously completed anywhere between an 8th-grade and a 12th-grade education. They tried to require that students be at least 15 or 16 years old, while many were a good bit older. And they asked for some evidence of "good moral character," for these students who would soon be expected to guide the moral as well as the intellectual development of the rising generation of the nation's citizens.[6]

Given the wide variations in the levels of prior education on the part of the entering students, the faculty of the normal schools always faced the challenge of adjusting the level of instruction. As the enrollments, and the size of the faculty, grew, normal schools were able to differentiate programs beyond a single curriculum. Many normal schools insisted on a standard baseline, what Minnesota called the "uniform course of study," and what many states called the "elementary course" because it prepared graduates to be elementary school teachers.

In the late 19th century the normal school course was usually 2 or sometimes 3 years in length. Rhode Island State Normal School in Providence had a 3-year curriculum, but students who arrived with a high school diploma only took the 3rd year. In 1874 Wisconsin mandated what became the standard in many normal schools, a two-stage curriculum in which the schools offered a 2-year elementary course followed by another 2 years for the advanced course. In a slight variation, Winona, Minnesota's normal school offered a 3-year elementary course followed by a 4th-year advanced curriculum. Students with a high school diploma entered the last year of the elementary program at Winona and could complete the full 4-year advanced curriculum in 2 years.

In the 1920s, W. P. Morgan, president of the Western Illinois State Teachers' College at Macomb, Illinois, saw a pattern in which normal schools started out as 1- or 2-year programs for students who had completed the 8th grade, then expanded the curriculum to 4 years, then began to shorten the curriculum as they implemented higher admission standards including a high school diploma, and finally started to lengthen the curriculum again as they moved toward 4-year college status. If one is to make comparisons—a dangerous move given a century of change in American education—the average normal school of 1900 may be seen as offering something like the last 2 years of high school and the first 2 years of college to those students who were willing to take the advanced course and complete the program. By 1920 most normal schools were offering 4 years beyond high school, although the number who completed the whole program was limited. In 1920, while 69 of the nation's 166 normal schools and teachers colleges offered a 4-year course, 136 also offered a 2-year course. And again, many more aspiring teachers began than completed either program.[7]

The result for those few who completed the full advanced curriculum was certainly a more advanced education than the majority of the nation's teachers received at the time. Unfortunately, only a few students actually completed the advanced course and indeed most normal students left, often for a teaching position, well before completing the elementary course. Ogren's look at two relatively representative examples may be illustrative. At Millersville, Pennsylvania, in 1905 only 5 percent of the graduates finished the advanced course, while 95 percent of those who graduated were from the elementary course. At Normal, Illinois, 10 percent of the graduates completed the advanced course, still a small elite. And states recognized the advanced work as such. Thus, Wisconsin stipulated that students who finished the elementary course at any of the state's normal schools were entitled to a certificate that allowed them to teach anywhere in the state for 5 years, and graduates of the advanced course receive a permanent, or lifelong, teaching certificate.[8]

Christine Ogren's research points to the conclusion that normal schools at different places and at different points in their history taught much the same basic curriculum. As courses of study were lengthened and admission requirements were raised, the material could certainly be taught at more advanced levels, but there seems to have been something in the core philosophy of normal school faculty and administrators that pointed in the same general direction. Ogren quotes William E. Wilson, principal of the State Normal School at Ellensburg, Washington, as in 1904 he explained his commitment to "general scholarship and broad culture":

> The education of the teacher must not be narrowed down to mere training in the work of school teaching. The Normal School must cultivate a lively interest in study, it must promote the spirit of investigation, it must beget enthusiasm for learning. To accomplish this it must provide for the vigorous pursuit under able instructors of substantial branches of learning.

Pedagogy was not enough. The curriculum would "not be narrowed down to mere training in the work of school teaching"; the normal schools were also committed to a level of academic learning far beyond what was needed merely to teach the common branches and to fostering a curiosity and a sense of a lively intellectual life among their students.[9]

Ogren's review of normal school catalogs shows required courses in not only the subjects taught in elementary school, but other matters also. A fairly typical list can be found in one especially detailed study of the normal schools of Wisconsin published in 1914. The author found that the basic academic course included specific courses in grammar, orthoepy and reading, composition, spelling, penmanship, literature, American history, civics, European history, a choice between economics or sociology, arithmetic, algebra, geometry plane & solid, geography, physiography or additional physics, physics, botany, physiology, chemistry or zoology, and agriculture, plus one elective. Students who stayed on for more advanced work could take a range of additional courses in the sciences, in mathematics including calculus and trigonometry, history, art, English composition and literature, the history of education, and either German or Latin.[10]

The science curriculum, at least according to the catalogs reviewed by Ogren, was expected to go well beyond the basics, even if schools had limited laboratory equipment, something that improved as the years went on. Bridgewater, Massachusetts, added a chemistry laboratory in 1872 and a separate building for labs in 1881, while by 1888–1889 Emporia, Kansas, noted that physics was taught, "as far as the size of the class permits, exclusively in the laboratory." By the 1870s most normal schools did have some laboratory space and equipment.

At Florence, Alabama, the catalogs in the 1880s stated that leading a student to understand "the fundamental principles of chemistry" received "special attention," while the natural science course was to "develop a spirit of investigation, train the powers of observation, and produce habits of independent thought." In 1894 Westfield, Massachusetts, added a requirement to the botany course that students were to "observe, draw, describe, experiment, and teach," while the physics course included "special attention . . . to elementary phenomena and to practical applications. In this subject everything is taught experimentally, pupils being required, as far as possible, to perform all important experiments for themselves." At San Marcos, Texas, Peru, Nebraska, and Oswego, New York, students and faculty collected biological and mineral specimens in the field. And in 1900 one member of the Las Vegas, New Mexico, faculty took students not only into nearby New Mexico Pleistocene beds but also to the Southern California coast to collect insects and marine fauna. These were not courses doing advanced research or taught by a research faculty, but in 1900 the number of colleges whose faculty were serious researchers could still be counted in very low numbers. For students who had never traveled far from home and who had only studied in a one- or two-teacher rural school, and who had previously experienced the sciences, if at all, as odd collections of facts, such laboratory and field experiences brought their intellectual development and life experience to a profoundly different level.[11]

The catalogs of the normal schools for the late 19th and early 20th century also reflect education courses that would sound familiar to anyone familiar with a 21st century school of education. The Florence, Alabama, catalog for the 1870s assured the reader that "In addition to a thorough knowledge of each subject embraced in the course, students will receive instruction as to the best methods of imparting information." This focus on the methods of imparting information was expected to be part of the academic/ content courses but also part of specialized courses in pedagogy, including:

- Principles and Methods of Instruction (Providence, Rhode Island)
- Methods of Teaching (schools in Oregon and Vermont)
- Primary Methods (San Jose, California)
- Theory and Art of Teaching, including "Specific Methods of Teaching Each Elementary Branch" (Oshkosh, Wisconsin)

As it emerged in the elite research universities, psychology, and the more specialized field of educational psychology, came to play a larger and larger role in the normal schools. So Bridgewater's principal Albert Boyden wrote, "The teacher as an educator must know what the different mental powers are, the order of their development, and how they are called into right activity." Whitewater, Wisconsin's Albert Salisbury said, "Practical and scientific study of the phenomena and development of the child-mind, [is] the true material of the teacher's art."[12]

Important as courses in pedagogy and psychology were, however, the heart of practical teacher preparation in the normal schools was what one historian, a century later, would call practice-oriented education.[13] In the words of the normal school leaders, work in the lab or training school was the "center and the core of school life," or "the body and soul of teacher training." Wherever one looked in normal school catalogs one found statements like the one in the 1901–1902 catalog for Tempe, Arizona, that "to enable one to arrive at a thorough understanding of education theories, an opportunity for observing their practical application and for assisting in it, is essential. To supply the opportunity a training school is provided." And at Florence, Alabama, the catalog said, "Their work is neither experiment, nor is it observation, but actual teaching, just as in the hospital the practitioners give actual medical or surgical treatment to their patients."

It was not just in the catalogs that student teaching was emphasized. Graduates routinely remembered, as one San Jose, California, graduate did, that wonderful and terrible moment when "Senior A was to go down stairs [to the lab school], for well we knew how much depended upon this test of our ability in school management." And in New York a state legislative committee investigating the normal schools in the 1870s—not usually the most friendly of observers—reported that "usually near the close of the day, these pupils who have been acting as teachers, as well as those who have been 'observing,' meet, and one of the normal critics who has been watching their work, reviews it, pointing out and explaining not only the errors, but the excellencies observed. . . . The committee were very deeply impressed with the great value of this exercise."

This emphasis on student teaching linked to close observation and follow-up evaluations had been true at normal schools since Massachusetts governor Edward Everett had opened the nation's second normal school in 1839 with a declaration that the normal school needed a link to a district school "as a school of practice, in which, under the direction of the principal of the Normal School, the young teacher may have the benefit of actual exercise in the business of instruction." Ironically, it had also been true in normal schools much longer than it had been in medical schools. By 1900, given the obvious differences in prestige between the two professions and their professional preparation, teacher educators sometimes sought to compare themselves to medical educators. But in the 19th century teacher educators had every reason to do so. Kenneth Ludmerer has summarized mid-19th-century medical education by noting that in most of the nation's medical schools in 1850, "Students would graduate without having attended a delivery, without having witnessed an operation, and often without having examined a patient. All emphasis was on committing to rote the onerous details of the lectures." No normal school graduate of 1850 or later would have the equivalent lack of experience in teaching.[14]

As was true of the earliest normal schools, and also of the academies for teachers like Emma Willard's, and the missionary schools for African-American teachers of the Reconstruction era, and the 19th-century teachers' institutes, the teachers of the normal schools also understood that there was more to teaching than academic knowledge and pedagogical skill. As Ogren reported, in 1901, Professor James E. Lough told the students at Oshkosh, Wisconsin, State Normal School that "The one who teaches merely because of the personal gain is a tradesman; the one who teaches because he loves, and has a heart and head interest in his vocation is a professional." Head, hand, and heart—content knowledge, practical skill, and a heartfelt commitment to teaching as a special calling that demanded one's best—were all considered essential in the normal school curriculum.

It was not just the faculty who said such things. Normal school newspapers echoed this same sense of commitment. Without embarrassment, what Ogren has called "the spirit of consecration" permeated their editorials. The Greeley, Colorado, paper, The Crucible, referred to normal school students as "co-workers in the cause of education," while the Ellensburg, Washington, Normal Outlook talked of student dedication "to the true cause of education." In The Pedagogue, published by students at San Marcos, Texas, graduating seniors declared, "I intend to represent the best there is in a teacher's life and work, and bring to my profession the nobleness and dignity of a high calling. . . . I shall remember my training and stick to my work and try to bring my little part of the world a step closer to knowledge and progress." Of course, such language is easy to dismiss as sentimental rhetoric, and some of it no doubt was. But the deeper one digs in the academic and student life and writings of the normal schools—and Ogren's book, for one, is certainly based on substantial digging—the more one becomes convinced that something important was part of the campus atmosphere, the classes, and the informal life of the students that reflected a community imbued with the "ozone of teaching," and a commitment to a successful outcome of one's preparation in the lives of one's own students.[15]

The authors of the Carnegie Foundation for the Advancement of Teaching's 1920 study, hardly a group in danger of falling into sentimental rhetoric, concluded their analysis of the students in the normal schools of the state of Missouri by writing:

> In or out of the classroom, whether in conversation or unconscious of the observer, these boys and girls produced the impression of unlimited industry and a consuming purpose. Much of this, perhaps, is the result of sheer vocational impulse; certificates must be earned and maintained. But the larger significance of their opportunity is seldom absent, and the influence of individual teachers as well as, usually, the spirit of the school as a whole, continually emphasizes it.[16]

There was something special in the commitment expected of normal school students and in the "ozone of teaching" that they breathed on the campus.

THE SEARCH FOR COLLEGE STATUS

Speaking to the National Education Association in 1897, H. H. Seerley saw an extraordinary diversity in the curriculum and purposes of the nation's normal schools. "I do not see," Seerley said, "how these variations could be either more marked or more definite if the plan was to put forth as many theories and experiments as the human mind could invent. There is no typical state normal school yet developed. It remains for the future to develop it."[17] But in fact the future had already begun to arrive, as a generation of normal school leaders had begun a campaign to achieve some element of standardization in admission requirements and curriculum and even, in time, to develop standards for accreditation.

The American Normal School Association had been organized in 1858, and in 1866 it became the Department of Normal Schools of the National Teachers Association, later the National Education Association. In 1885 the Department of Normal Schools appointed a committee to look at the curriculum of the normal schools, which urged in its 1886 report that the states should recognize a normal school diploma as a life certificate to teach, that the normal schools should maintain a single focus—preparing teachers—and that it was the responsibility of the normal schools, working together, to develop a clear body of principles and scholarly standards. Finally, the 1886 report concluded with a plea, repeated often in the next 120 years, that it was their responsibility to "insist upon professional training as a requisite for eligibility to educational offices."

Meeting in Los Angeles in 1899, the NEA Department of Normal Schools agreed to a more controversial report that set a high school diploma as a minimum admission requirement and a 2-year curriculum as the minimum acceptable offering of any normal school. The 1899 report also called for expanded training school facilities and minimum standards for student teaching as well as maximum teaching loads for the normal school faculty. Willing as they were to vote for such standards, however, the normal school leaders were exceedingly slow to implement them. They had little choice but to ignore admission standards if they wanted students. School boards, on the other hand, showed little preference for normal school graduates and no inclination to implement a requirement that professional training was a requisite for a teaching position.

A separate group, initially the North Central Council of State Normal School Presidents, was founded in 1902. It became the National Council of State Normal School Presidents and Principals, then the National Council of Teachers Colleges, and in 1923 it merged with the NEA Department of Normal Schools to become the American Association of Teachers Colleges, forerunner of the American Association of Colleges of Teacher Education, founded in 1948. Under its different names, this group was deeply committed to raising the standards for what constituted a quality normal school and a normal school education.

In 1919 the National Council of State Normal School Presidents and Principals appointed a Committee on Standards and Surveys. Four years later that committee, now part of the renamed American Association of Teachers Colleges, recommended offering only college-level programs at all normal schools. They said, "The Standard American Teachers' College or Normal school is a school with two-year, three-year, and four-year curriculums designed to afford such general and professional education as will best fit students for specific teaching in elementary and secondary schools." The admissions standard was now clear. "Such schools should require for admission the satisfactory completion of four years of work in a secondary school approved by a recognized accrediting agency, or equivalent of such course." The normal schools would now offer exclusively college-level work. In addition, the 2-year course would yield a diploma and the 4-year course a baccalaureate degree. Faculty, the committee said, should have a minimum of a baccalaureate degree and 3 years of teaching experience, preferably a master's degree. The AATC standards also included specifications for faculty workload and standards for student teaching and for libraries, laboratories, buildings, and financial resources.[18]

It was a level of standardization and of academic achievement that could not have been possible in any previous decade, but by the 1920s the committee was confident that three developments supported their recommendation:

1. The rapid increase in high schools in the various states has made possible requirements for entrance to Teachers' Colleges—graduation from a four-year high school or equivalent scholarship.
2. The great demand for high school teachers necessitates increased facilities in the teachers' colleges to meet the needs of the high schools.
3. Candidates for the Bachelor's Degree, now demanded of all teachers in high schools, must receive the same grade of instruction as those prepared in departments of education in universities.

There was great logic in the recommendations.

High schools had grown to the point where it was, for the first time, possible to envision requiring a high school diploma prior to admission to every normal school. In many places it would be late in the 1920s before this goal could be a reality, but it seemed within reach to most in the normal schools by the time of the 1923 report.

At the same time, high schools, as well as elementary schools, were experiencing a teacher shortage in large part because more students were attending school and were staying in school longer than any previous generation. The teacher shortage was one the normal schools could fill and wanted to fill. Indeed, if the normal school leaders were determined not to cede high school teacher preparation to the university education departments—and they were very determined—then they needed to adjust their curriculum so that they could offer a credible program for preparing high school as well as elementary school teachers. The division of responsibilities advocated by many university leaders, in which normal schools would prepare elementary teachers and university departments would prepare high school teachers, was never accepted by most normal schools.

Finally, the normal school degree would be meaningful only if it was, in every way, the equivalent of a collegiate baccalaureate degree. Normal schools had experimented with offering their own specialized degrees. In the 19th century Pennsylvania's Kutztown Normal School had offered a B.E. (Bachelor of the Elements) to those who completed a 2-year course. But these degrees had led to more derision than if they had kept to a simple diploma. By World War I normal school leaders wanted neither a specialized degree nor a diploma but a collegiate baccalaureate degree.[19]

There is deep irony in the normal school presidents' 1923 recommendations. They were recommendations for what normal schools should become, but they refer to standards and requirements of *teachers colleges*. In the 4 years during which the report was being generated, the association that created the Committee on Standards and Surveys changed its name from the National Council of State Normal School Presidents and Principals to the American Association of Teachers Colleges. As they sought, for better or for worse, to advance in the academic pecking order, to become an all-college institution, normal schools as such ceased to exist, replaced first by state teachers colleges and then by state colleges. The new institutions had a level of academic quality and status that their predecessors did not. But it was a quality and status that came at considerable cost in terms not only of institutional focus but also the breadth of the education offered to students and the commitment to teaching demanded of them.

In a brilliant review of the efforts by normal schools to shed their perceived lowly status and move up in the educational hierarchy Christine Ogren wrote:

> With each advance in the procession, these institutions breathed a sigh of relief. For example, a 1940s in-house history of the New York State College for Teachers at Albany (as it was then called) reported that in 1908, "the last two-year class was graduated. Rid at last of this final incubus of its normal school days, the institution in all its departments reached full collegiate stature." Other teachers colleges sandblasted buildings to remove the ignominious word "Normal," and saw to it that their town's Normal Avenue became College Avenue, and then University Avenue.[20]

With such changes in both substance and symbol, the normal schools disappeared from the American scene, transformed for the most part into state teachers colleges, well before the outbreak of World War II.

While the American Association of Teachers Colleges and its predecessor organizations were engaged in their long effort to develop standards for what should be in the offerings of a normal school or teachers college, the Carnegie Foundation for the Advancement of Teaching was engaged in one of the most detailed studies of what then existed in these schools. The Carnegie Foundation had come to prominence in American education when Henry S. Pritchett, its president, commissioned Abraham Flexner to write his famous report, *Medical Education in the United States and Canada*, which the foundation issued in 1910. It is ironic in light of the fact that virtually every subsequent generation has called for and commissioned its own "Flexner report on teacher preparation" that less than a decade after Flexner's medical report, Pritchett commissioned William S. Learned and William C. Bagley to write *The Professional Preparation of Teachers for American Public Schools*, a report that never came close to the Flexner medical report in terms of its influence.[21]

In spite of its august title, the Learned–Bagley report was much more limited in its focus. It was, as the subtitle acknowledges, only a study of the tax-supported normal schools in the state of Missouri. Nevertheless, it was an exhaustive study, and the Carnegie Foundation clearly saw the report's aim as being as broad in the field of teacher education as Flexner's had been in medical education. In 1914, Missouri governor Elliott W. Major asked the foundation to study the state university, 5 normal schools, and 75 high schools with teacher training courses to answer the question, "what is the best preparation and what is the duty of the State in meeting it, and how can the State secure the greatest benefit at a minimum expense." The report's authors decided to focus on the state normal schools, leaving the state university to another—yet-to-be commissioned—report and generally ignored the high school programs, though they noted that they prepared many Missouri teachers.

Missouri's first three normal schools for white students were typical of similar institutions in most other states. Established at Kirksville in the northern part of the state and Warrensburg in the southern in 1871 and then at Cape Girardeau in the southeast in 1873, they were part of the reorganization of Missouri's educational system launched by the Reconstruction legislature, and they barely survived the end of that era in the 1880s and 1890s. The Carnegie report noted that for their first 30 years of existence, these schools were essentially high schools, admitting students who had completed a common school education and offering a 4-year curriculum, though the largest number of students never stayed for more than 2 years.

In 1904 these three schools agreed to give high school students advanced standing and to make the last 2 years of the curriculum clearly postsecondary. Soon thereafter these schools also added 2 more advanced years of work and began offering a baccalaureate degree. Two more white normal schools, established at Springfield and Maryville in 1906, also adopted this new pattern. The authors of the report, however, clearly had doubts about the collegiate level of the coursework, noting the tensions between the normal schools and the university. While they voiced appreciation for the normal schools, the Carnegie researchers noted that if they wished to grant degrees and be viewed as college-level institutions, "the normal schools should demonstrate their fulfillment of the standards by which they seek to be judged. Such fulfillment can hardly be by affirmation merely; the burden of proof rests with them."[22]

The Carnegie report also noted in passing that the Reconstruction-era legislatures also launched a separate African American normal school, Lincoln Normal Institute in Jefferson City, in 1879. The authors saw that school as barely worthy of mention and did not include it in any of their general findings. In a separate two-page section they dismissed the Lincoln Institute, saying that "the 'college department,' for which an elaborate curriculum is set forth, does not exist; considered on its merits, all of the school's work, the normal department included, is on a secondary level or below, and has apparently always been so. . . . the training department is a pathetic delusion." The reasons for the starved resources available at Lincoln seemed beyond the scope of the report, though the authors did voice the hope that Lincoln might one day take its place as a peer of the other normal schools, but their final recommendations did not include any that would help accomplish this goal.[23]

When it came time to make their final recommendations, Learned and Bagley and their colleagues were much gentler in their assessment of Missouri's normal schools than Flexner had been a decade earlier with the nation's medical schools. If there was one overarching recommendation it was that "It should be considered a fundamental principle that state-supported agencies for preparing teachers should devote themselves exclusively and without reserve to that task." They also recommended a single state board and chancellor to avoid infighting—and competition for state and federal resources—among the different schools. They strongly recommended that the requirement of a high school diploma for admission be enforced and also recommended a more difficult goal, that all public school teachers in the state "from the first to the twelfth grade, urban and rural alike," be required to complete "four school years of organized professional preparation of collegiate character."

The report's authors recognized that for the time being, Missouri would continue to rely on high schools to prepare many teachers, though they were not happy about it. They recommended that the secondary-level professional courses should be limited only to the senior year of high school, that the primary emphasis should be on subject matter knowledge but there should also be student teaching and a course in "elementary pedagogy including the simpler principles of educational psychology," a course in rural school management, and a course in rural life problems. Most important, they recommended that as soon as possible, the whole teacher preparation enterprise should move from the secondary to the collegiate level. The authors knew that the future they wanted might be some years in coming, but there was no confusion in terms of what they wanted that future to look like.[24]

By the time of the 1920 Carnegie Report and the 1923 American Association of Teachers Colleges standards, it could safely be said that the confusing diversity of the late 19th century had been replaced by relatively clear standards, even if those standards were not yet enforced in all places. Normal schools were no longer to be in any way a substitute for high school, but, rather, a clearly postsecondary college-level institution. Their curriculum was to be clearly organized in 2-year and 4-year programs, preparing both elementary and secondary teachers and granting to those who completed the full 4 years a bachelor's degree parallel to that awarded by any other college. The leaders of these schools still recognized that they were only preparing a minority of the nation's teachers, but believed fervently that it was better to maintain standards for what a teacher should know and be able to do even if that meant preparing an elite minority who could help move the profession forward. Ironically, with the advent of such standards and expectations for themselves, the normal schools also ceased to exist as normal schools. If they were colleges in their admission standards, their curriculum, and their degree-granting authority, most also wanted to be colleges in name. And so within another two decades normal schools had disappeared from the American stage; replaced first by teachers colleges that were relatively quickly transformed into all-purpose state colleges or, occasionally, city colleges. Within 20 years of the agreement on the 1923 standards, hardly a normal school was left in the United States.

HOW IMPORTANT WERE THE NORMAL SCHOOLS
IN PREPARING THE NATION'S TEACHERS?

At the end of the 19th century, for the 1896–1897 school year, there were 403,333 teachers in the United States, most of them in elementary schools. High schools were still relatively few and far between, but elementary schools had become a common fixture on the nation's educational scene. But at the same time, the U.S. Commissioner of Education reported that nationally there were 8,188 graduates of the normal schools and 3,067 graduates of private academies entering teaching. This meant that not more than one in five or one in six of the expected 50,000 new teaching jobs that would be open for the following fall would be filled with a normal school graduate. In Massachusetts, where the normal schools had first begun and where they were still far more prominent than in many places, only 38.5 percent of the teachers had attended normal schools and only 33.5 percent had graduated from one. Obviously, between two-thirds and four-fifths of the nation's teachers had never attended a normal school, but had prepared for teaching in some other way, formal or informal.

As late as 1923 David Felmley of the State Normal University at Normal, Illinois, recognized this reality when he wrote that "The normal school is not the exclusive agency for the training of teachers." Indeed, he lamented the fact that "less than one-fourth of the elementary teachers in the Middle West are normal school graduates. . . . The vast majority of school boards do not require normal school training." He wished the situation were different, but nevertheless, Felmley did see a special role for the normal school. Because it was the primary agency controlled by state government, the normal schools had a special responsibility to "establish the standards, set up the ideals, build up the professional spirit, and send out the men and women whose call is to educational leadership." It might not educate the majority of teachers, but the normal school would prepare the leaders and the role models.[25]

In 1918, as many normal schools were beginning the climb to full collegiate status, a survey of rural teachers in Pennsylvania—certainly one of the nation's less isolated states—confirmed the limited impact of the normal schools on the professional lives of teachers, especially rural teachers. Some 1,400 of the 10,038 Pennsylvania teachers who were working in one-teacher schools responded to the study. These 10,000 teachers, who taught in every county in Pennsylvania outside of Philadelphia, constituted about a quarter of all of the teachers in the state.

When the survey asked the teachers about their professional preparation, 76 percent reported no state normal school education of any kind. The remaining 24 percent had attended normal school for time periods ranging from 6 weeks to 4 years, while only 18 percent of the total number were normal school graduates. For something approaching a quarter of these teachers, the normal schools had made a difference in their preparation. But the overwhelming majority of Pennsylvania's rural teachers had been prepared elsewhere if they had received any formal preparation. While high schools had played a more important role than normal schools, 39 percent of the teachers reported that they had no secondary education of any kind, high school, normal school, or academy. Those who had attended high school had done so for varying amounts of time—7 percent for less than 1 year, 4 percent for 1 year, 11 percent for 2 years, 17 percent for 3 years, and 22 percent for a full 4 years.

As the author of the study notes, Pennsylvania still had many rural high schools offering only 2- or 3-year programs, so the number of high school graduates was certainly higher than the 22 percent figure might imply. Nevertheless, the overall conclusions are relatively clear. At most a quarter of the rural teachers in Pennsylvania in 1918 had attended a normal school, and many of these had not graduated; something like 60 percent had attended high school for some period of time, but less than a quarter for 4 years; and almost 40 percent had no preparation beyond the eight grades of elementary school to which they had returned as teachers.[26]

In spite of their limited impact on the teaching profession, especially in rural areas, by 1900 the normal schools had become one of several important means of preparing teachers. There were some 140 of them across the country, a number that would grow to almost 200 in the 1920s. Still, the vast majority of the nation's teachers were prepared in other ways. Late in the 20th century, before the advent of alternative routes into teaching in the last decade of the century, one could reasonably assume that virtually any teacher had completed a program in a state-approved college or university teacher education program. Reading this assumption back to the beginning of the century, indeed to any time before the 1950s, is a serious error.[27]

Jurgen Herbst's critique that "By the end of the [19th] century, America's normal schools had failed to make themselves the reliable source of classroom teachers in the country's public elementary schools" certainly seems justified.[28] But perhaps it is not such a fair critique after all, even if it is an accurate statement of the facts. On the one hand, normal schools served effectively as "people's colleges," bringing at least the beginnings of a college education within the geographical and financial range of many who would never have been able to afford the time, the travel, or tuition, or the preparation to meet the admission requirements, at either public or private colleges and universities. Christine Ogren's research certainly makes a compelling case that during some of the most racist years in American history, normal schools were far more open than most white colleges and universities to people of color—African Americans especially in both integrated and segregated settings, but also Latino and American Indian women and men. They did offer practical training in the work of teaching, and they did prepare many teachers, but they also brought many more into a larger and livelier intellectual world than the terrible isolation of much of American life, especially rural life, imposed on many other citizens in the late 19th and early 20th centuries. As Ogren concludes:

> The men and women who attended state normal schools between the 1870s and the 1900s shared an extraordinary experience. As these institutions accommodated students' nontraditional backgrounds, normalites enjoyed a lively intellectual life and the opportunity to develop a professional spirit.[29]

Perhaps that is sufficient to ask of any one set of educational institutions.

8

Universities Create Departments and Schools of Education

1870–1930

In 1889 Lucia B. Downing was among the proud graduates of the University of Vermont. With her baccalaureate degree in hand, Downing moved to a teaching position in one of the nearby district schools in Vermont and later to Erie, Pennsylvania, where she continued a lifelong career in teaching. Unlike many teachers of her day, Downing did not merely teach for a few years before marriage but stayed in the profession for decades.

Important as the University of Vermont was to her, however, it was not the key to Downing's career in teaching. In fact, she had been a teacher for 7 years when she received her degree from the University of Vermont. Born in Essex Center, Vermont, in 1868, Downing had begun teaching in the nearby Keeler District School in 1882. Many years later she remembered, "In the days of my adventure, Vermont had no law restricting the age, or youth, of a teacher . . ." Her career began as a bit of a lark. In her town the village doctor also carried the duties of school superintendent. He had been her family doctor all her life. And so one day, "when my sister, already a teacher, went to take another examination, the spring I was thirteen, I went along too, and said to the doctor, who was only a superintendent that day, that, if he had enough papers, I should like to see how many questions I could answer." With a bit of smiling condescension, the doctor/superintendent allowed her to take the test along with her sister. The exam included arithmetic, grammar, geography, history, civil government, and physiology, all topics with which Downing was reasonably comfortable. Finally, in the section on school management, she "advocated a firm, but kind and gentle method, with dignity of bearing." A week later an envelope arrived at their house and "out fluttered two yellow slips— two certificates, entitling the recipients to teach in Vermont for one year. And one was in my name! I cannot recall any subsequent joy equal to what I felt at that moment—even a college diploma and a Phi Beta Kappa key, in later years, brought less of a thrill."

A short time after receiving her certificate, Downing heard that a nearby district planned to reopen a long-unused schoolhouse because there were children nearby and a school was needed. After some discussion in her family and with the committeeman in charge of the school, she was hired. Her 14th birthday came before the school term actually began in late August. She wondered at times how to pass the 6 hours a day with only four pupils and her pride "suffered several falls," but in the end the "glorious autumn days flew by and the ten weeks' term was drawing to a close." She was paid two dollars a week for her services, and the family that had given her room and board received an additional dollar and a half for each of her weeks with them.[1]

Downing's story has often been used for insight into what teaching was like for many young women in a one-room rural school in the last decades of the 19th century. But the story is equally useful for understanding the preparation of teachers at the time. Even though high schools offered specialized programs for urban teachers and by Downing's day these high school programs for teachers were beginning to appear in rural areas also; even though by the time she began teaching, the normal schools were in their heyday, offering programs that were the equivalent of high school and even beyond high school level; even though the first university departments of education had already been launched, the reality was that many teachers in many parts of the nation never attended any of these formal programs. Like Downing, they took an examination in the "common branches of learning," and perhaps in pedagogy. If they had received a good common schooling they probably passed the examination. And they began to teach. In many cases they might attend a teachers' institute for a week or two each year. In far fewer cases, they might later attend high school, normal school, or university. But well into the early decades of the 20th century, many of the young people of the United States were taught by teachers who themselves had no formal preparation prior to entering their classrooms and who, like Downing, made the best they could of the situation, and furthered their education when and if opportunities arose.[2]

In this context, understanding the development of university departments of education that formally began in Iowa in 1873 and that spread rapidly is very important. But for more than three-quarters of a century these university programs prepared only a tiny minority of the nation's teachers. Focus as they might on teacher preparation, university programs were quickly drawn into the preparation of high school teachers, superintendents, and researchers. Until almost the middle of the 20th century, most teachers were prepared elsewhere, though as the university programs grew they influenced all routes to teaching—preparing many of the normal school faculty who often taught the teachers, and the educating supervisors who would evaluate new teachers, long before they prepared significant numbers of teachers themselves.

COLLEGES AND UNIVERSITIES HAVE
ALWAYS PREPARED TEACHERS

When John Adams and the majority of his Harvard classmates in the colonial era went off to teach for a year or two they certainly drew on things they had learned in college, most likely both information that they had been taught and modes of instruction that they had experienced. In this way, at least in retrospect, these graduates transformed the colonial colleges into teacher preparation agencies, though the colleges themselves never saw that as part of their mission and did not give any attention to the topic. From their roots in medieval Europe, universities have always prepared teachers. And for most of their history their faculties have not given the practice of teaching much attention.

Early in the 19th century, however, several American colleges began to take their role in the preparation of teachers for the burgeoning common schools of the new nation more seriously. As the common school movement was taking root and gaining attention, various groups of faculty and trustees turned their attention to the preparation of teachers. While virtually nothing permanent was established in universities before the Civil War, and in time most colleges seem to have been quite happy to turn the whole matter over to the normal schools, the early starts—if false starts—deserve attention.

In 1826 the faculty at Amherst College recommended creating a department of the science of education, but the board did not act on the recommendation. Pennsylvania took some of the earliest state action, conditioning state charters for new colleges on their preparing teachers and offering state subsidies to those that did. One of the first schools to do so, Washington College, received a state appropriation in 1831 on the condition "that the trustees shall cause that there be instructed annually, gratis, 20 students in the elementary branches of education, in a manner best calculated to qualify them to teach common English schools." In 1838, Lafayette College built its own model school. The plan seemed a good one—poor students could get a college education at no cost and Pennsylvania would get a steady supply of well-prepared teachers. But little came of the effort. The districts did not care if the teachers were college-educated and the colleges seemed to see pedagogy as a marginal enterprise or, as James Wickersham, who had been Pennsylvania's state superintendent of education, said in 1886, "The experiment of educating teachers in the colleges failed—because there was not then much demand for teachers thus prepared, and for the stronger reason that the general work of a college and the special work of a teachers' school can never be made to harmonize." There have been those in every subsequent generation who agree with Wickersham's analysis.

Other colleges also offered a course or two in education. The University of the City of New York was supposed to have a chair in the philosophy of education from its founding in 1832. Wesleyan University in Middletown, Connecticut, briefly had a normal department in the 1840s. In 1851 the ever-inventive President Francis Wayland of Brown opened a department of didactics with Providence's superintendent as the professor. The course was suspended 4 years later, and it would be another 40 years before Brown again prepared teachers. Not surprisingly, when Horace Mann became president of Antioch College in 1853 he insisted on a course in "didactics, or the theory and practice of teaching." Indiana University opened a "normal seminary" within the preparatory or high school unit of the university.

One of the reasons it is difficult to pinpoint the beginning of university-level instruction in education is that until well into the 20th century, it was exceedingly difficult to pinpoint what a university was at all. The annual report of the U.S. Commissioner of Education for 1889–1890 listed 415 colleges and universities in the nation, with an additional 179 women's colleges listed separately. Among the first 415 more than one-fifth of the faculty taught in preparatory departments, essentially on-campus high schools that were conducted by colleges that recognized that the students who came to them were not ready for what they considered college-level work. There is good reason to believe that a far higher percentage of the students, and certainly a majority in many places, were in the preparatory departments; and that was often where the teachers were prepared. The 415 colleges reported a total of 118,518 students of whom between one-third and one-fourth were women, in addition to the 24,851 women in the separate women's colleges. In nearly all cases the programs in pedagogy, sporadic as their existence was, were offered in the preparatory departments, consistent with the 19th-century pattern of conducting teacher preparation at the secondary level whether in a high school, a normal school, or the preparatory department of an institution calling itself a college or university. One observer of these early normal departments reported to the Commissioner of Education that any high school graduate who had read a book on methods of instruction and another on psychology "might graduate immediately and with honor from the great majority of the normal departments or teacher's courses of our colleges or universities." In other words, the early university normal departments operated at about the same level as their competitors the normal schools, which were still, in 1890, considered the elite of teacher preparation in the United States.[3]

Wisconsin offers an example of the ambivalence that characterized 19th-century universities. In 1849, a year after Wisconsin had been admitted to the union, the Board of Regents for the still-to-be-opened university announced their intention to prepare teachers. They declared, "That there be hereby established a normal professorship; and that it be the duty of the chair to render instruction in the art of teaching, comprising the most approved modes of inculcating knowledge, and administering the discipline of the common school . . ." The board also said:

> That it is the fixed intention of the board of regents thus to make the University of Wisconsin subsidiary to the great cause of popular education, by making it, through its normal department, the nursery of the educators of the popular mind . . .

Such words gave Eleazer Root, the state's first superintendent of public instruction, high hopes except for "the probable inadequacy of the available means," an inadequacy that continued for many years.

Throughout the 1850s the regents talked of their commitment, but did little more. In 1855 English professor Daniel Read was appointed to the normal chair to teach one course in pedagogy, though the regents again stated their goal of having a professor whose undivided time and energy could be devoted to this work. However, in launching a new university other priorities always seemed to take precedence, and one wonders who in the university really wanted to be "subsidiary to the great cause of popular education." When Connecticut's Henry Barnard was chosen to head the University of Wisconsin in 1858 he led teachers' institutes in some 20 Wisconsin counties, but Barnard never took to the isolation of Wisconsin and by 1861 he resigned. During the Civil War, apparently in part in an effort to attract women students to replace the men who were off fighting, the University of Wisconsin in 1863 created a normal department and appointed a professor to lead it. That department continued until 1869.

Given the evident lack of enthusiasm for normal instruction or making the university "subsidiary to the great cause of popular education" that the authorities in Madison showed, the Wisconsin Board of Regents for Normal Schools eventually gave up on the university as a source of teachers. The separate board for normal schools had been created in 1857; but for most of its first decade the board appropriated state funds for teachers' institutes or "temporary normal schools," pinning most of its hopes on the university. By 1865, as it became clear that the university would not fulfill those hopes, the board turned to the model of many other states; solicited bids from towns willing to make the greatest town-level investment in land, buildings, and operating costs; and launched the Wisconsin normal schools at Platteville in 1866, Whitewater in 1867, Oshkosh in 1868, and River Falls in 1874. Additional normal schools would open in due course at Milwaukee in 1885, Stevens Point in 1894, Superior in 1896, La Crosse in 1909, and Eau Claire in 1917. All of these would follow the standard progression to teachers college and state college, and in 1972 they were all folded into a multi-campus University of Wisconsin system.

It would, however, be a long time after the launch of Wisconsin's normal schools before teacher preparation was again a fixture at Madison.[4]

UNIVERSITY CHAIRS, DEPARTMENTS, AND SCHOOLS OF EDUCATION

Many historians date the beginning of the formal engagement by American colleges and universities in teacher education from the time when the University of Iowa converted its normal school into a Department of Pedagogy between 1871 and 1873. In fact, the 1873 date was but one stop of many in Iowa's somewhat distinct approach to the study of education. When the 10-year-old state of Iowa launched its state university in 1856, it included a normal school as part of the university rather than the usual pattern of a complete institutional and geographical separation of state universities and state normal schools. Unlike other state universities that included attention to teacher preparation in their charters, but ignored the subject in practice, beginning in 1856 Iowa had a professor, first John Van Valkenburg and then D. Franklin Wells, who offered courses in the theory and art of teaching and, indeed, most of the standard normal school curriculum. Wells also opened a model school so that students at Iowa's normal school would have the opportunity for student teaching. And like most normal schools of the time, and many early university programs, the normal school offered courses at a secondary, pre-collegiate, level.

In 1867, however, the normal school became the Normal Department of the university with a clear goal of moving its work to the collegiate level, new courses were offered, and students were given the opportunity to earn a bachelor's degree in didactics—as education was called in many 19th century institutions—a process that led to its full recognition within the university a few years later.

Stephen N. Fellows, professor of didactics and moral and mental philosophy, led this transformation to collegiate status, and he also abolished the model school, asking students instead to observe in nearby local schools. Ironically, well after the department's university status was assured, Fellows was forced out, in 1886, by state lawmakers who felt that the program ignored the needs of schools, especially rural ones, in favor of a more academic approach to the study of education. The tension between university desires for academic respectability, which often meant a greater focus on theoretical research than on practical applications, and the need felt by leaders of schools and state legislatures for well-prepared teachers had an early beginning.[5]

Six years after Iowa, in 1879, the University of Michigan appointed a full-time professor in education. Unlike Iowa, which had created a normal school and then slowly transformed that secondary-level normal program into a university department, Michigan moved directly to university-level attention to education. After that, university interest—and competition—was intense, and by 1892 31 universities, including many of the best-known ones in the United States, had at least one full-time professor of pedagogy.

Benjamin W. Frazier traced true university engagement in the preparation of teachers to the creation of the University of Michigan's department in 1879 "because of its importance, influence, clear-cut organization, and exclusively college-grade work." It did not hurt that one of the department's later leaders, Burke Hinsdale, was an especially effective publicist. When Michigan appointed William H. Payne as its first professor of the science and the art of teaching, it also outlined the purposes of the department:

1. To fit university students for the higher positions in the public-school system.
2. To promote the study of educational science.
3. To teach the history of education, and of educational systems and doctrines.
4. To secure the rights, prerogatives, and advantages of a profession.
5. To give a more perfect unity to our State educational system by bringing the secondary schools into close relations with the university.

Read one way, these goals represented a powerful university commitment to improving the public schools of Michigan, especially the high schools, by linking the university more directly with them, including a university—as opposed to a normal school—role in the preparation of teachers. Read another way, these same five points represent a recognition by the university that public schools, especially high schools, were growth industries and that the university ought to seize the leadership of the movement, especially in the preparation of those slated for "higher positions in the public school system," which could include future high school teachers, superintendents, and normal school professors. Both readings are probably accurate for 1879 and almost every subsequent decade.[6]

From the beginning, Michigan's leaders were not shy about asserting the leadership role of the new department, even though Michigan's state normal school at Ypsilanti had been on the scene for a quarter-century. Michigan President James Angell told the university regents that his program's graduates would be "called directly from the university to the management of large schools, some of them to the superintendency of the schools of a town." While Michigan's first education professor, William H. Payne, was not able to convince the Michigan legislature to support his 1884 bill making the university teacher diploma a Michigan state teaching certificate, Burke A. Hinsdale, who had succeeded Payne in the chair of pedagogy, did persuade the legislature in 1891 to authorize the university itself to award teaching certificates, bypassing the local authorities who normally did so and enhancing the prestige of the university's programs.[7]

Among the courses offered in the early years at Michigan were The Art of Teaching and Governing, History of Education, School Supervision, and Comparative Study of Educational Systems, Domestic and Foreign. These courses represent some of the range of what universities thought they could do in the field. On the one hand, there were practical courses, parallel to those in the normal schools in the art of teaching or the methods of teaching. Also parallel to the normal schools were courses in the history of education, a field that in the early years happily dominated much of what was offered to aspiring teachers and educational leaders. There were also courses for which presumably the universities were especially well suited, such as school supervision, for after all the supervisors should come from the universities even as the supervised might come from the normal schools.

An examination of the catalogs of other late-19th-century universities shows similar lists of courses, with a heavy emphasis from the beginning on variations of educational psychology, but also theories of teaching, many courses in the history and philosophy of education, practical courses in the methods of teaching, supervision, and general overview courses of school systems. As Frazier noted, student teaching was generally absent from university programs, except at Cornell. After all, from the beginning, "Professional preparation for teaching was not yet in very wide demand among employers of high school teachers. Not a little of faith, hope, and tenacity sustained the early college teachers who endeavored to make a respected place for professional education in the regular college curriculum."[8]

Michigan's programs continued to evolve. In 1907 the Department of the Science and Art of Teaching became simply the Department of Education, with four full-time professors and an impressive range of courses. While most new courses in the department were in either the history and philosophy—and increasingly psychology—of education or in supervision, the department was successful in encouraging a number of other departments—chemistry, astronomy, mineralogy, and geology—to develop their own "teacher's course" for future high school teachers in those disciplines. Nevertheless, it was clear at Michigan that the science of education, and to a lesser degree educational administration and leadership, trumped any focused interest in the direct preparation of teachers. This, too, would be part of the national model of university-based education programs that, in the succeeding century, never fully changed.

In the 20th century Michigan's programs grew substantially. In 1921 President Marion L. Burton elevated the department to the status of a separate School of Education led by Dean Allen S. Whitney, who had come to Michigan as a junior professor in 1899. The new dean was delighted to be free of what he called the "academic domination" of the subject matter disciplines so that the school could "develop its work in accordance with its own standards and ideals." Whitney was committed to the preparation of teachers as well as administrators, but his focus for teachers was more on scientifically trained educators, which meant experts in psychology, than on subject matter experts. The undergraduate degree in education included 100 hours of academic work, including 31 hours in psychology and 15 hours in education, including the history of education, principles of teaching, educational psychology, and student teaching. During the decade of the 1920s the new school established not only the bachelor's but also master's and doctoral degrees, as well as partnerships with a University High School. Its leaders were determined to find their place within the university based on their expertise as scholars in the science of education. Professional preparation of teachers remained important at Michigan, but secondary to other faculty commitments.[9]

Other universities followed Iowa and Michigan, though at first only slowly. The new Johns Hopkins University began offering some studies in education in 1883, though it suspended them after G. Stanley Hall left in 1886. Wisconsin established—or reestablished—a chair in 1885, Indiana in 1886, and Cornell in 1887. Within a decade of Michigan's move, several major universities had either a chair, a department, or at least a set of courses in pedagogy or related fields, including the University of Minnesota, the University of California, Johns Hopkins, Ohio University, Northwestern, and at Columbia University the beginnings of what would become Teachers College. The University of the City of New York—now New York University—opened the first distinct school of education in the nation, originally the School of Pedagogy, in 1890, "to give higher training to persons who may have devoted themselves to teaching as their calling," and was among the first to offer graduate-level study in education leading to a master of pedagogy and a doctor of pedagogy degree.[10]

While Michigan may have offered the structural models for university-based education programs, the young G. Stanley Hall, writing and lecturing in education during the 1880s from his position at Johns Hopkins, offered much for the intellectual rationale for making education a subject of university study. In part, Hall argued that if German and English universities could create a range of courses in pedagogical theory and literature, then American universities should do the same. Hall drew on a range of disciplines, including history and philosophy, to develop what he saw as a new science of education. But most of all, Hall anchored the study of education in the newly emerging science of psychology and argued that psychology offered educators a solid scientific foundation for their work and study. Indeed, he sometimes spoke as of education as a subfield of psychology. And as his work continued, his focus became clearer and clearer. So he wrote about how he believed the psychology of the child must be understood:

> Here is the heart of the pedagogy of to-day and of to-morrow, where the science and philosophy of education join friendly hands with the practical teacher, and here he who would speak with authority and be heard in the new departure already ripening, must study with patience and love the psychology of the growing, playing, learning child and youth.

Hall also criticized school superintendents and supervisors for becoming so caught up in their day-to-day roles that they were failing to establish a profession; that is, a profession based on scientific professional knowledge. If education was to be a profession, Hall argued, then it needed to be anchored in science, in psychology, and in university programs that understood the hard science that was the professional root of schooling. Hall left Hopkins in 1888 to become president of Clark University in Worcester, Massachusetts, where, until his death in 1924, the president who first brought Sigmund Freud to the United States also worked to establish child study and the study of education as serious academic disciplines based in scientific psychology. Some of Hall's doctoral graduates also carried his views to the expanding education schools at Iowa, Indiana, Stanford, and Ohio State, and his influence on creating a separate academic field of education within 20th-century American universities is hard to overestimate.[11]

Parallel to Hall's efforts to establish a new science of education, Edmund J. James of the University of Pennsylvania, who had played a leading role in the development of the new academic discipline of economics, was also convinced that there was a science of education waiting to be discovered. James viewed normal schools as mere "distributing reservoirs," but someone else, in research universities, needed to develop the ideas to be distributed. James believed that education could be a liberal field of study, offering the same mental challenge as other disciplines, as well as a field for professional expertise. He was disappointed that some of the nation's leading universities, including Harvard, were not rising to the challenge of creating this new science.[12]

Not everyone accepted the efforts by Hall and his generation to create a new science and discipline of education. In 1924 the president of the University of Illinois said, "When one reads the literature of this field he is tempted, as he is when he reads some of the literature of sociology and psychology, to wonder whether after all the so-called field of study did not emerge into public attention largely because its devotees invented a terminology and then thought they had a science." Faculty in other disciplines not only criticized the new field of education, but also resented being pushed aside by the advocates of this new academic field. Henry Judson, professor of history at the University of Minnesota from 1885 to 1891 and later president of the University of Chicago, had begun his career as a public school teacher in Troy, New York, where he taught for 15 years. Thus when he offered lectures at Minnesota on "the science and art of teaching" he was drawing on both his expertise as a historian and his long career as a teacher. But once Minnesota appointed a professor of pedagogy, Judson's course seemed less important and less scientific than those emerging from the new professionals and was quietly pushed aside.

As Geraldine Clifford and James Guthrie have said, "While many nineteenth-century college professors and presidents identified themselves as participants and leaders in the various school movements of their age, increasingly after 1900, they were being told, in effect, to stand aside." This was not a good thing for schools, either intellectually or politically. It created a divide between the intellectual and political heart of the universities and the public schools. But in spite of such critiques education specialists used their writings and their ability to attract students and thus tuition income and legislative support to carve a larger and larger niche in 20th-century American universities and to use the space to expand their teaching and writing about the new science of education.[13]

If the University of Michigan offered the earliest structural models for a department or school of education within a research university, and if G. Stanley Hall did more than anyone else to develop education as a university discipline, Columbia University's Teachers College did more than any other institution to establish the place of the university-based school of education within the structure of American higher education. Teachers College did not have an easy birth. When he became president of Columbia College in 1864 Frederick A. P. Barnard proposed teaching "the Principles and Art of Education" as part of the college's mission, and in 1882 he proposed a chair or department for the study of education at Columbia. The trustees may have listened respectfully to the inaugural address, but 18 years later, when called on to act, they rejected Barnard's request. But Barnard explored another option. He focused his efforts not on the trustees but on a young doctoral candidate in philosophy at Columbia, Nicholas Murray Butler. Butler had grown up in Patterson, New Jersey, and attended the public schools there while his father was president of the town's board of education. After earning his Ph.D. at Columbia under Barnard's mentoring in 1884, he studied in Berlin and Paris, centers of the European study of educational theory, and then returned to Columbia as an assistant professor of philosophy in 1885. While teaching philosophy, Butler also gave Saturday lectures for teachers that were extremely popular—1,500 teachers were turned away from one lecture after the hall had filled up—but the trustees again rejected any proposal for education courses within Columbia, in large part because such instruction might bring women into the college in spite of "the fixed policy of the Board."

Their initial failures with the trustees, however, moved Barnard and Butler in another direction that was, in the long run, very beneficial. Butler had become the president of the Industrial Education Association in New York and made it his goal to create a new direction for this philanthropic organization—a focus on the education of teachers. If they could not act within Columbia, Barnard and Butler would start outside and "build up teacher's college outside the University, and to bring it later into organic relations with the University." The result was that the New York College for the Training of Teachers was founded in 1887 and chartered in 1889 as a purely professional school with the right to confer Bachelor, Master, and Doctor of Pedagogy degrees, something that the Columbia trustees never would have allowed. And the school kept its own tuition income, something that became terribly important as many another university turned to its education school as the "cash cow" for other programs. Butler himself was president of the new school from 1887 to 1891 and remained an important player in the life of the college, especially during his long tenure as president of Columbia University. In his 4-year tenure at the teacher education school, Butler recruited a growing student body, built the library, hired faculty who would become internationally famous educators, started publications including *Educational Leaflets* and *Educational Review*, and spoke before virtually every major education body in the United States. Enjoying the best of both independence and connections to Columbia, Teachers College—as it was renamed in 1892—became virtually the Mecca for progressive educators in the United States, most of all when John Dewey moved from Chicago to the Columbia Philosophy Department in 1905.[14]

While John Dewey was the most illustrious professor associated with Teachers College, his primary appointment was always in the philosophy department "across the street" at Columbia itself. But in his long Columbia career as a professor from 1905 to 1930 and a professor emeritus from 1930 to 1952, Dewey lectured at Teachers College, joined in the faculty debates, and helped attract others. Led by dean James Earl Russell from 1897 to 1927 and including such nationally respected leaders as Paul Monroe, Edward l. Thorndike, William Heard Kilpatrick, Patty Smith Hill, George D. Strayer, and eventually dozens of others, the Teachers College faculty set out to create a literature—practical and philosophical—for the field of education even while they fought and argued with one another over every aspect of American education. For the next century Columbia's Teachers College, along with education programs at Harvard, Ohio State, Stanford, the University of California at Berkeley, Chicago, Iowa, Michigan, Minnesota, and Yale, soon joined by the University of California at Los Angeles and the Universities of Illinois and Wisconsin, were rated as the top institutions of the profession, and in almost every list Teachers College usually ranked first among these equals.[15]

When Ohio State University opened its College of Education in 1907 its founders were clear on their purposes. Many other schools in Ohio were preparing teachers—state, private, and municipal normal schools, smaller colleges, and a number of high schools. But the flagship state university had a special role to play. There were three things that could be done especially well at the university. It could train qualified specialists, academic experts in the field of education. It could prepare high school teachers of academic and special subjects. And it could prepare normal school faculty members, school supervisors, and district superintendents. Like many other leading universities, Ohio State entered the new century determined to make use of the structures that emerged from Michigan, the scientific study of the new discipline of education pioneered by G. Stanley Hall, and the prestige demanded by Columbia University's Teachers College. As American education was becoming more hierarchical and bureaucratic, universities like Ohio State saw their role as preparing the top tier of the hierarchy.[16]

With the new century, more and more colleges and universities kept expanding their education programs. While in the earliest years many programs in pedagogy were adjuncts of the preparatory or high school departments, in the 20th century more truly college-level programs emerged in units of widely differing size and name. By 1930 more than 100 universities had schools or colleges of education, and 593 individuals were listed as either heads of education departments or deans of schools or colleges of education by the U.S. Office of Education. Many of these schools, colleges, and departments of education offered not only undergraduate and graduate programs but a wide variety of extension and continuing education opportunities, especially in summer schools for teachers, which often had a higher enrollment than the regular programs. Indeed, during the first third of the century the university programs began a process that would quickly squeeze the older school district–led teachers' institutes to the margins as continuing education courses and summer school on a university campus became a preferred means of professional growth for many teachers and many school districts.

There are a number of reasons for the growth of university education schools, colleges, and departments between 1890 and 1930. High on the list, often explaining nearly all of the early growth, was the rapid expansion of high schools. Universities quickly tried to take on the preparation of high school teachers as a university function, while they were often willing to leave the preparation of elementary teachers to the normal schools and teachers' colleges. Given the fact that university leaders and faculty often controlled the accreditation process for both colleges and secondary schools, and that they were quite willing to use that process to demand that high schools hire university, and not teachers college, graduates, the university–high school link was quite powerful. At the same time, university faculty were also clear that they were the appropriate people to prepare leaders, principals, supervisors, and superintendents just when the size of school bureaucracies was growing exponentially. Finally, research universities were the natural place for the burgeoning field of educational research. Normal schools had prided themselves on hiring a faculty who were primarily teachers to teach teachers. Universities, on the other hand, hired researchers, and educational research also grew significantly between 1890 and 1930.[17]

THE GROWTH OF HIGH SCHOOLS AND
THE NEED FOR HIGH SCHOOL TEACHERS

If there was one institution that had the greatest impact on the transformation of American teacher preparation in the teens and twenties of the 20th century, it was the phenomenal growth of the American high school. Between 1890 and 1930 the population of the United States approximately doubled. So did the enrollment of children in elementary school, from 12,519,618 in 1890 to 21,278,593 in 1930. However, the high school population increased from 202,963 in 1890 to 4,399,422 in 1930, an increase of more than 20 times the 1890 number. By 1930 approximately half of all high school–age youth were in high schools, an amazing change in just two decades.[18] The rapid spread of high schools impacted teacher preparation in many ways. As the high schools became more and more available in more and more cities but also in small towns, normal schools were able to move from secondary to postsecondary institutions by requiring what they never could have expected before, a high school diploma for admission. On the other hand, the growth of high schools transformed the teaching profession itself. What had been for a century a relatively homogeneous profession—teachers for elementary or common schools—suddenly became a highly differentiated profession, with secondary schools needing academic specialists whose preparation would differ markedly from the academic generalists of the lower grades.

While in the beginning university involvement in education and in teacher preparation and the phenomenal growth of the American high school were somewhat separate developments, they quickly became linked. High schools wanted college- and university-trained teachers. Universities wanted a niche that clearly separated them from—and elevated them above—the normal schools and teachers colleges. And the more specialized, and proportionally more male, high school teachers sought to differentiate themselves a notch above their elementary teacher sisters. According to many university and high school leaders, the perfect world could be found if there were an orderly division of responsibilities in which the university prepared the often male high school teachers while the normal schools graduated the increasingly all-female teachers for the lowly elementary schools. Such a division put the university education programs in the "higher" position, but also it put them on the cutting edge of growth. And, not surprisingly, the leaders of the normal schools never accepted the arrangement.

While high schools in the United States began in the 1830s, they were even slower than normal schools to take hold. And then, fairly suddenly, in the early decades of the 20th century, they took hold of popular interest with a vengeance. In commenting on this extraordinary growth of secondary education, in a speech he gave in 1923, Benjamin J. Burris, Indiana's state Superintendent of Public Instruction, noted both the growth and the changing function of American high schools. "In thirty years [from 1890 to 1920] the high school enrollment in the nation has increased from 200,000 to 2,000,000." At the same time high schools were offering a far more diverse set of programs in 1923 than in 1892. "No longer is the high school considered an institution for the favored few or for college preparation alone," Burris said. "The high school is now the people's college. The great mass of students passing through it go no further in school." No longer was the high school a college preparatory program, he was saying, but rather a replacement for apprenticeship in many fields. If one looked for a way to shape education in Indiana—or any other state—in 1923, what better place than the preparation of teachers for the rapidly growing high schools?[19]

Burris's analysis misses the point that high schools had always focused on a more diverse set of students than just the college-bound. Indeed, Boston's English Classical High School was specifically created for young Boston boys who did not want to go to college, but rather preparation for the world of commerce. In other cities such as Chicago or San Francisco, as described in chapter 5, high school prepared some students for college, others for commercial opportunities, and still others to be teachers. But while Burris may have missed the diversity of 19th-century high schools, he was right on target in understanding that they had served a small minority of high school–age youth, while in the 20th century high schools would serve the majority. And that majority of young people needed teachers.

ACCREDITATION—THE SEARCH FOR ORDER

While high schools searched for teachers and universities struggled with the place of education in a research university, prospective teachers used university programs, along with normal schools, high schools, and other agencies, to prepare for their work as well as to gain further preparation and status. Lucia B. Downing was hardly alone in entering teaching after some very informal early preparation and then some years later returning to a university to receive additional training and the legitimacy of a degree. When Abraham Flexner and Frank B. Bachman studied the preparation of teachers in Maryland for the General Education Board in 1914 and 1915, they found what looked to them like chaos, an "inconceivable confusion and lack of sequence and order," that left the preparation of teachers "heterogeneous to the last degree." They continued:

For example, some teachers had entered the normal schools after high school graduation, as they should; but some had entered from the first, second, or third high school year, and not a few went straight from elementary schools. Some went from elementary schools to college in order to study "education"; others spent a year or two in normal school and then entered college; still others reversed this last mentioned process.[20]

But what struck Flexner and Bachman as chaos may, in the case of thousands of Lucia Downings, have actually been a relatively thoughtful effort to take control of their own professional preparation, to seize the opportunity to work when a job was offered but to enhance one's professional expertise when the right institution opened its doors or life chances put one in a place to attend.

Having teachers take control of their own lives and use various institutions for their own ends did not sit well with people like Flexner and Bachman. And to be fair, the chaotic situation they saw in Maryland in 1915 meant that it was hard to know what standards, if any, were being applied to any institution or certificate. While the extraordinary interchangeability of names that had characterized the 19th century—when *college, university, academy, seminary, normal school, high school, institute,* and *preparatory department* could all be virtually interchangeable terms—had already begun to yield to some level of order, the situation in 1905 or 1915 might still seem very confusing to the 21st-century eye. Most normal schools still admitted many who were not high school graduates. Most school districts still hired elementary teachers who had not completed the equivalent of high school and high school teachers who had not completed a collegiate course. The examinations required for teaching certificates might or might not guarantee much in the way of higher standards, and in many places, urban and rural, political favoritism could trump whatever standards did exist.

The solution, or at least one early solution, that many saw to this confusing situation was a new system of accreditation for high schools and for colleges. Not surprisingly, some of the same leaders who helped create the School of Education at the University of Michigan also started to create a system of accreditation. The roots of the North Central Association of Colleges and Secondary Schools, the nation's first accrediting body, began as early as 1869–1870 when faculty from Michigan began visiting high schools to determine if the faculty and curriculum made the students eligible for admission to the university. Approved high schools were known as diploma schools, and that status was eagerly sought. While the system fostered uniformity and gave university faculty a significant say in the curriculum and the hiring at the high schools—too much, some districts said—many in the high schools enjoyed an external standard that they could use to prod local school boards for resources and that differentiated them from the unstandardized elementary schools. By 1895 these visits were formalized with the creation of the North Central Association, whose seal of approval became more and more important to high schools even as in 1908 it began accrediting colleges as well.

While accreditation was taking hold, it still remained true, as Edward Krug has noted, that in 1900 "The notion of college as something preceded by graduation from a four-year secondary school, familiar as it has been in recent times, was slow in developing, only partially understood, and in some quarters by no means appreciated." It took the Carnegie Foundation for the Advancement of Teaching, established in 1905 with Harvard president Charles Eliot as the first chair of the board, to develop new and more precise definitions for the terms *high school, college,* and *university.*[21]

The impact of the movement toward accreditation and of the work of the Carnegie Foundation, and of the orderly world that they created, was profound indeed. Accreditation created a powerful new link between high schools and colleges and gave universities a strong edge in claiming a monopoly in the preparation of secondary teachers. Indeed, in some cases, having a majority of, or all of, the teachers at a high school be university graduates became a condition for accreditation. Playing no part in the organizations like the North Central Association of *Colleges and Secondary Schools* [italics added] marginalized normal schools and their graduates in substantial ways.

Normal schools were not the only teacher preparation institutions marginalized by accreditation. When W.E.B. DuBois had studied African-American colleges in 1900 and again in 1910, his goal was to recognize the leadership of the "First-Grade Colored Colleges" like Howard, Fisk, Atlanta, Morehouse, and Virginia Union, and to push for consolidation so that resources would be used strategically. When Thomas Jesse Jones of the Phelps-Stokes Fund began his studies in 1917, the goal was more complex. Like DuBois, Jones also wanted to consolidate resources and focus on those places—he named Howard and Fisk—that had the greatest potential for excellence. But quite unlike DuBois, Jones also insisted that there be a complete separation of preparatory departments and college-level programs and that a college have an endowment of at least $200,000. Only Hampton and Tuskegee had such endowments, and Northern philanthropists were not likely to endow other schools that did not fit the Hampton-Tuskegee model. Ironically, then, early in the 20th century accreditation, along with the growing strength of racism and segregation, pushed historically black colleges that had offered future African-American teachers the most liberal education into the far more narrow Hampton-Tuskegee camp. It was the only way to gain the resources to receive the national approval that the colleges needed to stay in business, and that their graduates increasingly needed to gain certificates to teach.[22]

Finally, the rationalization of education brought about by accreditating bodies and philanthropic initiatives shifted a great deal of power from teachers to those who believed that they knew best how teachers should be prepared, certified, and supervised. The role of teachers in thoughtfully choosing to move in and out of various programs of education—an opportunity that was far greater before the systemization that took place in the United States during the second and third decades of the 20th century—is a subject worthy of far more study than it has received to date. It was probably a good thing when Vermont raised its standards to inhibit a 13-year-old Lucia B. Downing, fresh from her own elementary education, from taking an exam one day and beginning to teach a few weeks later. But the alternative need not have been the rigidity and top-down control that has become the reality for much of the next century.

TEACHERS COLLEGES FIGHT BACK

In 1923 Ambrose L. Suhrie, the dean of the Cleveland School of Education, Cleveland, Ohio's municipal normal college, attacked those who advocated moving the professional preparation of teachers from normal schools and teachers colleges to the colleges and universities, many of which in the last decade or two had established their own chair, department, or even school of education. But Suhrie did not trust them. He warned of those who were ready to turn teacher education over to universities:

> They do not seem to understand that the professed interest of these institutions is in large measure sinister and is definitely related to campaigns for endowment or for the support of legislature appropriation bills. They overlook the fact that these institutions, generally speaking, have no adequate equipment of the right sort, no program of studies and activities, and no professional staff for the training of teachers and that worse still the cardinal educational doctrines of the average academic professor include such as that (1) *he who knows a subject can teach it,* and (2) *the word pedagogy is anathema and should be stricken out of all reputable dictionaries.*[23]

Some of Suhire's words might be said some 90 years later by those defending education schools against their many attackers, but in 1923 they were an attack on university-based education schools themselves, coming from a defender of a single-purpose normal school or teachers college who believed that colleges and especially research universities would never be welcoming homes for those committed to the preparation of teachers.

Sharp criticism, however, could cut both ways. As more and more normal schools became teachers colleges and granted baccalaureate degrees, questions began to emerge about the equality of these degrees with the same academic degrees granted by American colleges and universities, especially when applications were being made to university graduate schools by degree-holders from the teachers colleges. In 1922 the Association of American Universities looked specifically at the quality of the degrees granted by the then

92 teachers colleges authorized to grant them. They did not like what they found. More than a third of the institutions, 33 of the 92, had no specific courses at an advanced or upper-division level, while 26 had no specific major or minor sequences for graduation. The university representatives thus concluded:

> The teachers colleges are at the present time unstandardized. In some cases these institutions are unorganized in the sequences of courses which they require for graduation and staffed by persons of inadequate scholarly training. In other cases the teachers colleges have successfully adopted the form of organization of the standard institutions of higher learning.

The report concluded with promise to continue an attitude of "pointed criticism" of all that did not meet the scholarly standards of the universities, while welcoming "into academic relations all students who come from teachers colleges which will adopt and maintain high scholarly standards."[24]

The 1922 report reflected a widespread attitude on the part of American colleges and universities, and much of the American public, toward the teachers colleges. There might be some strong schools among them, many conceded, but the lack of standards meant that one could not trust the academic quality of their programs or the academic competence of their graduates. And there was, indeed, much good reason for such a view. On the other hand, the leaders of the teachers colleges and normal schools now faced a dilemma. Not only were they being called on to raise standards, they were not sure they liked the specific standards being proposed. There was one single standard being held up to them: the standard of the research university, which was itself being transformed in these years. Where many colleges as well as normal schools might pride themselves on the focus on teaching of their faculty in 1890, by 1920 the leaders of American higher education prided themselves on having a faculty that was devoted to research and on preparing students who could follow in their footsteps. A focus on teaching in the faculty, and a focus on preparing students who could teach subjects well at the high school or the even more difficult elementary school levels, was never high on the university agenda. If this was to be the single model for the teachers colleges of the future, then there was much in Suhire's warnings about coming disaster that needed attention. Developments in the coming century would offer only partial resolution of the quandary.

9

Teachers for Cities, Teachers for Immigrants

1870–1940

When Leonard Covello, the legendary East Harlem high school principal, was himself a student at New York City's Morris High School, he concluded that school was not helping him get where he wanted in life, and so he simply left. As he recalled,

> What stands foremost in my mind concerning this decision was the indifference and the lack of guidance at the high school itself. I simply turned in my books at the school office and went away. That's all there was to it. No one spoke to me. No one asked me why I was leaving or discussed my problems with me.

On the street friends met him to celebrate. In response to his asking if anyone cared if he ever came back, one friend responded, "Come back? Does a jailbird wanna get back to prison?" In fact, Covello did return to high school and, at the prodding of an English teacher and his own girlfriend, reluctantly applied for a scholarship that sent him to Columbia College in the fall of 1907. At Columbia he majored in French and studied the Romance languages. Already the idea of teaching was developing in his mind.

Having graduated from Columbia in 1911, Covello was teaching night school and doing some tutoring when his friend Angelo Lipari left a job at DeWitt Clinton High School to accept a college teaching position. Lipari recommended Covello, and the next day Covello showed up for the interview with John L. Tildsley, the principal of De Witt Clinton High School. Tildsley read Covello's transcript and asked him only one question: "Where did you go to high school?" When Covello answered "Morris High," the response was, "Then you know what a high school job is like. Go upstairs to the lunchroom. Your class is waiting." Thus was launched one of New York's most impressive educational careers. The Columbia B.A. might meet the standards, but it was being a New Yorker, knowing the people and streets of an immigrant urban neighborhood and an urban high school that won Covello the job and that shaped his subsequent career most substantially.[1]

A more typical New York teacher of the turn-of-the-20th-century era might be Mary Ryshpan, born on the Lower East Side in 1880 to Solomon and Sheba Ryshpan, who had just immigrated to the United States from Russian Poland. While her father believed daughters should be prepared for home and marriage, her mother sought wider opportunities and arranged for three of her daughters, including Mary, to attend the Normal College of the City of New York, the school that would later be renamed Hunter College. Mary Ryshpan entered the Normal College at age 17, a bit older than some students, in 1897 and completed her course in 1900. While there she studied Latin, perhaps Greek, English, history, mathematics, and the sciences in a curriculum that covered high school and some college-level studies. She also prepared to be a teacher.

After graduation from the Normal College, Mary Ryshpan was hired as a teacher at Public School 12 in her home neighborhood of the Lower East Side. There she taught children who had grown up much as she had, in generally impoverished immigrant families. Ryshpan's starting salary in 1901 was $610 for the year and had increased to $773 for 1905, her last year of teaching. In 1906 Mary Ryshpan married Morris Raphael Cohen, destined to be a highly regarded author and defender of Jewish immigrant culture. At the time New York did not allow married women to teach, and so her formal teaching career, ended though she spent the next decades teaching English at the Educational Alliance and helping lead the Organization for Rehabilitation and Training, which assisted Jewish immigrants to settle into lives in New York. In the early years of the new century three-quarters of New York City's teachers were Normal College/Hunter graduates, making Ryshpan's experience far more common than that of Covello or others like him. On the other hand, both Covello and Ryshpan reflected other common characteristics of the majority of New York City's teachers, indeed the teachers in most large cities, in the early decades of the 20th century. They both had foreign-born parents and had grown up in homes where English was not the first language. City teachers as well as city students were products of the massive new immigration that the United States experienced between 1880 and 1920.[2]

HUNTER COLLEGE AND THE NEW YORK STORY

The nation's largest city moved more slowly than some of its counterparts in creating a high school–level program for the preparation of elementary teachers. As we have seen in chapter 5, Boston, Chicago, and San Francisco all had normal programs in their city high schools by the 1850s. However, New York City's Normal and High School for Females did not open until 1871, almost two decades later. (Prior to 1898 New York City only consisted of the current boroughs of Manhattan and the Bronx. Brooklyn was a separate city that did launch some teacher preparation programs ahead of New York, while Queens and Staten Island were a series of small independent rural towns.)

New York City, like other major cities across the nation, was changing the ways in which it prepared its teachers even as the cities themselves were being transformed. Between 1880 and 1920 millions of new immigrants entered the United States, most from southern and eastern Europe but some also from Asia. And within the United States, even more people were moving from rural farms to big cities. In 1890 30 percent of the nation's 63 million people lived in cities. In 1920 fully half of a much larger population of 106 million people lived in cities. The cities and their schools had been transformed, not only by the numbers but by the many new cultures represented in the nation and especially in places like San Francisco, Chicago, Boston, and New York.[3]

There had been small-scale movements to improve the preparation of teachers in New York City since the beginning of the 19th century. When the city's all-male Free Academy was established in 1847 its curriculum was supposed to include "Principles of Teaching," though little came of that plan. There had also been talk of a parallel female academy when the Free Academy opened, but it remained talk. The Free Academy, which became City College, briefly offered a course in pedagogy, but it was soon dropped for lack of interest. Only much later, in 1887–1888, was a more permanent set of lectures in "theory of pedagogics" launched, which did, by the beginning of the 20th century, become City College's Department of Education, qualifying young men for teaching.[4]

As in most cities, teaching at the elementary level in New York City was increasingly women's work. And in New York City, which also came late to founding its high schools, elementary teaching was all there was. Several of the female grammar schools—the higher-level elementary schools—did offer supplementary courses in pedagogy beyond the usual eighth grade curriculum, since the grammar school diploma was required for an elementary teaching position in New York. (In many 19th-century cities the 8 years of elementary school were divided between 4 years of "primary school," followed by 4 years of "grammar school.") A "Saturday Normal School" had also begun in 1834, which, except for a brief suspension during the Civil War, offered courses in both academic content and pedagogy for practicing teachers on their day off.

From the 1830s onward there had been proposals for more advanced training for New York City's teachers, but these had always been blocked. The primary opposition came from the ward leaders who were responsible for hiring and supervising the teachers in their ward, who did not want any external interference, such as educational requirements, with their patronage system. Ironically, the major change came about in 1868 when a new Board of Commissioners for the Schools, dominated by appointees favored by the notorious William Marcy "Boss" Tweed, decided to make substantial changes. As

Thomas Hunter, soon to lead the new effort, wrote, "The new board . . . partly to justify its existence and chiefly to improve the educational system, resolved to establish a normal and high school for the education and training of women teachers."

Where other reformers had failed, this board moved quickly. They not only voted to establish the Daily [as opposed to Saturday] Normal and High School for Females, but they also gave the school the authority to grant teaching certificates to its graduates, who could then teach without further examination. In addition, the board ordered that once the new school was organized "no teacher shall be appointed to teach in the common schools of this City and County of New York without a certificate duly signed by the Committee on the Normal High School." Thus, when it opened the new school not only offered a route to teaching, it suddenly offered the only route to teaching in New York City.

It was the school's good fortune that strong leadership was selected. Thomas Hunter, the well-known principal of one of the grammar schools for boys, was appointed president of the new school and Lydia Wadleigh, principal of Girls School No. 47, an illustrious grammar schools for girls, became Lady Superintendent. Hunter would serve as president for 37 years and do more than any other person to shape the school and the education of New York City's teachers. The new leaders visited other normal schools and designed a curriculum to offer both methods of instruction and a broad foundation in the sciences, mathematics, and languages so that new teachers would not merely draw on their own elementary schooling but transcend it. The Normal College founders also insisted on a training school for practice teaching adjacent to the new high school.

Much as he insisted on student teaching, Hunter also insisted that a "trained mind" was the most essential fixture of a teacher. He warned that "Practice teaching on a narrow basis of education is building a pyramid with its apex on the ground, a superstructure which is likely to topple over." In his presidential Annual Report for 1875, Hunter said:

> Practice in the training school is of course important: and it is necessary that theoretical knowledge obtained by lectures and study should be strengthened by experiment. Nevertheless the chief reliance must be placed upon the resources of cultivated minds. The prime requisite for the training of superior teachers is to give the Normal students a sound education.

Hunter thus cut through the major debate of 19th-century—and 21st-century—teacher education between those who focus on a strong liberal arts education and those who focus on practical preparation by answering, "both."

With its philosophy and curricular plans in place, the new Female Normal and High School opened in February 1871 with some 300 young women from Wadleigh's grammar school being joined by an additional 400 students from other female grammar schools from around the city in a 3-year curriculum that mixed academic study, courses in pedagogy, and student teaching and that guaranteed the graduates a teaching position in the burgeoning schools of New York City when they were finished.[5]

A year after the school opened it was renamed the Normal College of the City of New York to give it parity with the male College of the City of New York, though Hunter acknowledged that the name was "a misnomer . . . but it was something to work towards." Hunter was clear, however, that he wanted New York City's normal school to offer a higher academic standard than those he had seen in some other normal schools. He would not allow any short course. The curriculum at the Normal College was a full 3 years beyond elementary school. The first 2 years were the academic courses similar to other high and normal schools, including Latin. Only in the 3rd year did students start the study of pedagogy, including theories of instruction, as well as practice teaching. At Hunter's insistence admission was by examination, and students needed to pass other examinations to stay and to graduate. He wanted to be sure there was no taint of favoritism, either for the politically well-connected or the well-born.

Finally, Hunter used his political connections and the Board of Education's desire to act quickly, before Tweed might be indicted or they lost the next election, to gain a permanent campus for the school. With good reason, Hunter worried that the same reformers, the "shoddy aristocracy" he called them, who were bent on exposing the corruption of the Tweed circle would be far less supportive of the higher-level teacher education that had Tweed's backing. Construction began quickly on Park Avenue between 68th and 69th Streets at the edge of the current Hunter campus. The new building, with 30 classrooms, an art studio, 15-foot-wide halls, and a chapel seating 2,000 was dedicated at ceremonies featuring New York's mayor and governor and the U.S. Commissioner of Education in October 1873. After a late start, something permanent seemed to be in place in New York.[6]

During Hunter's long tenure as president, the curriculum was lengthened and the first academic degrees were offered. Hunter and his successors continued to stress the importance of a strong subject matter background for teachers as well as professional preparation. They also prided themselves on building a college for women. While they paid careful attention to the nation's normal schools, they also saw themselves as competing with the new women's colleges, Vassar, Wellesley, Smith, and Bryn Mawr, seeking to offer working-class New Yorkers the same opportunities that these colleges offered the daughters of the elite. In the process, Hunter created internal tensions that would continue throughout the college's life—tensions between a clear focus on preparing teachers and on offering a multipurpose curriculum and tensions between being a democratic school that served as many as young women as possible or a more selective school that served an intellectual, if not a financial, elite.

Within a decade of the school's founding the 3-year curriculum was extended to 4 years. Many students and parents were unhappy about this move, just as they had been unhappy with the original decision to avoid any shorter route to teaching at a time when most normal schools offered a 2-year course or less. But Hunter and his colleagues wanted a high standard, and they were able to stand firm. After 1878 Hunter's curriculum took 4 years to complete and after 1881 only 4-year graduates received recommendations for New York City teaching jobs.[7]

In 1888 the Normal College began to diversify its curriculum to serve young women who had interests other than teaching. Many recognized that for all of the focus on preparing teachers, the college—like normal schools across the country—actually had a broader mission if one looked at the professional lives of its graduates. In the early 1870s, an article in the *New York Times* noted that "of all the pupils in the Normal College, only about one-third become teachers . . . The Normal College is rightly held to be not only a training school for teachers but a high school to supplement the education in the grammar schools." Unlike some other normal schools, New York City's Normal College never demanded a commitment to teaching for admission, and the school continued to graduate more women than the city needed as teachers. In time, the course of study was split into two tracks, a 4-year "Normal Course" and a 5-year "Classical Course" that corresponded more closely to that offered at the still-all-male City College and that led to the college's first Bachelor of Arts degrees but not to a teaching license.[8]

New York City's Normal College, like many other normal colleges, also reflected a racial and class diversity not seen elsewhere in American higher education. While middle-class white Protestants were the majority in the early years, there were always Catholics and Jews among the normal students, as well as a smattering of African Americans. Only a few colleges, Antioch and Oberlin in Ohio, outside the historically black colleges of the South, admitted African American women when the Normal College was launched, but the records of the Normal College are clear. As long as New York maintained separate female Colored Grammar Schools, four or five of the graduates of these schools regularly appeared among the Normal College students. Photographs from the 1870s and 1880s also show African American students. Historian Carleton Mabee reported that by 1890, 56 black teachers had graduated from the college. While old New York City did not hire its first black teacher until 1895, Brooklyn and other cities and towns did hire Normal College graduates, including African American graduates.

In 1889 *The American Hebrew* praised the school for allowing students of all backgrounds to achieve academic distinction "irrespective of religious affiliation." And in 1891 one student wrote of the Normal College as a place where the daughter of the "manufacturer sits next to the child of the factory-hand." In fact, poorer students regularly dropped out for lack of funds, and the school had its share of racism and anti-Semitism. To say that the Normal College was better than most of American higher education in respect for diversity of race, religion, or social class in the late 19th century is to set a very low bar. But compared to other schools, the college did prepare future teachers for New York's heterogeneous students in an atmosphere of relative respect for and experience of diversity.[9]

As the Normal College entered its third decade, new challenges appeared to its monopoly position as the educator of New York's women teachers. Barnard College began granting degrees, backed by the prestige of Columbia University, in 1889. In 1892 the New York College for the Training of Teachers, which had opened in 1887, became Teachers College of Columbia University, granting B.A., M.A., and Doctor of Pedagogy degrees. And in 1890 the School of Pedagogy at New York University opened its doors, granting baccalaureate, master's, and doctoral degrees. Although all of these schools could easily work together, there was also competition, especially with Columbia. When Grace Dodge, the primary benefactor of Columbia's Teachers College, traveled to Albany to oppose giving the Normal College degree-granting authority, it led Thomas Hunter to write sarcastically that she did so "perhaps on the ground that it would tend to reduce the supply of servants and thereby increase their wages."

In the end, the phenomenal growth of New York City in the 1890s and beyond meant that there was more than enough work for those who were prepared for and who wanted to enter the teaching profession, though the turn-of-the-century progressive reforms championed by Columbia's Nicholas Murray Butler and others of his and Grace Dodge's social class often meant that Normal College graduates did the teaching while graduates of schools like Columbia did the supervision and set the curriculum.

Between 1888 and 1905 the college, still led by Hunter, went through a number of changes so that by 1905 the college offered a 7- or 8-year curriculum for elementary school graduates, or a 3- or 4-year curriculum for those who entered from high school, leading to both a B.A. degree and a New York City teaching license. While it would continue its own high school–level programs, by 1905 the Normal College had finally lived up to the name it had been given in 1872, when it was first called a college.

In 1872 the school had 700 students, the majority of whom did not complete the full 3-year curriculum. Nevertheless, by 1887 a total of 3,768 young women had graduated from the college, and by 1895 3,000 of New York City's 4,000 teachers were graduates of the Normal College. Many of the remaining thousand were male teachers, mostly high school teachers, a significant number of whom had graduated from City College. While New York had come late to offering high school–level normal instruction for prospective elementary teachers, it had caught up quickly.[10]

The greatest crisis in the life of New York City's Normal College came with the merger of New York and Brooklyn to create the new greater New York City

in 1898 and the subsequent victory of the political reformers whom David
Tyack and Elisabeth Hansot rightly named the administrative progressives—
people who believed that reform would be accomplished by centralizing control of all aspects of municipal affairs in the hands of "the best and brightest,"
namely themselves as Protestant Europeans whose parents were not immigrants. In New York City the administrative progressives included John Purroy
Mitchel, who would become mayor of the city, William Henry Maxwell, the
newly appointed superintendent of the expanded school system, and Nicholas Murray Butler, founder of Teachers College and soon to be president of
Columbia University. These administrative progressives took a dim view of the
Normal College and its graduates. As Katherina Kroo Grunfeld has noted, it
would have been hard for the Normal College to escape the reformers' wrath.
They were dissatisfied with the schools and the teachers, and the Normal College "had graduated over 75% of the teachers and a large number of the female principals and assistants." If the reformers wanted a target, this was an
easy one.

The split between the reformers, for whom Superintendent Maxwell was
the prime voice, and the Normal College, still led by Hunter, was complex.
Administrative progressives—a very different group than the more democratic and child-centered progressives, of whom John Dewey was a prime
philosopher—took a pretty dim view of teachers, at least teachers who wanted
to make decisions on their own. In the view of leaders like Maxwell and Butler,
knowledge of the right way to conduct schools flowed downhill from people
like themselves to their hand-picked assistant superintendents and principals—
mostly expected to be graduates of institutions like Columbia's Teachers
College—to the lowest level, the classroom teacher. In part this was a gender split,
in part a class split, and in very large part a split between different ethnic groups.
The administrative progressives were mostly male and generally from middle-
and upper-class Protestant families of many generations in the United States.
They were quite convinced that they were the best and the brightest that this
society could produce. The Normal College graduates, on the other hand, were
overwhelmingly female, from diverse religious and ethnic backgrounds, far less
well off, and generally, like many New Yorkers, first-generation Americans.

If in the eyes of the administrative progressives these teachers were to effectively "Americanize" the immigrants, they needed to do so closely following a script written by others. Teachers had a very different view of the situation.
Perhaps the most powerful voice of teacher resistance to the administrative
progressives was Margaret Haley, founder and leader of the Chicago Federation of Teachers. In 1904, in the midst of the Normal College's battles with
Maxwell, Haley gave a speech at the National Education Association that noted
"the increased tendency toward 'factoryizing education,' making the teacher
an automaton, a mere factory hand, whose duty it is to carry out mechanically
and unquestioningly the ideas and orders of those clothed with the authority

of position." Hunter and his colleagues had no intention of preparing automatons. Maxwell, on the other hand, wanted teachers who would not ask too many questions in carrying out his plans.[11]

As had been true from the school's opening in 1871, the heart of the curriculum of the college that by 1902 granted aspiring teachers a B.A. degree was in the arts and sciences, with the faculty careful to limit the professional courses and student teaching. Not everyone was happy with this focus. As early as 1895 the Normal College had run afoul of a state mandate that at least one full academic year be devoted exclusively to "the Art and Science of Teaching" at all normal schools and colleges in New York state.

Maxwell and his allies were not sure that they approved of the college's focus on the liberal arts. In 1899 the New York state superintendent prodded the college to offer at least 2 years of purely professional work toward the degree, more than the faculty wanted. And in 1902 Maxwell himself informed Hunter that he would no longer grant Normal College graduates the waiver from the city's teacher examinations that they had previously been given. From then on Normal College graduates would need to take the college's final exams, the state exams, and the city exams—the last dubbed "Maxwells" by unhappy students. While the faculty organized review courses to help students pass the city exams—and they generally did—Maxwell's real purpose was to change the curriculum of the college. As Grunfeld noted, this was part of a larger pattern in which "standardized regulations were being imposed which left schools the ability to certify a course of studies, but gave professional examining agencies . . . the power to grant licenses to practice. By controlling licensing examinations, these agencies were able to dictate the content of school programs." Hunter himself was more blunt, writing in his 1905 annual report that "the professional examinations have been warped to follow the course pursued in the city training schools . . . to determine whether the specific requirements of the city elementary course of study have been studied and memorized than to ascertain whether the applicants have acquired a broad knowledge of the recognized underlying principles of the science of education and the art of teaching."

Starting in 1897, the Board of Education examinations focused on "manual training, drawing (mechanical and free-hand), coloring, modeling in clay, and sewing." This was not the academic program that the faculty believed future teachers needed, but in controlling the examinations the superintendent could exert control over the curriculum. Though he was rebuffed in seeking direct control over admission and graduation requirements at the college, the power shift in Maxwell's direction was nonetheless clear. The college faculty protested what they saw as the superintendent's power grab, "not only because it would be illegal but because it would be degrading to the College and its faculty," but there was little they could do if they wanted to guarantee their graduates the New York City teaching jobs that were still the college's reason for being.[12]

Prior to the merger of Brooklyn and Manhattan in 1898, the City of Brooklyn had maintained its own Training School for teachers. After 1898 Maxwell established a similar training school in Manhattan. The New York and Brooklyn Training Schools required a high school diploma for admission, and they offered a 2-year professional program for these high school graduates that prepared them to be teachers. All aspects of the training schools—admissions, curriculum, and graduation requirements—were under the direct control of the superintendent. This program, far closer to an apprenticeship program preparing teachers for the schools as they were, or as Maxwell wanted them to be, than the Normal College's program for preparing tough-minded, independent professionals, was anathema to the Normal College faculty. But in the minds of leaders like Maxwell and Butler, they were preferable.

In his 1905 Annual Report Hunter was clear in his detailed condemnation of the Training Schools.

> It is obvious that the college presents greater inducements than those offered by the training schools to young women who desire to become teachers. It has a collegiate charter which places it in a position to grant degrees which are recognized and registered by the Regents of the University. Such a degree is always valuable to a teacher and it is especially so in the City of New York where the by-laws of the Board of education provide that a degree is a necessary qualification for many of the higher positions in the teaching and supervising staff. . . . The highest ambition of a training school graduate is limited to obtaining a position to teach in an elementary school. . . . It is a very grave question whether the City of New York should prepare persons for employment as teachers in a less period of time or with a less extensive training than is comprehended in and provided by the courses which have been adopted by the trustees of the Normal College.

Maxwell meant to do just what Hunter condemned. After all, if decisions were to be made at the top, if teachers were to follow the directives of their "betters," then the Normal College program, with its 4 years of study beyond high school and its focus on the academic disciplines, was an expensive way to prepare troublemakers. Far better, and cheaper, was the 2-year program that was fully integrated into the ways of the New York City Public Schools.[13]

Less threatening to the Normal College, but nevertheless a factor in its future, was the emergence of other high schools in New York. Brooklyn had its own high schools prior to the 1898 merger. And in its 1st year the new consolidated Board of Education also proposed a series of high schools for Manhattan and the Bronx. Hunter himself supported the move to expand educational opportunity in New York, but he also recognized that these schools offered competition with his own institution. No longer would the Normal College be the only high school for women in Manhattan.

One result of the great immigration of the 1890s and early 1900s was a desperate shortage of teachers that both helped and hurt the Normal College.

On the one hand, its faculty gained maneuvering room in the battles with Maxwell; the superintendent simply could not do without the college's graduates as New York City teachers. On the other hand, the shortage made it necessary for New York City to import hundreds of teachers from outside New York City when the Normal College could not produce enough graduates. It also made the Brooklyn and Manhattan Teacher Training Schools essential and made it relatively easy for graduates of other colleges to be certified in New York. Never again would one institution so completely dominate the preparation of New York City teachers as the Normal College had done in its first 35 years of existence. Nevertheless, the college and other parts of what became City University would be the major, if not the exclusive, provider of teachers for the New York City schools for the next century.[14]

By the time Thomas Hunter retired in 1906 the school he had founded in 1871 no longer had its monopoly position as the only high school or college for women in Manhattan or as the sole provider of teachers for the city. With Hunter's departure there were proposals to merge the Normal College either with the Training Schools or with the male City College or both and to remove the high school–level programs. These efforts were defeated, and the college maintained its autonomy. Indeed, through the next century Hunter College as a degree-granting institution with its own high school would continue to operate with a high level of independence. Recognizing the growing diversity of the student body's goals, there were proposals to rename the school the New York City College for Women, but instead in April 1914 it was named in honor of its President Emeritus as Hunter College of the City of New York.

After 1907 students could major in mathematics, classical languages, French, German, science, or history. All students took a heavy course load in English grammar and composition, and most students also took the pedagogical course leading to certification. After 1914 the M.A. was required for appointment to the faculty, and after 1918 a Ph.D. for promotion to the rank of full professor. While teaching remained a career of choice for many Hunter women, the new academic levels opened other options for others, and after 1910, when New York temporarily solved its teacher shortage, more Hunter graduates concluded that other fields were preferable to teaching. By the time of World War I the college had moved decisively away from being a single-purpose institution preparing teachers for its city to a multipurpose institution preparing teachers but also offering a collegiate education to New York women who met its standards and who sought careers ranging from secretarial work to lawyers and medical doctors. In the end, Hunter College's historian, Grunfeld, concluded that the college was never again able to "develop a coherent mission once it abandoned the primacy of normal-training."[15]

New York City and its public schools continued to grow through the early decades of the 20th century, and New York City's public university remained the primary provider of teachers. After World War I the need for teachers grew even more severe. Of the postwar era Rousmaniere writes, "Increased enrollment meant that New York schools needed teachers badly. The teaching force grew from 20,000 teachers in 1920 to 33,600 in 1930, with more than a thousand new teaching positions opening every year." The city's Board of Higher Education was created in 1926, and in 1929 the College of the City of New York came to include both City College and Hunter. Brooklyn College was founded in 1931 and Queens College in 1937 as outer borough campuses and only later became independent campuses. While all of these schools—Hunter, City College, Brooklyn and Queens Colleges—prepared students for many careers, they also prepared the vast majority of New York City's teachers. Each separate campus now had its own school of education, and they continued to prepare the majority of the city's teachers as other campuses were added to the system and as it was reorganized as the multicampus City University of New York in 1961.[16]

NEW YORK WAS NOT ALONE: CHICAGO, CINCINNATI, DETROIT

New York was hardly alone either in launching a municipal university or in developing its own municipal normal school or normal college. Other cities did not so much copy New York—indeed, New York had gotten a late start—as respond to similar pressures. As we saw in chapter 5, Chicago had included a normal course of study in the high school curriculum since the city launched its first high school in 1856. That program continued for 15 years, graduating between 20 and 35 new teachers each year.[17]

In 1893, Superintendent Albert G. Lane, who had himself graduated from the normal program at the old Chicago High School, established a new apprentice-style program called Cadet Teachers. At that time graduates of any Chicago high school could become teachers if they could pass an examination. Lane wanted to shift the emphasis to a more practice-based approach, and with Board of Education approval he created a program to "issue teachers' certificates to those graduates of high schools, who attained a scholarship average of ninety per cent for the four years' course of study, after they had acted as cadet teachers in the schools of Chicago for five months, and had demonstrated their ability to teach." Cadet teachers taught school for half of each day and took classes for the other half. After 5 months, if they had shown "sufficient ability to instruct a class and to manage a room," they could be assigned their own classroom.

In the first year of the program 176 young graduates of Chicago's different high schools spent the morning studying the methods of teaching, reading, writing, arithmetic, geography, history, music, drawing, and calisthenics, as well as psychology and school management, with two experienced teachers especially selected by Superintendent Lane. In the afternoon they were assigned to schools. Lane was proud of the program and of the improvement in the preparation offered teachers. He wrote in his 1894 annual report:

> For many years prior to the organization of the Training Class, inexperienced teachers were assigned to schools where they assisted regular teachers in the management of the rooms, and were called upon to substitute when teachers were absent. As soon as they demonstrated power to manage a room, they were appointed to positions in our schools. Since the organization of the Training Class the instruction which has been given to the cadets in the methods and principles of teaching has resulted in making them much more effective teachers.

While the cadet program was clearly an improvement over the "sink-or-swim" induction that Lane described, one wonders if there was opposition from more experienced teacher educators who could well have seen the cadet program as close to Superintendent Maxwell's New York efforts to control all aspects of a teachers' preparation. In any case, a much more thorough program for new teachers was developing.[18]

In 1867 the state of Illinois organized the Cook County Normal School to serve both Chicago and its surrounding towns, and in 1896 the Cook County Normal School and Lane's Cadet Teacher program were merged under the direct control of the Chicago Board of Education as the Chicago City Normal School. Cook County Normal and its successor Chicago City Normal School would play a very important role in shaping teacher education both in Chicago and nationally. Early in the 1880s Cook County Normal School began to emerge as one of the nation's premier teacher education programs in large part because of the prominence of its principal, Francis W. Parker.

Parker, a Civil War veteran and longtime educator had become superintendent of the Quincy, Massachusetts, public schools in 1873 after that town's school committee had been dismayed to find that youngsters knew the rules of grammar but could not write a letter and could read from textbooks but could not make sense of other sources. Parker's agenda was what a later generation would call teaching for understanding.[19]

Parker had moved from Quincy first to Boston and then to Chicago in the early 1880s. In his annual report for 1890 Parker noted that the school granted diplomas on the basis of a 1-year course of study beyond high school, and "satisfactory evidence of a high appreciation of the duties, responsibilities and possibilities of the teachers' profession, sufficient knowledge and skill to warrant the beginning of the work of teaching," and also, among other things, "ability to control, govern, and teach a school fairly well, [and] a knowledge of the principles of education, sufficient to guide a candidate to the discovery of right methods." While Parker was clear that he would have preferred to offer the normal curriculum to college graduates, who could combine the knowledge and the maturity to truly benefit from it, the reality was that he was "governed by circumstances, which do not admit of an ideal standard." Parker might want a collegiate program, but what he could offer was a 5th year of high school. In 1890 it was still true that most teachers lacked even a high school diploma and many had only "gone little beyond a grammar school." Given that reality, Cook County Normal set a high standard.[20]

In 1893 Parker became one of the best-known progressive educators in the nation when John Mayer Rice in *The Public-School System of the United States*—the book that some said launched the progressive education movement —described Parker and Cook County Normal School as the inspiration for what progressive teaching should look like, as its students were taught to use the familiar world to engage elementary school students in the study of literature, science, and the arts.[21] Soon after Cook County Normal School had become Chicago City Normal School, Parker outlined the core of his approach:

> The child in the primary school room is brought in contact with the elementary ideas underlying all truth. First through direct observation and subsequently by reading. . . . By giving thought, the art of expression, writing, making, modeling, drawing, painting, etc. are acquired. By the study of forms of life, real and conventional, geometry is begun; by measuring, weighing, uniting and separating objects of thought, the first steps in arithmetic are naturally taken. Thus the so-called branches of study which take up so much time and toil, are made necessary, auxiliary, accidental, and helpful in the study of the true objects of thought.[22]

No wonder John Dewey called Parker the "father of progressive education."[23]

Parker's brand of progressive education began with a focus on the child and the child's natural and growing curiosity about the world. But unlike some later—all too easily satirized child-centered progressives—Parker's progressivism never simply let the child's creative mind wander where it might. On the contrary, the teacher's job, as Parker saw it, was to link this young inquisitive mind directly with "the so-called branches of study" and to ensure that the child's interest in the world turned into an understanding of mathematics, botany, zoology, history, and so forth. Cultivating this sort of learning was no small task, and it required a teacher of high-caliber knowledge of all of these subjects as well as the pedagogical skill to lead young minds to this sort of engagement. Cook County/ Chicago City Normal was the premier place to prepare such teachers.

Parker constantly asked for more time in the preparation of teachers. There was so much to do. "There is no question, but that the fundamental cause of imperfect teaching is due to ignorance of the subjects to be taught, or that the abuse of text books is largely due to the same cause. And it is also true, that the mere study of methods, per se, can not be substituted for the deficiency in knowledge of subjects taught." Unless the teacher deeply understood the subjects to be taught, no real creative teaching could happen. On the other hand, there was a level of skill that was also essential. Future teachers needed to study psychology and what Parker called the science and art of education, and they also needed their own experience in practice teaching under strict supervision. Like Thomas Hunter, Francis Parker would not choose between content and methods. In the end, Parker pinned his hopes on bringing his students face-to-face with "the grave responsibilities and duties of the work which should be done in the school room." Like leaders of teachers' institutes three-quarters of a century before, Parker placed his ultimate hope in inspiring teachers, believing that the school would then arouse in its graduates "the incentives to determined effort in the right direction, as the deep feeling of personal responsibility."[24]

Parker retired from the school in 1899, but in that same year his goal of raising the standards began to show fruit as the school expanded its curriculum to a 2-year course after high school. In 1905 another famous Chicago progressive, Ella Flagg Young, became the principal and served until her election as the first woman superintendent of a large urban school system when she became Chicago's leader in 1909. Under Young's superintendence, the school was renamed the Chicago Normal College and in 1926 it expanded to a 3-year course. In 1938 the renamed Chicago Teachers College became an accredited degree-granting institution. Much later, in 1965, the school was transferred back to the state of Illinois and became the Illinois Teachers College: Chicago South, and then, as its academic programs diversified, it became Chicago State University in 1971. By then, like so many of its counterparts, not only in New York but in virtually every state of the union, the movement from normal school to teachers college to multipurpose college was complete. And, once again, the expanded opportunities for students also meant the marginalization of teacher education, no longer the primary purpose, not even a major purpose, of the institution of growing importance to the residents of the South Side of Chicago but of far less national importance in teacher education.[25]

Other cities also followed suit, although in each city the pattern was slightly different, depending on local conditions. The University of Cincinnati was officially chartered in 1819 to confer "all or any degrees usually conferred in any college or university in the United States," though in reality not much happened in Cincinnati until 1858 when a substantial bequest allowed the city to begin more substantial efforts. Late in the 19th century colleges of liberal arts, engineering, law, and medicine as well as a manual training high school became parts of Cincinnati's well-recognized municipal university. However, in Cincinnati it was only in 1905 that a college of education was added to the city university. Unlike the other constituent units, the university and the city board of education jointly governed the college of education until 1930, and its work was closely coordinated with the needs of Cincinnati's growing school system.

In Detroit the pattern was somewhat closer to New York City and Chicago, with teacher education gaining an early start. Detroit Teachers College traced its history to requests that the city's school superintendent, J. M. B. Sill, made in his annual report every year from 1864 to 1880. Finally in 1881, after 16 years of requests, the board agreed to support Sill in opening a class for new teachers more similar to a teachers' institute than a normal school. The program was expanded to two semesters in 1895, three semesters in 1904, and 2 full years in 1913. By 1914, when the new Normal School building opened, Detroit was offering future teachers a 2-year collegiate program that was also accepted by the University of Michigan, which granted its graduates junior standing at the university.

As in other places, Detroit's superintendents wanted further education for the teachers. In 1920 the superintendent recommended that "the name of the City Normal School be changed to Detroit Teachers College and that as soon as possible legislative action be secured empowering the college to offer 4-year courses and graduate work leading to appropriate degrees." The recommendation was accepted, and in 1921 the Detroit Teachers College was authorized to grant degrees. During the decade of the 1920s, also following the pattern in many state schools, the 2-year and then 3-year curricula were phased out, and starting in 1930 the only programs were those leading to the bachelor of arts in education and bachelor of science in education, while at the same time it expanded its affiliation with the College of the City of Detroit and after 1930 shared the same buildings.[26]

A similar pattern could be traced in a hundred other major U.S. cities. While there were many variations, the basic pattern was mostly the same. What began in the late 19th century as a series of high school–level courses for elementary or grammar school graduates who wanted to teach gradually expanded into a 2-year and then in time a 4-year postsecondary program leading to the baccalaureate degree and a teaching license at the same time. By 1930, while most cities still hired non–college graduates as teachers, most municipal colleges limited their own programs to those leading to a college degree. At the same time as New York City and Chicago, more and more of these municipal colleges became multipurpose institutions and, following the pattern of Chicago but not New York City, were transferred from city to state control. The result of all of these developments was a dramatic increase in the educational standards expected of future teachers, but also a loss of focus in the education offered to them as teaching became one among a dozen or more careers—and usually far from the most respected or well-paid one—for which the same college prepared its students.

THE KINDERGARTEN MOVEMENT
IN TEACHER EDUCATION

While public school leaders in cities like New York, Chicago, Cincinnati, and Detroit were creating their own high school and then college-level programs to prepare their own residents to be teachers, a very different group of people also came to focus on the preparation of a very different group of urban teachers. Equally concerned about raising the quality of education offered to the predominantly poor and immigrant children who made up city school students, a generation of philanthropic women created not only the kindergarten movement in the United States but also founded a national network of schools devoted to the preparation of kindergarten teachers.

As Barbara Beatty has noted, the kindergarten movement in the United States defined itself as over-against the public schools or, as Elizabeth Peabody said in her 1863 guide for kindergarten teachers, the kindergarten was "not the old-fashioned infant-school" nor was it a "primary school," but a community for young children to discover the world through play. While the kindergarten movement was also a Progressive-era reform and had much in common with the goals of other progressive educators like Francis Parker, the two movements also kept some distance from each other.

The kindergarten as it was first brought to the United States by Margarethe Meyer Schurz, wife of abolitionist and civil service reformer Carl Schurz, and then popularized by Elizabeth Peabody, Pauline Agassiz Shaw, and Lucy Wheelock, traced its origins to the educational romanticism of the French philosopher Jean-Jacques Rousseau, Swiss educator Johann Heinrich Pestalozzi, and most of all the German institution-builder Friedrich Froebel. In fact, Froebel's German kindergarten was a highly structured learning environment in which sequenced materials, including carefully designed blocks and activities along with opportunities in the arts and at play, were supposed to help expand children's lives. In the United States, Froebel's approach was followed quite literally at first but later more freely adapted to the American scene by a group of generally upper-class women, many veterans of the abolitionist and suffragist movements, who wanted to improve the lives of immigrants and take the edge off the pain of industrialization for the children of poor and working-class families.

Given the independence and critical approach of the kindergarten movement, the work of preparing kindergarten teachers fell almost completely outside the sphere of traditional normal schools and teachers colleges, especially public ones. The kindergarten reformers themselves simply started their own schools. Lucy Wheelock in Boston, Elizabeth Harrison in Chicago, and Maria Kraus-Boelte in New York City began offering classes until there was a similar school in most of the nation's major cities, many of which have emerged as small but important private colleges.[27]

The kindergarten movement always had something of an evangelical tinge to it. The psychologist G. Stanley Hall, who so admired Francis Parker, dismissed the kindergartners as people who practiced "Froebelolatry." One of Elizabeth Harrison's students remembered that studying with her "twas akin to getting religion," and the graduates felt "impelled to go out into the world with this new message of Friedrich Froebel and we were fired with the zeal and consecration of true missionaries."[28]

Elizabeth Harrison in Chicago, like Lucy Wheelock in Boston and many others, was both an evangelical missionary for a cause and shrewd institution-builders. Unlike some kindergarten advocates, Harrison herself did not have a great deal of money. But she had the good fortune to connect with others who did, especially Mrs. J. N. Crouse, who became the chief financial backer, co-associate principal with Harrison, and business manager of the school she founded. Harrison, it was always clear, was the chief teacher and guardian of the school's philosophy.

In her autobiography Elizabeth Harrison recalled that a large part of what brought her to the kindergarten movement was the dullness of her own education. Born in Davenport, Iowa, in 1849, she had a successful elementary and high school career but remembered that "Going to school was simply a duty that must be performed like the hanging up of my clothes or the making up of my bed." Her own ill health, and then that of her father, prevented her from attending college as she had planned, but eventually, in 1879, she was able to move to Chicago to study for 1 year in the school for kindergarten teachers managed by one of the pioneers of the kindergarten movement, Alice Harvey Putnam. At the end of that year, Putnam offered Harrison a job as her assistant. Further study with Susan Blow, who ran the only public school kindergarten at the time in St. Louis, and who would later lead the kindergarten program at Teachers College, Columbia, and then with the famed Maria Kraus-Boelte in New York City rounded out Harrison's education before she returned to Chicago and began her own lectures. At first Harrison simply offered instruction to any who were interested, but in the spring of 1885 Mrs. John N. Crouse attended one of Harrison's lectures, and within a very short time the two had agreed to launch their new school.[29]

What started as Miss Harrison's Training School in 1886 had by 1889 become the Chicago Kindergarten Training School and then in 1891 the Chicago Kindergarten College. By the 1897–1898 academic year it offered future kindergarten teachers multiple levels of preparation. Admission to all programs required "a good high school education, or its equivalent," and students had to be at least 18 years old to enroll. Students could take a 1-year course leading to a Freshman Certificate, since the school recognized that "a large number of women cannot plan in advance for so long a course of study and so wide an experience as is required to obtain a diploma," or they could continue for a second year for the Junior Certificate, while a third year of study led to a diploma and a fourth year to a Normal Diploma.

The curriculum was filled with references to "the gifts, games, occupations of the Kindergarten as taught by Froebel," and students were promised "talks and discussions on the practical carrying out of Froebel's method . . ." The more advanced normal course included more advanced "study of the

Froebelian theory," and students at this level were expected "to explain the true significance of the Kindergarten system to public audiences in order to acquire the clearness and confidence necessary to their future success." The course titles reflected the school's philosophy and included classes in Psychology, The Play Gifts of the Kindergarten, the Play Songs of the Kindergarten, Games, Drawing, and Color Work, but also the Philosophy of Literature, the Philosophy of Art and the Philosophy of History, Special Pedagogical Study of Method, and ample practice teaching. Froebel's birthday on April 21 was a major event at the school, parallel to the opening convocation in September and the presentation of certificates and diplomas in June. Here even more than at Cook County Normal under Francis Parker was an educational movement with a clear philosophical core and a sense of evangelical zeal.[30]

Like the high school and normal school programs with which it co-existed, Chicago's Kindergarten College also continued to raise its academic standards and the names of its degrees. Founded as Miss Harrison's Training School in 1886, the school changed its name yet again in 1912 when it affiliated with the National Kindergarten Association and became the National Kindergarten College. In the fall of 1916 it added a 2-year program for elementary teachers and in 1917 changed its name to the National Kindergarten and Elementary College. By that time the school was offering 2-, 3-, and 4-year diploma programs. Students who completed the 3-year program were eligible for teaching certificates in Illinois without further examination, and the four-year course led to a Bachelor of Education degree.[31]

Not surprisingly, expansion of the college did not stop with the addition of programs in elementary education or the new degree-granting authority. National prided itself on offering baccalaureate programs to teachers long before these were required, and so with the coming of the teacher surplus during the Great Depression, National graduates found jobs when others did not. The college was accredited in the 1940s, and after World War II National expanded what had been a large but informal continuing education program into a formally accredited graduate school that focused on improving teacher performance, offering courses to teachers who, according to the then-president, "wanted to become better teachers," but not necessarily "want to become theorists." By the 1970s the school was offering a Master of Arts in Teaching for liberal arts graduates who wanted to be teachers and a Master of Science in Education for current teachers.

In the 1970s National also moved into a wide-ranging set of extension programs. In 1984 it added doctoral programs in instructional leadership, reading, and school psychology. When the market for programs in education collapsed in the late 1970s and early 1980s, National responded by adding programs in whole new areas, first in allied health, applied behavioral sciences and human services, and then a separate School of Arts & Sciences, and finally in 1989 a College of Management and Business. In 1990 the name was changed to National-Louis University in recognition of the diversity of programs and the gift of a generous donor. The result of all of these changes and this growth was a diversification of programs and campuses that probably saved the school financially but certainly made clarity of purpose more difficult. The religious fervor with which every one of Elizabeth Harrison's graduates was expected to go out and change the world of young children could, at best, be one among many goals for the graduates of the school at the time of its centennial.[32]

The National story was repeated with slightly different details in many other places. Lucy Wheelock's school in Boston became Wheelock College, an institution that has retained more of its traditional focus on preparing teachers and people in related child-centered fields than many others. Wheelock's longtime cross-town rival, Edith Lesley, started Miss Lesley's School, an institution that has now expanded into Lesley University, a very large multipurpose institution with campuses across the country offering a wide range of educational opportunities. In New York Maria Kraus-Boelte's school did not continue but Lucy Sprague Mitchell, a later convert to the kindergarten movement, also much influenced by Maria Montessori, launched Bank Street College, a school that also continued to offer a curriculum for educators in a range of fields. Whether multipurpose like National-Louis and Lesley or smaller and more closely focused on education like Wheelock and Bank Street, these schools are all degree-granting colleges that decades ago shed any tradition of shorter curricula for aspiring teachers who could not devote more than a year or two to preparation. Any study of the history of teacher preparation in the United States would ignore them at its peril.

10

Every Teacher a College Graduate

1920–1965

In June 1955, just as the baby boom was at its peak and schools were bursting at the seams and in desperate need of more qualified teachers, 50-year-old Thelma Pairsh applied for an elementary teaching position in Albuquerque, New Mexico. Those responsible for staffing the schools must have been delighted. Her transcript included an A.B. degree from the New Mexico Normal University, as well as advanced work at the University of New Mexico at Albuquerque and institutes in California. She had taught successfully in elementary schools in the small town of Carrizzo, New Mexico, for 13 years. And in response to questions that would never be asked a half-century later, she reported that she regularly attended a house of worship, had no noticeable defect in sight, hearing, speech, or body, was married, and weighed 140 pounds.

A further examination of Pairsh's application reveals other characteristics of many who taught in the schools of the United States at mid-20th century. As Thelma Zuber before her marriage, she had attended high school in Las Vegas, New Mexico, from 1922 to 1926. She then enrolled at the then New Mexico Normal University in Las Vegas in the fall of 1926 and studied full-time for the 1926–1927 academic year. She took courses on and off in 1928 and 1929, studied full-time again in 1931–1932, took a few courses at the University of New Mexico at Albuquerque between 1932 and 1936, and finally completed the required coursework for graduation, including an Introduction to Philosophy course and courses in Principles and Practices of Teaching and Methods of Teaching, in the spring semester of 1939. Thirteen years after she began, Zuber received her degree with a major in Education and minors in Social Sciences and Spanish. She was hardly alone in this checkered university career. Through the years of the Great Depression, many Americans moved in and out of college as they could afford to and as other opportunities opened or closed for them. Given the fact that New Mexico was also many years away from requiring a college degree for elementary teachers, the young Zuber could easily have taken the state examinations, gained her license, and taught school during any of these years, although if she did she did not report it on her Albuquerque application.

The other interesting thing about Thelma Zuber's transcript is the fact that while she graduated from New Mexico Normal University in 1939, when the transcript was issued in 1942 the word *Normal* had a large black stamp across it, nearly blotting the word out. Above it, in large type, was the word *Highlands*. Following the rules of every registrar's office in the United States, everything else on the transcript was exactly as it had been at the time it was entered—the school had changed from percentage to a letter grading system and from a quarter to a semester system during her student years—but no effort was made to account for these changes on the transcript. But the name change of the university was a different matter. Already, a few months after the name had been changed, it was essential to blot out the word *normal* and replace it with the university's new and more respectable name. In this way, too, Thelma Zuber Pairsh's record reflected some of the major currents of the history of the preparation of teachers in the middle years of the 20th century.[1]

NORMAL SCHOOLS BECOME TEACHERS COLLEGES

As we saw in chapter 7, across the nation, as normal schools sought college status, they also became teachers *colleges* rather than *schools* of any sort. Different places made the shift at different times and in different ways. Sometimes the normal school followed the 1923 American Association of Teachers' Colleges recommendations and took on the attributes of a college—requiring a high school diploma for admission and offering a 4-year baccalaureate program—and then changed their name. In other cases, the normal school made the name change first and then tried desperately to live up to the academic standards implied in the college name.

In 1932 the state of Massachusetts declared that beginning in 1933, all of the state normal schools would become state teachers colleges. This change had long been in the works, and for some of the normal schools, such as Bridgewater, it was overdue recognition of changes that had already come about. As a result, in the fall of 1933, students returned to the century-old campus at Bridgewater but to a new academic institution, Bridgewater State Teachers College. As early as 1894, Massachusetts, the state that had founded the first normal schools in 1839, declared that thereafter none of the normal schools could admit a student who did not hold a high school diploma even though some Massachusetts schools would allow exceptions for years. This was quite a step for a state that 60 years earlier had offered a 1-year normal curriculum to common school or elementary school graduates. In these 60 years the starting point for normal school study had moved from something approximating a 9th-grade level to a postsecondary level. But more change was soon to come.[2]

Some of the pressure that led to the requirement of a high school diploma for admission to normal school came indirectly from the high school leaders themselves. Many high school leaders preferred to hire only university graduates to teach in high schools. In 1890 the high school masters of Massachusetts (as that state called its male high school teachers) called a conference "to consider founding a training school for high school teachers which would accept only college graduates." In that model, which was never implemented, high school teachers would earn a university degree and then add some postgraduate coursework in pedagogy at a new state institution to prepare for their lofty careers. It was a plan that would have offered both a high-level academic preparation for these teachers and, equally important to the high school masters, would have clearly differentiated high school teachers from their elementary sisters.

In 1915 Massachusetts high school masters began to study the growing movement toward junior high schools in some other states. They had reservations about the new kind of school, but most of all they worried about the need for additional "well-trained departmental teachers," a need that they felt the normal schools certainly could not fill.[3] At Bridgewater, the faculty responded quickly. Bridgewater had offered a small 4-year curriculum leading to a diploma for high school teachers since the latter part of the 19th century. Between 1918 and 1921, in response to the high school masters' study, the Bridgewater faculty also created a 4-year program for junior high school teachers. Chester R. Stacy, who led the effort at Bridgewater, was clear that "The four-year course should be entirely professional in its motive and those graduating from it should be granted a professional degree." By casting its lot with the movement for postsecondary programs, Bridgewater meant to claim the turf of preparing junior and senior high school teachers—a constituency they were not going to cede to the universities—and at the same time raise the status of their own school to a full collegiate level.[4]

While the faculty was focused on the curriculum and on matters of professional status, others in Massachusetts were focused on consolidating state government. In 1909 the state board of education took over complete control of the normal schools. The various boards of visitors for the schools were abolished, and the schools now reported to the state commissioner of education. The board and the commissioner then worked to standardize the offerings at the various normal schools. They outlined a plan by which all normal schools would offer a 2-year post–high school course for teachers of the first six grades and three of them—Bridgewater, Fitchburg, and Salem—would offer a 3-year course for teachers in grades 7 through 9. Between 1917 and 1921 the 4-year course and the focus on high schools was temporarily dropped from all of the normal schools. Such a rationalized and specialized approach to the state's need for teachers would not last long.[5]

In 1918 a special legislative commission recommended establishing one "State Normal College with the power of granting degrees." Rather than establish a new school, however, it seemed more logical to elevate one of the normal schools. Politics made it hard to select just one school and in 1921, five were given degree-granting authority, if not the collegiate name. Bridgewater and Worcester were authorized to offer a 4-year course leading to a Bachelor of Education degree for elementary, junior high, and senior high teachers beginning in 1921 (changed to a Bachelor of Science in Education in 1929). Framingham and Salem Normal Schools were authorized to offer degrees in limited subject areas and the Normal Art School in Boston to grant the degree in art education. Individuals earning a 2- or 3-year diploma from any of the other state normal schools could complete their degree at one of the five offering degrees.

The program grew slowly, with 2 candidates for the degree at Bridgewater in 1922, 6 in 1923, up to 54 in 1929, 60 in 1930, and a total of 109 in 1933, the last normal school graduation. Only one new faculty member was added at Bridgewater to accommodate the new programs, keeping happy those concerned with the cost of state institutions but giving ammunition to the critics who saw the new programs as expansions in time more than in quality.

While Bridgewater and some of the other Massachusetts normal schools were expanding the length of their programs and offering degrees, they were also seeking to eliminate the shorter programs. The 2-year elementary course was abolished in 1929; thereafter the minimum program was a 3-year course for elementary teachers. After 1935 Bridgewater limited admissions to those seeking a 4-year baccalaureate degree, whether in elementary teaching or any other field. By the mid-1930s, then, Bridgewater had already taken on nearly all of the attributes of a college-level program in terms of admissions, length of its curriculum, and offering academic degrees. As a catalog from the 1940s noted, the name change to Bridgewater State Teachers College was really recognition that these changes had already taken place and that "the needed prestige and the privilege of granting the degree [is] now considered essential to graduates."[6]

In nearby Pennsylvania, Keystone State Normal School in Kutztown became Kutztown State Teachers College in 1928, 5 years earlier than Bridgewater, but the route from normal school to state teachers college was quite different in Kutztown's case. Where Massachusetts allowed some normal schools, especially Bridgewater and Worcester, to take on more and more of the attributes of a college and then changed the names of all of the schools by state action, Pennsylvania made the name changes first, reflecting hopes ahead of realities.

The differences in the two states were rooted in the differing origins of normal schools. Where Massachusetts had created three state-controlled and state-funded normal schools in 1839 and 1840, Pennsylvania's normal school legislation of 1857 was simply permissive. The bill that authorized the schools was seen as "a visionary project," and no state funds were involved. Normal schools in Pennsylvania would be private or local affairs with a state blessing.

In 1866 a group of citizens in Kutztown, in the heart of the German-speaking region of Pennsylvania, came together to create a school to prepare local youth to teach in German-speaking schools of their isolated part of the state. One Keystone principal estimated that in 1872 "two-thirds of the students had an inadequate knowledge of English." But this was not necessarily a problem. After all, "well-trained Pennsylvania German teachers did more effective work in teaching Pennsylvania German children than non-German teachers could."[7]

As they entered the 20th century, most of Pennsylvania's normal schools were still private schools offering something equivalent to a high school education for future teachers. At the normal school at Kutztown, most students took the 2-year elementary course, and this course did not require a high school diploma for admission. In 1909 the school's superintendent defended the policy, saying that "it will be apparent that Pennsylvania is not ready to impose a four-year high school training as a condition for entering the normal school." Indeed, he feared such a requirement, for in his judgment, "Wherever this policy has been adopted, the normal schools have become ladies' schools to a large extent, the young men going to professional and technical schools which they can enter with the same preparation," and he was determined to attract men as well as women, future teachers and many others. Keeping the admission standards low, he could maintain a more healthy tuition income. The unfortunate by-product was a low standard for Pennsylvania's teachers.[8]

In 1911 the state of Pennsylvania started a slow process of acquiring the private normal schools. In November 1917, just after the United States had entered World War I on the side of England, the state acquired the German-language-speaking school in Kutztown and it became the Kutztown State Normal School. German was quickly exorcised from the curriculum. Pennsylvania's new Superintendent of Public Instruction, Thomas E. Finegan, also moved to consolidate the programs and elevate the status of the normal schools. He saw one of the key problems he faced as "the low standards set for beginning teachers and the closely related problem of low salaries, short minimum terms, poorly enforced attendance laws, inadequate state appropriations to the public schools and normal schools, and provisional certificates issued by the county superintendents." Finegan not only diagnosed the problems, he pushed for rapid change. In 1921, the Pennsylvania legislature adopted his recommendations to increase the length of the school year, increase teacher salaries, and require a minimum of 2 years of study beyond high school for all new teachers. The reform legislation also moved control of teacher certification from the county superintendents, who were famous for granting waivers, to the state department of education. Finally, the legislation provided badly needed state funds for the support of the now state normal schools.[9]

Superintendent Finegan used the new authority and the new funds to standardize the offerings at the state normal schools. A high school diploma was now expected for admission. Specialized programs were offered for future kindergarten, early elementary, more advanced elementary, junior high school, and rural teachers. While Massachusetts changed the name of all of its schools at one time, Pennsylvania reviewed each of the 14 schools separately. Kutztown received approval from the state council on education to make the name change in December 1926, and in May 1928 Kutztown State Teachers College awarded the first Bachelor of Science in elementary and junior high school teaching to four seniors.

Unfortunately for the new state teachers college, the change came with the onset of the Great Depression. Many in Pennsylvania argued against spending the money needed to offer future elementary teachers a 4-year college degree when a 2-year program had seemed sufficient in the past and colleges and universities had prepared the teachers for the high schools. One newspaper argued that "the Pennsylvania State Teachers Colleges were a product of the inflation of the 1920's when they acquired their fancy names while expanding in the 'grand manner.'" It would be a long time before Kutztown could reach the full potential that its new name seemed to indicate. As Karen Hallman has noted, "In Massachusetts the state normal schools had been granting degrees for eleven years before they changed their names. In Pennsylvania, the name change was one more change on top of many and it happened at a time when money was tight. . . . This transition did not come simply or quietly."[10]

In the segregated South, there were both similarities and differences in the story. Alabama State College in Montgomery, a segregated school preparing African American teachers, claims a special place in American history for its own reasons. At close to midnight on December 1, 1955, Jo Ann Robinson, a member of the faculty, and a few of her friends met in her college office. They pretended that they were working late grading papers, but they were really there for a very different reason. That afternoon, Rosa Parks had been arrested for refusing to give up her seat on the city's segregated buses. On that fateful night, Robinson and her colleagues drafted a leaflet that began:

> Another Negro woman has been arrested and thrown into jail because she refused to get up out of her seat on the bus and give it to a white person. . . . Until we do something to stop these arrests, they will continue. . . . We are, therefore, asking every Negro to stay off the buses on Monday in protest of the arrest and trial.

And with that leaflet, the Montgomery bus boycott entered the nation's history.[11]

The school where Robinson and her colleagues worked traced its roots to the creation of Lincoln Normal School in Marion, Perry County, Alabama, in 1867. Just 2 years after the end of the Civil War, black leaders in this county started their own school for the preparation of teachers. Like many of the small elementary-level schools that emerged immediately after Emancipation, Lincoln Normal School was initially a product of local black initiative. A year later, in 1868, the American Missionary Association took over the financing—and the management—of the school and sought further funds from the Freedman's Bureau and the "colored people of Alabama." In 1870, with Reconstruction still under way, the Alabama state legislature began support for the school. In 1871 Peyton Finley, the first black elected member of the State Board of Education, sought expanded state funding and petitioned the legislature to establish a "university for colored people," and in 1873 the state established the State Normal School and University for the Education of Colored Teachers and Students on the condition that the Lincoln school turn its facilities over to the state. The trustees agreed, and in 1874 the school became the first state-supported school for African Americans in the United States. More state funding and a move to Montgomery, Alabama, came in 1887 when the school was transformed into Alabama Colored People's University with a faculty of nine. At this point in history the distinctions between normal school, high school, college, and university were all still quite vague, in black and white schools. Nevertheless, the teacher education programs were, as in most universities, offered at the pre-college level.

In 1889 the school changed its name to the Normal School for Colored Students. On the eve of World War I it was one of only seven state normal schools serving African Americans in the South and the only one in the Deep South.[12] As chapter 6 has shown, the majority of African American teachers in the Jim Crow South were prepared at county training schools, missionary colleges, or institutes like Hampton and Tuskegee. But in Alabama there was a state normal school for blacks. John William Beverly, the school's first black president, took office in 1915, and he and his successors restructured it as a full 4-year teacher preparation high school and then added a 2-year junior college. In 1928 the school expanded to a 4-year college and granted its first degrees in 1931; as the State Teachers College, it awarded its first master's degree in 1943. Almost a decade before Robinson wrote her historic leaflet in the school's offices, it had also followed a national pattern and had dropped its *teachers college* name in 1948, first becoming Alabama State College for Negroes and then, in 1954, Alabama State College. This school in Montgomery, Alabama, had evolved from a school offering at best a high school–level education for a handful of future elementary teachers, to a normal school offering at least some college-level work, to a collegiate-level degree-granting institution for teachers in less than a century.[13]

SNAPSHOT—STATE TEACHERS COLLEGES DURING THE 1930–1931 ACADEMIC YEAR

During the 1930–1931 academic year Esther Marion Nelson visited a total of 57 state teachers colleges offering 4-year collegiate-level teacher preparation programs. The schools were in 27 different states and offered a cross-section of American teacher education from the San Diego and Santa Barbara State Colleges in California, to the Wisconsin State Teachers Colleges at Eau Claire, La Crosse, Milwaukee, Oshkosh, River Falls, and Superior, to four state teachers colleges in Pennsylvania, three in Tennessee, Alabama State Teachers College at Florence, Virginia State Teachers Colleges at East Radford, Farmville, and Fredericksburg, and the James Ormond Wilson Teachers College in Washington, D.C. What Nelson found was extraordinary variety.

While all of the 57 teachers colleges that she visited offered a 4-year program, she found that 80 percent of them also offered a 2-year program that met the standards for certification as an elementary teacher in that state. Indeed, of the 57 colleges, 46 offered a 2-year (or shorter) program leading to certification, 6 offered a 3-year program, and only 5 offered only the 4-year program. Clearly, while baccalaureate programs were available at nearly all teacher preparation schools by the 1930s, they were far from being the norm. Indeed, 2 years of study beyond high school remained much more popular for preparation for elementary teaching in most parts of the United States in spite of the more vaulted course offerings that were used by only a small minority of future elementary teachers.

Nelson also found great variety in the requirements for future teachers even within the 2-year and 4-year programs. She studied the requirements for student teaching and found such a great range that averages were almost meaningless. One college required only 60 hours of student teaching and another required 432 hours in its 2-year programs. The required hours of student teaching were generally more extended in the 4-year baccalaureate programs, but 10 percent required less than 120 hours while about half required more than 240 hours of student teaching at this level.[14]

Nelson also found much that bothered her in the teacher preparation programs. She praised teachers colleges for the effort to lengthen their elementary programs and to "make more nearly adequate provision for cultural background, well-rounded general education, the essential tools of learning, professionalization, technical skills, and a variety of social and physical activities." But she was not satisfied with the results. She noted that in "some teachers colleges many of the student-teachers had taken courses that were very restricted in outlook and narrow in scope; that were in no way related to the problems of modern life or to the current social trends . . ." Student teachers, she found, came to end of their preparation, in both 2- and 4-year programs, with inadequate general education and inadequate professional preparation. That the teachers colleges had failed to meet all of these challenges hardly made them unique in comparison to the more informal routes still in use by many in 1930.[15]

THE NATIONAL SURVEY OF THE
EDUCATION OF TEACHERS

While Nelson was examining the curriculum of state teachers colleges around the nation, the U.S. government conducted the most exhaustive study of all aspects of teacher education ever done in this country. Ever since Abraham Flexner published his famous *Medical Education in the United States and Canada* in 1910, people frustrated with the quality of teacher education had called for a "Flexner report" in that field. In fact there have been many such reports, at least one a generation for the past century. The Carnegie Foundation for the Advancement of Teaching, which had published Flexner's original report, also sponsored *The Professional Preparation of Teachers for American Public Schools* in 1920, a report described in chapter 7 that focused on the state of Missouri but whose authors happily made national recommendations. In 1916 Abraham Flexner himself, along with Frank P. Bachman, published *Public Education in Maryland*, a study they had conducted that examined the preparation and work life of teachers in the schools of that state. Former Harvard president James Bryant Conant's *The Education of American Teachers* was, with Carnegie support, supposed to be the Flexner report of the 1960s. The list continues.[16]

In reality, however, the *National Survey of the Education of Teachers*, published as a series of six volumes by the federal government through the early 1930s, represented a far more thorough study of teacher education than Flexner's highly subjective though very influential 1910 study of medical education could possibly match. Early in the Great Depression, the 71st Congress authorized a study of "the qualifications of teachers in the public schools, the supply of available teachers, the facilities available and needed for teacher training, including courses of study and methods of teaching." The result was a 3-year study led by E. S. Evenden of Teachers College, Columbia. Those who call for a "Flexner Report on teacher preparation" need look no further than the *National Survey* for a report far more thorough if less opinionated than Flexner's more famous study of medical schools.[17]

The authors of this Depression-era study were fairly clear on what a reasonable standard of preparation for a teacher looked like. They acknowledged that standards had traditionally been low. "Even at the turn of the present century many States were admitting prospective teachers who had finished the eighth-grade work to 1- and 2-year courses in normal schools, the completion of which entitled them to some form of teacher certification. Less than a decade ago [that is, during the 1920s] half of the States, representing all sections of the country, were preparing teachers in secondary schools." But while in 1900 8th grade or 8th grade plus 1 or 2 years of high school–level study were considered sufficient for teaching and in the 1920s half the states still considered a high school–level normal program to be sufficient, by the 1930s these authors wanted a higher standard. "Since the period immediately following the World War [World War I]," they wrote, "it has been generally accepted that the desirable minimum of educational preparation for elementary teachers was 2 years beyond the completion of high school while the desirable minimum for secondary teachers was 4 years of college work." This was the minimum that some schools happily exceeded with their baccalaureate degrees. On the other hand, it was a minimum that was not met by at least a quarter of the nation's teachers.

While in 1935 they could advocate for a standard of at least 2 years of true college-level, postsecondary education for elementary teachers and a baccalaureate degree for high school teachers, the authors of the Office of Education report understood that though progress had been made, there were still many teachers who needed much more preparation to meet this standard. The *National Survey of the Education of Teachers* found that in 1930 approximately half of the nation's elementary school teachers did have the 2 years of college minimum, another quarter had surpassed the standard, and another quarter (26.2%) had less than the minimally acceptable level of preparation. The quarter of the people in the teaching profession whom the study's authors deemed as underprepared—sometimes greatly underprepared—were also not evenly distributed around the nation. The urban-rural split remained especially serious. While both small-town and city teachers had more preparation, more than 60 percent of the teachers in what were called "open country" one- and two-teacher schools reported less than the 2 years of college-level preparation. But across all parts of the country and from big cities to the most rural schools, only one elementary teacher in eight had a college degree. For secondary teachers the numbers were more encouraging, although almost 40 percent of junior high school teachers and 12.9 percent of senior high school teachers still needed further study to complete their baccalaureate degrees.[18]

The authors of the *National Survey* offered a thoughtful reflection on the standard assumption that the Great Depression—which was fully under way as they wrote—allowed states to raise the standards for teaching, as people who lost jobs in other areas were attracted to the work. While they acknowledged that this was partly true, there were two problems with the conclusion. First, the success of teacher education programs, normal schools, municipal programs, and college and university departments had created an oversupply of teachers in the United States by the mid-1920s, well before the stock market crash and the beginnings of high unemployment in other fields that accompanied a national depression. And second, the report's authors bemoaned the fact that too often the usual response to an oversupply of teachers was not necessarily an increase in standards but rather "a lowering of salaries until some of the surplus teachers withdraw from the profession or the teacher market." This latter option was especially appealing to many cash-strapped cities and towns in the midst of the Depression, and the authors saw the danger that even in the midst of the worst economic times, the result could be that "the more ambitious and able 'prospects' for the profession enter more promising fields of work." Much as they might speculate about that issue, other indicators of rising standards for new teachers were coming into sharp focus.

The evidence for an increase in the minimum standards for becoming a teacher between 1920 and 1930 was clear. In 1921, 30 of the 48 states had no definite requirement for teachers, while by 1926 that number had dropped to 15 and by 1930 to 12. On the other hand, in 1921 14 states had required simply a high school diploma in order to teach but in 1926 in only 6 states was this sufficient and in 1930 only in 5. At the highest level in 1921 no state required as much of 2 years of education beyond high school, the minimum education that the authors of the report wanted to see established, but in 1926 four states required at least 2 years beyond high school and in 1930 seven states required either 2 or 3 years beyond high school. The trend was clear, though at the time of report not a single state required a college degree for elementary teachers. The researchers also happily found that by 1930, 31 states had separate requirements for high school teaching and most of these states required a college degree for high school, while almost half, 21 states, required some specific combination of courses in an academic discipline and in education for high school teachers.[19]

One very valuable feature of the *National Survey* is the fact that an entire volume is devoted to "The Education of Negro Teachers." In prior reports, indeed in too many subsequent reports, the pattern of the 1920 Carnegie study of Missouri, which saw the education of African American teachers as "outside the scope of the report," remained the norm. The *National Survey* did not fall into the trap of surveying only white teachers. Its volume, written by Ambrose Caliver, Senior Specialist in the Education of Negroes in the U.S. Office of Education, is indeed a significant exception. In 1930 there were almost 12 million African Americans, about one-tenth of the nation's population, and 80 percent of these still lived in 16 southern states and the District of Columbia, with their children generally attending legally segregated public schools. The report began by noting the extraordinary educational gains achieved by African Americans in the previous 70 years. At the time of the Civil War not more than 5 to 10 percent of African Americans could read and write, but by 1930 illiteracy had been cut to 16 percent. In 1865 2 percent of newly freed slaves were in school, but in 1930, 78 percent of African Americans attended school for at least some period of time.

Beginning with these accomplishments, Caliver turned to the stark reality faced by African American students and their teachers in Jim Crow and Depression-era America. Comparing African American and European American teachers, the researchers found that in the segregated schools of the South some 22.5 percent of black teachers but only 5.7 percent of white teachers had a high school diploma or less. There was less discrepancy at the other end of the spectrum, where 20.7 percent of black teachers and only 25.7 percent of white teachers had completed 3 or more years of college. Only 1.1 percent of black teachers and 1.9 percent of white teachers had attended graduate school, hardly a meaningful difference nor one that would impact the education of many students of any race. The greatest discrepancies in education were found in teachers in one- or two-room rural schools, called open country schools, where only 4.5 percent of the white teachers but 35.8 percent of the black teachers had a high school diploma or less. The report also examined the curricula of the county training schools, high schools, and colleges offering teacher preparation programs and found many wanting.

Far greater than the disparities in preparation were the differences in salaries, where, across the South, the report found that white teachers were paid more—much more—than black teachers. In Alabama the median annual salary for white women teachers was $425 while the median for black teachers—females and males—was $253.69. In Georgia the median white woman's salary was $670, the median for blacks $453.

In the end, the report recommended that "Teacher-preparing institutions for Negroes should raise their entrance requirements making them more selective," and "More uniformity should exist in curricula for the education of Negro teachers in the amount of work required, the courses prescribed, and their sequence, content and methods." The authors also recognized that if separate and equal was to be equal, then very far-reaching changes were needed across the educational spectrum, concluding:

> Equalization of educational opportunity applies to all levels of education. Teacher-preparing facilities for Negroes cannot be equalized without first equalizing the elementary- and high-school facilities for Negroes. It is urgently recommended that all possible effort be made to hasten the improvement of education for Negroes at all levels.

While serious attention to implementing this obvious recommendation is impossible to find, the Caliver report is by far the most thorough study of African American teacher education prior to the civil rights era.[20]

TEACHERS COLLEGES BECOME "JUST COLLEGES"

The state teachers colleges that virtually replaced all of the nation's normal schools in the 1920s were a relatively short-lived phenomenon in American higher education. In 1960 Bridgewater State Teachers College became Bridgewater State College. It had been Bridgewater Normal School for more than 90 years, but a state teachers college for only less than 30. In the same year, 1960, Kutztown changed its name to Kutztown State College and then in 1983 to Kutztown University of Pennsylvania, following the pattern of most of the Pennsylvania schools. Alabama school for African American teachers had more name changes, though they pointed in the same direction. It had become the State Teachers College in 1929, the Alabama State College for Negroes in 1948, the Alabama State College in 1954, and finally Alabama State University in 1969. And earlier, in 1941, the New Mexico state legislature renamed the New Mexico Normal University the New Mexico Highlands University, an all-purpose university thriving today as one of the strongest multipurpose Latino campuses in the United States.

Between 1941 in New Mexico, 1948 in Alabama, and 1960 in Pennsylvania and Massachusetts, each of these schools dropped the word *teachers* or *normal* from its name. By 1940 virtually the last normal school had become a state teachers college, and within 20 years another even more significant change had taken place as the last of the state teachers colleges took on various names as state colleges or regional state universities, indicating a shift from a more or less single-minded focus on teacher education to being a multipurpose university serving a wide range of students with many different programs, and far too often marginalizing teacher education as not only one among many parts of their mission but one that was far from the top of the priority list.[21]

While the move from state normal school to state teachers college was not without controversy, it was a change of status but not a change of direction. This was not surprising because in the 1920s many used the names *normal school* and *teachers college* interchangeably. As high schools became more widespread and normal schools were able to build on rather than duplicate their work, and as more students—even if not a majority—were willing to stay long enough at these now college-level institutions, it was not surprising that the schools sought the status they felt was their due and changed their name to *teachers college.*

Something quite different took place in the 1940s and 1950s. The move from teachers college to college was not just a logical extension of long-term developments. It was, on the contrary, a radical break with the past and a turn in a quite different direction. In 1920 the Carnegie Foundation for the Advancement of Teaching put its prestige behind a recommendation that "It should be considered as a fundamental principle that state-supported agencies for preparing teachers should devote themselves exclusively and without reserve to that task."[22] The Carnegie reporters did not have a preference as to whether the institutions called themselves normal schools or teachers colleges as long as they met collegiate-level standards, but they were clear that they should not be diverted from the preparation of teachers by taking on other tasks.

While they challenged the normal schools to use the same standards to judge their work that were being used at the flagship state university in Missouri, William S. Learned and William C. Bagley were dismissive of the movement prevalent in normal schools to become all-purpose institutions for their region of the state. They noted the 1909 catalog of one that said, "It cannot be denied that the Normal School comes nearer the people than other schools and may therefore be justly called the People's College," while another announced, "The Normal School has a larger mission in Southeast Missouri than that of a state college for teachers." Learned and Bagley disliked such talk and such plans. It was their conclusion that "institutions established by the state to prepare teachers as public servants for its schools should make that business their sole purpose and concern." Anything else was a dangerous diversion, and "no consideration whatever should divert such schools from their task." It was a clear conclusion and a losing proposition.[23]

As strongly as many argued for a separate single-purpose institution for the preparation of teachers, such single-purpose schools virtually disappeared from the American scene in the decade after World War II. In 1935 the state of California, which had renamed its State Normal Schools State Teachers Colleges, changed the name yet again. Humboldt State Teachers College became Humboldt State College, San Jose State Teachers College became San Jose State College, and so on down the coast to San Diego, where the school's name was now San Diego State College. (A final rise in status came in 1972 when all of these schools became state universities, but by then their teacher preparation past had long been marginalized.) In this, as in many other things, where California led, the nation followed.

While California made the move in 1935, many other states waited until after World War II. Christine Ogren reported these changes. Arizona's old normal schools at Flagstaff and Tempe became Northern State College and Arizona State College, respectively, in 1945. In Texas different schools changed their names at different times. North State Teachers College in Denton and West State Teachers College in Canyon, both of which had been elevated from normal schools in 1923, became North State College and West State College in 1949, while Lyndon Johnson's alma mater, Southwest State Teachers College, became Southwest State College in 1959. North Carolina reflected great diversity as schools shifted in name between 1951 and 1967. One segregated white school, East Carolina State Teachers College in Greenville, became East Carolina College in 1951, while in Boone Appalachian State Teachers College became Appalachian State University only in 1967. Indiana, one of the last, changed the name of Ball State Teachers College to Ball State University and the State Teachers College in Terre Haute to Indiana State University in 1965. Indiana's eastern neighbor had been among the first to make the shift when Kent State Normal College had become Kent State College and Bowling Green State Normal College had become Bowling Green State College in 1929, and both were promoted to university status in 1935.[24]

Between the 1920s when the movement began and 1965 when it was complete, however, something very substantial had happened in the preparation of American teachers. For 100 years large numbers of the elite of the nation's elementary teachers, and a good number of high school teachers, had been educated in institutions dedicated primarily, if not exclusively, to the preparation of educators. After 1965 virtually no future teachers received such an education. For better or worse, future teachers were now prepared in schools, colleges, or departments of education in large multipurpose colleges and universities. Whether the origin of these universities was as a normal school or a research university, after 1965 virtually nowhere was teacher education the prime mission of the schools that prepared the nation's teachers.

Looking at these changes in teacher education in 1990, John Goodlad wrote, "It was not uncommon for academic administrators to view the decline of teacher education on their campuses virtually as evidence of a rite of passage signifying a coming of age for their institutions."[25] Certainly the change in name from teachers college to just "college" or perhaps to a regional university represented a clear and deliberate decision by the college officials and the state legislatures that held not only their purse strings but often much greater control of their institutional directions, to reject the Carnegie recommendation and move toward being what many of them had already become— multipurpose institutions in which teacher preparation was but one of many aspects of the mission of the school. Almost without exception, teacher preparation suffered as a result.

The reason most commonly given for the shift from teachers college to multipurpose college was the impact of the post–World War II GI Bill that sent thousands of recent veterans back to college campuses in the late 1940s and early 1950s. Certainly the state colleges and regional universities welcomed these students and the federal tuition dollars that they brought with them, and opportunity in American society was vastly expanded for one segment of the population because of this federal program. But the dates of the changes would indicate that the reasons for the shift were far more complex than anything that could be explained by the GI Bill alone. William Learned and William C. Bagley published their report warning against such a movement in 1920. California and Ohio, among others, had changed the name and mission of their schools in the mid-1930s, long before a promise of new benefits for veterans was on anyone's mind. On the other hand, many other states—Indiana, North Carolina, Pennsylvania, and Massachusetts, among others—were changing institutional names and purposes long after the influx of war veterans was a distant memory. Much more was going on in American teacher education.

Karen Hallman has argued convincingly that the Soviet launch of Sputnik in 1957 and the subsequent National Defense Education Act of 1958 must be considered if one is to understand the shift in institutional names and public resources from preparing teachers to preparing a more diverse population, especially scientists and engineers as well as other cold warriors. Certainly if one looks at the expansion of programs in science and mathematics at the new Bridgewater State College or the programs in foreign languages at Kutztown State College, which established its modern languages department the year it became a full-scale college, there is ample evidence for such a conclusion.[26]

In the end, however, David Riesman probably explained the change best, though he did not specifically attend to it. In his brilliant *Constraint and Variety in American Higher Education*, Riesman wrote of the "institutional homogenization" that was overtaking American higher education. The perhaps unintended result of a process that had begun in the early 1900s, as some leading universities and philanthropic agencies sought to raise standards and clarify terms for what it meant for a school to call itself a college or a university, as opposed to an academy, high school, or normal school, and to accredit those that truly fit the mold, had also set off a never-ending struggle by virtually all higher education institutions to not only meet the new standards but to do so in a way that would put them at the top of a new pecking order. At the time when Riesman wrote his book, when the process of shifting from teachers college to college was still under way, Riesman himself was clear that while the procession was long, at its lower end were such institutions as technical schools and teachers colleges, which he said were "colleges only by grace of semantic generosity." No college wanted to retain that status. No president wanted to lead a school at the end of the procession. And no route to advancement seemed faster than jettisoning the much-maligned "teachers" part of the teachers college name. That it took until the middle of the 1960s to complete the process may be the only surprise.[27]

A COLLEGE DEGREE BECOMES THE NORM

While the normal schools were becoming teachers colleges and the teachers colleges were dropping word "teachers" as quickly as possible, another parallel development was changing the options available to those who wanted to be teachers in the elementary and secondary schools of the United States. In the century between 1830 and 1930 the requirements for a teaching job had generally increased from completion of the level of school in which one wanted to teach, to some or all of a high school-level program, to 2 or 3 years beyond high school. As late as the early 1920s, when a post–World War I teacher shortage forced school districts to lower standards or, as Michael Sedlak put it, "to round up someone to sit in each classroom," several surveys found that of the nation's 600,000 teachers perhaps 30,000 or 5 percent had no schooling beyond 8th grade, while, perhaps even more troubling, some 300,000 or half of the nation's teachers had no more than a high school education. Against this standard, the *National Survey* was reporting significant progress when its researchers found that in 1930 some three-quarters of the nation's teachers had at least 2 years of education beyond high school. The selectivity that the Depression of the 1930s allowed school districts accounted for part of this difference from the days of the desperate shortage of teachers that the nation experienced in 1920. But standards had been rising rapidly through the decade of the 1920s; states had taken a stronger role in setting minimum educational qualifications for all teachers; and equally important, a variety of programs in major universities, municipal colleges, and state teachers colleges were being revised to offer more opportunity to those who wanted more study.

Nevertheless, the *National Survey of the Education of Teachers* researchers who called for a floor of 2 years beyond college in 1930 would have been amazed to look ahead and learn that between 1930 and the late 1950s the standard moved from a goal of 2 years of college-level study prior to beginning a teaching career to an almost universal requirement across the United States, in urban and rural areas, and rich and poor states, that every teacher, virtually without exception, was expected to have a college degree. In 1937 five states already required a college degree for elementary teaching where none had done so in 1926. In 1940, 11 states required a college degree for elementary certification, by 1950 the number had risen to 21 or almost half of the then–48 states, and by 1964 46 of the 50 states required a bachelor's degree of all new teachers. The high school standard had been set earlier, since in 1940 40 states already required a college degree for secondary teaching and by 1960 it was all 50 states. What would have pleased the authors of the *National Survey of the Education of Teachers* in the early 1930s—a preparation program that included high school and 2 years of college-level study—was by the 1950s far below the minimum requirement for licensure in any state of the union.[28]

Michael W. Sedlak has traced one essential piece in the dramatic rise in the educational qualifications—as measured in years of schooling and academic degrees demanded—for a teaching position that occurred in nearly all parts of the United States in the 30 years prior to 1965. An understanding of these changes is essential to any meaningful analysis of the role of various programs for the preparation of teachers. In Sedlak's story, "Up through the mid-nineteenth century, recruiting and hiring teachers was almost entirely a private, negotiated procedure which occurred between someone with authority to employ and pay a teacher, and someone willing to accept whatever instructional—and maintenance—responsibilities were wanted." As a result, local school board representatives might give preference to a teacher who had studied for a shorter or longer period of time in a normal school, or a high school that offered a normal curriculum, they might prefer someone with experience or who had attended a teachers' institute, but in the end they also might not care, might not be able to find someone who had met that standard, or might have a relative who needed a job.

After the mid-1800s states did begin to set *some* standards, most of all by creating county superintendents and vesting these officers with authority over granting teaching certificates and by instituting various forms of state examinations for teachers. As the case study of New Mexico's certification examinations and standards will show, these state standards offered a fairly low minimum threshold for entry into the profession, but they did encourage some level of study to meet at least the minimum—often through a teachers' institute—and they also offered some limited rewards—often in the form of a certificate that lasted longer or could be renewed more times without further study or examination—for those who met a higher threshold of preparation. Nevertheless, in this era, while completing high school, a normal school, or even a university program could yield one a higher-level certificate or prepare one more effectively for the state and local exams, there were certainly no minimally effective standards in terms of basic preparation in effect in most parts of the United States.

The situation started to change further in the 1920s as "the vast majority of states" began rejecting "examinations in favor of evidence of educational attainment for certification." Such moves allowed states, for the first time, to start to enforce actual standards for a minimum educational preparation for teaching, be that minimum the high school diploma or some level of normal school or college study.

The U.S. Office of Education's Benjamin Frazier summarized the new consensus in 1938, writing that the "best interests of American childhood demand that certification of teachers be based on something more substantial than mere success in passing an examination." By that time, few disagreed. According to Frazier's study, at the start of the school year in September 1937, 28 states certified teachers based solely on credits or credentials issued by academic institutions, while the remaining 20 states used some sort of mix of examinations and credentials. A few, such as Massachusetts, still left local school committees to make nearly all of the certification decisions, but by 1937 most states had taken on this responsibility.[29]

This new level of state control of teacher certification was coming into force at the same time that the range of teacher preparation programs across the country was being narrowed. Thus Sedlak concluded,

> The variety of institutions entitled to offer legitimate professional education gradually narrowed as collegiate-level programs eclipsed the two year normal schools as the dominant preparatory model . . . By the early 1930s, as a consequence, virtually all states required four years of college for secondary certification, and a rapidly growing number required it for elementary teachers as well.[30]

The national norm that a college degree represented the minimum for any teaching job that reigned from the late 1950s onward was thus well launched as the only possible direction by the 1930s. If states could set the standard for every new teacher a local school or district wanted to hire, and by the 1930s nearly all of the states did that, it was easy enough for the states to raise the requirement to include a B.A. or B.S. degree, and by 1960 they were all well on their way to doing that also.

The state of New Mexico represents a useful case study of Sedlak's three stages, as it did for the interplay of teachers' institutes and certification examinations reported in chapter 4. States moved from complete local autonomy to some level of state oversight, primarily through state examinations, to minimum state educational requirements that eventually came to include a college degree. Each state also moved through the stages somewhat differently, and often the new requirements were phased in slowly even as older ones disappeared, sometimes even more slowly. Thus, while the national generalizations are useful, so is a look at the unique characteristics that can be found by more careful examination of a case study.

As we saw in chapter 4, New Mexico's first Superintendent of Public Instruction, Amando Chaves, moved quickly after his appointment in 1891 to begin to create a unified territorial system of education and to improve the standards for teachers in the territory, demanding that county superintendents conduct oral examinations and launching three normal schools, two within 2 years of his appointment.[31]

The next logical step came in 1898 when a new superintendent of public instruction proposed the creation of a board of territorial examiners so that the examination questions would not simply be left to the imagination of the county superintendents. Three years later, in 1901, the examination process had moved from oral examinations administered by the county superintendent to written examinations issued twice a year by the territorial board of education.[32]

A first tentative step toward the final stage in Sedlak's schema came to New Mexico in 1905 when the territorial legislature gave the Board of Education authority to issue territorial teachers certificates, which were meant to be a cut above the county certificates earned by the examinations. Territorial certification required graduation from one of New Mexico's normal schools or holding a diploma from a normal school or a college in another part of the United States, a prize that they hoped would encourage immigration of qualified teachers to New Mexico. Here was an important beginning, if only a beginning, of a move from licensure by examination to licensure by academic credential. In January 1908 a total of 48 teachers held territorial certificates based on academic accomplishments, while 564 teachers, over 10 times as many, held county certificates based solely on examinations.[33] It would be a long time before the majority of New Mexican teachers would reach the higher standard.

In his annual report for Taos County for 1910, a report typical of many that came to the territorial board from the county superintendents, the Taos leader complained, "The teachers of the county are of excellent moral worth, but, unfortunately, many of them do not have proper school advantages and preparation for the teacher's work." Complicating the work in Taos and most of New Mexico was the need to find teachers who could communicate with students whose native language was Spanish.[34]

In 1923 two changes in the certification laws were made. From then on all the certificates would be given by the state (New Mexico had become a state in 1912), even those based on examination scores, and not by the different counties. High school certification was also separated from elementary, and having all of its teachers be certified became a requirement for any high school seeking accreditation.

During the Great Depression, in June 1932, the state joined the list of states—more than half in the mid-1930s—that made certificates conditional on educational attainment, not examinations. The minimal certificate now required a high school diploma and 6 semester hours of college credit, while higher-level certificates required a high school diploma and 2 full years of college work—the minimum asked for by the *National Survey*. High school teachers needed at least 135 academic credits, essentially 3 years of college, and they needed a B.A. for the highest-level certificate.

Georgia Lusk, the long-serving state superintendent, proudly reported the changes that had come in the educational qualifications of New Mexico's teachers. In the 1924–1925 academic year, 909 of the state's 2,923 teachers, or 31 percent, had less than a high school diploma. In the 1931–1932 year that number had dropped to 293 out of 3,738 teachers, or 8 percent. On the other hand, in 1924–1925 only 12 percent of the state's teachers had been college graduates, while in 1931–1932 25 percent of the teachers had a college degree. The numbers would keep getting better. By 1934, 312 of the new certificates granted were high school certificates for college graduates, and the majority of the elementary certificates, 794 out of a total of 1,168, were of a grade that required at least 2 years of college. With more than half of its teachers having more than 2 years of college education, by 1932 New Mexico ranked quite well in terms of the national averages reported by the *National Survey of the Education of Teachers*.[35]

World War II temporarily slowed the effort to raise the academic standards for teachers in New Mexico, as elsewhere. As late as the fall of 1940, standards were still rising. In that year all new teachers were required to have a minimum of 2 years of college training, and all high school teachers had to have a college degree. But the war created a new crisis-level shortage of teachers. A new certificate was created: "To meet the critical shortage of teachers during the biennium, War Emergency Certificates were issued on a temporary basis." At first, during the 1942–1943 year, War Emergency certificates required high school graduation and 30 semester hours (1 year) of college and a request from the school district. By the 1943–1944 year the rules were broadened in shortage areas. And in addition, Substitute and Permit certificates could be issued "when a regularly qualified teacher could not be found." In the war emergency, as in earlier emergencies of the beginning of the century, if a qualified teacher could not be found, someone who could cover the classroom would be. In the face of a real shortage, those who hire teachers have always lowered the standards when all else failed. War Emergency certificates would continue to be issued in New Mexico well into the early 1950s. If only on a temporary basis, many of the stricter standards of the 1930s seemed to slip away for the wartime and immediate postwar era.[36]

Nevertheless, a statewide review of the credentials of all teachers in New Mexico who were actually teaching, as opposed to those who were certified to teach, in 1948–1949 found that of 1,515 teachers, 693 held a B.A., 59 held an M.A., and 2 held a Ph.D., meaning that almost half of the teachers held a college degree. Of those who did not hold a degree, most had 3 years of college, and only 128 or 8 percent had less than 2 years of college. Reality was overtaking the rules in a way that gratified many, though the divide between more urban schools, where the B.A. was now the norm among elementary as well as high school teachers, and the isolated rural areas, where a college educated teacher was much less common, persisted well into the 1950s.[37]

A final step in teacher certification came to New Mexico in 1956. As of July 1, 1956, a new set of regulations that had been formulated by the New Mexico Commission on Teacher Education and Professional Standards went into effect. For new teachers, the college degree was no longer optional but the only route to a teaching career. Teachers who held earlier certificates would be allowed to continue to renew them, but for new entrants college was *the* way. The Division of Teacher Certification that had begun in 1949 was also growing in strength. By the mid-1950s this office was no longer simply soliciting teachers' opinions and offering advice to the teacher preparation programs. The staff of the office saw certification as a state function and saw themselves as an essential link in the chain that also included accreditation of individual colleges and universities as the key to quality teachers. For the modern teacher or teacher educator, the regulations in place in New Mexico after 1956 would be familiar in terms of both the academic qualifications expected of individual teachers and in terms of the role of the state in assuring that all teachers met those qualifications in a way that the procedures of any earlier decade would not. After 1956 the "one best system" in which a college education was the only acceptable route to a teacher certificate was firmly in place. This was the norm for teacher preparation in the United States for the second half of the 20th century as it had not been before or might not be in the future.[38]

It is important to remember that given the length of many professional careers, it takes decades before a requirement to *enter* the profession becomes universal *within* the profession. In the early 1960s, when every state had already required a college degree, most for a decade or more, 15 percent of the nation's teachers still did not hold a college degree. That number then dropped steadily for the next two decades. On the other hand, as a college degree became the minimum requirement, more and more teachers sought graduate degrees, in part to qualify for increasingly popular salary boosts based on such degrees, and perhaps also to set themselves off from those who merely met the new professional minimum or to achieve higher levels of certification. Perhaps these teachers also simply wanted to improve the knowledge base for their practice of their profession. Table 10.1, adapted from a 1987 National Education Association report, summarizes the changes in education levels of teachers once a college degree became a requirement. (Note that the chart indicates the highest degree held. Thus, as more teachers earned graduate degrees, the percentage for whom the bachelor's was the minimum decreased even as the standards rose.)[39] Something very significant had happened to the educational standards for teachers. Although no state actually required a master's degree in order to begin teaching, by 1986 half of the nation's teachers held the degree. Even more significant, by 1986 less than one-half of 1 percent of the nation's teacher had not graduated from college.

Two significant trends had transformed the ways in which teachers were prepared in the decades between the late 1930s and the 1960s. On the one hand, not only the normal schools but also the teachers colleges had disappeared. With rare exceptions, the places where teachers were taught—to use John Goodlad's felicitous phrase—were in schools, colleges, and departments of education that existed within the context of much larger multipurpose colleges and universities. Whether those colleges and universities had emerged from a normal school past or had only recently added education to the curriculum mattered far less than the role of the teacher education program as one among many units of the institution of higher education. And during the same decades, virtually all of the states had moved to require a college degree for those who would enter teaching. The college degree was also becoming highly regulated. States had started adding requirements—a major in a subject and a certain number of professional courses for high school teachers—in the 1940s and by the 1950s had a state bureaucracy that worked with the colleges and universities making recommendations and, soon enough, adding requirements to the curriculum for teachers. The college degree that a teacher needed to have in the 1950s and beyond came from a unit of a larger university, but state education department standards governed the nature of that degree. It was a situation that easily led to a clash of cultures.

Table 10.1. Changes in Education Levels, 1961–1986

Highest degree held	1961	1966	1971	1976	1981	1986
Less than a bachelor's degree	14.6	7	2.9	0.9	0.4	0.3
Bachelor's degree	61.9	69.6	69.6	61.6	50.1	48.31
Master's degree or 6 years	23.1	23.2	27.1	37.1	49.3	50.7
Doctorate	0.4	0.1	0.4	0.4	0.3	0.7

11

A New Status Quo and Its Critics

1960–1985

Judy Logan spent her career as a high school teacher in San Francisco. She remembered her preparation vividly. By the time Logan began her formal preparation for teaching in 1965 the rules and the opportunities were different than they had been for previous generations of aspiring teachers. By the early 1960s when Logan was in college, the route to teaching—the only route—included a college degree, a reality that had not been the case in many states even a decade before.

Logan's interest in teaching began early. She remembered that although her parents had not attended college, "Somehow my parents conveyed to me that there was no question but that I would go to college and, in my mind, there was never a question that I would grow up to be a teacher." The inspiration for college came from her parents' ambition for a better life for their daughter. The daughter's inspiration for teaching came from experience. Logan was clear: "Since second grade, when I fell in love with the kindness of my instructor, Miss Miles, I had wanted to be a teacher." Even as a child, Logan also had a pretty clear sense of the options available to women in postwar Eisenhower America. "In the 1950s, this was the best career I could imagine for myself. Teaching was a traditional woman's profession at that time, but in my family it was still traditional for a woman to be a homemaker."

Logan attended San Francisco State College but did not take the education courses that the school offered, indeed, that it had been founded to offer. But there were other options. "After I graduated from San Francisco State in 1964," she wrote, "I worked for a year, then took a government loan and returned to State to get my teaching credential." Her graduate experience confirmed something that had been brewing for her.

> While I always knew I wanted to be a teacher, it wasn't until I taught that I realized how right this was for me. I can't explain this. I was a potter who had discovered clay, a swimmer in water, a gardener with her hands in dirt.

She was a teacher for life.

Logan turned down a teaching position in the suburbs to return to the city where she had grown up but to a school that was radically different from her own. At Bayview Junior High School in Hunter's Point, "I was the only white person in my classroom. I wasn't the expert I thought I was. I had some students in my room who couldn't read and write, and I didn't know what to do about that. I couldn't remember how I had learned to read and write. Shakespeare was no help. And worst of all, many of these students didn't like school, didn't like me, sometimes didn't like themselves." This was where Logan knew she had the most to learn. "I had to learn how to teach reading, how to confront my own and others' racism, how to deal with violence, and how to expand my notion of teaching beyond the content of the curriculum." Logan's autobiographical *Teaching Stories* recounts her continuing struggle over the next 24 years as she came to terms with the crisis in American education that she had faced as a young teacher in San Francisco beginning in the turbulent 1960s.[1]

A MIDCENTURY CONSENSUS ABOUT THE EDUCATION OF TEACHERS?

To a casual observer it might seem that by about 1960, for the first time in the nation's history, a new uniformity had been created in the nation's structures for preparing teachers. Virtually every state in the union required a college degree in order to teach, culminating a process that had been building during the latter stages of the Great Depression, as college graduates who needed jobs edged noncollege graduates out of any openings in the nation's teaching force. This had been temporarily slowed by the incredible labor shortages of World War II, when emergency wartime certification was given to virtually anyone over the age of 18 who was willing to teach and who had not been drafted into the army or some other form of more immediate wartime work. But in the 1950s, as the national economy returned to a peacetime mode, as women were driven out of many of the jobs they had held during the war, teaching again became one of the limited number of professions open to women, and women in large numbers as well as more limited numbers of men were willing to follow the path and complete a college degree prior to entering teaching.

At the same time, in a parallel development, both the municipal programs for teachers and the state normal schools had become degree-granting teachers colleges, generally by the 1930s if not much earlier, and then, by the 1950s, multipurpose institutions of higher education in which a school or department of education competed with programs in the arts and sciences and often in a range of other professional fields for the attention of students and the allocation of ever-scarce funds. While a few state teachers colleges kept the "teachers" name into the 1960s, the future was clear. It was only a matter of time before the last of the schools would follow where the majority had already led and drop any pretense of a primary focus on the preparation of teachers.

The result of these two very significant changes—the requirement that every teacher have a college degree and the restructuring of the institutions that offered these degrees—was a level of seeming uniformity that would have amazed teacher educators of any previous generation. After 1960, preparing teachers was a university monopoly. As the perceptive Paul Woodring understood, the seeming uniformity masked a deep divide within these institutions of higher education between the teacher education faculty who had dominated the normal schools and the now dominant faculty from more traditional university disciplines, especially in the arts and sciences. Woodring wrote of these programs, "The teacher education found in the university schools of education is an unsuccessful marriage of the two which has failed so far to synthesize the two philosophies. This failure may be seen in the sharp conflicts of view which may be found between professional educators and academic professors in many an American university." Indeed! Some of the tensions of the coming decades might have been easy to predict.[2]

The 1950s have often been thought of as a time of great stability. Yet just under the surface historians have found the decade to be one of extraordinary changes. Certainly that was the case in teacher education. On the surface it seemed that things were about to be settled forever. Separate institutions for the preparation of teachers were gone or fast disappearing. Teachers would be prepared in—only in—education departments and schools of large, multipurpose colleges and universities. And at almost exactly the same time virtually every state legislature mandated that every new teacher, no matter what district or grade level, would need a college degree. And at the same time as this new status quo was taking form, more critical voices called for dramatic change.

THE FUND FOR THE ADVANCEMENT OF EDUCATION

Perhaps the most significant and certainly the most well-funded effort to rethink teacher education in the 1950s came from the Fund for the Advancement of Education, a major initiative in the field of education that was the product of the reorganization of the Ford Foundation after Henry Ford's death in 1947. The new fund was in the hands of its president, Clarence Faust, and vice president, Alvin C. Eurich. Eurich, himself an educational psychologist, had a deep and well-informed distrust of most educational research and of traditional approaches to teacher education. As provost and acting president of Stanford he had advocated abolishing the school of education, and as chancellor of the State University of New York he had made the same proposal regarding the state's teachers colleges. Eurich was not opposed to preparing teachers within major universities; on the contrary, it was only when the whole university took on responsibility for teacher education, he believed, that could it be done well. At the same time, Faust and Eurich understood that there was a desperate need for more teachers as school enrollments boomed, and this need would allow for experimentation. It also represented an opportunity that if missed would not come again soon.[3]

With some general ideas about what needed to be changed and with extraordinary new resources behind them, Faust and Eurich set out to change the world of teacher education. From the beginning, Ford's leaders based their work on the assumption that faculty from across the university—from education and from the arts and sciences—needed to work together much more effectively than they had in the past, that the tradition of each side accusing the other of engaging too much of a student's educational time and the general ill will between factions needed to stop. They saw the teacher education they wanted as including four interrelated parts:

1. Liberal education;
2. An extended knowledge of the subject or area taught;
3. Professional knowledge, as distinguished from professional skills;
4. Skills in managing a classroom.

They did not claim to know what institutional arrangements would best accomplish these goals as they set out on their enterprise.[4]

Eurich later wrote about his commitment to using the Ford endowment to ensure that "assumptions underlying selection, education, and utilization of personnel" were thoroughly reexamined. The way to do that, he was convinced, was to support "a wide variety of explorations, experiments, and new ideas." The Fund's leaders were not going to invest in projects that maintained a status quo with which they were thoroughly dissatisfied. The degree to which they succeeded or failed has been subject to much debate. Eurich himself understood that while their grants had certainly created ferment, "ferment does not necessarily result in progress or improvement," but any failures were not for want of trying. Between 1951, when they began their work, and 1957 the Fund for the Advancement of Education spent $57 million, an extraordinary investment, most of it directly on efforts to create and test new models of teacher preparation.[5]

The Fund's approach was based on an understanding that teacher preparation in the United States had changed dramatically by the 1950s and that some new approaches needed to be tried if the critics were ever to be answered. The ever-perceptive Paul Woodring warned that many critics of teacher education, especially critics of the teachers' colleges, had missed the most important recent developments. "The critic who attacks teacher education in terms of the teachers college is likely, when he looks around him, to find that he is attacking a ghost rather than a reality." After all, Woodring understood, by the 1950s the independent institution for teacher preparation was rapidly becoming a thing of the past.

> It seems a safe guess that within twenty years, perhaps within ten years, the sepa-
> rate undergraduate teachers colleges will have gone the way of the dodo. The state
> college which replaces it is a generalized institution in which only a fraction of
> the students are preparing to become teachers.

It was to these more generalized institutions that the fund was turning its attention.[6]

Given the extraordinary changes that had come about in the institutional arrangements for teacher education in the United States between 1930 and 1950, the Fund's leaders wanted first to understand the situation and then to change it. They knew, as Woodring said, that "At the time the Fund began its work, teacher education in the United States was rapidly becoming standard-ized despite the sharp differences of opinion which continued to exist within the profession and within the colleges and universities." And this newly stan-dardized pattern, with education programs embedded in larger academic in-stitutions with faculty in different units fighting over the allocation of students' time and state agencies playing a growing role in approving the curriculum for aspiring teachers, "was not entirely satisfactory to anyone concerned."

> Academic professors, who constituted the larger part of the faculty even in the
> teachers colleges, protested that the professional courses were taking so much time
> as to emasculate the liberal arts program. . . . Professional educators, on the other
> hand, insisted that the amount of time allotted to professional courses and to
> practice teaching was so small as to make it impossible to provide prospective
> teachers with the professional preparation needed.

And the students were caught in the middle. Indeed, Woodring wondered how many students said, "a plague on both their houses," and chose some other profession.[7]

The Fund's leaders set out to find new models. They were immediately attracted to various ideas for 5-year or 5th-year programs in which some of the time problems would be solved by adding 20 percent more time to the teacher preparation plan but in which the formal professional in education could be moved to a year of graduate study that could also involve far more time spent directly in schools, observing teachers and teaching under supervi-sion, than was possible in any existing undergraduate curriculum.

By far the largest amount of the Fund's resources were invested in 5th-year programs, most of all in a program designed to make the state of Arkan-sas the site of an experiment with a new and different state-wide model. Even before the Fund was formally launched, they were negotiating a planning grant with the president of the University of Arkansas. "The purpose of the project," the initial proposal said, "is to launch a large-scale attack on the problem by setting up and carrying forward a program of teacher education based upon a four-year program of broad liberal education to be followed by a period of combined internship and professional study as a requirement for certification." Eventually the Fund spent over $3 million revising teacher preparation in Arkansas.

In Arkansas students were expected to complete a 4-year undergraduate college curriculum with virtually no attention to education. Then, in their 5th year, students engaged in a yearlong internship in the public schools from September to June where they observed, taught under careful supervision, and studied "the problems of education at the same time." Along with the internship, 5th-year students took a series of seminars that covered the material normally associated with education courses. At the end of the year, students were certified by the state of Arkansas.

The Fund invested in the project in a variety of ways. The University of Arkansas and 14 other liberal arts colleges in the state received a total of over 200 distinct grants to revise the undergraduate curriculum to strengthen it in terms of breadth and appropriateness for covering the subject matter needed for future teachers. The Arkansas experiment began in the fall of 1952 with its first cohort of paid interns. Beginning in the fall of 1955, interns became full-time salaried teachers in the schools with an increase in responsibility and a loss in the time they could observe and ask critical questions. The substantial supervision and the seminars continued, with the focus of the seminars becoming increasingly on "problems met in the first year of teaching."

Even before the first interns began their work in September 1952, the Arkansas program had received national publicity and extraordinary amounts of both praise and critique. Liberal arts faculty members and critics of teacher education generally loved the idea. Faculty in education departments and schools naturally feared being displaced and had serious reservations as to whether an ongoing seminar for interns could cover the work of more extended education courses. It was noted that "The plan seemed to deny the values of *courses* in education and to reduce all professional education to training in methodology." There was certainly the danger of creating an internship where students learned the "tricks of the trade," but not the philosophical, theoretical, and ethical underpinnings that would allow them to be reflective professionals. On the other hand, the Arkansas experiment represented a way to reduce the seemingly neverending proliferation of education methods courses that the turf wars engendered by the creation of university departments of education seemed to spawn. The program seemed to work especially well for future high school teachers, where the link of liberal arts subject matter and the teacher's work is most obvious.

Based on their own sense of success, the leaders of the Fund for the Advancement of Education awarded grants to others who wanted to replicate the program. Temple University in Philadelphia received $350,000 to develop and administer a 3-year on-the-job Master of Education degree that recruited high-achieving undergraduates without prior professional education and helped place them in teaching jobs while offering a series of courses and seminars that both supported the novice teachers and enriched their professional base. Cornell, the University of Louisville, and Goucher College also developed programs, each with their own specific variations, that received support from the Fund. None of these experiments were institutionalized as deeply as the Fund's leaders would have wanted. Nevertheless, because of the Arkansas experiment and similar ventures, the notion of a 4-year liberal arts undergraduate program followed by a 5th or 6th year of professional study with heavy attention to the internship was embedded in the consciousness of teacher educators as one significant approach, even if always a controversial one.[8]

While the heart of their work involved direct investments in a wide range of experiments with new approaches to the education of teachers, the Fund also invested in studies that evaluated these projects and that asked larger questions about the current state of the field of education. In his 1957 study, Paul Woodring noted another emerging problem in teacher education. By the time he wrote, state certification requirements, still relatively recent in many states, were coming to be seen as more and more burdensome by many educators. While states had used examinations to certify teachers, state authorities had generally trusted that the exams themselves would guide those offering teacher education—in normal schools, teachers' institutes, or colleges—since they all obviously wanted their students to pass the examinations. With a movement away from examinations to certification based on years and credits earned in college, state authorities began to specify in more and more detail just what sorts of credits a future teacher needed. States might require a major or minor in the liberal arts, but they specified quite specific courses and numbers of credits in education. Some university faculty complained, some outside of education saw a conspiracy of professional educators to control the college curriculum through state regulation, and some saw these developments as a logical extension of the academic community's lack of interest in preparing teachers. "There was no conspiracy, of course, but it is quite true that the responsibility for teacher education had been allowed to slip out of the hands of the academic scholars," Woodring wrote. "What happened was that while the liberal arts colleges were preoccupied with other things, while they ignored the problems of teacher education, a like-minded group of school administrators and other professional educators came to agreement among themselves on the necessity for professional preparation for teachers and transmitted their convictions into law." Except in the case of Arkansas, where all of the players were working closely together, these laws often hindered experimentation far more than they fostered it.[9]

Woodring was raising a substantial red flag. More than 30 years later, the usually mild John Goodlad also challenged the impact of overly detailed state regulations on the quality of teacher education and equally challenged those in authority in the universities to have the courage to do something about the situation:

> States have a responsibility to assure their people that persons coming through teacher education programs are literate, and the states are well within appropriate bounds of authority and responsibility in setting licensing requirements. States endanger quality and make a mock of professionalism when they take it on themselves to specify the curricula to be followed. College and university boards of trustees, administrators, and faculty members are derelict in their responsibilities when they sit idly by—as they usually do when teacher education programs are being savaged by state edict—while institutional autonomy is seriously eroded. The fact that they rarely become aroused over just one more familiar intrusion into the curriculum of teacher education is another sad reflection on the low status of this enterprise and the long road yet to be traversed in making teaching a profession and schools of education professional.[10]

Beyond the voices of Woodring in the 1950s and Goodlad in the 1990s, all too few of the friends or critics of teacher preparation have focused on the over-regulation of teacher education, and it remains a serious concern to some. Only at the very end of the 20th century did a new generation of voices again engage this issue, with some—from right and left—proposing that state regulations of teacher education be abolished altogether, with others—also representing all parts of the political spectrum—advocating with equal energy that the state requirements ought to be strengthened as the only sure guarantee of teacher quality.[11]

In the end of a thoughtful review of the development of the Ford Foundation–sponsored efforts to improve teacher preparation during the 1950s, Paul Woodring concluded by recognizing what too few other critics seemed to recognize, that teaching is very hard work. Speaking of the ideal elementary teacher, he said:

> She would, first of all, have a masterly understanding of the learning process and would know how to arouse and sustain the interest of children from a wide variety of social, economic, and intellectual backgrounds and how to motivate all to maximal individual achievement. . . . Being responsible for the teaching of all subjects taught in the elementary school, she should command a scholarly knowledge of mathematics, literature, history, science, geography, government, music, and art.

No wonder, Woodring concluded, so many were so dissatisfied with the nation's teacher preparation programs.[12]

THE MASTER OF ARTS IN TEACHING DEGREE— AN EFFORT TO BRIDGE THE GAP

Judy Logan was hardly the only teacher of the 1960s to prepare herself for teaching in a graduate program. By the 1960s about a quarter of the nation's teachers had not only graduated from college but had earned a master's degree. Some of these had graduated from an undergraduate teacher education program and then earned a degree later in their professional lives as a way to enhance their professional skills and their seniority within a school district. But many, like Logan, were drawn to teaching late in their academic careers and took their first education course and experienced their first student placement as a graduate student, whether in a formalized 5th-year program or another graduate-level option. And many leaders in the field, not only those at the Fund for the Advancement of Education, thought that this was the best way to prepare to teach.

There were also many within the higher education and especially the teacher education community who hoped that by making teacher preparation a graduate program, the status of this most female of professions could be elevated. Moving teacher education out of the undergraduate experience and into specialized graduate programs also offered the promise of bypassing the seemingly intractable divides between the arts and sciences and education faculties. It was a hope that was not fulfilled, though it absorbed the professional energies of many and an extraordinary outpouring of faculty energy and philanthropic dollars.

One of the major efforts to bridge the great divide between faculty in the arts and sciences disciplines and those concerned with the professional preparation of teachers came with the development of a new academic degree, the Master of Arts in Teaching, initially at Harvard University. Since the 1880s, as other universities began programs in education, that most elite of American universities, Harvard, struggled with the place of education in its midst. In 1920 the Division of Education at Harvard College had been elevated to a Graduate School of Education. At the ceremony creating the new school the aging Paul Hanus, who had been the sometimes lone voice of education at Harvard since 1891, spoke angrily of the attitude of his Harvard faculty colleagues, saying, "We have received their scrutiny, sometimes their suspicion, always their criticism." The divisions at Cambridge, it seemed, went very deep.

A decade later, in 1933, as the full impact of the Great Depression was being felt across America, a still-young chemist, James Bryant Conant, was inaugurated as Harvard's new president. Unlike his predecessors, Charles William Eliot and A. Lawrence Lowell, Conant came to the presidency with no particular inclinations and relatively little interest in the preparation of teachers. Two developments quickly focused Conant's interest.

The first concern to come to Conant's desk was a direct impact of the Great Depression itself as well as of the management of the first education dean, Henry Wyman Holmes. The now 12-year-old graduate school was broke. In addition, Conant discovered deep tensions about the education of teachers across the university. As many teachers and future teachers seemed to prefer the A.M. degree offered by departments of the Graduate School of Arts & Sciences as were enrolled in the Graduate School of Education for an Ed.M. degree for teachers. Conant also suspected a lack of intellectual coherence in the School of Education.

Within 3 years, in 1936, Conant persuaded the faculty of arts and sciences and the faculty of education to turn their efforts to a new academic degree, the M.A.T., to be jointly administered by a new universitywide coordinating committee. Perhaps as much to bridge the campus political divides as for coherent intellectual reasons, Harvard's M.A.T. included equal numbers of courses in the disciplines and in education, examinations were given by both faculties, and the degree took at least 2 years to complete.[13]

The initial response to the M.A.T. was not enthusiastic. An average of one M.A.T. a year was awarded in mathematics for several years, leading one observer to wonder if there was any "point in Harvard's having a program without a product." The M.A.T. program continued, but the continuing Depression and the rise of fascism led Conant, and many others at Harvard, to turn their primary interest to research that would serve a nation on the brink of war and, at the same time, land the massive new federal contracts that were becoming available. In his 1938 annual report, Conant wrote, "The study of education as a social process—quite apart from the training of teachers—is as important as the study of law or of business administration." The education of teachers, though not abandoned, certainly took a back seat. No one pointed out that true as Conant's statement might be, no one was likely to advocate dropping the preparation of lawyers from the law school because of the need for new research studies. Nevertheless, in the aftermath of World War II the graduate faculty of education—such as it was; there were only five tenured professors—gave serious consideration to dropping the M.A.T. degree, indeed, to abandoning teacher preparation altogether. Only a persuasive argument by the school's new dean, Francis Keppel, kept the M.A.T. alive.[14]

Keeping the M.A.T. turned out to be a wise move. In the 1950s, with the postwar baby boom in full swing, schools were bursting at the seams, teachers were desperately needed, and Harvard was well positioned to prepare the best and brightest of the professionals. The faculty even launched a new Ed.M. degree for elementary teachers while it expanded the M.A.T. substantially, convincing other prestigious universities, notably Yale, to launch their own M.A.T.s. A degree program that had been invented to solve internal institutional problems in the 1930s became in the 1950s a very popular national model of the right way to prepare teachers—in the academic disciplines at the highest level and in the techniques of teaching.

The real success of Harvard's M.A.T., however, lay in Francis Keppel's extraordinary skill in fundraising. Early in his tenure as dean, Keppel, along with President Conant, had approached the Ford Foundation for support for the social science research being conducted on their campus. They found little interest. Faust and Eurich had very little faith in the value of social science education research, but they were very interested in teacher preparation. Having been rebuffed in his effort to interest the Foundation's leaders in his faculty's beloved social science research, Keppel asked Faust and Eurich to support Harvard's M.A.T., arguing that it was the ideal complement to the Arkansas experiment. After all, he said, the M.A.T. also recruited undergraduates whose college careers had included no study of education. And unlike the Arkansas experiment, Harvard recruited some of the nation's most elite students who had attended elite undergraduate institutions. In addition to direct support for Harvard, Ford spent some one-half million dollars supporting a feeder system in which 29 "distinguished undergraduate institutions" agreed to recruit among their students for the Harvard graduate program, guaranteeing Harvard a steady stream of students and, while perhaps absolving the other colleges of their own responsibility to prepare teachers, certainly ensuring "an interest in teaching on the part of able liberal arts students in colleges of the kind which have not, in recent years, provided many teachers."

If one looked carefully at the Harvard M.A.T. in 1960, it was quite similar to what it had been since the 1930s, a degree that offered in-depth preparation in both academic content and pedagogy. Since the 1940s it could be completed in 1 year. But in the 1950s it had also recruited degree candidates with a kind of "missionary zeal," as Keppel's successor Theodore Sizer noted, and the M.A.T., like other Harvard programs, also recruited those who by both background and accomplishment reflected the elite of the nation. By 1960, 242 of the 293 students in the program were graduates of the most prominent of the nation's private universities. If others followed where the elite led, there was no question where the elite was to be found.[15]

The M.A.T., indeed any commitment to teacher preparation, did not continue to thrive at Harvard. The Ford Foundation's direct support allowed the Graduate School of Education to grow dramatically. Preparing the children of the nation's educational and financial elite—not normally a group attracted to teaching—to return to their own communities fit the mold espoused by Keppel and to some extent by Sizer. The M.A.T. not only drew from the well-off, it served the well-off. Three-quarters of the 1954 alumni of the program reported that their own students were from professional, executive, or white-collar families, and the same was true throughout the life of the M.A.T. For the most part, Harvard M.A.T.s taught in the most prosperous suburbs.

In the 1960s, Lyndon Johnson's War on Poverty pushed the national interest in education in a different direction. On the one hand, there was more federal money than ever before flowing into educational research, and many on the Harvard faculty could justify complete indifference to teacher education because of the size and prestige of their federal grants. On the other hand, there was great unease with a teacher preparation program that focused on preparing teachers for the well-off when schools in Harvard's immediate neighbors in Cambridge and Boston were in desperate need of teachers who could elevate the academic programs being offered to poor students, deal forthrightly with the intractable racism that divided both cities, and transform long-neglected urban classrooms into centers of excellence. There was little reason to see in the M.A.T., as it had developed, a model for such engagement. Harvard, of course, had no immediate obligation to prepare teachers at all—it was a private university—and so in 1973 the faculty turned its attention to more basic urban research in the hopes of having a national impact. The M.A.T. was abolished, and Harvard entered a decade-long period of politely ignoring teacher education altogether until another dean, historian and former teacher Patricia Albjerg Graham, began a new teacher education program based on the novel assumption that a serious research focus on education would not have intellectual or ethical coherence without some immediate effort at teacher preparation.[16]

While the M.A.T. was Harvard's—and specifically James Bryant Conant's —invention, it was an invention that was adopted with substantial local modifications by many others. Writing for the Fund for the Advancement of Education in 1957, Paul Woodring attempted to define the unique essence of the M.A.T. degree. At its core the degree was an effort to bridge the traditional divide between education and the disciplines by creating a new program that was "Planned and sponsored jointly by the Faculty of Arts and Sciences and the Faculty of Education." In place of the more traditional arts-dominated M.A. or the education-dominated M.Ed., the M.A.T. included courses—usually equal numbers of courses—in both. Another aspect of the degree was equally important to Woodring. Where many 5th-year programs, including those sponsored by the Fund for the Advancement of Education, assumed that the best preparation of teachers was a 4-year program in the liberal arts untainted by professional concerns, followed by a year of study in education, preferably with a heavy clinical or school-based component, the M.A.T. tried to blend the two arenas at the same time.[17]

In addition to Yale, other institutions adopted the M.A.T. Vanderbilt University, in cooperation with the then-independent George Peabody College for Teachers, recruited from among the best liberal arts graduates, especially from colleges across the South, though students came from 71 undergraduate institutions in 30 states. The Ford Foundation also supported M.A.T. programs at Brown University and a very similar program leading to an M.Ed. degree at Johns Hopkins University. Other universities adopted the M.A.T. on their own. In all of the early programs, the basic characteristics of professional preparation, including substantial classroom experience, strong academic courses, and avoidance of "the duplication and unnecessary proliferation of professional courses," all under the joint control of faculties in education and the arts and sciences, remained the core of the program. And in most places, the very elitism of the programs, as well as the complex institutional arrangements, drastically limited the pool of candidates and in time led to the demise of the programs. The bridge that Conant wanted to build between his differing faculty groups was both expensive and shaky. It provided a promising model, but not broad impact in terms of preparing substantial numbers of teachers, especially teachers for the urban and rural schools that most needed them.[18]

THE NEW CRITICS: ARTHUR BESTOR, JAMES D. KOERNER, JAMES BRYANT CONANT

Although it may not have been very visible to Judy Logan as a graduate student at San Francisco State College in 1965 or to her counterparts across the country in M.A.T. programs at Harvard, Yale, or Vanderbilt, the world of teacher education that she had entered was a world that to many, especially the faculty, seemed to be in a state of siege. Just at the moment when the nation had moved to require a college degree of every future teacher and when the programs that offered these degrees had been consolidated into one basic form—a school or department within a larger university—when things seemed to be settled forever, these teacher education programs came under intense scrutiny and, indeed, attack, some informed and thoughtful, some vicious and mean-spirited.

The critique of the teacher education offered at the nation's colleges and universities had been building for a decade. In 1953 Arthur Bestor published *Educational Wastelands: The Retreat from Learning in Our Public Schools.* While Bestor had a wide-ranging critique of the state of American public schools in the postwar era, the institutions that trained the teachers came in for more than their share of blame. Basically Bestor had two complaints.

First, Bestor believed that as it had developed in the schools and departments of education, the academic study of education had become detached from its roots in the academy and in academic disciplines. John Dewey himself was a philosopher, but by the time Bestor wrote he feared that far too many philosophers of education had failed to follow in Dewey's footsteps and had instead studied a more narrow subject only with other philosophers of education and had become disconnected from the main currents of American philosophy. And the same problem existed in every other discipline. "Cross-fertilization," Bestor wrote, "the original purpose of departments of education, has ceased, and we are up against the fact that the products of cross-fertilization—the hybrids— are frequently sterile."

The result of this insular separation of the field of education was a narrow vocationalism in education departments and schools. Thus:

> University and graduate departments of education were founded with the idea of raising school teaching from a vocation to a profession. This was to be accomplished—it could only be accomplished—by requiring a thorough training in the liberal arts before permitting a student to embark upon specialized training in pedagogy.

In this claim Bestor seemed to be endorsing the work of the Fund for the Advancement of Education. But Bestor had a more far-reaching distrust of education faculty than his counterparts at Ford. He continued:

> Instead of a new and genuinely professional approach to education there was a mere upgrading in the numbering of the old courses in pedagogical method. For most students these courses were apt to be piled, layers thick, upon an undergraduate major in pedagogy, not upon a major in one of the liberal arts. In the end, so-called graduate work in education tended to become merely a prolonged and attenuated program of vocational training.

And in Bestor's mind this was not a training of much rigor or intellectual coherence or professional value.

Not only had the field of education become isolated within the university, but also it had developed what Bestor saw as an unholy alliance with school administrators, superintendents, and principals, in an "interlocking directorate" that controlled the rules for teacher education and silenced educational researchers as effective critics of the schools. Both parts of the bargain represented huge problems for Bestor. On the one hand, he argued that "It was peculiarly necessary for professors of education to maintain their independence from such pressures, since one of their major responsibilities was to examine, criticize, and judge with scholarly impartiality the programs that school administrators were carrying out." But in addition to shedding their scholarly impartiality for a questionable alliance, Bestor believed that education professors had used the alliance to protect their turf within the university. Thus, he charged, "State educational officials exert control over such programs by the requirements they lay down for the certification of teachers, and these universally include substantial course work in pedagogy. . . . educationists are quite ready to invoke the coercive power of the state to compel every prospective teacher to take a specified number of courses in pedagogy. Protected behind state requirements which no department but itself can satisfy, the department is able to defy, or even to wage aggressive warfare against, the academic standards of the university."[19]

Critics quickly challenged Bestor. Writing in *Teachers College Record*, Karl Bigelow, who had himself led one of the major studies of teacher education, the eight-volume American Council of Education study, reminded readers that in the judgment of many, Bestor "grossly underestimates the quantity and quality of special knowledge and skill that good teaching requires." Looking at the inevitable compromises that make up any undergraduate or graduate curriculum, Bigelow also felt that if one looked at the actual situation in most colleges and universities, the allocation of courses among general education, specialized work in an academic discipline, and in professional studies hardly representative of the "megalomaniac imperialism that Professor Bestor declares in his writings to be the educationists' chronic characteristic."

For Bigelow, as for Paul Woodring and for many who worked in the nation's classrooms in midcentury, it was clear that teaching was more complex and needed more complex preparation than people like Arthur Bestor understood. Bigelow wrote:

> A teacher as such must have a clear idea of educational purpose, a considerable understanding of children, a grasp of social realities and their implications for the schools, resources of scholarship, and ability to use those resources to facilitate the growth of children according to guiding purpose.[20]

And, of course, in Bigelow's mind this meant substantial though never exclusive professional study in education. Nevertheless, Bestor had struck a chord, and many, at the Ford Foundation and elsewhere, would spend much of the decade of the 1950s trying to respond. In his critique of what he saw as both the low standards and the proliferation of regulations and courses in pedagogy, Bestor had also outlined what would be the core of most critiques of teacher education for the coming half-century.

Bestor's critique was far from the end of the criticism heaped on schools of education and the professors who taught in them, however. The early 1960s saw far more thoroughgoing assaults than anything that Bestor or other critics of the 1950s represented. In 1963 two books shook the world of teacher education to its roots.

James D. Koerner's *The Miseducation of American Teachers* was the more biting of the two. Koerner had visited 63 college campuses, interviewed recent teachers and obtained questionnaires from 827 recent graduates, and published articles in *The Atlantic Monthly*, *The Saturday Evening Post*, and *The Saturday Review* for some time. No one was much surprised by the content of his 1963 book. But Koerner's critique was joined by the carefully reasoned work of James Bryant Conant in the similarly named *The Education of American Teachers*. Conant was now retired from the presidency of Harvard and a term as U.S.

High Commissioner and then ambassador to Germany. His previous books on American education, *Slums and Suburbs* and *The American High School Today,* had established Conant as a nationally respected voice that could not be dismissed as easily as Koerner alone might have been.

As part of his study of teacher education, Koerner spent time interviewing education students and recent graduates of the programs who were already teaching in the schools. One response by a young teacher summarizes much of Koerner's anger at what he found in schools of education:

> The courses are one dull, repetitious thing after another. I had 3 courses [she had 45 semester hours of Education, total] in a row which were straight repeats, Statistics, Teaching and Guidance (the last two under the same professor, a psychological testing bug). Every course starts out with 6 weeks of "developmental psychology"—which means such labored truisms as "The whole child comes to school," "Children develop at different rates," "You have to start where the child is," etc.

Koerner's interviewee was not only critical of the dull and boring nature of her education courses—though both she and Koerner were that—but also of their lack of relevance to future professional work as a teacher. The same student continued that her courses contained:

> Not one thing about how you go about teaching—you are left to find out the practical, down-to-earth dealings with children completely on your own. Generalities are all right for a base, but do you little good when a supervisor is looking over your shoulder.

Finally, this interviewee, clearly one whose opinions Koerner embraced, made her own recommendations for transforming teacher preparation:

> My prescription would be: good, heavy content courses for most of three years—history, science, literature, geography, some of the newer math, English composition. Perhaps a basic "Psychology of Learning" and "Backgrounds of Modern Education" in the third year. Then I would like to see methods courses coordinated with student teaching in a laboratory school situation, where the student observed a master teacher, planned a similar or follow-up lesson and taught it, then evaluated it with the teacher-professor.

Koerner could not have said it better himself, which is presumably why he cited this student at such length.[21]

In the end, Koerner's judgments were even harsher than those of his favorite interviewees. While he did happily find "a greater ferment throughout teacher education now than has been evident for a very long time"—perhaps Bestor's critique and Ford's efforts had made a difference—he did not find much else that satisfied him. Among his many complaints, Koerner found "an appalling lack of evidence to support the wisdom of this or that kind of professional training for teachers." Lacking such evidence, Koerner argued, as others would 40 years later, that "there should be many routes, not just one, to the teaching license." Like Bestor, he also found that departmental status "does not make Education a genuine discipline; it only makes possible the building of more academic empires on sandy foundations." Also like Bestor, Koerner found that the links between education programs and schools and state agencies created "an immense academic industry with a top-heavy bureaucracy," and he greatly feared that the creation of NCATE (The National Council for Accreditation of Teacher Education) as a national accrediting agency would only foster even more centralization and uniformity unaccountable to standard academic norms. Finally, and most damning, he found both the students and the faculty in education programs to be wanting. "It is an indecorous thing to say and obviously offensive to most educationists, but it is the truth and it should be said: the inferior intellectual quality of the Education faculty is *the* fundamental limitation of the field, and will remain so, in my judgment, for some time to come."[22]

Writing for the *Harvard Educational Review*, E.V. Johanningmeier aimed his own criticism at what he saw as the core problem with Koerner's book. While he found the book full of critique, Johanningmeier found little in terms of an intellectually coherent new model for what teacher education should look like in the last third of the 20th century. So Johanningmeier wrote, "One wishes that Koerner had used the famed Flexner report for a model. Flexner began his survey of medical schools with an idea, a defensible conception of what a medical school should be. Mr. Koerner had no such model."[23] If some wished that Koerner had offered a book more like Abraham Flexner's work on medical education, the other major critique to appear in 1963, Conant's *The Education of American Teachers*, was specifically commissioned by the Carnegie Corporation to be that "Flexner report on teacher education."

When James Bryant Conant began his study in 1961, he found that the division and distrust that he had seen in the Harvard faculty in the 1930s were alive and well across the country. The most progress he actually found in healing the divide was a remark by one education dean that "The boys have at least agreed to check their hatchets with their hats at the Faculty Club coatroom when they lunch together." But everywhere Conant looked, the hatchets were still being sharpened. He remarked:

> While I am not prepared to say that there was, or is, actual hostility between educational and academic professors on every campus, there has always been a considerable gap between the two groups in a majority of institutions. Such a gap often exists in spite of fine words spoken by administrators about "an all-university approach" to the education of teachers, and existence of a committee that symbolized the approach.

Conant then launched into a brilliant analysis of this hostility between the education faculty and the arts and sciences faculty as he experienced it on the campuses he visited in the early 1960s.

More than 40 years after Conant wrote, virtually every word, except for the importance of the Russian success with their Sputnik satellite, could still be true. The education professors Conant spoke with felt both defensive and angry about the neverending criticism of their work. "We who have shaped and improved our public schools are now being unfairly attacked," Conant heard them say. These professors, and here Conant fully agreed with them, were also angry that "the faculties of arts and sciences had shown little interest in school problems. . . . With few exceptions, college professors turned their backs on the problems of mass secondary education . . ." In light of this irresponsible behavior, it was galling to hear only criticism of their work from members of the arts and science faculty.

On the other hand, Conant was unhappy with much in the nation's schools, and he gave at least partial blame to the educators for "the failure to challenge the academically talented youth." He reported, and one senses his agreement, that "Many academic professors believe that the courses given by professors of education are worthless, and that the degrees granted students who have devoted much of their time to these courses are of little value." He did note that "It is generally the case that the academic professors who advance these arguments know far too little about education courses," but it was also true that "what some professors of education have written about education can be labeled anti-intellectual." Perhaps most aggravating to liberal arts faculty, and here Conant the chemist is clear where he stood, was the assumption that only the education faculty knows what good teaching looks like. After all, Conant and many of his colleagues prided themselves on being good teachers without having taken any education courses. And one supposes Conant could have added that he had been a very successful college president without any courses in educational administration.

Finally Conant, like Woodring before him and Goodlad later, saw in "the issue of state requirements" something that stirred deep anger in many quarters.

> Time was, not long ago, when in some states a school board could hire a teacher, and give him a permanent position, even if he had never even seen a professor of education. But those days are past. As a consequence, a graduate who has majored in an academic field must by hook or by crook meet the state requirements in education. . . . The fact that schools of education are beneficiaries of a high protective tariff wall is the single aspect of the present-day education of teachers that is most maddening to the academic professors.

And to varying degrees that, too, would remain true for the next 40 years.[24]

More deeply than Koerner, Conant moved beyond critique, though his book also has plenty of critique, if usually in a more gentle voice than Koerner's. In

the end, however, Conant's recommendations did not represent an intellectually coherent new model for teacher education but rather something of a tacit
admission of defeat. He concluded that the knowledge base simply did not exist
for the development of a new model, and so the good scientist urged maximum
freedom for the greatest new level of experimentation. He concluded:

> In view of the great diversity of opinions and practices to be found in the leading
> institutions, I conclude that neither a state authority nor a voluntary accrediting
> agency is in a position to specify the amount of time to be devoted to either aca-
> demic or educational courses. What is needed is on the one hand for the state to
> allow freedom for institutions to experiment, and on the other for academic pro-
> fessors and professors of education in each institution to take joint responsibility
> for the reputation of their college or university in training teachers.

Beyond that there was little that Conant would commend, not even his own
creation, the M.A.T. degree.

He did urge states to develop financial incentives to recruit more able students into the profession. He was convinced that some form of student teaching was essential, and that the faculty of the university as a whole should have
to justify the requirements for the bachelor's degree in terms of both depth
and breadth of subject matter knowledge. He recommended that NCATE and
other accrediting or legislative agencies be advisory only. And finally, on the
same note of freedom, he recommended that:

> Each college or university should be permitted to develop in detail whatever pro-
> gram of teacher education it considers most desirable, subject only to two condi-
> tions; first the president of the institution on behalf of the entire faculty
> involved—academic as well as professional—certifies that the candidate is ade-
> quately prepared to teach on a specific level or in specific fields, and second, the
> institution establishes in conjunction with a public school system a state-approved
> practice-teaching arrangement.

Here was a proposal for a level of freedom and academic responsibility that
many could only envy even if it represented a frightening level of permissive-
ness to others.[25]

THE POWER OF THE STATUS QUO

One can read the critiques of teacher education from the 1950s and 1960s with
a sense that exceedingly little has changed in the language of teacher education's
toughest critics in subsequent decades. What is equally amazing to the historian
looking at these decades is how very little impact these reports had on the actual
practices on college campuses or on the actual experience of those preparing for

careers in teaching. The reports sold by the thousands. They were discussed across the country. And not much happened. Students continued to major in education. The arts and sciences faculties continued to complain about the number of education courses as well as the academic caliber of the education students and faculty. States continued to regulate the education curriculum, usually in greater and greater detail. The machine kept going.

One substantial reason for the power of the status quo and the tenacity of education programs in holding onto their academic and financial turf was the continuing teacher shortage, combined with the glass ceiling experienced by women in many other fields well into the 1970s and beyond, a reality that made teaching a very appealing profession to large numbers of young women who wanted a career. As a result, education schools became the cash cow of the colleges that contained them; there were lots of students and lots of tuition money; and complain though the arts and sciences faculty might, few trustees, presidents, or chief financial officers were willing to tamper with the unit that paid the bills. It was an era of benign neglect.

Throughout the decade of the 1970s the sense of complacency continued on many campuses. Reviewing the curricula at some 100 education schools he had visited in the 2 years after Conant and Koerner published their reports, Walter K. Beggs concluded with some understatement, "There is no indication at present that any major changes will be made in this general format . . ."[26] Certainly there continued to be proposals for drastic reshaping of teacher education. Legislatures in Oklahoma, California, Michigan, and New Jersey considered proposals to eliminate their state's schools of education, to limit the number of credit hours for any education courses, and to create alternative routes outside the schools of education. The Florida legislature considered a bill to abolish the College of Education at the University of Florida. But mostly these proposals seemed like the normal background noise that schools of education had successfully ignored for so long. David C. Smith, dean of the College of Education at the University of Florida—the school his state legislature once tried to eliminate—from 1978 to 1994 reflected on the year 1980, when, he recalled, "At first, the demand for change made little impression on SCDEs [schools/colleges/departments of education] where confidence prevailed that preparation programs were inherently strong. The teacher education community argued that there was little evidence to support the critics' contentions and that what evidence did exist was largely anecdotal." Such a self-satisfied and self-confident response, Smith understood, would not work in the long run. So he noted, "Rather than quelling the critics, this attitude fueled the flames of discontent, making the calls for reform more strident." But it would be another half-decade and more before the ongoing calls for reform would turn into the kind of groundswell for change that would make more significant changes in the field a reality.

12

Preparing Teachers in the Era of *A Nation at Risk*

1965–2000

Ashallah Williams grew up poor and black and always wanted to teach, but her teachers in New York City had targeted her for success, which to her and to them meant something much more lucrative and prestigious than teaching. She followed their advice and attended Princeton University with scholarships and pursued a premed program. After receiving her B.A. from Princeton, she decided that a master's degree in biology from Hampton would help her in applications to medical school. However, while at Hampton she also, for the first time, found teachers who appreciated her desire to teach. She shifted to Hampton's teacher education program and after successfully completing it began teaching 5th grade in Baltimore, Maryland.[1]

At the same time, Teach For America, an organization that proudly recruits from among the best of the nation's college students, describes some of those who are currently teaching as TFA corps members. Sanford Johnson, an African American who graduated from Auburn University with a major in political science, spent the next 2 years teaching in rural schools in the Mississippi Delta. He remembered, "I was born in the Mississippi Delta and lived here until I was nine. It was during a trip back to the Delta the summer before my senior year of college that fueled my desire to change things." According to TFA's own report, when Johnson started teaching, 54 of his 65 students were failing social studies. In the end, all 65 students passed the state U.S. history test. Of course, TFA, like any more traditional organization, advertises its successes far more than those who have found the program problematic, but clearly there are many successes to celebrate.[2]

THE TEACHER CORPS

Teach For America and other 1990s alternative routes to teaching do not represent the first time that teachers have been prepared and licensed to teach outside university-based education programs. Of course, throughout most of the nation's history most teachers came through what might now be labeled alternative routes. But even in the decade of the 1960s, as the last separate teachers college was becoming a multipurpose college and the last state required a college degree for every teacher, a major route into teaching bypassed the new standard arrangement.

In the late 1960s and through much of the 1970s, those who wanted to transform the preparation of teachers generally bypassed the undergraduate programs that were the core of where the nation's teachers were prepared. If the criticism from people like Koerner and Conant could not bring about change, some reasoned, perhaps the education faculty and their allies in the state program approval agencies were simply too powerful to challenge. The experimentation that Conant wanted would have to happen elsewhere. The Master of Arts in Teaching was far from being the only program aimed at bypassing undergraduate programs in the preparation of teachers. But others wanted to bypass university education programs altogether. One of the major complaints about M.A.T. programs was that they used the resources of some of the nation's most elite colleges to prepare teachers for some of the nation's most elite and prosperous suburbs. Something else was needed if the increasingly urgent needs of the nation's cities and the schools and children of those cities were to be addressed, needs that were beginning to get much more attention in the activist 1960s than they had in the complacent 1950s. There was no shortage of ideas or programs.

One of the most innovative and still-beloved programs for the education of teachers outside the confines of traditional university programs was the National Teacher Corps. The Teacher Corps was born out of the intellectual energy and moral fervor of the Great Society. As Donald M. Sharpe said, "The Teacher Corps was to do for the slums of America what the Peace Corps ideally did for the underdeveloped nations. There were high hopes that it would appeal to the young idealistic reformer." By not only recruiting young, well-educated idealists and placing them in teaching positions as interns, but also immersing them deeply in the communities near their schools—something that few teacher education programs had done—and also engaging them in graduate courses in education to expand their teaching expertise, there was a hope that a new kind of teacher could be recruited and perhaps a new model developed that would in time transform even the education schools in the process.

In 1965 Massachusetts Senator Edward M. Kennedy proposed creating a corps of experienced teachers who would devote a year or two to schools attended by poor children, and at about the same time Wisconsin Senator Gaylord Nelson proposed expanding a program that already existed in Washington, D.C., the Cardozo Peace Corps Program in Urban Teaching, which focused on recent college graduates, into a national program. The timing could not have been better. In January 1965 President Lyndon Johnson had proposed the most far-reaching investment of federal funds in the public schools ever offered, and only 3 months later he signed the first Elementary and Secondary Education Act, of which he said, "As President of the United States, I believe deeply no law I have signed or will ever sign means more to the future of America." Education was on the front burner. Commitment to urban and rural communities, communities of color and communities of poverty, was something that many Americans cared about. At the same time, as Bethany L. Rogers has noted, "For Great Society liberals, the system of professionalism—an interlocking chain of education, training, credentials, experience—had ceased to function as the path of talent to power." A new cadre of teachers who came from different and more privileged backgrounds and who would ask different questions would, the corps' sponsors were sure, be warmly welcomed by communities and schools across the country.[3]

As it emerged from Congress, the goal of the Teacher Corps was to recruit both young and energetic liberal arts graduates and experienced teachers who would make a commitment of 1 or 2 years, and who would be placed as a cohort as interns in the schools while at the same time taking classes in one of the many education schools that eventually came to partner with the program. They would also work in the communities near the schools, engaging in activities as diverse as voter registration or leading a Boy or Girl Scout troop. While the goal shifted over time, a more subtle goal was also to transform the stodgy ways of teacher education by this infusion of new blood, and indeed, some saw this as a prime benefit of the program.

Donald M. Sharpe, who directed the Teacher Corps program at Indiana State University, called it "Possibly the most radical experiment in teacher education ever tired." Sharpe explained, "It can teach the profession a lot. At one and the same time it was trying to prepare teachers for roles that had not previously existed by means that had never been tried." Linking serious engagement in and respect for the diverse cultures of urban communities of color and rural communities, black and white, with a cohort-based internship moved teacher education out of the university classrooms and not only into the schools but the sidewalks and homes of some of America's poorest citizens. Another education school administrator said it was "very safe to predict that the fringe benefits of the Teacher Corps money will be to revitalize teacher education in the United States." The program's national office preferred to focus on the Teacher Corps' role as a component in President Johnson's War on Poverty. In 1966 they issued a press release that said:

> Teacher Corps men and women will be pioneering experimental programs that the schools have had neither the time nor staff to develop. They will make inventive use of the curriculum, approaching it from new angles that may "connect" for the hard-to-reach youngster. They will extend teaching beyond the classroom, and look for new ways to involve parents in the mysteries of the learning process.

Where the young interns or even the more experienced teachers would get the expertise to do all of this was less clear.

The Teacher Corps began operation in 1966. In its first 8 years more than 3,000 young interns and 600 experienced teachers completed its 2-year cycle. Nearly 250 school systems in 27 states and Puerto Rico participated, including large urban districts such as New York, Chicago, Detroit, Philadelphia, and Los Angeles as well as small rural school districts in Appalachia, the Ozarks, the rural South, Indian schools, and Spanish-speaking communities in the Southwest. The program attracted many who completed a term of service and who, like returning Peace Corps volunteers, took that experience into their future careers. It also attracted many others who in the end made a lifetime commitment to teaching and became educational leaders in the future.

The Teacher Corps created significant conflict on many of the college campuses where the interns studied. Highly educated, young, idealistic, and often politically radical, they were not about to accept the status quo at many of the education schools where they found themselves. An evaluator of the Teacher Corps found, "Because the interns thought their coursework was unrelated to the needs of students from low-income families, they tried to change the courses. Their basic strategy was to challenge the instructors. Some instructors said this made them think; others were simply distressed; others defensive."

Of course, the education professors facing Teacher Corps interns were not the only college professors of the 1960s and 1970s era who were being challenged, sometimes politely and sometimes not very politely at all. It was a time of upheaval in America, most of all on the nation's college campuses. As in many other cases, the NEA evaluators found, "One defense reaction was to label the interns as *hippies*, or to call them *rude*; once they were labeled, their professors no longer felt it necessary to take them seriously." The evaluators did find some of the interns difficult. "Interns were also regarded as anti-intellectuals who had no interest in studying. The interns countercharged that professors penalized those who openly disagreed with them." In some ways, the Teacher Corps brought the late 1960s crisis on the nation's college campuses directly into the education schools. Many came from undergraduate educational experiences in schools where the debates about civil rights and the war in Vietnam had been most intense. It would have been amazing if they had not challenged the graduate schools where they found themselves.[4]

Teacher Corps interns also transformed the schools where they taught, sometimes easily and sometimes with great struggle. And some of the changes were lasting, while in other cases the school's old guard of teachers and administrators closed ranks and relatively quickly excluded the interns and any change they might have advocated. Certainly it was the case that the Teacher Corps was designed not only to recruit a new cadre of teachers, people who might not otherwise have entered teaching, but also to use these new teachers to transform the schools. As the NEA evaluators said, "One premise of the Teacher Corps is that the education of poor children can be improved by recruiting people with backgrounds different from those of most teachers in the profession." The evaluators found less evidence to support this premise than they, or the corps' founders, might have wished. What they found was that, in fact, "the greater the difference between interns and teachers in social attitudes or in status, the less change took place." To a good sociologist, this ought not to have been all that surprising. "The interns aroused defensive reactions from teachers and professors, yet they themselves had neither the numbers nor the authoritative position to overcome those reactions." It was not, in the end, a surprising result.[5]

In the late 1960s there were also many Teacher Corps–like programs. The New York City public schools, in cooperation with New York University, created a program in which the city of New York initially paid the tuition for qualified college graduates to attend an extended summer school at NYU, including 4 weeks of student teaching, in a program that led to provisional certification to teach by summer's end. In return, graduates of the program were expected to commit to teach for at least 1 year in the New York City public schools. If they fulfilled their commitment, their tuition was forgiven. In an era of high need for teachers and deep frustration with the traditional models of teacher preparation, such models thrived. In the late 1960s, with the war in Vietnam expanding and more and more young men facing the draft, the fact that public school teaching also created an automatic draft deferment made the programs very popular and dramatically increased the male participation in these programs above anything seen in teaching for many years.

The Teacher Corps and similar programs thrived for a decade, but then they shrank and disappeared. A number of factors were involved in the end of these experiments that had begun with such high hopes. At a basic level, the Teacher Corps was asking people to do very hard work. One intern said, "I'm not sure that it's the university that's to blame. It may be a general problem. No one knows how to teach disadvantaged children." High hopes, high ideals, and deep commitment, while terribly important, were not enough. And the result too often was cynicism and frustration. In addition, the years were hard on all programs like the Teacher Corps. What had begun at the height of the Great Society sank like most of the Great Society into the mud of Lyndon Johnson's Vietnam adventure and then the Watergate scandal of the Nixon years. After the war, after the "credibility gap" that both Johnson and Nixon earned for themselves, any government program seemed doomed, especially any federal program aimed at changing society's ways. And ongoing federal budget cuts helped fuel this sense of doom. Finally the Teacher Corps, like many of the most traditional programs on college campuses, ran directly into the sudden teacher glut of the late 1970s. Where in the early 1960s school districts, especially urban and rural districts, had been desperate for teachers and were willing to try any experiment that might yield more, the nation's changing demographics—which reduced the school-age population as the last of the baby boomers finished high school, and encouraged a generation of teachers to stay in their work, deferring retirement or other ventures—led to a virtual closed door at the personnel offices of school districts. Why spend federal money to meet a need that no longer existed? Indeed, many students asked, why study to be a teacher at all? There were no jobs to be had at the end of the preparation, however long or short it might be.[6]

THE CENTER FOR EDUCATIONAL RENEWAL AND A NEW SENSE OF URGENCY

Perhaps the most sustained effort at reforming teacher education during the last 3 decades of the 20th century was led by John I. Goodlad at the Center for Educational Renewal, the Institute for Educational Inquiry, and the National Network for Educational Renewal. In 1970, while he was still dean of the School of Education at the University of California at Los Angeles, Goodlad wrote, "Nothing short of a simultaneous reconstruction of preservice teacher education, inservice teacher education, and schooling itself will suffice if the [educational] change process is to be adequate." Goodlad then devoted the rest of his career to creating that simultaneous reconstruction.

In 1984 John Goodlad, joined by Kenneth Sirotnik and Roger Soder, created the Center for Educational Renewal at the University of Washington. The Goodlad, Sirotnik, and Soder team published three major works in 1990, all focused on teacher education and all aimed at joining inquiry and research with the transformation of practice. *Places Where Teachers Are Taught* (1990) examined the historical background of a number of the institutions—former normal schools, liberal arts colleges, and flagship universities—that were then preparing the bulk of the nation's teachers. *The Moral Dimensions of Teaching* explored a larger discourse too often excluded from the conversations about teacher education, examining the moral purposes of schools in a democratic society and the ethical responsibilities that teachers needed to enter into those institutions. Finally, *Teachers for Our Nation's Schools* (1990), solo-authored by Goodlad, outlined his overarching plan for the transformation of the teaching profession and specifically the preparation of those who would enter it.[7] The trio would continue their work together well into the next century.

In spite of a determinedly upbeat and optimistic stance, in the end the three volumes are not encouraging about the state of teacher education during the decade of the 1980s when the research work was done. Goodlad understood better than most observers the deep divide between elite graduate schools of education that too often "prepared no teachers or just a few," while the faculty devoted themselves to higher-prestige research and while the nation's teachers were prepared in not only less prestigious but less intellectually rigorous places. At the same time, education faculty, whether they were in elite or nonelite schools of education, "suffer from congenital prestige deprivation." In the end, Goodlad argued, teacher education must be transformed. "Programs for the education of the nation's educators must be viewed by institutions offering them as a major responsibility to society and be adequately supported and promoted and vigorously advanced by the institution's top leadership." Whether they would be, however, remained an open question to any reader of the three books.[8]

Writing in the Center's volume, *Places Where Teachers Are Taught,* of the marginalization that happened to teacher education when it became one among the many functions of multipurpose colleges and universities, historian Robert A. Levin has written persuasively that we must ask why "some teacher education programs faded with their boots on and were given a decent memorial in a positive, restructured program, while other trailed off in unresolved bitterness." There are many villains in the story. As Levin tells it, "It is hard to avoid the impression that few will mourn for education faculties' hurt feelings or entertain their nostalgia for the good old days. (Goodlad, in fact, questions how good the old days were; his work elsewhere suggests that better old days in teacher education might have facilitated more democratic and innovative public schooling by now.)" But whether teacher preparation programs were marginalized because of their own failure to reach the standards that should have been asked of them or because of the prejudices of the lager university world, or both, is not the most important question. In the end it does not matter to Levin, who reminds us that "The real question seems to be about the extent to which the community of scholars cares a whit about mass democratic education for the nation's children, beyond slinging barbs at the schools and/or education faculties."[9] Given the likely answer to Levin's question, so reminiscent of similar questions asked by Conant a quarter-century earlier, there was little reason to assume that the 1990s would see much in the way of important developments in the field. But more voices were joining the chorus in demanding change.

In 1988 Geraldine Joncich Clifford and James W. Guthrie reflected on the bitter battles that had taken place at the University of California at Berkeley to maintain an education department, where they had both served terms as chairs of the much-maligned unit. Their frustration was clear as they wrote the first page of their book, *Ed School:*

> Our thesis is that schools of education, particularly those located on the campuses of prestigious research universities, have become ensnared improvidently in the academic and political cultures of their institutions and have neglected their professional allegiances. They are like marginal men, aliens in their own world. They have seldom succeeded in satisfying the scholarly norms of their campus letters and science colleagues, and they are simultaneously estranged from their practicing professional peers. The more forcefully they have rowed toward the shores of scholarly research, the more distant they have become from the public schools

they are duty bound to serve. Conversely, systematic efforts at addressing the applied problems of public schools have placed schools of education at risk on their own campuses.[10]

Few faculty in similar departments across the country would have disputed the analysis of the situation for the 1980s or, in many places, for the following decades. The only strong dissent might have come from the faculty in the relatively newer education departments and schools, who would want to delete the reference to "those located on the campuses of prestigious research universities." This was a national problem among the elite and those much further back in the academic procession.

Two years later, as John Goodlad's colleagues reviewed their own detailed study of the recent history of "places where teachers are taught," they came to a similar conclusion. When Soder and Sirotnik looked at the institutions they had been studying, their conclusions reflected the same pessimism, the same sense of being caught in a double bind between the demands of the university and the demands of the schools that Clifford and Guthrie described. They concluded:

> As William Johnson notes, "the history of twentieth-century teacher training can be seen as a series of institutional displacements, with normal schools becoming state teachers colleges, then multipurpose liberal arts colleges, and now, in many instances, regional state universities." The displacement, for all types of institutions with teacher training programs, has been in the direction of research and away from traditional teaching and service activities. . . . The university schools of education "have consciously distanced themselves from training and serving classroom instructors" and the "university research agenda produces little useful knowledge for the practitioner or scholarship respected by members of traditional academic disciplines." . . . The shift from a teaching and service emphasis to a research emphasis continues. . . . That which was honored no longer is, leading to a sense of betrayal and resentment.

Report after report, commentator after commentator found the university-based schools of education—and nearly all teachers were being prepared in such programs—in a state of intellectual disarray. Faculty were deserting teacher preparation to engage in more high-prestige and university-rewarded fields, be they education policy studies, statistical research, or the ongoing efforts at educational studies.

Goodlad and his colleagues were hardly the only ones to identify this problem. Judith Lanier, education dean at Michigan State University and the leader of the group that wrote the Holmes Report, wrote on another occasion, "There is an inverse relationship between professorial prestige and the intensity of involvement with the formal education of teachers."[11] The Goodlad team noted that though they were housed in schools of education, many faculty members identified with the liberal arts disciplines, and from the safe perspective of those disciplinary departments studied the field of education. For those who remained in directly in teacher preparation, there was a loss of identity, a loss of prestige and recognition, and, as Soder and Sirotnik conclude, "a major consequence of loss of identity (for individuals and for groups), in addition to low morale and resentment, is a sense of powerlessness, a sense of the futility of involvement in the enterprise." It was, to put it mildly, a sorry state of affairs. And yet something was brewing that might lead to better days, even as Goodlad, Soder and Sirotnik and Clifford and Guthrie were writing.[12]

HOLMES AND CARNEGIE—WHAT THE REPORTS RECOMMENDED AND WHAT THEY CHANGED

In the spring of 1986, two education reports appeared almost simultaneously that, taken together—as they almost always were—redefined teacher education in the United States. For a decade after the publication of *A Nation Prepared*, the report of the Carnegie Forum on Education and the Economy, and *Tomorrow's Teachers*, from the Holmes Group of Education Deans in 1986, both of which called for a significant restructuring of teacher education, these reports set the agenda.[13] Even for the harshest detractors of the reports, there was a sense that they had focused the nation's attention in a way that nothing else had done in decades. Since the publication of *A Nation at Risk* in 1983, there had been a plethora of reports about the problems of American education, but not, for a long time, teacher education. Then the tidal wave hit.[14]

Longtime education dean Gary R. Galluzzo described the context in which the Holmes and Carnegie reports appeared. In spite of the impact caused by *A Nation at Risk*, in 1983 many teacher educators felt that with the consolidation of their work in schools, colleges, and departments of education in larger colleges and universities, their own battles were in the past. "Comfort and complacency perhaps best describe the condition of teacher education prior to the fateful shockwave," Galluzzo wrote. Once the 17 Holmes deans—education deans at some of the most elite of the nation's universities—began to make their own views public, joined by the leaders of the Carnegie Forum, the situation was very different. As Galluzzo said:

> The challenge Holmes [and I would add Carnegie—they were hard to separate for many observers] laid down generated both academic and emotional reactions. . . . Many chuckled over whether the faculty at these flagship universities could ever really attend to the world of practice. At the same time, the most visible leader of the Holmes Group, Michigan State's Dean Judith Lanier, was raising a great deal of money and allies to support the initiative. . . . Moving quickly from a study group to a national organization, Holmes invoked exclusive membership criteria that omitted all state regional colleges and universities—

former teachers' colleges that had produced annually about two-thirds of the nation's teachers—and all private liberal arts colleges.

To many this felt like one more top-down elite effort to separate the winners and the losers in teacher education and to marginalize those institutions that prepared the vast majority of the nation's teachers.

Nevertheless, these new reports were different from previous reports. They moved from critique to proposing solutions. And the solutions they proposed—though far from universally accepted—were based on the kind of intellectually coherent view of teacher education that Koerner and Conant and others of their generation have been properly criticized for missing. At the core of the Holmes report was a central, non-controversial goal, "to make the education of teachers intellectually more solid." In the end, for all of its problematic vagueness, it was a goal that was hard to resist.[15]

The two reports, apparently developed somewhat separately—although Judith Lanier was part of both groups—are surprisingly similar in the basic reforms that they call for. The basic list, as summarized in the Carnegie report, includes the following:

- Create a National Board for Professional Teaching Standards . . . to establish high standards for what teachers need to know and be able to do . . . [While the National Board was a Carnegie proposal, the focus on establishing high standards and a differentiated professional hierarchy was the core of Holmes.]
- Restructure schools to provide a professional environment for teaching.
- Restructure the teaching force, and introduce a new category of Lead Teachers.
- Require a bachelor's degree in the arts and sciences. [Holmes was clearer in wanting to move all professional study to the graduate level.]
- Develop a new professional curriculum in graduate schools of education leading to a Master in Teaching degree, based on systematic knowledge of teaching and including internships and residencies in the schools.
- Mobilize the nation's resources to prepare minority youngsters for teaching careers. [The initial Holmes report was silent on this issue, but subsequent reports by the Holmes Group gave significant attention to the issue.]
- Relate incentives for teachers to school-wide performance . . .
- Make teachers' salaries and career opportunities competitive with those in other professions.[16]

For the rest of the decade of the 1980s, and well into the 1990s, the pages of scholarly journals and popular publications in education were filled with debates about these recommendations, but the recommendations dominated the discussion. Initially the options in teacher education seemed to be limited to either the complete implementation of the Holmes and Carnegie proposals or to casting a critical eye on the reform efforts in a way that, given the absence of alternative reform visions, simply supported the maintenance of the status quo. In reality the world was more complex, as people like John Goodlad had been making clear for years. Nevertheless, there were plenty of defenders and critics, and for a time the teacher education world seemed ready to divide into a new set of hostile camps. More nuanced responses to the reports and to the intellectual and political ferment they launched did appear in time. Many found some parts of the reports' recommendations that they favored, even if they opposed others. And the intellectual and political ferment that they launched certainly transformed the landscape in the late 1980s and early 1990s.

It is important to note that though the diagnosis of the problem in the Holmes and Carnegie reports was similar to earlier diagnoses offered by John Goodlad, Geraldine Clifford, and James Guthrie, their proposed cure was quite different. As David Labaree has written, there was a fundamental tension in the reform agendas, with "the Holmes Group advocating a strategy that would tie teacher education more closely to the university and Clifford and Guthrie advocating a strategy that would ally the programs more closely with the teaching profession." Labaree himself had serious doubts that either direction would work. In *The Trouble with Ed Schools* he argued:

> A professional school cut off from the profession, offering only a pale reflection of disciplinary scholarship, provides no rationale for its continued existence, which is one reason that high-end education schools are the most frequent to bite the dust. And an education school that pursues the professional role, while taking on a bit of research and doctoral study ends up coming off as lowbrow to the university and as pretentious to the profession.

Until some quite different ways of looking at the place of education schools develops, it seems that every proposal will be caught in the tension Labaree describes.[17]

While the debates have continued for decades, however, many of the proposed reforms were implemented at breakneck speed in the 1980s. While teacher education did not follow the medical or legal norm and become an all graduate school enterprise, the role of the liberal arts, often meaning a required major in a liberal arts discipline, the strengthening of clinical experiences, and the raising of academic standards in the late 1980s and early 1990s are all developments that can be traced at least in part to the impact of Holmes and Carnegie. The history of education reform movements in the United States has often been one of much national rhetoric and little action at the local level. For all the pages of print generated by the Koerner and Conant books, it is hard to locate a campus where the curriculum changed because of what they said. The Holmes and Carnegie reforms were different. An amazing number of states and individual institutions became involved in changing at least some parts of their systems for preparing teachers. Within the first 2 years of the publication of the Holmes and Carnegie reports, the majority of the 50 states had made some kind of change in their certification laws. This speed in actual implementation of reform proposals stands in sharp contrast to many reform efforts conducted earlier in the 20th century.[18]

For all of the local variety, there was a coherence in the direction of the changes—more study in the academic content areas, more time in student teaching or other internship placements, reduction in the proliferation of education courses—that would have encouraged critics stretching back at least as far as Arthur Bestor, though few remembered what he had written 30 years before. Two years after the reports appeared, the *Chronicle of Higher Education* reported that "Twenty-six states have stiffened the requirements for admission to teacher education programs," and "Thirty-two states have revised the curriculum for students who plan to become teachers. Some have abolished the undergraduate degree in education and now require prospective students to major in an academic subject area. . . . Other states have increased the number of courses in pedagogy that teacher education majors must take."[19]

While state agencies were changing the rules of the game, the Carnegie Corporation continued to build a national base for institutionalizing the proposals through its funding of the National Board for Professional Teaching Standards, chaired by North Carolina Governor James Hunt, which began issuing its first certificates for "Board Certified Teachers." With Carnegie support, the Carnegie Forum on Education and the Economy was transformed into the National Center on Education and the Economy, an independent advocacy agency based in Rochester, New York. One of the advantages of a foundation with the resources of the Carnegie Corporation of New York is that it can both propose major reforms and simply pay for the implementation of at least some of its recommendations.[20]

IMPLEMENTATION IN MASSACHUSETTS—A CASE STUDY

Among the states that moved decisively to implement some of the recommendations that came from the Holmes Group and the Carnegie Forum was Massachusetts, the state where the normal schools had been born. In 1986, as the national reports were being released to great fanfare, Massachusetts found itself with three new leaders in education. Robert Schwartz was appointed as the Education Advisor to Governor Michael Dukakis, who was then seriously exploring what would be a successful run for the Democratic nomination for president in 1988 and who wanted to make education one of his key issues. At the same time, the state board of education appointed Harold R. Raynolds, formerly the commissioner of education in the state of Alaska, as the Massachusetts commissioner of education, successor in the office first held by Horace Mann. And the new position of Chancellor of the state Board of Regents of Higher Education, a body that directly oversaw the state colleges—the former teachers colleges—was filled by Franklyn Jennifer, a leader in higher education recruited from New Jersey. Schwartz, Raynolds, and Jennifer liked each other personally, wanted to work together, and saw in the national reports an agenda for change in the regulations governing the education of teachers in Massachusetts that could create desperately needed quality controls.

There was good reason for the state's education leaders to be concerned. In the previous year, while the Holmes and Carnegie reports were in the making, a team of senior educators from outside the state, led by former New York University dean Daniel E. Griffiths, visited the teacher preparation programs in Massachusetts. Their report was not encouraging. They found, "Most of the units try to do too much with too little" [and] "very few minority students and proportionately even fewer minority faculty members." Most of all, the team said, "Teacher education programs can be characterized as too much Education, too little liberal arts." It was a blunt call for change.

The Griffiths team found that "elementary education majors often take up to 60 semester hours of Education (far too much) with the result that there is too little time for liberal arts courses, while there are so few secondary teacher education students that the institutions cannot offer proper classes in Education, particularly special methods. Basic to the elementary education major problem is an erroneous interpretation of the requirements for state certification (interpreted by some institutions to mean between 50 and 60 semester hours in Education) and poor advisement which allows students to take Education courses instead of the appropriate liberal arts courses." They also found the national tensions replicated on many campuses, "The perceptions expressed by students were supported by the visiting team's impression that academic professors were not very interested in Education students. The impression was also conveyed that the relationship between academic professors and Education professors was 'not all that good.'" No wonder the state's education leaders felt change was urgent.[21]

The Schwartz, Jennifer, and Raynolds team wanted to move quickly. They appointed a 31-member Joint Task Force on Teacher Preparation, drawn from college presidents, school superintendents, college faculty, classroom teachers, and state union leaders, and decided to personally co-chair it. The group was given a mandate to develop a report regarding a fundamental restructuring of teacher education in Massachusetts and to do so in 4 months. Timing, the leaders understood, was everything. Too much deliberation would only sink the process into a never-ending political quagmire.

The task force called for "a solid foundation in the liberal arts and sciences," and defined this foundation as "a major in the liberal arts and sciences, or an appropriate interdisciplinary major, as well as broad distribution of liberal arts courses." If any campus retained an education major—and several did—it would have to be a dual major program. Once adopted, the JTTP (as the task force came to be known) recommendation meant that every future teacher in Massachusetts would have a liberal arts major. Of all the recommendations, this was the most controversial and the most far-reaching.

The task force also argued that "the heart of the teacher preparation process should be in the schools where teachers will practice their profession," including a new level of mentoring for first-year teachers. Arguing that "today's teachers are a great untapped resource in training the next generation of teachers," they created a new category of mentor teacher. Finally, the report insisted that in order to design and implement these new requirements, a new level of partnership between school districts, arts and sciences faculty members, and education professors would be required so that every new teacher could work with a team of a mentor teacher and faculty experts in both pedagogy and content.[22]

The report was met with very mixed reviews. Some hailed it as the most significant advance in standards for teacher preparation in decades, while others saw it as "destroying teacher education" in Massachusetts. Some of the report's recommendations, such as those about developing more integrated undergraduate experiences, were vague enough that everyone could claim immediate success, while others—most of all the requirement of an arts and sciences major for every teacher—were so explicit that they had to be accepted or rejected. The commitment to the arts and sciences major stuck. Other recommendations were implemented for a time and then faded. But as with the nation, some things, especially a growing focus on the need for more arts and sciences courses as well as more school-based experiences for future teachers, remained.[23]

Other states followed similar patterns and would continue to do so for the rest of the century and beyond. The state of Illinois was one of 14 states to enter into a formal partnership with NCTAF (The National Commission on Teaching and America's Future, described later in this chapter) to develop clear performance standards for students, teachers, and teacher preparation programs. The result, published as the Illinois Framework for Restructuring the Recruitment, Preparation, Licensure and Continuing Professional Development of Teachers in 1996, also moved that state closer into the Holmes-Carnegie fold. Among other things, the 1996 Illinois reform involved implanting a three-tiered certification system in Illinois that includes initial certificate, a more permanent standard certificate, and finally a rank of Master Teacher that would be awarded when a teacher was certified by the National Board for Professional Teaching Standards, the organization originally established at the recommendation of the Carnegie Forum. Many other states followed the same pattern, using task forces, either state-mandated or private, partnerships with national reform groups like NCTAF, the National Board, or the Holmes Partnership, and legislation by state oversight bodies to move teacher education in the direction of standards that would, for the most part, have seemed logical to any member of the initial Holmes Group or Carnegie Forum.[24]

A CRISIS IN RACIAL DIVERSITY IN THE TEACHING PROFESSION

In their reports the authors of *A Nation Prepared,* the Carnegie Forum, had one recommendation completely missing from the first Holmes report. Carnegie said that it was essential to "Mobilize the nation's resources to prepare minority youngsters for teaching careers." In the heart of the report they also elaborated on this recommendation:

> The education available to minority and poor children is often lacking in quality compared to that offered to others. They drop out of the education "pipeline" much faster than other children. The result is that obtaining adequate numbers of minority teachers requires more than making teaching an attractive career. There are simply not enough minority students graduating from college with strong academic records to meet the growing need for minority teachers. Only a massive effort to improve the education of minority and poor students from elementary school through graduate school will effectively address the problem.[25]

Although they probably did not realize it, these authors were saying almost exactly the same thing that Ambrose Caliver had in his report on "The Education of Negro Teachers" in the early 1930s (see chapter 10). The Carnegie authors had named a reality that the nation could not continue to ignore if the schools were to be effective places of learning for all of the nation's children.

In the 5 years between 1978 and 1983 the number of new teachers graduating from historically black colleges that were members of the American Association of Colleges for Teacher Education decreased by almost half. And the number of African American teachers had been dropping in the United States for some time. In the decade and a half after the U.S. Supreme Court's 1954 *Brown v. Board of Education* decision that outlawed school segregation, some 31,584 African American teachers had lost their jobs in the schools of the Southern and border states most impacted by the initial implementation of *Brown,* which far too often meant integrating white schools and closing black ones.[26]

In 1987, a year after the Carnegie recommendations appeared, the American Association of Colleges for Teacher Education hosted a gathering at the Wingspread Conference Center in Wisconsin that resulted in a report, *Minority*

Teacher Recruitment and Retention: A Public Policy. AACTE continued to attend to the issue, and in 1992 Mary E. Dilworth, then the organization's senior director for research, edited an influential volume, *Diversity in Teacher Education: New Expectations,* that added urgency to the discussion and proposed promising practices that could address the concern for a more diverse teaching force in the nation The Dilworth volume also broadened the discussion from one that had begun as a focus on African American teachers to include recruiting and supporting Latino and Asian teachers.[27]

Some states took up the challenge offered by the Carnegie report and the discussions generated by it, but in general the political will to make real change was lacking. Some individual colleges and universities did develop their own creative programs to recruit more African American and Latino, and occasionally Asian, teachers, but of all of the recommendations that received so much attention in the 1980s, this one had probably the least to show in terms of measurable outcomes some 20 years later.[28]

THE HOLMES GROUP BECOMES
THE HOLMES PARTNERSHIP

Within months of the publication of the first Holmes report, its implementation became the work of the Holmes Group, an alliance of some 100 research universities in the United States "dedicated to applying the intellectual and material resources of those powerful yet often rigid places to the deep and permanent improvement of the education of teachers," as one of the group's major outside observers, Oxford University's Harry Judge, put it. Some also said that the group was dedicated to preserving the elite status of their own institutions over the regional universities that still produced most of the teachers. But in the minds of the Holmes leaders, the key to improving the education of teachers, and therefore the education offered to American youth, was to improve the intellectual seriousness and professional relevance of education in the best places and—as had happened in medical education after the 1910 Flexner report—to close the places that could not measure up.[29]

This expanded Holmes Group published a second and third Holmes report. *Tomorrow's Schools,* published in 1990, called for shifting much of the core of teacher preparation into Professional Development Schools and for a much more in-depth connection between schools of education and elementary and secondary schools. These new Professional Development Schools were meant to be the focus of educational research, thoughtful, long-term inquiry into the teaching and learning process, as well as places for internships and joint faculty planning. While the report was long on expectations, it left open the debate as to whether a professional development school had to fit exactly into the Holmes mold, what Frank Murray called an "all-or-none" criteria for a

Professional Development School, or whether they were simply "an ideal type toward which reform-minded schools are striving."[30]

The third Holmes Group report, *Tomorrow's Schools of Education,* was not published until 1995, in large part because of major disagreements within the Holmes Group about just how specific to be in terms of what constituted the kind of education school that would fulfill the mandate of the original report to foster a continuing process of reform in the best education schools and close the rest. One reviewer called *Tomorrow's Schools of Education* "a curious mixture of scathing self-criticism, high ideals, revolutionary talk, timid reform proposals, and stunning omissions." While probably too harsh, the reality was that the best ways to link universities to professional development schools—given the huge differences in the culture of higher education and K–12 education—and to find the best ways to engage the arts and sciences faculty in teacher education have yet to be found. *Tomorrow's Schools of Education* did not find them.[31]

In the process of developing its three reports, the Holmes Group had also gone through substantial changes not only in leadership but in philosophy. While the first Holmes Report focused on the importance of education schools—or at least elite education schools—gaining prestige within the university, by the third report the authors seemed much less interested in the pursuit of academic credibility. Thus they wrote critically of those who sought it, "Many professors go about their teaching and research with hardly a nod toward the public schools, seldom ever deigning to cross the thresholds of those 'lowly' places." By Holmes III the schools, not the universities, had become the proposed center of the action. Perhaps Clifford and Guthrie, as well as Goodlad, were winning the argument after all.[32]

When *Tomorrow's Schools of Education* finished its long gestation and finally saw the light of day, there was a widespread sense that things needed to change at the Holmes Group. There had been considerable accomplishments. The Group had reframed the debate about teacher education, not only introducing the notion of a Professional Development School but also raising the standards for both the clinical experience and the intellectual discourse of teacher education. Through its emphasis on equity and diversity in the two later reports and through the creation of the Holmes Scholars program, which supported over 100 doctoral candidates of color in a mentoring and networking system designed to create a pool of new faculty of color in education schools, the Holmes Group tried to make up for the omissions of the first report.

By 1995, however, the members of the Holmes Group were feeling marginalized, perhaps stalled in their efforts, and indeed, beginning to think that their elite status and emphasis on report-writing was working against them. The group restructured itself as the Holmes Partnership, a much-expanded alliance of education schools, professional organizations, schools, and school districts. The goal of the new partnership was to take the core of their work—

an emphasis on high-quality professional preparation and institutional renewal in K–12 schools and education schools, a deep commitment to equity
and diversity as well as scholarly inquiry and research—and turn all of that
into a series of policy initiatives. The fact that this set of changes took place
at the same time as the launch of the National Commission on Teaching and
America's Future (NCTAF) and the last Clinton-era reauthorization of the
Higher Education Act that included Title V, "Shaping the Profession that
Shapes America's Future," a section that put federal dollars behind the
NCTAF agenda, meant that renewed attention to teacher education seemed
promising.[33]

One major study of the decadelong life of the Holmes Group, of which
Galluzzo was also a co-author, concluded, "We have a chance for the first time
of really bringing the teaching profession into the postmodern age. We could
do this but then again, we may not." Harry Judge, with characteristic blunt-
ness, concluded his evaluation of the same 1986–1996 decade by saying, "The
effort stalled (which is not to say terminated) when the colleges and schools of
education had to think seriously about reforming themselves. They will change
only when they really wish to, and not enough yet do." The future, as always,
was impossible to predict.[34]

Afterword:
Teachers for a New Millennium

2000–

Gretchen Wilkinson received her second academic degree from the University of Washington in 2003 just as the university was being awarded one of the Carnegie Corporation of New York's prestigious Teachers for a New Era grants. The $5 million grant came to the university with the expectation that it would dramatically improve its teacher education programs. But the Carnegie grant was also a vote of confidence in what was already happening at Washington, in the education that had been given to Wilkinson and to students at the other schools that received similar funds.

One result of the Carnegie grant was that Wilkinson and other recent graduates were eligible to participate in Washington's new Center for Teaching and Learning, designed to support recent graduates in their early years of teaching. While Wilkinson came to teaching with more life experience than many—she had previously taught in rural upstate New York and then run her own business for 12 years—she could not have agreed more with those who called for such an initiative. "No one should be put out there without a really tight mentor who is encouraging, supportive and lets them know what is possible," she said. "It can be really discouraging, and yet, teachers are just sent out there and told to go do it. I just don't think it is fair."[1]

Wilkinson's experience makes her representative of several emerging trends in teacher education in the 21st century. Carnegie's Teachers for a New Era is but one of several new initiatives designed to dramatically improve the quality of teacher preparation and respond to many of the longstanding critiques of the enterprise. Even among places that are recognized as national leaders, few were satisfied with the status quo in teacher education as the new millennium opened. The University of Washington's development of a program to mentor its graduates is also representative of programs being developed in several places. Teaching may have long been something that people, especially women, did for a few years before moving on, but many have come to worry about the rapid turnover in teaching, and mentoring programs are one way to slow the exodus while also linking education schools and school systems in a closer partnership to support novice teachers. To what degree these sorts of initiatives will continue, or will be displaced by other currents, is impossible to know. But any careful look at the status of teacher preparation in the middle of the first decade of a new century would include a number of important organizations and trends for which Wilkinson's education could be illustrative.

WHAT MATTERS MOST—THE NATIONAL COMMISSION ON TEACHING AND AMERICA'S FUTURE

In September 1996, a decade after the Holmes and Carnegie reports had appeared, the National Commission on Teaching and America's Future released its long-anticipated report, *What Matters Most: Teaching for America's Future.* Chaired by North Carolina governor James B. Hunt, who had also been a leader in the earlier Carnegie efforts, including some of the nation's most distinguished educators, and funded by the Rockefeller Foundation and the Carnegie Corporation of New York, the commission was well placed to attract public notice. The report itself, written by a team led by Linda Darling-Hammond, then of Teachers College, Columbia University, made a series of dramatic recommendations, including a call for state and school districts to "get serious about standards for both students and teachers"; for a thorough restructuring of teacher preparation, recruitment, and professional development; for encouraging and rewarding teacher skills; and for ensuring that schools are structured for success.

In offering the media a combination of dramatic examples of current failure—over one-third of mathematics teachers have not had a major or a minor in the subject; the majority of teacher education institutions are not accredited—and in calling for sweeping change and an "audacious goal—by the year 2006, America will provide all students in the country with what should be their educational birthright: access to competent, caring, and qualified teachers," the report generated immediate notice. Ironically, neither the publicity around the report nor the report itself gave significant attention to the fact that it was, in fact, taking its place in a long series of reports stretching over decades. While the authors of *What Matters Most* made respectful reference to some of the most influential reports of the past decade, those previous efforts are hardly central to the argument of *What Matters Most.* No wonder that some of the more experienced, or perhaps jaundiced, of observers asked, what is different this time?[2]

In fact, several things were different in the implementation of the National Commission on Teaching and America's Future report. The report called for the development of what came to be called the "three-legged stool," linking the teaching standards of the National Board for Professional Teaching Standards (NBPTS) to a more consistent national pattern of state program approval devised by the Interstate New Teacher Assessment and Support Consortium (INTASC), and to accreditation by the National Council for Accreditation of Teacher Education (NCATE). By linking initial licensure, advanced national board certification, state program approval, and professional accreditation, the National Commission was proposing a strong, coherent, standardized system for evaluating the success and failure of the nation's teacher preparation efforts.[3]

There were those who questioned whether in creating such specific standards and developing such tight institutional linkages NCTAF—as the report came to be known—was creating an overly rigid system, a kind of "one best system," to use David Tyack's felicitous term, that might hinder innovation. Indeed, that was exactly the worry about national accreditation that James Conant had voiced in 1963. While voluntary accreditation has certainly helped many institutions improve their teacher preparation programs, requiring everyone to be accredited by a single accrediting agency ran the risk, some argued, of fostering bureaucracy and uniformity. The conservative tilt of early-21st-century politics also led some to question linking state program approval to national standards when different ideological approaches to education changed the state and federal standards depending on the most recent election.[4]

Nevertheless, NCTAF represented something different from its predecessors. The stirring language of the report's goals, and the spotlight on the very real problems—the huge numbers of American youth being taught by teachers not certified or not expert in the subject matter—generated the initial publicity. But what really made a difference was the fact that the National Commission (which took on the NCTAF name) became a permanent organization fostering a series of national meetings and state partnerships "to create new policies and practices for dramatically improving the quality of teaching."[5] NCTAF, it seemed, was now a permanent fixture on the national scene.

REGULATION AND DEREGULATION IN A CONSERVATIVE ASCENDANCY

In 1990, a young Princeton senior, Wendy Koop, used her undergraduate thesis to propose a new program to attract some of the nation's most able undergraduates, perhaps Princeton seniors like herself, to careers—at least, short-term careers—in teaching. The program struck a chord among many who wanted to see higher standards for those who entered the teaching profession and who believed that state program approval requirements as well as college curricula imposed far more in the way of quantity than they did quality. As a result, Koop was able to quickly amass the necessary funds and to launch Teach For America, perhaps the most successful of the myriad of alternative routes to teaching that sprung up in a development that was parallel in time to the NCTAF-led reforms while reincarnating the spirit of the Teacher Corps.

United States Secretary of Education Rod Paige described what he liked about Teach For America in 2003:

> Since 1990, Teach For America has placed more than 9,000 college students in schools from the Mississippi Delta to Los Angeles. In that time it has become one of the nation's largest suppliers of teachers; according to the American Association of Colleges for Teacher Education, only 10 percent of institutions produce more new teachers each year. Teach For America's recruits are precisely the type of candidates the nation needs to attract to teaching: the typical member has a 3.5 GPA and 89 percent have leadership experience. These teachers receive five weeks of training during the summer and take courses toward certification during the year while they teach full time.

Having described TFA's approach, Paige also cited Hoover Institution research that was to him quite convincing as to the program's effectiveness:

> In mathematics, students of new Teach For America recruits finished 12 percent of a standard deviation higher than students of other new teachers. Teach For America recruits were also much more consistent than other teachers; for instance more than 60 percent of Teacher For America teachers performed better than the median non-TFA teachers in reading. The study's authors concluded, "If you were choosing between two math teachers and the only thing you knew about them was that one was a TFA member and one was not, you would choose the TFA member. This would give you the best chance of selecting a good teacher."[6]

If only it were that easy. Other researchers drew quite different conclusions.

Linda Darling-Hammond, a leading critic of TFA, disputed every part of the research offered by Paige and the Hoover-based research team. Darling-Hammond accused the researchers who wrote such glowing reviews of TFA's graduates of failing to make the right comparisons. If one were to compare TFA graduates against those who have completed rigorous, accredited "traditional" teacher education programs, then, Darling-Hammond argued, it was essential to compare them with certified teachers, not the whole of the teacher force in any city, many of whom may have also entered teaching through alternative routes or with temporary credentials. The issue was not how TFA graduates do in comparison with all teachers but against fully certified teachers. Darling-Hammond and her colleagues made their own analysis of Houston, where the Hoover research was done, and their findings could not have been more different:

In a series of regression analyses looking at 4th and 5th grade student achievement gains on six different reading and mathematics tests over a six-year period, we find that certified teachers consistently produce significantly stronger student achievement gains than do uncertified teachers. These findings hold for TFA recruits as well as others. Controlling for teacher experience, degrees, and student characteristics, uncertified TFA recruits are less effective than certified teachers, and perform about as well as other uncertified teachers.

Thus Darling-Hammond and her colleagues conclude, "Teachers' effectiveness appears strongly related to the preparation they have received for teaching."[7]

In the end, this competing research left most citizens, educators and noneducators alike, in a quandary. When Rod Paige, long known to like Teach For America, found research that indicated that TFA graduates do much better than other teachers and Linda Darling-Hammond, who has if anything a longer track record as a detractor of TFA, found research that the program was ineffective, who is to be believed? The research duel is likely to continue, and it will be an unusual moment when any researcher accepts research at odds with his or her views.[8]

For most people, the one sure thing is that TFA and other programs like it are going to continue to be a major part of the configuration of teacher education in the United States for a long time to come. In its first 15 years, TFA has attracted over 12,000 participants. Many only stay for their 2-year term, and TFA proudly announces the post-TFA careers of their corps members who go on to be doctors, lawyers, engineers, civil rights leaders, and long-term teachers. But in a profession where the majority leave within 5 years, no matter what entry route they take, and in a nation that has become convinced that high academic standards are needed for teaching, TFA offers to recruit some very bright people to spend some part of their lives teaching others. Because of its success and size, it is also the symbol for many, supporters and detractors, of the many alternative routes into the teaching profession that have come to be a permanent part of the 21st-century educational scene.[9]

The debate between advocates for a NCTAF-like approach who seek excellence through high standards and TFA advocates who seek to "let a thousand flowers bloom" is based on their differing reading of the research. In part, however, it is based on even more fundamental views of the definition of educational excellence. One perceptive observer of the battles over teacher education at the beginning of the 21st century has said, "There is no one who is more prescriptive than a libertarian with power." With the contested presidential election of 2000, a new generation of libertarians and other conservatives came to power in the nation's capital and in many of the states. These conservatives had an agenda for teacher education, as they did for many aspects of the nation's life, one that they had been developing for years, if not decades, in such think tanks as the American Enterprise Institute, the Manhattan Institute, and similar places.

One element in the conservative agenda was a reduction in the standards for credentialing and licensure of teachers, the barriers to entry into teaching, as they called them, exactly the standards that NCTAF advocates wanted to raise. In these terms the battle lines were fairly clear. As Frederick M. Hess, certainly one of the more conservative voices in the debate, described the split, "One reasonable response to this challenge [the concern over educational quality that began with the 1983 publication of *A Nation at Risk*] was to seek to specify new guidelines that would toughen up the existing licensure and preparation systems. Most famously this was the tack of the reports of the Carnegie Task Force on Teaching as a Profession (1986) and the Holmes Group." On the other hand, Hess saw those, including himself, "who would strip down much of the existing licensure apparatus . . . [which] leaves established gatekeepers unchallenged, dissuades talent from entering the field, stifles challenges to the reigning orthodoxy, and inflates the cost of educational provision. Such critics would pursue new structural arrangements that would allow aspiring educators to bypass traditional preparation institutions and, thus, diminish the influence of existing stakeholders." As summarized by Hess, this seems like a fairly straightforward split. On the one hand are people, and Linda Darling-Hammond certainly comes to mind, who believe that the key to future progress is tough and consistent high standards and structures to enforce them, and on the other hand are people like Hess himself, who see the very same standards as "unnecessary, ineffectual, or an obstacle to recruiting talented candidates."[10]

At the same time that Hess and some of his colleagues gathered at the American Enterprise Institute to urge on the decentralizing and less rigid agenda, other conservatives were coming to power in the U.S. Department of Education and in state departments and were using that power to move in exactly the opposite direction, to impose new and quite rigid curricular standards—phonics was in, whole language was out; direct instruction was in, constructivist approaches were out; American history was to teach an appreciation of the heroes of the past, not a questioning attitude toward governments past and present. And teacher education programs were to be held accountable for the success of their students in passing tests often based on some of the same ideological standards, the state program approval process was to be used to ensure conformity to the reigning curricular ideology, and research was to be defined as only that research that met the "gold standard" of being scientifically based including random assignment of youth to control groups. It is an odd juxtaposition with the more libertarian call for tearing down the walls that surrounded professional practice or the call by NCTAF's leaders for high but very different standards. Yet all of these trends seemed to exist simultaneously and be supported by many in authority, and teacher educators, once again, felt buffeted in the process.[11]

TOWARD THE FUTURE—CLARITY, DIVERSITY, AND NEW TENSIONS

While the political battles were raging, one of the most venerable players in generations of reform efforts, the Carnegie Corporation of New York, launched a major new initiative, Teachers for a New Era, targeted specifically at improving the quality of teaching by improving teacher education. Led by Daniel Fallon, former dean of the College of Liberal Arts at Texas A & M University and founder of Project 30 Alliance of some 30 colleges and universities that committed themselves to expanded partnerships between education and arts and sciences faculty members, Carnegie committed itself to six to nine—eventually 11—awards of $5 million each to select colleges of education that could represent exemplary practice.

From its inception in 2001, Teachers for a New Era was organized by three design principles—that teacher education programs should be guided by evidence, including evidence of pupil learning gains under graduates of the program; engagement of the arts and sciences disciplinary faculty in the preparation of teachers; and that teacher education should be a clinical practice profession requiring close cooperation with schools, master teachers, and residencies for beginning teachers. The call for engaging the arts and sciences faculty in teacher education and the demand for more clinical practice could certainly be dated at least to the mid-20th-century work of James Bryant Conant and others. The call for evidence reflected an increasing distrust of assertions that could not be measured.

In time eleven very different schools of education from across the United States were selected to lead the Teachers for a New Era experiment including Bank Street College in New York, California State University at Northridge, Michigan State University, the University of Virginia, Boston College, Florida A & M University, Stanford University, the University of Connecticut, the University of Texas at El Paso, the University of Washington, and the University of Wisconsin-Milwaukee.

Teachers for a New Era was different from other grants to schools of education because of the amount of money involved—$5 million from Carnegie or other funders to be matched by $10 million raised by each campus—but also because the schools formed a network and promised transparency in regular reports to the larger education world on the success and failure of their efforts.[12]

In an attempt to clarify the meaning of best practices in teacher education, the American Educational Research Association appointed its own expert panel in 1999, led by Marilyn Cochran-Smith and Kenneth Zeichner. That panel's report on research and teacher education was published in 2005. In the end, the panelists concluded that while "reviews of this kind are likely to conclude with definitive recommendations," the depth of the debates in teacher education made that impossible. As one example, Marilyn Cochran-Smith and Kim Fries note that while virtually everyone, from those on campuses to those in the halls of Congress and the federal Department of Education, focus on and call for guarantees regarding "teacher quality," the meaning and measures of that term can be elusive. For some, teacher quality is measured in terms of student achievement—"good teachers are ones who get large gains in student achievement for their classes; bad teachers are just the opposite"—while for others teacher quality is measured by the standards of preparation and the qualifications of the teacher. Cochran-Smith and Fries also note that depending on the issue, the lines can shift again and again. For example, some who are deeply concerned with social justice for those often excluded in American schools because of race, poverty, or gender see justice being achieved best through tough high standards, while others, equally committed, see the same standards as closing the doors either on teachers of color or on programs that give particular attention to the kinds of urban partnerships that will produce the most effective teachers.[13]

The AERA panel also noted that the debate about just what constituted research, described so well in Ellen Lagemann's *An Elusive Science: The Troubling History of Education Research*, had only expanded in the half-decade since Lagemann had published her book. While the federal government had narrowed the definition of acceptable research in education to what was called "scientific research," defined as experimental research with control groups of other pupils in place, many if not most in the educational research community rejected such a narrow, deterministic approach to research about the teaching and learning process while questioning the ethics of maintaining control groups in some educational settings. The ways in which that debate will develop, and the impact of the debate itself and the research generated on the more immediate work of preparing teachers, is yet to be known.[14]

On February 21, 2005, David G. Imig stood before the members of the American Association of Colleges for Teacher Education to deliver the association's Charles W. Hunt Memorial Lecture. It was an emotional moment, for it was also David Imig's own farewell to an organization that he had led for a quarter-century. In that speech Imig outlined what he saw as a likely agenda, for his organization and for the whole of American teacher education in the coming decades of the 21st century. Imig painted a sometimes stark agenda for the assembled education deans and professors. He offered a long list of challenges he saw on the horizon, including the facts that, "Accountability demands will escalate . . . Challenges to the social justice agenda and multicultural ideology will intensify . . . Calls for new forms of scholarship will escalate . . . Competition among providers will intensify as school districts bid teacher preparation and principal preparation among all providers and gain the right to award certification at the district level." He also predicted, "Resources will stagnate." For many in the room it was a sobering list, not only the note about stagnating resources, but the prediction of increased federal and state intrusion into the work of the schools and the schools of education while the same government bodies would pour resources into alternative means of entry into teaching.

In the end, while Imig pleaded with his colleagues to recommit to being a community of common interest in protecting their efforts and resisting most of the current directions, he also pleaded for "a new progressivism that truly values all children and youth," that would create a new center of gravity in the teacher education field. He urged teacher educators not to get distracted and not to turn into negative defenders of their ways of doing things, but to stay focused, above all, on "The democracy and education agenda [that] has shaped teacher education for more than a century." "We must create a new democratic ideal," he said, "and prepare teachers to engage all students in reaching that ideal."

For this leader, these were not merely high ideals, but a pragmatic response, closely anchored in his own career, and also in a tradition that had been part of the history of teacher education in the United States since at least the 1830s. In proposing that agenda, Imig was joining a long line of teacher educators beginning with Emma Willard and Henry Barnard, and including among many others Ella Flagg Young, Charlotte Hawkins Brown, and Thomas Hunter, all of whom saw teaching as fundamentally a moral enterprise as much as one of an exchange of knowledge, and who therefore advocated a kind of teacher education including attention to the teacher's ethical commitment to "teach every child," a commitment that in any generation could only be met with a mix of knowledge, skill, and moral fervor. Sometimes the agenda had been overshadowed by other voices, sometimes it was the dominant one, but linking reform in teacher education to a larger agenda of moral reform through the schools has been on the scene for a long time.[15]

Whether the early decades of the 21st century will witness a flowering of Imig's hopes for a "new progressivism" or some yet unimagined direction is, of course, beyond the current judgment of anyone. Whether the places where teachers are taught will be able to meet the concerns of their critics and transcend some of the historical problems that have afflicted the enterprise remains an open question. Will university faculty members, especially in the arts and sciences disciplines, be able to welcome colleagues who are committed to attending to the world of pedagogy as much as content or to the realm of practice as much as theory? Will teacher educators be able to hold themselves accountable to the highest of university standards without getting caught up in a quest for status that pulls them away from teachers and schools? Will they be able to avoid a romantic attachment to process alone, while keeping a clear focus on the preparation of expert teachers who know both what to teach and how to teach it? Will school leaders be able to appreciate the preparation of thoughtful and critical teachers who have had an education that prepares them to ask hard questions as well as to deliver effective services? And will everyone engaged in the enterprise have the moral courage to demand something better for all of the nation's children? These are among the questions that will determine what sort of preparation the American teachers of the early 21st century receive. It is a story to be watched carefully.

Notes

Introduction

1. David F. Labaree, *The Trouble with Ed Schools* (New Haven: Yale University Press, 2004), 2–3.

2. Ellen Lagemann, *An Elusive Science: The Troubling History of Educational Research* (Chicago: University of Chicago Press, 2000), xv.

3. Larry Cuban, *How Teachers Taught: Constancy and Change in American Classrooms, 1890–1990, 2nd ed.* (New York: Teachers College Press, 1993), xix.

4. John I. Goodlad, "Connecting the Present to the Past," in John I. Goodlad, Roger Soder, & Kenneth A. Sirotnik, editors, *Places Where Teachers Are Taught* (San Francisco: Jossey-Bass, 1990), 3–4; Ellen Condliffe Lagemann, *Private Power for the Public Good: A History of the Carnegie Foundation for the Advancement of Teaching* (New York: College Entrance Examination Board, 1983), 3.

5. Goodlad, 87.

6. *Report of the President of Cook County Board of Education and the Principal of Cook County Normal School for 1890* (Chicago: Cook County Board of Education, 1890), 12.

7. William S. Learned, William C. Bagley, et al., *The Professional Preparation of Teachers for American Public Schools* (New York: Carnegie Foundation for the Advancement of Teaching, 1920), 78.

8. See Labaree's brilliant discussion of these issues, both the tendency of education professors to create their own discipline and their tentative relationship to issues of social justice, in *The Trouble with Ed Schools*, especially chapter 6, "The Ed School's Romance with Progressivism," pp. 129–169. In the end I am more optimistic about the future of teacher preparation that Labaree seems to be, but only if the issues he raises are addressed forthrightly.

9. Labaree, p. 163.

Chapter 1

1. John Adams, *The Autobiography of John Adams*, in L. H. Butterfield, editor, *Diary and Autobiography of John Adams*, Volume 3 (Cambridge: The Belknap Press of Harvard University Press, 1961), 263. In this and subsequent quotations I have silently updated Adams's 18th-century spelling and capitalization.

2. David McCullough, *John Adams* (New York: Simon & Schuster, 2001), 37–44.

3. John Adams, entries for Saturday, February 21, Saturday, April 24, and Monday, March 15, 1756, in L. H. Butterfield, editor, *Diary and Autobiography of John Adams, 1755–1770*, Volume 1 (Cambridge: The Belknap Press of Harvard University Press, 1961), 9–22. See also McCullough, 35–38.

4. Christopher J. Lucas, *American Higher Education: A History* (New York: St. Martin's Press, 1994), 108.

5. John L. Rury, "Who Became Teachers? The Social Characteristics of Teachers in American History," in Donald Warren, editor, *American Teachers: Histories of a Profession at Work* (New York: Macmillan, 1989), 14; James Axtell, *The School Upon a Hill: Education and Society in Colonial New England* (New Haven: Yale University Press, 1974), 187–188.

6. The famous Yale Report of 1828, cited in Lucas, *American Higher Education*, 133. While there has been much debate about the influence—positive or negative—of the Yale Report, it did make a most articulate case for the virtues of a broad liberal undergraduate education, with professional studies postponed until the graduate level.

7. For the early development of professional preparation for the Protestant ministry and specifically the founding of Andover Theological Seminary, see my *Schooling the Preachers: The Development of Protestant Theological Education in the United States, 1740–1875* (Lanham, MD: University Press of America, 1988).

8. Dan C. Lortie's in-depth study of 20th-century teachers, *Schoolteacher* (Chicago: University of Chicago Press, second edition, 2002), 66, indicates that even with highly developed programs of teacher preparation, teachers, unlike other professionals, reflect "no great divide between preentry and postentry evaluations. Training (and even subsequent experience) is not a dramatic watershed separating the perceptions of naïve laymen from later judgments by knowing professionals." After all, Lortie concludes, these modern teachers have also been observing classrooms long before they entered teacher preparation programs.

9. Theodore Rawson Crane, editor, *The College and The Public, 1787–1862* (New York: Teachers College Press, 1963), citation p. 5; Lucas, *American Higher Education*, 116–121; Donald G. Tewksbury, *The Founding of American Colleges and Universities Before the Civil War, With Particular Reference to the Religious Influences Bearing on the College Movement* (New York: Teachers College Press, 1932). Tewksbury's 70-year-old volume remains a gold mine of detail on the antebellum college.

10. See Lucas, *American Higher Education*, 121–122; and also Jonathan Messerli, *Horace Mann: A Biography* (New York: Alfred A. Knopf, 1972) for detail on Antioch that Lucas does not include.

11. Lawrence A.Cremin, *American Education: The Colonial Experience, 1607–1783* (New York: Harper & Row, 1970), 189–191, citing Cotton Mather, *Corderius Americanus: An Essay upon the Good Education of Children* (Boston: John Allen, 1708).

12. Cremin, 167–195; William J. Reese, *The Origins of the American High School* (New Haven: Yale University Press, 1995), 22–25.

13. Reese, *Origins of the American High School*, 127.

14. Douglas Sloan, *The Scottish Enlightenment and the American College Ideal* (New York: Teachers College Press, 1971), 38.

15. George Frederick Miller, *The Academy System of the State of New York* (Albany: J. B. Lyon Company, 1922), 131.

16. See Douglas Sloan, "Harmony, Chaos, and Consensus: The American College Curriculum," *Teachers College Record* 73:2, December 1971, 221–251; and Theodore R. Sizer, *The Age of the Academies* (New York: Teachers College Press, 1964), 1–48. See also the new work by Margaret A. Nash, *Women's Education in the United States, 1780–1840* (New York: Palgrave Macmillan, 2005), 7.

17. Sizer, 19–20.

18. Catalogue of the Barre (Vermont) Academy, n.p., cited in Sizer, 20.

19. Miller, 19–29.

20. Miller, 133–134.

21. Miller, 131–162.

22. Miller, 167.

23. Miller, 137–141, 167–171.

24. Sizer, 35.

25. Most of the material on Andover's Teacher's Seminary is taken from Claude M. Fuess, *An Old New England School: A History of Phillips Academy Andover* (Boston: Houghton Mifflin, 1917), 204–219. See also Sizer, 35.

26. Nancy F. Cott, *The Bonds of Womanhood: "Woman's Sphere" in New England, 1780–1835* (New Haven: Yale University Press, 1977), 104.

27. Cott, 113.

28. Thomas Woody, *A History of Women's Education in the United States*, Volume 1 (New York: Science Press, 1929, reprinted by Octagon Books, 1966), 138.

29. David Tyack and Elisabeth Hansot, *Learning Together: A History of Coeducation in American Public Schools* (New Haven: Yale University Press, 1990), 19; see their pp. 13–27.

30. Woody, 138–141.

31. *New York Gazette* cited in Woody, 194; also Woody, 178–179, 202–203.

32. Tyack and Hansot, 13, 20–21. The citation about "a new kind of prestige" is taken by Tyack and Hansot from Kathryn Kish Sklar, "The Founding of Mount Holyoke College," in Carol Ruth Berkin and Mary Beth Norton, editors, *Women of America: A History* (Boston: Houghton Mifflin, 1979), 181.

33. Cremin, 499–500.

34. Cremin, 172–188.

35. Samuel Eliot Morison, *The Intellectual Life of Colonial New England* (Ithaca, NY: Cornell University Press, 1956), 82–85; Kenneth A. Lockridge, *Literacy in Colonial New England: An Enquiry into the Social Context of Literacy in the Early Modern West* (New York: W. W. Norton, 1974), 38; see also Tyack and Hansot, 16.

36. Christopher J. Lucas, *Teacher Education in America: Reform Agendas for the Twenty-First Century* (New York: St. Martin's Press, 1997), 4.

37. Tyack and Hansot, 302–303.

38. Woody, 131.

39. Jon Reyhner and Jeanne Eder, *American Indian Education: A History* (Norman: University of Oklahoma Press, 2004), 14–39, quotation on p. 32.

40. Carlos Fuentes, *The Buried Mirror: Reflections on Spain and the New World* (Boston: Houghton Mifflin, 1999), 119–147; John Calam, *Parsons & Pedagogues: The S.P.G. Adventure in American Education* (New York: Columbia University Press, 1971), 31.

41. Herb Boyd, editor, *Autobiography of a People: Three Centuries of African American History Told by Those Who Lived It* (New York: Anchor Books, 2001), 13–30.

42. Cited in Manning Marable and Leith Mullings, editors, *Let Nobody Turn Us Around: Voices of Resistance, Reform, and Renewal* (Lanham, MD: Rowman & Littlefield, 2000), 41.

43. Thomas L. Webber, *Deep Like the River: Education in the Slave Quarter Community, 1831–1865* (New York: W. W. Norton, 1978), 131–133.

44. Carl F. Kaestle, *Pillars of the Republic: Common Schools and American Society, 1780–1860* (New York: Hill and Wang, 1983), 20.

Chapter 2

1. Devon A. Mihesuah, *Cultivating the Rosebuds: The Education of Women at the Cherokee Female Seminary, 1851–1909* (Urbana: University of Illinois Press, 1993), Appendix B and C.

2. Mihesuah, 26–27.

3. Mihesuah, 27–32.

4. Mihesuah's book, of course, offers a much more detailed analysis of the opportunities and contradictions embedded in the Cherokee school system and especially the teacher preparation program of the Cherokee Female Seminary. See also Anne Ruggles Gere, "Indian Heart/White Man's Head: Native-American Teachers in Indian Schools, 1880–1930," *The History of Education Quarterly*, 45:1 (Spring 2005), 38–65.

5. Marylynn Salmon, "The Limits of Independence, 1760–1800," in Nancy F. Cott, editor, *No Small Courage: A History of Women in the United States* (New York: Oxford University Press, 2000), 109–178; see also Nancy F. Cott, *The Bonds of Womanhood: "Woman's Sphere" in New England, 1780–1835* (New Haven: Yale University Press, 1977), 104–125, for more on the earliest academies for women (not particularly women wanting to teach); see Margaret A. Nash, *Women's Education in the United States, 1780–1840* (New York: Palgrave Macmillan, 2005), 36–41.

6. Henry Fowler, "Education Services of Mrs. Emma Willard," Chapter 7 in Henry Barnard, *Memoirs of Teachers, Educators, and Promoters and Benefactors of Education, Literature, and Science*, Volume 1 (New York: F. C. Brownell, 1861), 129–130.

7. The biographical material on Willard and the description of the launching of Troy Female Seminary is taken from Anne Firor Scott, "The Ever Widening Circle: The Diffusion of Feminist Values from the Troy Female Seminary, 1822–1872," *History of Education Quarterly* (Spring 1979), 3–25; Mrs. A. W. Fairbanks, *Emma Willard and Her Pupils or Fifty Years of Troy Female Seminary, 1822–1872* (New York: Mrs. Russell Sage, 1898), 9–24; Henry Fowler, "Educational Services of Mrs. Emma Willard," Chapter 7 in Henry Barnard, *Memoirs of Teachers, Educators, and Promoters and Benefactors of Education, Literature, and Science*, Volume 1 (New York: F. C. Brownell, 1861), 125–168.

8. For a specific analysis of the speech, see Scott, pp. 6–7.

9. Emma Willard, "An Address to the Public, particularly to the Legislature of New York, proposing a Plan for Improving Female Education," in Fowler, 137–142.

10. Fowler, 133–138.

11. Fairbanks, 16.

12. Fowler, 135.

13. Fowler, 153, 141.

14. Fowler, 134–135; see also p. 153.

15. Fowler, 135, 146, 148, 153–154; Nash, p. 67.

16. Scott, 8–9, 16; Cott, 124–125.

17. Scott, 9–12.

18. Elizabeth Alden Green, *Mary Lyon and Mount Holyoke: Opening the Gates* (Hanover, NH: University Press of New England, 1979), 38–60, 98, 123, 370; Polly Welts Kaufman, *Women Teachers on the Frontier* (New Haven: Yale University Press, 1984), 5.

19. Michael Goldberg, "Breaking New Ground," chapter 4 in Cott, *No Small Courage,* 197–198; Green, p. xvi; Nash, 82, 89, 93.

20. Thomas Woody, *A History of Women's Education in the United States* (New York: Science Press, 1929), 418. For more on Mary Lyon see also Nash, 108–110.

21. Green, 85–86, 265–267. See also Nash, 108–109, for a slightly different interpretation.

22. Nash, 109.

23. Kathryn Kish Sklar, *Catharine Beecher: A Study in American Domesticity* (New York: W. W. Norton, 1973), 59–97.

24. Sklar, 97–104, also 76.

25. Sklar, 169; see also 102–109. For an analysis of Beecher's father's educational and reform efforts see my *Pedagogue for God's Kingdom: Lyman Beecher and the Second Great Awakening* (Lanham, MD: University Press of America, 1985).

26. Sklar, 112–115, 131.

27. Sklar, 115.

28. Catharine Beecher, "An Essay in the Education of Female Teachers" (New York: Van Nostrand & Dwight, 1835) in James W. Fraser, *The School in the United States: A Documentary History* (New York: McGraw-Hill, 2001), 61–66.

29. Sklar, 97, 168–178.

30. Sklar, 178–181.

31. Kaufman, 19–23, 102–115.

32. "The diary of Arozina Perkins, September 5, 1850–October 2, 1850" in Kaufman, 102–115.

33. Ronald E. Butchart, *Northern Schools, Southern Blacks, and Reconstruction: Freedmen's Education, 1862–1875* (Westport, CT: Greenwood Press, 1980), 124; Jacqueline Jones, *Soldiers of Light and Love: Northern Teachers and Georgia Blacks, 1865–1873* (Chapel Hill: University of North Carolina Press, 1980).

34. David Tyack and Elisabeth Hansot, *Learning Together: A History of Coeducation in American Public Schools* (New Haven: Yale University Press, 1990), 43.

35. Keith Melder, "Women's High Calling: The Teaching Profession in America, 1830–1860," *American Studies,* 13 (1972), 19–32, cited in Tyack and Hansot, 43; see also Tyack and Hansot, 41–45.

36. Tyack and Hansot, 49; Sklar, 180. For much more on the changing gender demographics of the teaching profession, see Joel Perlmann and Robert A. Margo, *Women's Work? American Schoolteachers, 1650–1920* (Chicago: University of Chicago Press, 2001), as well as John L. Rury's important work in both "Who Became Teachers?

The Social Characteristics of Teachers in American History," chapter 1 in Donald Warren, editor, *American Teachers: Histories of a Profession at Work* (New York: Macmillan, 1989), 9–48, as well as John L. Rury, *Education and Women's Work: Female Schooling and the Division of Labor in Urban America, 1870–1930* (Albany: State University of New York Press, 1991).

37. Sklar, 113.

38. Scott, 25, note 39; Keith Melder, "Masks of Oppression: The Female Seminary Movement in the United States," *New York History*, 55 (July 1974); Geraldine Joncich Clifford, "Man/Woman/Teacher: Gender, Family and Career in American Educational History," in Warren, 293–344; Jackie M. Blount, *Fit to Teach: Same Sex Desire, Gender, and School Work in the Twentieth Century* (New York: State University of New York Press, 2005); and also Sari Knopp Bilken, *School Work: Gender and the Cultural Construction of Teaching* (New York: Teachers College Press, 1995); Nash, 110. Special thanks to Diana C. D'Amico and Christine Ogren, who have pointed me to much of this literature.

39. Nancy Hoffman, *Woman's "True" Profession: Voices from the History of Teaching* (Cambridge: Harvard Education Press, 2003), 43–44. See also Dan C. Lortie, *Schoolteacher* (Chicago: University of Chicago Press, 1975, 2002). For a very different perspective than Hoffman's see Redding Sugg, *MotherTeacher: The Feminization of American Education* (Charlottesville: University Press of Virginia, 1978).

Chapter 3

1. Charlotte L. Forten, *The Journal of Charlotte Forten*, edited with an introduction and notes by Ray Allen Billington (New York: W. W. Norton, 1953), 82; for the biographical information on Forten, see Billington's introduction, 7–41.

2. Billington, "Introduction," *Journal of Charlotte Forten*, 20–24.

3. *Journal of Charlotte Forten*, 71, 79, 82–83.

4. Arthur O. Norton, editor, *The First State Normal School in America: The Journals of Cyrus Peirce and Mary Swift* (Cambridge: Harvard University Press, 1926), 83.

5. *The Journals of Cyrus Peirce and Mary Swift*, 84–90, 95.

6. Jonathan Messerli, *Horace Mann: A Biography* (New York: Alfred A. Knopf, 1972), 239.

7. Messerli, 240–242.

8. Carl Kaestle, *Pillars of the Republic: Schools and American Society, 1780–1860* (New York: Hill & Wang, 1983), 79, 95.

9. Jurgen Herbst, *And Sadly Teach: Teacher Education and Professionalization in American Culture* (Madison: University of Wisconsin Press, 1989), 18–21.

10. Horace Mann, *Lectures on Education* (Boston: Ide & Dutton, 1855), 19, cited in Lawrence A. Cremin, *American Education: The National Experience, 1783–1876* (New York: Harper & Row, 1980), 155.

11. Cremin, 155.

12. Christine A. Ogren, *The American State Normal School: An Instrument of Great Good* (New York: Palgrave Macmillan, 2005), 11. Ogren's book now represents the definitive account of the history of the normal schools and the foundation for much that appears in this chapter and in chapter 7. I am in her debt.

13. Messerli, 261–262; see also Herbst, 21.

14. Messerli, 298–301.

15. Arthur O. Norton, Introduction to James G. Carter essay in Norton, 227, and Messerli, 298–299. Though Messerli is clear that Brooks overstated his own influence in the creation of normal schools (see footnote 2, p. 298), Messerli himself understates the influence of Carter and others in the development of the idea of some sort of specialized state-sponsored institution for teachers in the decade between 1825 and 1835.

16. James G. Carter, "Outline of an Institution for the Education of Teachers," *Boston Patriot*, February 1825, reprinted in Norton, 227–245; see especially 227, 228, 231. See also Norton, xxxiv.

17. G. E. Maxwell, "Standards for Teachers Colleges," in *Indiana State Normal School*, Volume XVII, Number 1 (December 1923), 100.

18. For an excellent overview of these developments and the citations in this paragraph, see Ogren, 13–15; see also Norton, xxxiv–xxxv and, for Hall's experience at Concord and Andover, chapter 1 of this volume.

19. Horace Mann, "History, Regulation and Curriculum of the First Normal Schools: Narrative and Documents," *Common School Journal*, February 1, 1839, reprinted in Norton, 253–263; Norton, xlvi–xlvii.

20. Ogren, 24; Herbst, 60–63.

21. Messerli, 324; Norton, xlvi–lvi, including a copy of the letter from Cyrus Peirce to Henry Barnard of January 1, 1841.

22. Robert T. Brown, *The Rise and Fall of the People's Colleges: The Westfield Normal School, 1839 to 1914* (Westfield: Institute for Massachusetts Studies, 1988), 22.

23. Ogren, 29. Ogren offers a detailed accounting of Everett's speech from which the following pages are drawn. I am indebted to her research for this material. See Ogren, 29–33, 38–41.

24. Ogren, 29–35.

25. Ogren, 29–44; see also Brown, 20–21; Norton, 45; Carter in Norton, 228; Swift in Norton, 100, 133.

26. *Catalog of the Teachers and Students of the Westfield Normal School for the Term Ending November, 1844* (Northampton, MA: Metcalf, 1844), 8–9, cited in Brown, 17.

27. Ogren, 9.

28. All citations of the committee's report are from *The Common School Journal*, Boston, August 1, 1840, Volume II, Number 15, 225–240, reprinted in part in Norton, 265–268 and in more detail in James W. Fraser, editor, *The School in the United States: A Documentary History* (New York: McGraw-Hill, 2001), 66–74. For an excellent study of the legislative debate, see Charles Leslie Glenn Jr., *The Myth of the Common School* (Amherst: University of Massachusetts Press, 1988).

29. Ogren, 24–25.

30. Ogren, 55; also 25–29.

31. For the best analysis of the ways in which students used normal schools in the service of their own ends, and in the process brought about a differentiation among different normal schools in different parts of the country, see Jurgen Herbst, *And Sadly Teach: Teacher Education and Professionalization in American Culture* (Madison: University of Wisconsin Press, 1989).

32. Herbst, 77.

33. Brown, 32–33.
34. Ogren, 46.
35. Brown, 46.
36. Herbst, 84.
37. Herbst, 74–75.
38. Ogren, 46, 52.

Chapter 4

1. Carmon Ross, *The Status of County Teachers' Institutes in Pennsylvania* (Philadelphia: Ph.D. dissertation, University of Pennsylvania, 1922), 103.
2. Ross, 1–2.
3. Paul M. Mattingly, *The Classless Profession: American Schoolmen in the Nineteenth Century* (New York: New York University Press, 1975), 63–64; see also Ross, 7–8.
4. Ross, 2, 11.
5. Ross, 5–6.
6. Mattingly, 84–115.
7. James W. Fraser, *Pedagogue for God's Kingdom: Lyman Beecher and the Second Great Awakening* (Lanham, MD: University Press of America, 1985), 186–188; Kathryn Kish Sklar, *Catharine Beecher: A Study in American Domesticity* (New York: W. W. Norton, 1976), 111.
8. Ross, 1–4
9. Ross, 8–9.
10. Henry Barnard, editor, *Normal Schools, and Other Institutions, Agencies, and Means Designed for the Professional Education of Teachers* (Hartford, 1851), 76, cited in Mattingly, 63.
11. Mattingly, 62–63, 67–68; Samuel P. Bates, *Method of Teachers' Institutes and the Theory of Education* (New York: A. S. Barnes & Burr, 1862), 39.
12. Robert W. Lynn, *Protestant Strategies in Education* (New York: Association Press, 1964), 57; see also Fraser, 181–197; Mattingly, 62–68.
13. Letter of Emma Willard, November 19, 1847, cited and described in Mattingly, 65
14. *American Journal of Education*, Volume 15, cited in Ross, 10.
15. Willard S. Elsbree, *The American Teacher: Evolution of a Profession in a Democracy* (New York: American Book Company, 1939), 361, 554.
16. William Russell, *Suggestions on Teachers' Institutes* (Boston: Tappan, Whittemore & Mason, 1848), 10, 50.
17. Bates, 22–23.
18. Russell, 15–25; Bates, 38–49, Elsbree, 158.
19. Bates, 12–13, 17–19.
20. Christine A. Ogren, *The American State Normal School: "An Instrument of Great Good"* (New York: Palgrave-Macmillan, 2005), 21.
21. Mattingly, 71.
22. *Nineteenth and Twentieth Annual Reports of the Territorial Superintendent of Public Instruction to the Governor of New Mexico for the years 1909–1910* (Santa Fe: The New Mexican Printing Company, 1911), 12, 47.

23. *1907 Course of Study for County Institutes of the Territory of New Mexico compiled by the Territorial Superintendent of Public Instruction,* Published by the Territorial Board of Education, 1907, 7–11; Compilation of the School Laws of the Territory of New Mexico (Las Vegas: The Optic Company, 1905), 128–129, 153, 186.

24. *Nineteenth and Twentieth Annual Reports of the Territorial Superintendent,* 47.

25. Ross, xii–xiii, and William S. Learned, William C. Bagley, et al., *The Professional Preparation of Teachers for American Public Schools: A Study Based Upon an Examination of the Tax-Supported Normal Schools in the State of Missouri* (New York: Carnegie Foundation for the Advancement of Teaching, 1920), xv.

26. Tom Wiley, *Politics and Purse Strings in New Mexico's Public Schools* (Albuquerque: University of New Mexico Press, 1968), 30–31.

27. Wiley, 32–35.

28. *Report of Superintendent of Public Instruction Amado Chaves* (Santa Fe: New Mexican Publishing Company, 1892), 6–7; *Annual Report of the Superintendent of Public Instruction for 1893* (Santa Fe: New Mexican Publishing Company, 1894), 6–9; Ogren, 224–225; Northern New Mexico Community College web site (nnmcc.edu), April, 2005. The school at Silver City continues as Western New Mexico University, the one at Las Vegas is now New Mexico Highlands University, and the school at El Rita is now Northern New Mexico Community College.

29. *Nineteenth and Twentieth Annual Reports of the Territorial Superintendent of Public Instruction, 1909–1910,* 30.

30. *Nineteenth and Twentieth Annual Reports of the Territorial Superintendent of Public Instruction, 1909–1910,* 30, 62–63.

31. *Nineteenth and Twentieth Annual Reports of the Territorial Superintendent of Public Instruction, 1909–1910,* 30.

32. *Nineteenth and Twentieth Annual Reports of the Territorial Superintendent of Public Instruction, 1909–1910,* 30–31.

33. *Eleventh Annual Report of the Territorial Superintendent of Public Instruction, December, 1901* (Santa Fe: The New Mexican Publishing Company, 1902), 19–21.

34. *1907 Course of Study for County Institutes of the Territory of New Mexico,* 6, 56–57. 94–99.

35. Elsbree, 365–366; Ross, 135–145.

36. *Forty-Fourth Annual Report of the Board of Education,* Chicago Public Schools, Chicago: the Board of Education, June 1898, 111, 115; Leo Ray DeLong, *City School Institutes in Pennsylvania,* Ph.D. dissertation, Columbia University, 1930.

37. Ross, iv–xiii.

Chapter 5

1. Mary J. Herrick, *The Chicago Schools: A Social and Political History* (Beverly Hills, CA: Sage Publications, 1971), 72.

2. William J. Reese, *The Origins of the American High School* (New Haven: Yale University Press, 1995), 2; David F. Labaree, *The Making of an American High School* (New Haven: Yale University Press, 1988), 10. See also David Tyack and Elisabeth Hansot, *Learning Together: A History of Coeducation in American Public Schools* (New

Haven: Yale University Press, 1990); Alexander James Inglis, *The Rise of the High School in Massachusetts* (New York: Teachers College, Columbia University, 1911).

3. Labaree, 67.

4. Reese, 53.

5. Reese, 35

6. Edward A. Krug, *The Shaping of the American High School*, two volumes (New York: Harper & Row, 1964, 1972); see above for Reese and Labaree.

7. Labaree, 72, 106–107.

8. Reese, 226.

9. *Fifth Annual Report of the Superintendent of Public Schools* (Chicago: Department of Public Instruction, February 1, 1859), 25–26.

10. U.S. Bureau of Education, Bulletin Number 6, *Public and Private High Schools* (Washington, D.C.: Government Printing Office, 1912), Table 3, p. 16, cited in Krug, 290.

11. Herrick, *The Chicago Schools*, 41–42.

12. Jurgen Hergst, *And Sadly Teach: Teacher Education and Professionalization in American Culture* (Madison: University of Wisconsin Press, 1989), 89; *Report of the President of the Board of Education and Fifth Annual Report of the Superintendent of Public Schools for the Year Ending Feb. 1, 1859* (Chicago: Department of Public Instruction, 1859), 15.

13. Reese, 56; *Fifth Annual Report of the Superintendent*, 25–26.

14. Herrick, p. 42; *Eighth Annual Report of the Board of Education for the Year Ending December 31, 1861* (Chicago: Department of Public Instruction, 1862), 26–27.

15. James Pyle Wickersham, *A History of Education in Pennsylvania* (Lancaster, PA: Inquirer Publishing Company, 1886), 610–613.

16. William Warren Ferrier, *Ninety Years of Education in California, 1846–1936* (Berkeley: Sather Gate Book Shop, 1937), 81–83; "Introduction," San Francisco Unified School District Records, SFH 3-October 8, 2004, San Francisco History Center, San Francisco Public Library.

17. Reese, 226; Ferrier, 85–86.

18. David Tyack, *The One Best System: A History of American Urban Education* (Cambridge: Harvard University Press, 1974), 58–59.

19. John L. Rury, *Education as Women's Work: Female Schooling and the Division of Labor in Urban America, 1870–1930* (Albany: State University of New York Press, 1991), 21–22.

20. Tyack and Hansot, 114–116.

21. Tyack and Hansot, 114–117.

22. *Forty-Fourth Annual Report of the Board of Education* (Chicago: Department of Public Instruction, June 1898), 20.

23. Tyack and Hansot, 114–117.

24. Edward J. Larson, *Summer for the Gods: The Scopes Trial and America's Continuing Debate Over Science and Religion* (New York: Basic Books, 1997), 24–25.

25. Willard S. Elsbree, *The American Teacher: Evolution of a Profession in a Democracy* (New York: American Book Company, 1939), 326–329.

26. Edward E. Redcay, *County Training Schools and Public Secondary Education for Negroes in the South*, Ph.D. dissertation, Columbia University, New York, 1935, 8.

27. Francis S. Murphy, Jr., "A History of Teacher Training in the City of Boston and The Role of the Laboratory School as an Integral Part in the Preparation of Teachers," unpublished Ed.D. dissertation, University of Massachusetts, Amherst, 1989, 15–19.

28. Murphy, 11–12.

29. "Boston State College Historical Materials," www.lib.umb.edu/archives/boscoll.html

30. Chicago Normal College: Announcement, 1931–1932, 6; "The History of the University," Chicago State University web site, www.csu.edu; *Fifth Annual Report of the Superintendent of Public Schools*, 1859, 77; *Forty-fourth Annual Report of the Board of Education*, 1898, 93–95.

31. Elsbree, 351.

32. Chart and discussion adapted from Elsbree, 351 and 352. Since in 1937 Massachusetts required a minimum of 3 or 4 years beyond high school, I moved it from the "no definite scholarship" to the 3-year minimum column. In 1937 Oklahoma, which is listed in the no definite minimum column, had actually adopted a requirement that teachers attend 2 years of high school prior to teaching. See also Benjamin W. Frazier, *Development of State Programs for the Certification of Teachers*, U.S. Office of Education, Bulletin 1938, Number 12 (Washington: Government Printing Office, 1938), 73.

33. Elsbree, 329–330.

Chapter 6

1. Mamie Garvin Fields with Karen Fields, *Lemon Swamp and Other Places: A Carolina Memoir* (New York: The Free Press, 1983), 114; Michael Fultz, "African American Teachers in the South, 1890–1940: Powerlessness and the Ironies of Expectations and Protest," *History of Education Quarterly*, Volume 35, Number 4 (Winter 1995), 403–404. Fultz, who first led me to Mamie Garvin Fields's wonderful autobiography, also cited Ambrose Caliver, *Rural Education Among Negroes under Jeanes Supervising Teachers*, U.S. Office of Education Bulletin, No. 5 (Washington, DC: Government Printing Office, 1933), 45–47.

2. Fields with Fields, *Lemon Swamp and Other Places*, especially 83–84, 90, 98–99; Thomas Jesse Jones, *Negro Education: A Study of the Private and Higher Schools for Colored People in the United States* (Washington, D.C.: Government Printing Office, 1917), 59.

3. Fields, 99, 241.

4. Thomas L. Webber, *Deep Like the Rivers: Education in the Slave Quarter Community, 1831–1865* (New York: W. W. Norton, 1978), 131–135.

5. Webber, 133; Fields, 2.

6. Carter G. Woodson, *The Education of the Negro Prior to 1861* (New York: The Arno Press, 1968; originally published Washington, DC: Associated Publishers, 1919), 215–219. See also James Anderson, *The Education of Blacks in the South, 1860–1935* (Chapel Hill: University of North Carolina Press, 1988), 7. The material on Deveaux is from Heather Andrea Williams, *Self-Taught: African American Education in Slavery and Freedom* (Chapel Hill: University of North Carolina Press, 2005), 104. Williams's new

book is now the definitive work on the informal preparation of black teaches before and after the Civil War.

7. Williams, 96–99. Anderson, 4–6.

8. Jones, *Negro Education*, 71.

9. Anderson, chapter 2, 33–78, especially 33–35 and 73. See also Booker T. Washington, *Up from Slavery: An Autobiography* (New York: Doubleday, Page, 1902).

10. Anderson, 34–35.

11. Anderson, 34–36, 54–55, 75.

12. Anderson, 52.

13. Jon Reyhner and Jeanne Eder, *American Indian Education: A History* (Norman: University of Oklahoma Press, 2004), 115–116, 96–98, 132–149.

14. Anderson, 115–130. Anderson's analysis of Fort Valley and other schools that experienced the same fate between 1900 and 1930 is a significant story and, as he notes, the role of white Northern philanthropy in Southern black teacher preparation deserves far more attention than it has received.

15. Anderson, 86–95. A significant literature, of which Anderson's book is probably the most significant, has analyzed the impact of Northern philanthropy in both building up a system of education for African Americans in the post–Civil War South and in using considerable influence to ensure that this system of education was focused much more on creating a docile labor force than on democratic schools or social systems. Exploring the issues in appropriate depth is beyond the scope of this study, but I am grateful to my colleague Joan Malczewski for opportunities to discuss it in detail.

16. Anderson, 52–62.

17. Anderson, 66–68.

18. Anderson, 66–72.

19. Williams, 38–39; Joe M. Richardson, *Christian Reconstruction: The American Missionary Association and Southern Blacks, 1861–1890* (Athens: The University of Georgia Press, 1986), 4–5.

20. Richardson, 113–114.

21. Richardson, 114–119.

22. Richardson, 123–135.

23. Richardson, 138–139, vii–ix; Jones, *Negro Education*, 59.

24. Anderson, 70–71; Richardson, 138–139, viii–ix. For a case study of one black-led school that moved in and out of the AMA orbit, and also Booker T. Washington's orbit, see Charles W. Wadelington and Richard F. Knapp, *Charlotte Hawkins Brown and Palmer Memorial Institute: What One Young African American Woman Could Do* (Chapel Hill: University of North Carolina Press, 1999).

25. Richardson, 126–127.

26. Jones, *Negro Education*, 59.

27. Anderson, 244–245.

28. Ambrose Caliver, Volume IV of *The National Survey of the Education of Teachers* (Washington: Government Printing Office, 1933), 1.

29. Edward E. Redcay, *County Training Schools and Public Secondary Education for Negroes in the South* (Washington, DC: The John F. Slater Fund, 1935, reprinted Westport, CT: The Negro Universities Press, 1970), 8.

30. Redcay, 2–3, 8–9. Precise numbers, indeed the precise meaning of terms like *high school*, is always difficult in these years. One well-researched report by Thomas Jesse Jones is the source of the 64 high schools for blacks in 1916 number, while *The National Survey of Secondary Education* reported 1,150 "Negro high schools" in the United States in 1930, of which the 612 Slater Fund–supported County Training Schools would be a majority. See also Anderson, 138.

31. Redcay, 30–36.

32. Redcay, 29

33. Redcay, 38.

34. Joan Malczewski, "Black Educators as Change Agents: Frame Alignment Processes and North Carolina Education Reform," unpublished paper, The Steinhardt School of Education, New York University, March 2005, 33.

35. Anderson, 140–144. While my analysis of the County Training Schools is strongly influenced by James Anderson, in the end I believe that the leaders of these schools were able to use distance to escape more of the philanthropic control than he does, and as a result, their impact on teacher preparation was more positive.

36. Redcay, 37–39, 50.

37. Anderson, 278.

Chapter 7

1. Kathleen Weiler, "The Struggle for Democratic Public Schools in California: Helen Heffernan and Corinne Seeds," in Margaret Smith Crocco, Petra Munro, and Kathleen Weiler, *Pedagogies of Resistance: Women Educator Activists, 1880–1960* (New York: Teachers College Press, 1999), 83–87; William Warren Ferrier, *Ninety Years of Education in California, 1846–1936* (Berkeley: Sather Gate Book Shop, 1937), 322, 333.

2. In fact, there have been surprisingly few studies of the history of teacher education in the United States at all, though there have been some excellent studies of the history of normal schools. Merle L. Borrowman's classic, *The Liberal and Technical in Teacher Education* (New York: Teachers College Press, 1956), is, as the subtitle suggests, "A Historical Survey of American Thought" about teachers and their preparation, but one could still easily assume that the normal schools were the 19th-century equivalent of the 20th-century university programs. Christopher J. Lucas, in one of the most recent studies of this history, *Teacher Education in America: Reform Agendas for the Twenty-First Century* (New York: St. Martin's Press, 1997), is primarily concerned with the future reform agendas, and his excellent two-chapter historical review does note the importance of teachers' institutes, but the story line is from normal school to state teachers college to university programs.

3. This paragraph is a quick summary of chapter 3. See that chapter for details. The citation is from the journal of Mary Swift in Arthur O. Norton, editor, *The Journals of Cyrus Peirce and Mary Swift* (Cambridge: Harvard University Press, 1926), 95–96.

4. Christine A. Ogren, *The American State Normal School: An Instrument of Great Good* (New York: Palgrave-Macmillan, 2005), 57–61, 213–235.

5. Kenneth M. Ludmerer, *Learning to Heal: The Development of American Medical Education* (Baltimore: Johns Hopkins University Press, 1985), 3, 11, 43.

6. W. P. Morgan, "The Growth of the State Normal School," *Indiana State Normal School*, Volume XVII, Number 1 (December 1923), 56–65; Ogren, 77–78.

7. Morgan, 57–63; Ogren, 86–89.

8. Ogren, 86–89, 104.

9. Ogren, 85–86.

10. A. N. Farmer, *Conditions and Needs of Wisconsin's Normal Schools* (Madison: State Board of Public Affairs, 1914), 404–407.

11. Ogren, 87, 93–94, 96, 104.

12. Ogren, 125–129.

13. The phrase, meaning the integration of practice and traditional academic study in a curriculum that fosters rigorous reflection on practice in light of theory, was coined by Richard M. Freeland, president of Northeastern University in Boston. See *The Atlantic*, Volume 294, Number 3 (October 2004).

14. Ogren, 136–141, 40; Ludmerer, 12.

15. Ogren, 121, 149.

16. William S. Learned, William C. Bagley, et al., *The Professional Preparation of Teachers for American Public Schools* (New York: Carnegie Foundation for the Advancement of Teaching, 1920), 127.

17. H. H. Seerley, speech at the National Education Association, 1897, p. 713, cited in *Indiana State Normal School*, Volume XVII, Number 1 (December 1923), 98.

18. G. E. Maxwell, "Standards for Teachers Colleges," *Indiana State Normal School*, Volume XVII, Number 1 (December 1923), 100–113. See also Edward R. Ducharme and Mary K. Ducharme, *The American Association of Colleges for Teacher Education: A History* (Washington, DC: AACTE, 1988).

19. H.C. Minnich, "The History of Normal Schools in America," in *Indiana State Normal School*, Volume XVII, Number 1 (December 1923), 38. *Note*: At the time he wrote this article, Minnich was both the Dean of the Teachers College at Miami University, Oxford, Ohio, and the Secretary of the American Association of Teachers' Colleges. See also L. Graver, *Beacon on the Hill: A Centennial History of Kutztown State College*, State College Bulletin, Volume 99, Number 1 (Kutztown, PA: The State College, 1966), 79–80.

20. Ogren, 2–3.

21. Abraham Flexner, *Medical Education in the United States and Canada* (New York: The Carnegie Foundation for the Advancement of Teaching, 1910). See also Ellen Condliffe Lagemann, *Private Power for the Public Good* (New York: College Entrance Examination Board, 1983), 59–74, 86–89.

22. Learned, Bagley, et al., xv–xvi, 1, 19, 34–38, 41.

23. Learned, Bagley, et al., 34, 385–386.

24. Learned, Bagley, et al., 387–397. My read of the report differs slightly from that offered by Ellen Lagemann, 86. What she saw as an effort to narrow or limit the preparation of teachers I tend to see as a call for focus and clarity of purpose in the institutions offering the preparation.

25. David Felmley, "The Collegiate Rank of the Normal School," *Indiana State Normal School*, Volume XVII, Number 1 (December 1923), 41–45.

26. Leroy Albert King, *Status of the Rural Teacher in Pennsylvania*, United States Bureau of Education Bulletin, 1919, Number 34 (Washington, D.C.: Government Printing Office, 1922), 1–5, 30–33.

27. Willard S. Elsbree, *The American Teacher: Evolution of a Profession in a Democracy* (New York: American Book Company, 1939), 313–314.

28. Jurgen Herbst, "Teacher Preparation in the Nineteenth Century: Institutions and Purposes," in Donald Warren, editor, *American Teachers: Histories of a Profession at Work* (New York: Macmillan, 1989), 231.

29. Ogren, 151, 200.

Chapter 8

1. Lucia B. Downing, "Teaching in the Keeler 'Deestrict' School," *Vermont Quarterly, a Magazine of History*, Volume XIX, Number 4 (October 1951), 233–240, reprinted in Barbara Finkelstein, *Governing the Young: Teacher Behavior in Popular Primary Schools in Nineteenth-century United States* (New York: Falmer Press, 1989), 175–182.

2. Clearly Finkelstein is using the story as an illustration of what teacher life was like, as did Nancy Hoffman, who included it in her pathbreaking *Woman's "True" Profession: Voices from the History of Teaching*, second edition (Cambridge: Harvard Education Press, 2003), 58–66. The story serves well as an illustration of both teachers' lives and their education.

3. Benjamin W. Frazier et al., "History of the Professional Education of Teachers in the United States," in Volume V of the *National Survey of the Education of Teachers*, Bulletin 1933, Number 10 (Washington, D.C.: Government Printing Office, 1935), 33; also citing Addis Wellford, *Curricula of Professional Schools*, in U.S. Bureau of Education, Report of the Commissioner of Education, 1889–1990, two volumes (Washington, D.C.: Government Printing Office, 1893), volume 2, 1020.

4. Albert Salisbury, *Historical Sketch of Normal Instruction in Wisconsin* (n.p., 1893), 9–12, 16–19, 31, 36–41.

5. Lester F. Goodchild, "The Beginnings of American Education as a Field of Study: Curricular Conflicts over Pedagogy as a Science or Practice, 1856–1940," unpublished paper, History of Education Society, Kansas City, Kansas, 2004, 7–8. I am very grateful to Lester Goodchild for sharing this paper with me in its current form, which is currently in press and will be available soon as a chapter in Bernard Schneuwly and Rita Hofstetter, editors, *New Education and Educational Sciences* (New York: Peter Long, 2006). See also Frazier, 20–21.

6. Frazier et al., "History of the Professional Education of Teachers in the United States," 33–35.

7. Geraldine Joncich Clifford and James W. Guthrie, *Ed School: A Brief for Professional Education* (Chicago: University of Chicago Press, 1988), 64; Christine A. Ogren, *The American State Normal School: An Instrument of Great Good* (New York: Palgrave Macmillan, 2005), 221; Goodchild, 14.

8. Frazier et al., 35–37.

9. Goodchild, 13–19. While Goodchild's careful research is key to this section of the chapter, he may not fully agree with the interpretations offered.

10. Frazier et al., "History of the Professional Education of Teachers in the United States," 35–37, 72–74.

11. Goodchild, "The Beginnings of American Education as a Field of Study," 2–3, 20–24.

12. Edmund J. James, *Chairs of Pedagogics in Our Universities* (Philadelphia, 1887), cited in Arthur G. Powell, *The Uncertain Profession: Harvard and the Search for Educational Authority* (Cambridge: Harvard University Press, 1980), 39.

13. Clifford and Guthrie, 76, 133.

14. Lawrence A. Cremin, David A. Shannon, and Mary Evelyn Townsend, *A History of Teachers College Columbia University* (New York: Columbia University Press, 1954), 10–27.

15. Cremin, Shannon, and Townsend, 27–58; Clifford and Guthrie, 51–52.

16. Clifford and Guthrie, 53–54.

17. Frazier et al., "History of the Professional Education of Teachers in the United States," 72–83; Clifford and Guthrie, 47–55.

18. Emery M. Foster et al., *Statistics of State School Systems, 1929–1930*, U.S. Office of Education, Biennial Survey of Education in the United States, 1928–1930, two volumes, Bulletin, 1931, Number 20 (Washington, D.C.: Government Printing Office, 1932), Volume II, 28–29, cited in Frazier, 43.

19. Benjamin J. Burris, "The Next Step Toward Better Schools," *Indiana State Normal School*, Volume XVII, Number 1 (December 1923), 94–97.

20. Abraham Flexner and Frank B. Bachman, *Public Education in Maryland* (New York: General Education Board, 1916), 58–60, cited in Clifford and Guthrie, 61.

21. Edward A. Krug, *The Shaping of the American High School* (New York: Harper & Row, 1964), 146–168; Goodchild, 14.

22. James Anderson, *The Education of Blacks in the South, 1860–1935* (Chapel Hill: University of North Carolina Press, 1988), 249–255.

23. Ambrose L. Suhrie, "The Teachers College as a Professional School," *Indiana State Normal School*, Volume XVII, Number 1 (December 1923), 77.

24. Cited in *Indiana State Normal School*, Volume XVII, Number 1 (December 1923), 111.

Chapter 9

1. Leonard Covello, *The Heart Is the Teacher* (New York: McGraw-Hill, 1958), 52–53, 61–62, 67–70, 77, 87, 92–93.

2. Lawrence A. Cremin, *American Education: The Metropolitan Experience, 1876–1980* (New York: Harper & Row, 1988), 3–4, 622–626; Kate Rousmaniere, *City Teachers: Teaching and School Reform in Historical Perspective* (New York: Teachers College Press, 1997), 32–38.

3. Cremin, 3–4.

4. United States Department of the Interior, Office of Education, *The History of the Municipal University in the United States*, Bulletin, 1932, No. 2 (Washington, D.C.: Government Printing Office, 1932), 39, 53–54, 61–72.

5. Katherina Kroo Grunfeld, "Purpose and Ambiguity: The Feminine World of Hunger College, 1869–1945," unpublished Ed.D. dissertation, Teachers College, Columbia University, 1991, 23–32; Miriam Balmuth, "The Hope of Our Humanity: Beginnings of the Teacher Education Program at Hunter College, 1870" (pamphlet issued by the School of Education, Hunter College, June 2003), 10.

6. Grunfeld, 33–38; Balmuth, 6–7.

7. Grunfeld, 39–44, 54–55.

8. Balmuth, 12–14.

9. Grunfeld, 93–99.

10. Balmuth, 12–14; Grunfeld, 48, 58–62, 68–74.

11. Grunfeld, 115–128, quotation on 118. For the discussion of the administrative progressives, see David Tyack and Elisabeth Hansot, *Managers of Virtue: Public School Leadership in America, 1820–1980* (New York: Basic Books, 1982); Margaret Haley, "Why Teachers Should Organize," 1904 speech to the NEA, reprinted in James W. Fraser, *The School in the United States: A Documentary History* (New York: McGraw-Hill, 2001), 187–191. See also Rousmaniere, especially chapter 2, 28–53.

12. Grunfeld, 105–130, citations on 121–122; *Thirty-Fifth Annual Report of the Normal College, 1905*, 15–17, cited in Grunfeld, 129.

13. Grunfeld, 122–126; *Thirty-Fifth Annual Report of the Normal College, 1905*, 14–15, cited in Grunfeld, 129–130. My analysis differs somewhat from Rousmaniere's. She writes that "the increased years in teacher education furthered the socialization of prospective teachers into the occupational identity that was promoted by school administrators" (p. 34). My own sense is that it was the short course supported by Maxwell that was designed to promote the most socialization. The longer course of study supported by Hunter fostered much more independence on the part of teachers.

14. Grunfeld, 111–120.

15. Grunfeld, 141–150, 249–252.

16. Rousmaniere, 32; Balmuth, 14; Grunfeld, 131–142.

17. See "Historical Sketch," *Chicago Normal College Announcement, 1931–1932* (Chicago: The Normal College, 1931), 6; Shepherd Johnson, *Historical Sketches of the Public School System of the City of Chicago* (Chicago: Clark & Edwards, 1880), 52.

18. Public Schools of the City of Chicago, *Thirty-Ninth Annual Report of the Board of Education*, June 30, 1893, 44–45; *Fortieth Annual Report of the Board of Education*, June 29, 1894, 48–49.

19. Lawrence A. Cremin, *The Transformation of the School: Progressivism in American Education, 1876–1957* (New York: Vintage Books, 1961), 128–135; "Historical Sketch," *Chicago Normal College Announcement, 1931–1932*, 6.

20. Cook County Normal School, *Report of the President of Cook County Board of Education and the Principal of Cook County Normal School for 1890* (Chicago: Cook County Board of Education, 1890), 10–11.

21. Cremin, *American Education: The Metropolitan Experience*, 227.

22. Public Schools of the City of Chicago, *Forty-Fourth Annual Report of the Board of Education*, June 1898, 95.

23. Cremin, *The Transformation of the School*, 129.

24. *Report of the President of Cook County Board of Education and the Principal of Cook County Normal School for 1890*, 12.

25. "Historical Sketch," *Chicago Normal College Announcement, 1931–1932*, 6; "Historical Sketch," *Chicago Normal College Announcement, 1934–1935*, 6; *Annual Report of the Chicago Superintendent of Schools, One Hundred Years of Educational Progress: Chicago Public Schools, 1845–1945* (Chicago: Chicago Public Schools, 1945); Chicago State University web site, www.csu.edu/President/history.htm

26. United States Department of the Interior, Office of Education, *The History of the Municipal Universities in the United States*, 80–83, 98–99, 143–145.

27. See Barbara Beatty, "Child Gardening: The Teaching of Young Children in American Schools," in Donald Warren, editor, *American Teachers: Histories of a Profession at Work* (New York: Macmillan, 1989), 65–97.

28. Janet Graveline Messenger, "The Story of National College of Education, 1886–1986," unpublished manuscript for the Centennial Celebration, September 1985, The Library, National-Louis University, Evanston, Illinois, 24.

29. Elizabeth Harrison, *Sketches Along Life's Road* (Boston: Stratford,) 27, 51, 178; Messenger, 3–7, 11–14.

30. Chicago Kindergarten College, 1897–1898, published by the College, 6, 8, 12–15, 25–27; Chicago Kindergarten College, Catalog, 1903–1904, 10–14; Harrison, 178.

31. National Kindergarten & Elementary College, Catalog, 1917–1918, 6–11.

32. Messenger, 138–146; National-Louis University, Undergraduate Catalog, 2004–2005, 10, National-Louis University web site www.nl.edu/about/history.

Chapter 10

1. Thelma Pairsh's Albuquerque application, transcripts, and many other family records are on file in the New Mexico State Archives and Records Center, Santa Fe, New Mexico.

2. Bridgewater State Teachers College *Catalogue*, 1931–1932, 4; E. S. Evenden, *National Survey of the Education of Teachers*, Bulletin 1933, Number 10, six volumes (Washington, D.C.: Government Printing Office, 1935), Volume 6, ix; Ogren, 15–16. I am deeply indebted to my former undergraduate student assistant at Northeastern University, Karen Hallman, for research on Bridgewater and Kutztown State Teachers Colleges. Hallman's research was presented as part of a panel discussion of "Rethinking the History of Teacher Preparation in the United States" at the History of Education Society meeting, November 7, 2004, Kansas City, Missouri.

3. Jurgen Herbst, *And Sadly Teach: Teacher Education and Professionalization in American Culture* (Madison: The University of Wisconsin Press, 1989), 173; A. C. Boyden, *The History of Bridgewater Normal School* (Bridgewater, MA: Bridgewater Normal Alumni Association, 1933), 119–121.

4. Boyden, 121–122.

5. Boyden, 114–115.

6. Boyden, 143–146; see also Bridgewater State Teachers College *Catalogue*, 1929–1930, 11; *Catalogue*, 1942–1943, 3.

7. Lee Graver, *Beacon on the Hill; A Centennial History of Kutztown State College*, Bulletin, Volume 99, Number 1 (Kutztown, PA: The State College, 1966), 41–44, 135–137.

8. Graver, 124–129.

9. Graver, 109–113.

10. Graver, 101–104, 135–137; Hallman, "Rethinking the History of Teacher Preparation in the United States."

11. Taylor Branch, *Parting the Waters: America in the King Years, 1954–1963* (New York: Simon & Schuster, 1988), 131–132; Douglas Brinkley, *Rosa Parks* (New York: Penguin Putnam, 2000), 121–123, and most important, Jo Ann Robinson, *The Mont-*

gomery Bus Boycott and the Women Who Started It (Knoxville: University of Tennessee Press, 1989).

12. James Anderson, *The Education of Blacks in the South, 1860–1935* (Chapel Hill: University of North Carolina Press, 1988), 113.

13. "History of Alabama State University," www.alasu.edu/about/history/htm

14. Esther Marion Nelson, *An Analysis of the Content of Student-Teaching Courses for Education of Elementary Teachers in State Teachers Colleges* (New York: Bureau of Publications, Teachers College, Columbia University, 1939), 5–7, 13–16.

15. Nelson, 263–265.

16. See Ellen Condliffe Lagemann, *Private Power for the Public Good: A History of the Carnegie Foundation for the Advancement of Teaching* (New York: College Entrance Examination Board, 1983), 59–93; William S. Learned, William C. Bagley, et al., *The Professional Preparation of Teachers for American Public Schools* (New York: The Carnegie Foundation for the Advancement of Teaching, 1920); Abraham Flexner and Frank P. Bachman, *Public Education in Maryland* (New York: General Education Board, 1916); James Bryant Conant, *The Education of American Teachers* (New York: McGraw-Hill, 1963).

17. U.S. Office of Education, *National Survey of the Education of Teachers*, Bulletin 1933, Number 10, in six volumes (Washington, D.C.: U. S. Government Printing Office, 1933–1935), Vol. II, vii–viii; Abraham Flexner, *Medical Education in the United States and Canada* (New York: Carnegie Foundation for the Advancement of Teaching, 1910).

18. Edward S. Evenden, Guy C. Bamble, and Harold G. Blue, *National Survey of the Education of Teachers*, Bulletin 1933, Number 10, Volume II (of six volumes): *Teacher Personnel in the United States* (Washington, D.C.: U.S. Government Printing Office, 1935), 40–42.

19. *The National Survey of the Education of Teachers*, Volume V, 44–48. See also Benjamin W. Frazier, *Development of State Programs for the Certification of Teachers*, U.S. Office of Education, Bulletin 1938, Number 12 (Washington, D.C.: U.S. Government Printing Office, 1938), 73–75.

20. *The National Survey of the Education of Teachers*, Volume IV, vii, 1–11, 21, 117–123.

21. By far the best and easiest to use source for the evolving name changes of these schools can be found in the appendix of Christine Ogren, *The American State Normal School: "An Instrument of Great Good"* (New York: Palgrave MacMillan, 2005), 213–235. Nevertheless, it is useful to consult the histories of individual schools for the detailed stories.

22. William S. Learned, William C. Bagley, et al., *The Professional Preparation of Teachers for American Public Schools* (New York: The Carnegie Foundation for the Advancement of Teaching, 1920), 391.

23. William S. Learned, William C. Bagley, et al., 71–72, 78.

24. Ogren, 213–235.

25. John Goodlad, *Places Where Teachers Are Taught*, edited by John I. Goodlad, Roger Soder, and Kenneth A. Sirotnik (San Francisco: Jossey-Bass, 1990), 21.

26. Hallman presentation, History of Education Society, November 7, 2004.

27. David Riesman, *Constraint and Variety in American Higher Education* (Garden City, NY: Doubleday, 1956, 1958), 21, 43, 61–62.

28. Michael W. Sedlak, "'Let Us Go and Buy a School Master' Historical

Perspectives on the Hiring of Teachers in the United States, 1750–1980," in Donald Warren, editor, *American Teachers: Histories of a Profession at Work* (New York: Macmillan, 1989), 257–290, especially 271 and 282; Frazier, *Development of State Programs for the Certification of Teachers*, p. 73.

29. Sedlak, 257–259, Frazier, 40–45.

30. Sedlak, 258–259.

31. *Report of the Superintendent of Public Instruction*, March 1, 1891–December 31, 1891 (Santa Fe, NM: New Mexican Printing Company, 1892), 5–7. *Report of the Superintendent of Public Instruction*, December 31, 1892, 5–7; *Report of the Superintendent of Public Instruction*, December 31, 1893, 5–7. New Mexico Normal School at Las Vegas, *Catalog*, 1898–1899, 6–9, 16–17; New Mexico Normal University at Las Vegas, *Bulletins* for April 1913, 20–21; March 1916, 18–55; November 1922, 22–25; November 1928, 23–30. See also Ogren, 213–235.

32. *Report of the Superintendent of Public Instruction*, December 31, 1898, 7–9; *Report of the Superintendent of Public Instruction*, December 31, 1901, 19–21.

33. *Fifteenth Annual Report of the Superintendent of Public Instruction*, December 31, 1905, 10, 13–14; *Seventeenth and Eighteenth Annual Reports of the Superintendent of Public Instruction*, January 1, 1909, 37.

34. *Nineteenth and Twentieth Annual Reports of the Territorial Superintendent of Public Instruction*, 1909–1910, 92–93.

35. *Report of the State Superintendent of Public Instruction for July 1, 1930 to June 30, 1932*, 36–38; *Report of the State Superintendent of Public Instruction for July 1, 1932 to June 30, 1934*, 30–31.

36. *Report of the State Superintendent of Public Instruction for July 1, 1940 to June 30, 1942*, 10–11, 20–22; *Report of the State Superintendent of Public Instruction for July 1, 1942 to June 30, 1944*, 10–11, 22, 48, 55–59.

37. *Twentieth Biennial Report of the Superintendent of Public Instruction, July 1, 1948 to June 30, 1950*, 83–88, 94–95, 136.

38. *Twenty-Third Biennial Report of the Superintendent of Public Instruction for July 1, 1954 to June 30, 1956*, 27–29, 32–33, 256–265.

39. National Education Association, *Status of the American Public School Teacher, 1985–86* (Washington, D.C.: NEA, 1987), reproduced in Geraldine Jonçich Clifford and James W. Guthrie, *Ed School: A Brief for Professional Education* (Chicago: University of Chicago Press, 1988), 20.

Chapter 11

1. Judy Logan, *Teaching Stories* (New York: Kodansha International, 1990), xiv–xv.

2. Paul Woodring, *New Directions in Teacher Education* (New York: The Fund for the Advancement of Education, 1957), 17.

3. Arthur G. Powell, *The Uncertain Profession: Harvard and the Search for Educational Authority* (Cambridge; Harvard University Press, 1980), 248

4. Woodring, 11.

5. Alvin C. Eurich, "Foreword," in Woodring, vii–viii.

6. Woodring, 21.

7. Woodring, 29–30.

8. Woodring, 29–37, 85–88, 124–125.

9. Woodring, 20–23.

10. John I. Goodlad, "Connecting the Present to the Past," in John I. Goodlad, Roger Soder, and Kenneth A. Sirotnik, editors, *Places Where Teachers Are Taught* (San Francisco: Jossey-Bass, 1990), 34.

11. See, for example, Frederick M. Hess, Andrew J. Rotherham, and Kate Walsh, *A Qualified Teacher in Every Classroom: Appraising Old Answers and New Ideas* (Cambridge: Harvard Education Press, 2004).

12. Woodring, 71–82.

13. Powell, 177–195.

14. Powell, 197, 206–208, 213, 229.

15. Powell, 244–253.

16. Powell, 270–279.

17. Woodring, 45–46.

18. Woodring, 52–55.

19. Arthur Bestor, *Educational Wastelands: The Retreat from Learning in Our Public Schools* (Urbana: University of Illinois Press, 1953), 104–114, 120–121, reprinted in David B. Tyack, editor, *Turning Points in American Educational History* (Waltham, MA: Blaisdell Publishing, 1967), 453–461.

20. Karl Bigelow, "How Should America's Teachers Be Educated?" *Teacher College Record*, LVI (October 1954), 20–24, reprinted in Tyack, pp. 462–465; see also Karl W. Bigelow, *Report of the Commission on Teacher Education*, 8 volumes (Washington, D.C.: American Council on Education, 1944–1946).

21. James D. Koerner, *The Miseducation of American Teachers* (Boston: Houghton Mifflin, 1963), 109–110.

22. Koerner, 12–21.

23. Sterling M. McMurrin, "Introduction," Koerner, ix–xiv; E.V. Johanningmeier, "Review of Koerner, *The Miseducation of American Teachers*," in *Harvard Educational Review*, Volume 34, Number 1 (Winter, 1964), 99, cited in William R. Johnson, "Teachers and Teacher Training in the Twentieth Century," in Donald Warren, editor, *American Teachers: Histories of a Profession at Work* (New York: Macmillan, 1989), 239. Johnson's discussion of both the Koerner and Conant reports is most helpful, as is the more detailed discussion found in Christopher J. Lucas, *Teacher Education in America: Reform Agendas for the Twenty-First Century* (New York: St. Martin's Press, 1997), 72–80.

24. James Bryant Conant, *The Education of American Teachers* (New York: McGraw-Hill, 1963), 1–8.

25. Conant, 209–218.

26. Walter K. Beggs, *The Education of Teachers* (New York: Center for Applied Research in Education, 1965), 25–26, 31–37, 42.

Chapter 12

1. Michelle Foster, *Black Teachers on Teaching* (New York: New Press, 1997), 183–188.

2. "Corps member profiles," found at www.teachforamerica.org.

3. Roy A. Edelfelt, Ronald Corwin, and Elizabeth Hanna, *Lessons from the Teacher*

Corps (Washington, D.C.: National Education Association, 1974), 8, 14–15; Lyndon B. Johnson, "Remarks in Johnson City, Texas, upon signing the Elementary and Secondary Education Bill, April 11, 1965," reprinted in James W. Fraser, *The School in the United States: A Documentary History* (New York: McGraw-Hill, 2001), 298; Bethany L. Rogers, "Better People, Better Teaching: The National Teacher Corps, Professional Authority, and the Dilemmas of Great Society Liberalism, 1965–68" (unpublished paper, 2006) 3.

4. Edelfelt et al., 15–16, 27–38.

5. Edelfelt et al., 36, 47.

6. Edelfelt et al., 28; Rogers, 19–24.

7. All three of the Goodlad, Soder, and Sirotnik volumes are (San Francisco: Jossey-Bass, 1990). See also Kenneth A. Sirotnik, *Renewing Schools & Teacher Education: An Odyssey in Educational Change* (Washington, D.C.: American Association of Colleges of Teacher Education, 1991), especially 1–5.

8. Goodlad, Soder, and Sirotnik, *Teachers for Our Nation's Schools*, 76, 228, 271.

9. Robert A. Levin, "Recurring Themes and Variations," in John I. Goodlad, Roger Soder, and Kenneth A. Sirotnik, editors, *Places Where Teachers Are Taught* (San Francisco: Jossey-Bass, 1990), 46.

10. Geraldine Joncich Clifford and James W. Guthrie, *Ed School: A Brief for Professional Education* (Chicago: The University of Chicago Press, 1988), 3.

11. Judith E. Lanier and Judith Warren Little, "Research on Teacher Education," in Merlin C. Wittrock, editor, *Handbook of Research on Teaching*, 3rd edition (New York: Macmillan, 1986), 527–569, specific cite on p. 530, cited in David F. Labaree, *The Trouble with Ed Schools* (New Haven: Yale University Press, 2004), 5.

12. Roger Soder and Kenneth A. Sirotnik, "Beyond Reinventing the Past: The Politics of Teacher Education," in John I. Goodlad, Robert Soder, and Kenneth A. Sirotnik, editors, *Places Where Teachers Are Taught* (San Francisco: Jossey-Bass, 1990), 386–388. Johnson citation is from W. R. Johnson, "Teachers and Teacher Training in the Twentieth Century," in Donald Warren, editor, *American Teachers: Histories of a Profession at Work* (New York: Macmillan, 1989), 243.

13. *A Nation Prepared: Teachers for the 21st Century: The Report of the Task Force on Teaching as a Profession* (New York: The Carnegie Forum on Education and the Economy, 1986); *Tomorrow's Teachers: A Report of the Holmes Group* (East Lansing, MI: The Holmes Group, Inc., 1986). My analysis of the Holmes and Carnegie reports draws on longer analytic pieces I did regarding these reports that were published as "Preparing Teachers for Democratic Schools: The Holmes and Carnegie Reports Five Years Later, A Critical Reflection," *Teachers College Record*, Volume 94, Number 1, 7–55 (Fall 1992) and a chapter on "Preparing Teachers for Democratic Schools" in James W. Fraser, *Reading, Writing, and Justice: School Reform as if Democracy Matters* (Albany, NY: State University of New York Press, 1997), 159–195.

14. Among the best known of the "first stage reports" issues in 1983 and 1984 were National Commission on Excellence in Education, *A Nation at Risk* (Washington, D.C.: U.S. Government Printing Office, 1983); and The Twentieth Century Fund, *Making the Grade: Report of the Twentieth Century Fund Task Force on Federal Elementary and Secondary Education Policy* (New York: The Twentieth Century Fund, 1983). Also included in the public discussions of education reform in the early 1980s were John I. Goodlad, *A Place Called School: Prospectus for the Future* (New York: McGraw-

Hill Book Company, 1984); and Theodore R. Sizer, *Horace's Compromise: The Dilemma of the American High School* (Boston: Houghton Mifflin Company, 1984). Still, when one talks of the reform reports of 1983 and 1984, *A Nation at Risk* is the one that usually comes to mind first.

15. Gary R. Galluzzo, "The Holmes Group," in Susan Cimburek, editor, *Leading a Profession: Defining Moments in the AACTE Agenda, 1980–2005* (Washington, DC: American Association of Colleges for Teacher Education, 2005), 28–29. For what is probably the most thorough review of the 1980s debates about reform efforts in teacher education, see Margo Okazawa-Rey, James Anderson, and Rob Traver, *Teachers, Teaching, & Teacher Education* (Cambridge: Harvard Educational Review, 1987); and Thomas S. Popkewitz, *Critical Studies in Teacher Education: Its Folklore, Theory and Practice* (London: The Falmer Press, 1987).

16. Carnegie, 3.

17. David Labaree, *The Trouble with Ed Schools* (New Haven: Yale University Press, 2005), 121–127.

18. For example, most studies of the Progressive era point to an amazing lack of impact on school classroom practice—as opposed to administrative structures—of all of the Progressive era publications. See Lawrence Cremin, *The Transformation of The School: Progressivism in American Education, 1876–1957* (New York: Random House, 1961).

19. Courtney Leatherman, "Reforms in Education of Schoolteachers Face Tough New Challenges," *The Chronicle of Higher Education*, April 20, 1988.

20. In two very thorough studies, Ellen Condliffe Lagemann has traced the role of Carnegie money in the transformation of many institutions in this society throughout the 20th century. See Ellen Condliffe Lagemann, *Private Power for the Public Good: A History of the Carnegie Foundation for the Advancement of Teaching* (Middletown, CT: Wesleyan University Press, 1983) and Ellen Condliffe Lagemann, *The Politics of Knowledge: A History of the Carnegie Corporation of New York* (Middletown, CT: Wesleyan University Press, 1987).

21. Daniel E. Griffiths et al., "Teacher Education in Massachusetts: A Report for the Board of Regents of the Commonwealth of Massachusetts," unpublished draft report, April 5, 1986, vi, 7, 26, 128.

22. "Making Teaching a Major Profession: Recommendations of the Joint Task Force on Teacher Preparation" (Boston: Massachusetts Board of Regents of Higher Education and Board of Education, October 1987).

23. The author was staff director of the Joint Task Force on Teacher Preparation and later directly involved with the implementation of the report's recommendations on a number of Massachusetts campuses. This material is drawn from direct experience.

24. Task Force on Teacher Preparation and Initial Professional Development of the Civic Committee of the Commercial Club of Chicago, *Improving Results: Transforming the Teaching Profession in Illinois* (Chicago: The Commercial Club of Chicago, 2004).

25. The Carnegie Forum, *A Nation Prepared*, 3, 40–41.

26. Elaine P. Witty, "The Norfolk Conference on Diversity," in Cimburek, *Leading a Profession*, 18–19.

27. See Witty, 18–20; Mary E. Dilworth, editor, *Diversity in Teacher Education: New Expectations* (San Francisco: Jossey-Bass, 1992).

28. See, for example, "Recruitment and Support of Minorities in Teacher Education Programs," The University of the State of New York, The State Education Department, Albany, New York, September 1989 and "The Recruitment and Retention of People of Color in the Teaching Profession in Massachusetts," A Report Prepared by the Statewide Committee on the Recruitment of Minority Teachers for the Board of Regents and the Board of Education of Massachusetts, March 1990, and also June A. Gordon, "Why Students of Color Are Not Entering Teaching: Reflections from Minority Teachers," *Journal of Teacher Education,* Volume 45, Number 5 (November–December 1994), 346–353.

29. Harry Judge, "Foreword: A Beginning or An End?" in Michael Fullan, Gary Galluzzo, Patricia Morris, and Nancy Watson, *The Rise and Stall of Teacher Education Reform* (Washington, D.C.: American Association of Colleges for Teacher Education, 1998), vi.

30. Fullan et al., *Rise and Stall,* 21–22

31. Fullan et al., *Rise and Stall,* 23–26.

32. *Tomorrow's Schools of Education,* cited in Labaree, 7. My own analysis of these issues has been greatly informed by David Labaree's thoughtful work.

33. Fullan et al., *Rise and Stall,* 26, 40–41, 52, 60–64.

34. Fullan et al., *Rise and Stall,* 70, xiii.

Afterword

1. Jon Marmor and Steve Hill, "Prep School," *Columns: The University of Washington Alumni Magazine,* December 2004, 1–2.

2. *What Matters Most: Teaching for America's Future* (New York: National Commission on Teaching and America's Future, 1996).

3. *What Matters Most,* 62–111.

4. For a detailed analysis of my own fears that NCTAF's agenda goes too far in the direction of creating "one best system," for teacher preparation, see my "Notes Toward a New Progressive Politics of Teacher Education," *Journal of Teacher Education,* Volume 56, Number 3, May/June 2005, 279–284.

5. Linda Darling-Hammond, *National Commission on Teaching and America's Future: Final Progress Report* (New York: Teachers College, Columbia University, 1997), cited in Fullan et al., *Rise and Stall,* 63–64.

6. U.S. Department of Education, *Meeting the Highly Qualified Teachers Challenge: The Secretary's Second Annual Report on Teacher Quality* (Washington, D.C.: U.S. Government Printing Office, 2003), 30–31.

7. Linda Darling-Hammond, Deborah J. Holtzman, Su Jin Gatlin, and Julian Vazquez Heilig, "Does Teacher Preparation Matter? Evidence about Teacher Certification, Teach for America, and Teacher Effectiveness," unpublished research paper, 2005.

8. For more on the debate see "Response to Recent Linda Darling-Hammond Study: Letter from Abigail Smith, Vice President of Research and Policy," Teach For America web site, www.tfanewsletter.teachforamerica.org.

9. Bethany L. Rogers, "The Roads Less Taken: Alternative Routes to Teaching— The American Debates, 1995–2005," unpublished paper; "Alumni Profiles," at www.teachforamerica.org.

10. Frederick M. Hess, "The Predictable, but Unpredictable Personal, Politics of Teacher Licensure," *Journal of Teacher Education*, Volume 56, Number 3, May/June 2005, 192–198.

11. See David Imig, "Beyond Protect and Defend: An Agenda for AACTE for the 21st Century," 2005 Charles W. Hunt Memorial Lecture, American Association of Colleges for Teacher Education Annual Meeting, February 21, 2005, Washington, D.C., and my own "Notes Toward a New Progressive Politics of Teacher Education," *Journal of Teacher Education*, Volume 56, Number 3, May/June 2005.

12. The best source for information on the Teachers for a New Era initiative is its web site, www.teachersforanewera.org.

13. Marilyn Cochran-Smith and Kenneth Zeichner, editors, *Studying Teacher Education: The Report of the AERA Panel on Research and Teacher Education* (Mahwah, NJ: Erlbaum, 2005), 7–8, 17–18. I am grateful to Marilyn Cochran-Smith for sharing parts of this report with me prior to its publication.

14. Ellen Condliffe Lagemann, *An Elusive Science: The Troubling History of Education Research* (Chicago: University of Chicago Press, 2000).

15. Imig, "Beyond Protect and Defend: An Agenda for AACTE for the 21st Century," 2005 Charles W. Hunt Memorial Lecture.

For Further Reading

I have not tried to list here all the sources in the notes, which are complete in themselves. Rather, I have noted the books that offer an especially useful next step for those wishing to explore the themes of any chapter in greater depth.

Chapter 1: Schooling Teachers for a New Nation, 1750–1830

The best overview of the state of schooling at the time of the Revolution remains Carl F. Kaestle's *Pillars of the Republic: Common Schools and American Society, 1780–1860* (New York: Hill and Wang, 1983).

Two books that offer a very useful analysis of schooling in New England, both formal and informal, and of the teachers who taught there are Nancy F. Cott, *The Bonds of Womanhood: "Woman's Sphere" in New England, 1780–1835* (New Haven: Yale University Press, 1977), and James Axtell, *The School Upon a Hill: Education and Society in Colonial New England* (New Haven: Yale University Press, 1974).

For an analysis of those who taught and those who learned in slave communities, the best place to start is Thomas L. Webber, *Deep Like the River: Education in the Slave Quarter Community, 1831–1865* (New York: W. W. Norton, 1978).

Chapter 2: Educating Women, Women as Educators, 1800–1860

Three books that are essential reading for understanding the major topics of this chapter are Margaret Nash, *Women's Education in the United States, 1780–1840* (New York: Palgrave, 2005); David Tyack and Elisabeth Hansot, *Learning Together: A History of Coeducation in American Public Schools* (New Haven: Yale University Press, 1990); and Nancy Hoffman, *Woman's "True" Profession: Voices from the History of Teaching*, which has just been revised and expanded from Cambridge: Harvard Education Press, 2003. All of these volumes are also relevant to several subsequent chapters.

For a wonderful analysis of the Cherokee school, see Devon A. Mihesuah, *Cultivating the Rosebuds: The Education of Women at the Cherokee Female Seminary, 1851–1909* (Urbana: University of Illinois Press, 1993).

For Catharine Beecher, the best source remains Kathryn Kish Sklar, *Catharine Beecher: A Study in American Domesticity* (New York: W. W. Norton, 1973).

For the women who prepared in Beecher's Hartford institutes and then went west, an ideal source is Polly Welts Kaufman, *Women Teachers on the Frontier* (New Haven: Yale University Press, 1984).

Chapter 3: The Birth of the Normal School, 1830–1870

Happily, there is now one logical place for anyone interested in the history of the normal schools to begin, Christine A. Ogren, *The American State Normal School: "An Instrument of Great Good"* (New York: Palgrave Macmillan, 2005).

Anyone wishing more information on the normal schools will still be well served by examining Jurgen Herbst, *And Sadly Teach: Teacher Education and Professionalization in American Culture* (Madison: University of Wisconsin Press, 1989).

Chapter 4: Teachers' Institutes, 1830–1920

Publishing a major study of teachers' institutes would constitute a significant service and fill a major gap in the history of education. Among the few authors who do give some attention to teachers' institutes is Paul H. Mattingly, *A Classless Profession: American Schoolmen in the Nineteenth Century* (New York: New York University Press, 1975).

It says a lot about the lack of attention to teachers' institutes that one of the best sources remains Carmon Ross, *The Status of County Teachers' Institutes in Pennsylvania*, Ph.D. dissertation, University of Pennsylvania, 1922.

Chapter 5: High Schools and City Normal Schools, 1830–1920

No book has focused specifically on the use of 19th-century high schools to prepare teachers. Two books, however, offer an excellent introduction to the development of the American high school in this era: David F. Labaree, *The Making of an American High School: The Credentials Market and the Central High School of Philadelphia, 1838–1939* (New Haven: Yale University Press, 1988); and William J. Reese, *The Origins of the American High School* (New Haven: Yale University Press, 1995).

Chapter 6: Normal Institutes, Missionary Colleges, and County Training Schools: Preparing African American Teachers in the Segregated South, 1860–1940

Anyone wanting to learn more about the themes of this chapter should, without question, start with James D. Anderson, *The Education of Blacks in the South, 1860–1935* (Chapel Hill: University of North Carolina Press, 1988).

For insight into the early informal preparation of teachers in the era of slavery and Reconstruction, a terrific new book is Heather Andrea Williams, *Self-Taught: African American Education in Slavery and Freedom* (Chapel Hill: University of North Carolina Press, 2005).

For missionary colleges for teachers Joe M. Richardson, *Christian Reconstruction: The American Missionary Association and Southern Blacks, 1861–1890* is an excellent place to start. Although Richardson focuses exclusively on the AMA and thus misses the work of other denominations, especially black-led ones, his insights into the missionary schools is extremely valuable.

Two much earlier studies remain of great value and have never been replaced in terms of their coverage of their material: Edward E. Redcay, *County Training Schools and Public Secondary Education for Negroes in the South* (Washington, D.C.: The John F. Slater Fund, 1935, republished Westport, CT: Negro Universities Press, 1970); and Ambrose Caliver, *Education of Negro Teachers*, Vol. IV of the *National Survey of the Education of Teachers* (Washington, D.C.: U.S. Government Printing Office, 1933; republished Westport, CT: Negro Universities Press, 1970).

There are also many excellent overviews of American Indian education. While to my knowledge there is no study that focuses primarily on an overview of American Indian teachers, anyone wanting to explore the topic in depth should read Jon Reyhner and Jeanne Eder, *American Indian Education* (Norman, OK: University of Oklahoma Press, 2004).

Chapter 7: The Heyday of the Normal School, 1870–1920

The two books listed for chapter three, Christine Ogren's *The American State Normal School* and Jurgen Herbst's *And Sadly Teach*, are also the primary sources for any examination of the normal schools during their heyday. Indeed, this era is at the heart of Ogren's work.

Although now half a century old, Merle L. Borrowman, *The Liberal and Technical in Teacher Education: A Historical Survey of American Thought* (New York: Bureau of Publications, Teachers College, Columbia University, 1956) remains a gold mine of information about the intellectual currents and educational debates among normal school leaders as well as university-based educators. Far more intellectual history, or as the subtitle says "a historical survey of American thought," than a history of institutional developments or student experiences in preparing for teaching careers, no scholar who is seriously interested in the development of teacher education in the United States should fail to consult it.

Chapter 8: Universities Create Departments and Schools of Education, 1870–1930

Perhaps the best overview of the movement toward university-based programs to prepare teachers can be found in Christopher J. Lucas, *Teacher Education in America: Reform Agendas for the Twenty-First Century* (New York: St. Martin's Press, 1997).

Of course, to understand the cost of these developments, the place to start is Geraldine Jonçich Clifford and James W. Guthrie, *Ed School: A Brief for Professional Education* (Chicago: The University of Chicago Press, 1988).

To understand the impact of university expectations regarding research, one must look to Ellen Condliffe Lagemann's *An Elusive Science: The Troubling History of Education Research* (Chicago: The University of Chicago Press, 2000).

Chapter 9: Teachers for Cities, Teachers for Immigrants, 1870–1940

Kate Rousmaniere's *City Teachers: Teaching and School Reform in Historical Perspective* (New York: Teachers College Press, 1997) does a very nice job of setting the context for a discussion of the issues in this chapter.

Chapter 10: Every Teacher a College Graduate, 1920–1965

The shift from normal schools to teachers colleges to all-purpose colleges has received surprisingly little study. Christine Ogren's *The American State Normal School* is, again, probably the most useful place to start to understand the context for these developments.

To place the Carnegie studies in context, the best source by far is Ellen Condliffe Lagemann, *Private Power for the Public Good: A History of the Carnegie Foundation for the Advancement of Teaching* (New York: College Entrance Examination Board, 1983).

Lucas, *Teacher Education in America*, is also very helpful here.

Chapter 11: A New Status Quo and Its Critics, 1960–1985

The primary sources indicated in the chapter, most of all the work of John Goodlad, remain essential reading here.

Chapter 12: Preparing Teachers in the Era of *A Nation at Risk*, 1965–2000

Most of the major reports discussed in this chapter remain easily available.

Although his focus is broader, David Labaree's new *The Trouble With Ed Schools* (New Haven: Yale University Press, 2005) is very helpful in understanding the context for most of the recent debates about teacher preparation.

An excellent source for the Holmes group and by extension other reform efforts is Michael Fullan, Gary Galluzzo, Patricia Morris, and Nancy Watson, *The Rise and Stall of Teacher Education Reform* (Washington, D.C.: American Association of Colleges for Teacher Education, 1998).

Afterword: Teachers for a New Millennium, 2000–

Just as this book was going to press, a new report appeared that is sure to impact the discussion of teacher preparation in the next years of the new millennium, Arthur Levine's *Educating School Teachers* (Princeton, NJ: The Education Schools Project, 2006).

Index

About the Author

James W. Fraser has recently joined the faculty of the Steinhardt School of Education at New York University, where he will teach courses in the History of American Education and Inquiries into Education, as well as lead the school's History and Democracy Initiative. From 1993 to 2006, he was Professor of History and Education and founding dean of the School of Education at Northeastern University in Boston, Massachusetts. Previous to his appointment there, Dr. Fraser was dean and professor at Lesley University. He has also taught at the Harvard University Divinity School, the University of Massachusetts at Boston, Boston University, and Wellesley College. In 1987–1988, he served as special assistant for teacher education to the Massachusetts Chancellor of Higher Education. While in Boston, Dr. Fraser was a member and chair of the Commonwealth of Massachusetts Education Deans Council, and observer at the Boston Plan for Excellence Board of Directors. For ten years he served on the Boston School Committee Nominating Committee. He was also a member of the American Association of Colleges for Teacher Education's Committee on Multicultural Education, and pastor of Grace Church in East Boston and Union Congregational Church in Winthrop. His first teaching position was at Public School 76 in Manhattan, where he taught fourth grade.

Dr. Fraser holds a Ph.D. from Columbia University, and an M.Div. from Union Theological Seminary in New York City, and a B.A. degree with honors in American History from the University of California, Santa Barbara. He is the author of numerous books and articles, including *A History of Hope: When Americans Have Dared to Dream of a Better Future* (Palgrave Macmillan, 2002), *The School in the United States: A Documentary History* (McGraw-Hill, 2001), *Between Church and State: Religion and Public Education in a Multicultural America* (Palgrave Macmillan, 1999), and *Reading, Writing, and Justice: School Reform as if Democracy Matters* (State University of New York Press, 1997). He is also editor of the "Transforming Teaching" series published by Routledge, New York.